Hong Kong
& Taiwan

Fred S. Armentrout and Ann Williams

GW00708178

Mitchell Beazley

THE AMERICAN EXPRESS ® TRAVEL GUIDES

Published by Mitchell Beazley International Ltd, Michelin House, 81 Fulham Road, London SW3 6RB

Edited, designed and produced by Castle House Press, Llantrisant, Mid Glamorgan CF7 8EU, Wales

ISBN 1 85533 955 1

The editors, authors and publisher thank the Hong Kong Tourist Association in London, the Free Chinese Centre in London, the Taiwan Tourism Bureau in Hong Kong, Michelle Liao, Darlene Lee, Neil Hanson, David Haslam and Hilary Bird for their assistance during the preparation of this edition — and baby Irene Isidora for waiting.

Fred S. Armentrout's research associate was Rodelia Delizo, Sheen Co. Ltd, Hong Kong

FOR THE SERIES:
General Editor:
  David Townsend Jones
Map Editor: David Haslam
Indexer: Hilary Bird
Cover design:
  Roger Walton Studio

FOR THIS EDITION:
Edited on desktop by:
  David Townsend Jones
Associate editor: Robin Reeves
Art editor: Eileen Townsend Jones
Illustrators:
  Sylvia Hughes-Williams,
  Karen Cochrane, David Evans
Gazetteer: Anne Evans
Cover photo:
  Tony Stone Worldwide

FOR MITCHELL BEAZLEY:
Art Director: Tim Foster
Managing Editor: Alison Starling
Production: Sarah Schuman

PRODUCTION CREDITS:
Maps by Lovell Johns, Oxford,
  England
Hong Kong KCR/MTR map
  by TCS, Aldershot, England
Typeset in Garamond and
  News Gothic
Desktop layout in Ventura Publisher
Linotronic output by
  Tradespools Limited, Frome,
  England
Printed and bound in Great Britain
  by HarperCollins Manufacturing,
  Glasgow

Contents

Hong Kong *by Fred S. Armentrout*

Taiwan *by Ann Williams*

Maps

How to use this book

Few rules and pointers are needed to understand how this travel guide works. Your enjoyment and efficiency in reading and using it will be enhanced if you note the following remarks.

HOW TO FIND WHAT YOU WANT

- For the general organization of the book, see CONTENTS on the pages preceding this one.
- Wherever appropriate, chapters and sections are arranged alphabetically, with headings appearing in **CAPITALS.**
- Often these headings are followed by location and practical information printed in *italics*.
- As you turn the pages, you will find subject headers, similar to those used in telephone directories, printed in CAPITALS in the top corner of each page.
- If you still cannot find what you need, check in the comprehensive and exhaustively cross-referenced INDEX at the back of the book.
- Following the index, a LIST OF STREET NAMES provides map references for all roads and streets mentioned in the book that are located within the areas covered by the main city maps.

KEY TO SYMBOLS

☎	Telephone	🚗	Secure garage
Tx	Telex	☺	Quiet hotel
Fx	Facsimile (fax)	♿	Facilities for disabled
★	Recommended sight		people
♣	Good value (in its class)	✿	Garden
⟵	Parking	⟨⟩	Outstanding views
☰	Building of architectural	≋	Swimming pool
	interest	⌁	Tennis
☷	Free entrance	⟿	Sauna
☵	Entrance fee payable	⚶	Spa
✗	Guided tour	∷	Golf
☐	Cafeteria	⛷	Riding
✦	Special interest for children	⟝	Fishing
☙	Hotel	⛾	Gym/fitness
⛔	Simple (hotel)		facilities
⛫	Luxury (hotel)	☷	Conference facilities
▢	Cheap	▭	Minibar
▨	Inexpensive	⌨	Business center
▥	Moderately priced	⇉	Restaurant
▦	Expensive	☗	Simple (restaurant)
▩	Very expensive	△	Luxury (restaurant)
AE	American Express	⊑	Good for wines
◉	Diners Club	⟐	Open-air dining
◐	MasterCard	●	Disco dancing
VISA	Visa	♩	Nightclub

CROSS-REFERENCES
These are printed in SMALL CAPITALS, referring you to other sections or alphabetical entries in the book. Care has been taken to ensure that such cross-references are self-explanatory. Often, page references are also given, although their excessive use would be intrusive and ugly.

FLOORS
We use the American convention in this book: "first floor" means the floor at ground level.

PRICE CATEGORIES
These are denoted by the symbols ▢ (cheap), ▢ (inexpensive), ▢ (moderately priced), ▥ (expensive) and ▥ (very expensive). For **hotels** and **restaurants** they correspond approximately to the following actual local prices, which give a guideline **at the time of printing**. Naturally, prices rise, but hotels and restaurants tend to remain in the same price category.

HONG KONG	Corresponding to approximate prices	
	for **hotels**	for **restaurants**
	double room with bath	*meal for one with service, taxes and house wine*
	(Hong Kong dollars: HK$)	
▥ very expensive	over $1,500	over $600
▥ expensive	$1,000-1,500	$400-600
▥ moderately priced	$700-1,000	$300-400
▢ inexpensive	$500-700	$200-300
▢ cheap	under $500	under $200

TAIWAN	Corresponding to approximate prices	
	for **hotels**	for **restaurants**
	double room with bath	*meal for one with service, taxes and house wine*
	(New Taiwan dollars: NT$)	
▥ very expensive	over $5,000	over $1,800
▥ expensive	$4,000-5,000	$1,000-1,800
▥ moderately priced	$2,500-4,000	$600-1,000
▢ inexpensive	under $2,500	$400-600
▢ cheap	under $1,000	under $400

About the authors

Fred S. Armentrout was born in the US and has lived in Hong Kong for 15 years. He has traveled widely in Asia as the editor of numerous regional arts, business and travel magazines. Books he has written include *Images of Hong Kong; Taipan Traders* (to which he was contributing author); *Spirit of Yenan, A Wartime Memoir,* and, in this series, *Singapore & Bangkok* (1992) and a predecessor volume, *Hong Kong, Singapore & Bangkok* (1988, with Keith Addison and Brian Eads). Forthcoming is *Outlier's Island: The Secret Life of Cheung Chau.*

He has also edited some 20 books on Asian arts, business and politics, including *China: The Long March; Bayan Ko: The Aquino Revolution; Living in Hong Kong; Doing Business in Guangdong Province* and *Who's Who in Hong Kong Communications.* His newspaper and magazine assignments have included work for the *International Herald Tribune, Asian Wall Street Journal* and *Fortune* magazine.

British-born **Ann Williams** is a food, fashion and travel writer who worked with numerous British newspapers before moving to Hong Kong, where she has lived for five years. Her articles for such publications as *Departures, The Regent* and *Orient* are widely admired.

A message from the series editor

In designing *American Express Hong Kong & Taiwan* we aimed to make this brand-new edition simple and instinctive to use, like all its sister volumes in our new, larger paperback format.

The hallmarks of the relaunched series are clear, classic typography, confidence in fine travel writing for its own sake, and faith in our readers' innate intelligence to find their way around the books without heavy-handed signposting by editors.

Readers with anything less than 20:20 vision will doubtless also enjoy the larger, clearer type, and can now dispense with the mythical magnifying glasses we never issued free with the old pocket guide series.

Our authors **Fred S. Armentrout** and **Ann Williams** and their editors have worked enormously hard to make this edition as accurate and up to date as possible at the moment it goes to press. But time and change are forever the enemies, and in between editions we appreciate it when you, our readers, keep us informed of changes that you discover.

As ever, I am indebted to all readers who wrote during the preparation of this book. Please remember that your feedback is extremely important to our efforts to tailor the series to the very distinctive tastes and requirements of our sophisticated international readership.

Send your comments to me at Mitchell Beazley International Ltd, Michelin House, 81 Fulham Road, London SW3 6RB; or, in the US, c/o American Express Travel Guides, Prentice Hall Travel, 15 Columbus Circle, New York, NY 10023.

David Townsend Jones

Hong Kong
& Taiwan

Hong Kong and Taiwan

Hong Kong has evolved in the past 40 years into one of the world's most vibrant cities, a center of intense capitalist enterprise on the edge of Communist China, a place that combines aggressive modernity with a rich panoply of tradition. It is a free port and a shopper's paradise. Its emporiums overflow with every kind of merchandise, from watches to couturier dresses, from gems to electronic equipment.

Beneath all the glitz, Hong Kong is also a great conservator of Chinese cultural traditions and world capital of the Overseas Chinese, a global community of about 13 million people spread among 174 countries, many of whom still maintain economic and social ties with their motherland. Since 1841, when Hong Kong was first established as an international trading center, the city has also been an artistic and intellectual sanctuary in troubled times and barometer of events in mainland China.

The people of Hong Kong know better than most that it is the business of the future to be dangerous, and they are poised for perhaps the greatest adventure this *de facto* city-state has ever undertaken. After 150-odd years as a British Crown Colony, Hong Kong is to return to Chinese jurisdiction in 1997, when it will become the economic capital of a region of South China with a population totaling some 120 million. To Hong Kong's own population of nearly 6 million people will be added the more than 440,000 people of Macau, the 62 million of Guangdong province and the 30 million of Fujian province. Alternatively, the area may develop as two regions: one led by Hong Kong with about 70 million people and another by Taipei with about 50 million, should the political divide between Taiwan and mainland China also be brought to an end.

China's recent political leaders came to power as revolutionaries and know full well how small numbers of people can effect great social change. So they too are anxious about the impact of Hong Kong's return to Chinese jurisdiction in July 1997 and Macau's in December 1999.

The joint declarations of China's leaders and the British and Portuguese governments on the future status of Hong Kong and Macau talk of creating "one country, two systems." Veteran Chinese Communist leader Deng Xiaopeng declared, "To get rich is glorious," and this has become the drum roll of a new generation of mainland Chinese. The net result is that "Socialism with Chinese characteristics" is becoming less and less distinguishable from Capitalism with Western characteristics.

Taiwan too has been undergoing significant political change, moving away from a 40-year-old martial law environment toward participatory democracy. Its rulers have even allowed the subject of Taiwanese independence from China to be raised. The founders of Taiwan's ruling party, the Nationalist Party of China or Kuomintang (KMT), took over the government of the island after being driven from the mainland by the Communists in 1949. Reared in many cases by the same Russian agents and German generals as the Communist leaders, they traditionally used many of the same methods of political control. But economically, they have had far greater success. Taiwan today has one of the highest levels of cash reserves in the world, a much appreciated New Taiwan dollar,

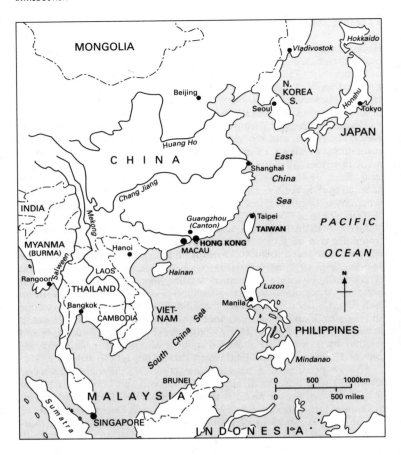

the beginnings of a consumer society, and the potential to become a major player in the economic life of the mainland — notably with Fujian province, which has cultural and linguistic ties with the island province.

The artificial divide between culture and politics on the one hand, and commercial life on the other, which has dominated relations between Hong Kong, Macau, Taiwan and the People's Republic of China (PRC), is now eroding daily. Replacing it are debates, commercial ventures and commitments from which natural leaders are emerging. Throughout the region, there is a tense excitement that did not exist a decade ago.

The changes will not be painless, nor always pretty, as the repugnant 1989 massacre of students in Tiananmen Square proved beyond doubt. But there has not been a more absorbing time to be in this part of Asia since the late 1970s. Tiananmen swept aside the belief that business success can be bought without reference to human rights and politics, a notion that had been gospel in this part of the world for at least 30 years.

Hong Kong's Legislative Council (Legco) now has 18 popularly-elected members, in a territory that has no tradition of democratic elections whatsoever. The elected members are challenging the assumptions of both mainland China and the Colonial Governor about what to make of Hong Kong's future. So are active local and foreign business organizations such as the Federation of Hong Kong Industries and the Hong Kong General Chamber of Commerce.

An assertive American Chamber of Commerce mounts regular lobby campaigns with governments in Hong Kong, Beijing and Washington, DC on such current thorny issues as Hong Kong air rights, US protectionism and post-1997 concerns like China's respect of intellectual property laws, Hong Kong's COCOM status, an independent Hong Kong judiciary and a free press. All of these bodies adhere to, and are buoyed by, the stipulations of the 1984 Joint Declaration of Chinese and British governments, which guarantees Hong Kong will be a "Special Administrative Region" (SAR) of China for 50 years beyond 1997.

Beneath all the political fencing which must characterize the territory's future if it is to have one worth arguing about, China's continued public adherence to its stipulations is heartening. China has continued to encourage investment in Hong Kong by Japan and concluded an agreement with the British government covering the massive public expenditure that will result in a new airport for the territory. Located on Lantau Island, the new airport, due to come into service in 1997, also involves construction of major new road and rail, tunnel and bridge links. Disputes continue about the existing utility monopoly in telecommunications and composition of the post-1997 court of final appeal. But all parties agree they are part of the sovereignty transfer negotiating process that must continue.

Meanwhile, a new generation of Chinese looks back to Dr Sun Yat-sen (1866-1925), the father of modern China, for inspiration. In a speech shortly before he died, the man who plotted the overthrow of the hated Qing dynasty while a student of medicine in Hong Kong made an observation that now vibrates with fresh resonance in China's coastal colonies and territories:

> "The question I am often asked is where did I get my revolutionary and modern ideas: the answer is that I got my ideas in this very place, in the Colony of Hong Kong. [In China] there was disorder instead of order, insecurity instead of security... Afterwards I saw the outside world and began to wonder how it was that foreigners, that Englishmen could do such things as they had done within 70 or 80 years, while China in 4,000 years had no place like Hong Kong... Immediately after I graduated I saw that it was necessary to give up my profession of healing men and take up my part to cure my country."

There are more than a billion people in China and the Chinese coastal territories poised to ask of themselves the same question, perhaps replacing "Englishmen" with "Cantonese" or "Taiwanese." The incumbent powers can only wonder about the answers they will give.

Hong Kong

Chinese dreams, cosmopolitan chaos

Hong Kong has always stretched the limits of probability. For ages it was a feudal backwater of walled villages and fortified government outposts in a no-man's-land of pirates and brigandry. British colonial traders and civil servants imposed their imperialism on a land of peasants, fishermen and renegades.

In more recent times, it has been called the world's largest transit lounge. Tourist or resident, everyone seems to be passing through. The faces, the destinations, the architecture are forever changing. But for all its cosmopolitan chaos Hong Kong is a Chinese city whose people dream Chinese dreams of making money and giving the next generation a flying start. It is a rags-to-riches society, where every coolie believes that with hard work and some luck he too can join the jet set.

The colony's birth was hardly auspicious. The main British trade with China was opium, grown in the Indian colonies and sold illegally in China, with proceeds of this sale paying for huge British purchases of Chinese tea. This unequal and turbulent arrangement was approved by Britain's Parliament and backed by the Royal Navy — even imperial mandarins took their cut. A crisis was triggered in 1839 when the firebrand Imperial Commissioner Lin Tse-hsu seized and burned an opium shipment of 20,000 chests, drove the traders out of Canton and Portuguese Macau to the anchorage at Hong Kong, and there cut off their food supplies. This provoked a Royal Navy attack on Chinese Navy junks, starting the first Opium War. This ended in 1842 with a treaty which ceded Hong Kong to Britain and established British trading rights in five Chinese ports, which, in turn, led to an enormous increase in the opium trade.

Hong Kong flourished as entrepôt for the China coast trade and a stopover on the trade route between India and Japan via Singapore and Penang. It retains that position today: Hong Kong vies with Singapore to boast the world's busiest container terminal, and its entrepreneurs own some of the largest shipping fleets.

In the 1850s the Taiping Rebellion in China drove thousands of refugees into the colony, an event which established a pattern of population influx that has lasted to this day; the refugees were fodder to the coolie foreign contract labor system, the basis of the Chinese remittance economy, which is now perpetuated by millions in Chinatowns all over the world (many of whose ancestors embarked from Hong Kong). In 1860 China signed away Kowloon Peninsula to Britain, and in 1898 the territory was completed with the 99-year lease on the New Territories beyond Kowloon.

Since its foundation, Hong Kong has experienced much turbulence, yet it survives and thrives. Hostilities between China and the European nations frequently led to civil strife in Hong Kong, with boycotts, strikes and riots. There was a virtual siege in 1857; in 1884 a dockers' strike saw the government's Sikh soldiers firing into the crowds; and further upsets occurred in 1905 and 1907. In 1911 the Chinese revolution against the foreign (Manchu) Qing Dynasty's rule sparked anti-British riots in the colony, culminating in an attempt to assassinate the Governor. In 1925-26 a strike-boycott paralyzed the city as a large portion of the population left for China in disgust.

In the late 1930s, Hong Kong's population almost doubled as refugees poured into the city to escape the Japanese armies invading and occupying South China. When Japanese troops took over Hong Kong in 1941, they sent a million people back to China, leaving only 600,000 in the city. Many returned after the Japanese surrender in 1945, and by 1948 the population had risen back to 1.8 million. Fresh waves of refugees after the Chinese Communist victory in 1949 boosted the total population to $2\frac{1}{4}$ million by the early 1950s. In 1953, a squatter-hut fire left 53,000 refugees homeless, forcing the colony to institute a public housing program which has turned the Hong Kong Government into the world's biggest landlord; today, it provides accommodations for $2\frac{1}{2}$ million tenants. Even so, following another influx of economic migrants from China in the late 1970s, about half a million people still live in squatter huts.

The Korean War (1950-53) led to a UN embargo on international trade with China, which hit Hong Kong's entrepôt trade badly. The colony's industrialists, many of whom had fled Shanghai in 1949, rushed to diversify into manufacturing, again using refugee labor. Their ability to respond rapidly to changing international trade trends, and slip past trade barriers, has been the secret of Hong Kong's success ever since; they have switched with breathtaking agility from manufacturing products as varied as plastic flowers and wigs, to designer jeans and fur coats, from quartz watch movements and toys to transistors and microchips, according to international trading conditions and opportunities.

In 1966-67 the city and its economy were badly shaken by a year of riots and bombings, a spillover of China's Great Cultural Revolution. But recovery was rapid. In the 1970s Hong Kong, thanks to its status as an international free port without financial restrictions, developed as an entrepôt for money, gold and diamonds. Combined with the growth in satellite communications and an open press environment, it was soon established as one of the world's largest financial, gold and gem trading centers. It also became Asia's English- and Chinese-language regional publication and printing center. Such was the growth in prosperity in this period that Hong Kong's balance of payments surpluses became an important factor propping up the value of Britain's pound sterling.

In 1974 an Independent Commission Against Corruption (ICAC) was formed in response to public anger at widespread police and official corruption.

Hong Kong moved into the 1980s on the crest of a real estate boom, with a growing class of "super-rich" citizens, and a very healthy budget surplus. Significant new areas of land were reclaimed from the harbor, opening the way for major new residential and commercial developments. Satellite factory towns of up to 500,000 people in the New Territories were completed by the 1990s. Tunnels were constructed under the harbor, to Aberdeen, and through the wall of mountains to the north, and the MTR subway network and an electrified train system to the China border came into full operation, completing Hong Kong's transformation from a harbor city to an island-peninsula metropolis.

Culture, history and background

A brief history of Hong Kong

Hong Kong has been occupied since before the dawn of history, although by whom is not clear. The archeological records suggest that some 6,000 years ago the coastal areas were inhabited by Stone Age tribes called the Yueh, fishermen living on the beaches who began to move into farming. Later evidence suggests people of a high culture, in contact with South China. Yueh chieftains are known to have attained military and administrative status in the Han Dynasty (**206BC-AD220**).

The first regular settlement of Hong Kong occurred during the Sung Dynasty (**AD960-1280**). The Tang and Chan clans settled in the northern New Territories, where they still reside today. The Tangs in particular prospered: a royal marriage made Tang Tse-ming of Kamtin the son-in-law of Sung Emperor Kao Tsung (reigned **1127-62**). Other locals were not so fortunate: discontented Tolo Harbour pearl divers (the Tsung rulers' technique was to tie a heavy stone to a local barbarian and throw him in) fled to Lantau, which became a pirate stronghold, apparently with Siamese connections.

In the **13thC** China was invaded by Genghis Khan's marauding Mongols, and Kublai Khan completed the conquest 45 years later. This was one of the most poignant periods in Chinese history. In **1276** the Sung Court was besieged in its capital at Hangchow and Emperor Kung Ti surrendered. Pursued by the Mongol army, Sung ministers fled to the south with the Emperor's two young half-brothers, Prince Cheng and Prince Ping, and joined the remnants of the Sung forces. Cheng, a boy of nine, became the Emperor Ti Cheng. Driven ever southward, the "Wandering Court" reached Hong Kong and set up "Temporary Palaces" in Kowloon, Mui Wo on Lantau and in Tsunwan. Ti Cheng fell ill on campaign and died a year later, aged 11. Ping, aged eight, succeeded him as Emperor Ti Ping. The following year, **1279**, the Mongol navy attacked Sung forces in Hong Kong, and by the end of the day Ti Ping was dead, and with him the Sung Dynasty.

The Mongol conquest threw South China into the melting pot. Many aboriginal communities, including the Hong Kong tribes, emerge at the close of the short Mongol reign (Yuan Dynasty, **1280-1368**) as Chinese, speaking Chinese dialects. The Yuan government was efficient and preserved the peace. "It shakes our preconceptions of the 'ruthless hordes' to find the Mongols in **1319** prohibiting the Tolo Harbour pearl fisheries on humanitarian grounds," one historian notes. To this day local

Hoklo fishermen like to recall where the pearls were found and how their ancestors suffered. Many died due to the primitive method of pearl-fishing used — divers were tossed overboard weighted with rocks and were not allowed to signal themselves to be hoisted until their oyster baskets were full. Those lacking lung capacity or good harvest ground often drowned.

Hong Kong suffered neglect, oppression and regular famines under the succeeding Ming Dynasty (**1368-1644**). Discontent led to an increase in lawlessness, and Lantau became a pirate stronghold. In **1557** the Portuguese were given permission to occupy neighboring Macau, in return for helping to control the piracy. The fall of the Ming to the Manchu invaders (Qing Dynasty, **1644-1911**) brought worse troubles: fighting and disruption continued in the Hong Kong area (then known as San On), and in **1648** a famine wiped out half the population. Loyalist forces based in Formosa (Taiwan) continued raiding coastal towns, with local support, until, in **1662**, the Manchu government ordered that the entire coastal population be driven inland on pain of death. The toll of suffering and death was immense: when the order was rescinded eight years later, only one in ten returned.

The British connection began in **1714** when China opened Canton port to foreign traders, and the British East India Company established itself as the principal European agency trading with China. The Pearl River Estuary was still terrorized by Lantau pirates, but in **1809** their chief, the notorious Cheung Po-tsai, was captured: extraordinarily, the Chinese government appointed him chief customs collector of Macau. Piracy nevertheless continued, even into the **20thC**. Some village elders can still remember pirate attacks in their youth, more than a century after the British had taken over — and some don't deny having taken part. Macau even has a feast day on Taipa island which celebrates the defeat of a pirate fleet in **1911**.

By the **1970s**, Hong Kong's children started to drift back from foreign universities, having had a taste of life overseas, the first generation with a self-conscious Hong Kong identity and a certain pride in the world stature of their birthplace. In the past decade they (and the city's young Westerners) have had a growing impact — out of all proportion to their numbers — on the cultural scene and the tone of street life. They have tried to translate the ambience of European, American and Japanese cities into a Hong Kong context with restaurants, discotheques, boutiques and arts projects. The bigger hotels, the business community and the leaders of the city joined in the push for an international cultural climate. It is not just a facade, although most of the community is unmoved. The older generation still prefers racehorses, *mahjong* and Chinese opera; most of the children of the **1950s** baby boom are locally-educated factory and office workers whose enthusiasm for Cantonese movies and "Canto-pop" music, sport and mass barbecues in the countryside is undented by visiting Western celebrities.

The Tourist Association has increasingly emphasized Hong Kong's rural past, actively promoting folk culture and the traditional festivals. The rural hinterland is itself more accessible; there are now 21 officially designated Country Parks, representing 40 percent of the total land area, as well as controlled nature reserves, several of considerable ecological interest. Meanwhile the city has become more comfortable, more exciting and more expensive. The territory as a whole is now a more relaxed and interesting stopover for adventurous travelers than it has ever been.

THE 1997 AGREEMENT

In **1984**, the British and Beijing Governments signed a unique agreement under which Britain agreed to transfer full sovereignty over the Hong Kong Islands and New Territories to China in **1997** in return for a Chinese assurance that Hong Kong's social and economic freedom and capitalist lifestyle would be preserved for at least 50 years. There has never been any question in the minds of Hong Kong Chinese to whom Hong Kong ultimately belongs: it belongs to them and to their motherland, China. In the common view of Chinese everywhere, Britain imposed unequal treaties on China in the **19thC**, as had Russia, Japan, Germany and France. According to the original treaties, the rest of Kowloon and Hong Kong Island were Britain's forever, but the Crown authorities announced early on in the negotiations with Beijing that they would not attempt to stay on without the New Territories, where much of the colony's manufacturing capability and work force has been relocated and where much of its food is grown.

How will Hong Kong prosper under Chinese rule? The territory has long enjoyed the joint support of both China and Britain. They have cooperated for years in keeping the border closed to illegal immigrants. China has a massive financial stake in its trade through Hong Kong and is an indirect owner-operator of numerous Hong Kong companies — shipbuilders, the largest chain of department stores, banks, publishing houses and others. It also provides half of Hong Kong's food and significant amounts of its fresh water and power.

Since the early 1980s, Hong Kong industrialists have begun investing heavily in Shenzhen, China's Special Economic Zone adjoining the New Territories, while hedging their bets by investing even more heavily overseas. In the mid-1980s, the city's financiers suffered a crisis of confidence: local reinvestment fell and major companies "moved offshore" as the property market, the stock market and the value of the HK$ plunged. The government stepped in to halt the slide; the budget went into deficit for the first time in years (although an accumulated surplus estimated at HK$36 billion was invested overseas), and major projects were shelved. But the crisis in confidence did not last. Hong Kong continues to ride the waves; the perennial boom bustles on.

Most painful of all was the mainland government's crackdown on China's student-led "Democracy Movement," which culminated in the massacre in Tiananmen Square on **June 4, 1989** and brought more than a million Hong Kongers out onto the streets in sympathy with the protestors. This endangered Hong Kong on two counts.

The revulsion in the world community, and especially in the United States, has left China's continued access to the American market as a country with "Most Favored Nation" trade status in doubt. That status, which guarantees that an "MFN" country will be treated no worse than the "most favored nation" with which another country trades, has to be renewed annually by the US. A powerful coalition in the US Congress wants this privilege withdrawn from Communist China or at least linked to the performance of the Beijing government on human rights issues. Since more than half of Hong Kong's wealth is derived by re-exports from China, and a large portion of the other half derived from direct and indirect business and financial services to the mainland, loss of MFN status would decimate the territory's economy — estimates put the loss as high as 10 percent of GDP.

Coincident with the threat to China's MFN status in the United States has been the hard line taken by China's leaders since the **1989** crack-down. It included a more abrasive insistence on new forms of power-sharing with the British colonial government during the transition period to **1997**. In the first half of **1991**, the territory waited in considerable suspense for the conclusion of negotiations about the creation of a new Hong Kong airport. The Beijing authorities insisted on being consulted, since the new airport not only requires massive new infrastructure developments in the western harbor area, but also has serious implications for the cash reserves they will inherit from the British.

An agreement was finally hammered out between Whitehall and the Great Hall of the People in July 1991. "LIFT OFF — AT LAST!" shouted a banner headline in the local *South China Morning Post* daily newspaper, suggesting the collective sigh of relief felt by residents.

Such tense negotiations are a portent of Hong Kong's future and would break the spirit of a less ambitious people in a less determined place. Hong Kong, however, continues to ride the waves; the perennial booms, busts and case studies in crisis economics bustle on.

The **1997** questions now being asked are: how capable are Britain and China of making a mutually beneficial transition of power? How much does Hong Kong owe its prosperity to British colonial law, order and commitment to entrepreneurial opportunity; and how much of that prosperity will remain under Chinese administration? Will the children of the refugees, whose skills and energy have built modern Hong Kong, stay and prosper, or will they try to uproot themselves again? No person in Hong Kong seriously pretends to know the answers.

Hong Kong's architecture

Hong Kong will be a wonderful place, runs a local joke, if they ever get it finished. In a city full of entrepreneurs who define long-term investments as those that take three years to recoup, architectural esthetics and history usually take a back seat to profitability. A notorious example of this bottom-line pragmatism occurred in the early 1980s when a brand-new Wanchai apartment block was demolished less than a month after completion to make way for an office building; commercial accommodations promised a better return than the residential property market.

The **railway clock tower** in Tsimshatsui, former **Supreme Court building** and **Flagstaff House** in Central, and **Ohel Leah synagogue** on Robinson Rd., in Mid-Levels, are notable exceptions and prove that some buildings of architectural worth and historical interest have survived the wreckers' hammer. In recent years major Hong Kong corporations have sought to match their global reach with prestigious and imaginative property developments at home.

Architectural styles in the territory fall into four categories: **traditional Chinese**, **colonial**, **postwar**, and the **ultramodern** style of the 1980s and '90s.

TRADITIONAL CHINESE ARCHITECTURE

By far and away the best examples of this style are found in the New Territories, and most are connected with Hong Kong's five great clans: the Tangs, the Haus, the Pangs, the Lius and the Mans.

These families migrated s throughout the Sung Dynasty (AD960-1279) and later when the area of modern Hong Kong was relatively uninhabited. They built themselves villages, ancestral halls, study halls and temples. All are solidly built structures, with sun-dried brick laid on granite foundations. The doorposts and lintels are dressed granite slabs; floors are paved with red brick; rafters are of China fir; and the pitched roofs are tiled. Invariably the style is symmetrical. Buildings are rectangular, usually grouped around a courtyard: the guiding principles are balance and simplicity.

Two prime considerations inform the traditional architecture. First is *fung shui,* literally "wind and water." Chinese geomancers rule on how to achieve the most harmonious relationship between a building and its natural surroundings. Usually this involves its facing s, toward the source of "male energy." Second is the weather. Thick walls ensure insulation against extremes of heat and cold, and can withstand the buffeting of typhoons. Pitched roofs are required to shrug off monsoon rains, and the southern aspect brings the benefit of cooling summer breezes and protection from chilling winter winds.

But the buildings are not all stern practicality. Even in disrepair they are rich in decoration, from carved wooden door screens (to keep out evil spirits, who travel only in straight lines) to ornate roof brackets, elaborate friezes, panels and grills. Brightly-decorated tiles depict legends and the exploits of the eight Taoist Immortals. The **Tang Ancestral**

Hall (1550) at Hang Mei Tsuen, Ping Shan, New Territories, is considered one of the finest examples of traditional Ming dynasty (AD1368-1644) architecture.

Few traditional buildings of value are to be found on Hong Kong island, although several 18thC and 19thC temples — notably the **Tin Hau Temple** in Causeway Bay and the **Man Mo Temple** on Hollywood Rd. — have a certain rococo charm, as do the traditional **3- and 4-story Chinese shophouses** which still survive on the steep hills above Central and Western districts.

Po Lin Monastery

A major new addition to the territory's religious architecture is to be found at **Po Lin Monastery** on Lantau Island. In 1990, the monks and their benefactors unveiled the world's tallest bronze **figure of Buddha**, constructed by engineers brought from the People's Republic of China. Mounted on a platformed altar, the figure stands 34 meters (111 feet) high, weighs well over 250 tons, and is visible from Macau, some 40 miles away across the great Pearl River. See illustration on page 76.

THE COLONIAL PERIOD

Colonial buildings of the 19thC and early 20thC have not fared much better than older Chinese structures, but some interesting examples survive. In the heart of Central district is the refurbished **Legislative Council Building** (illustrated on page 62) built between 1903 and 1912. The squat, domed building, formerly the Supreme Court, is a fine example of British colonial architecture. Above Central, on Upper Albert Rd., is **Government House** (illustrated overleaf), the residence of Hong Kong's British Governors since 1855. A ballroom was added in 1890, and during the World War II Japanese occupation a Japanese architect, Seichi Fujimura, remodeled the building, adding some Asian touches, such as a central pagoda-roofed tower.

St John's Cathedral (1849) on Garden Rd., thought to be the first Anglican Cathedral in East Asia, might have been transplanted from an English county town. Elsewhere, **Flagstaff House** (1846), one-time

Government House

residence of the Commander-in-Chief of British forces, and the **Marine Department HQ Building** (1906) near Western Market on Connaught Rd., afford a glimpse of how Hong Kong lived and worked in more leisurely non-air-conditioned days.

On the heavily redeveloped Kowloon Peninsula, there are two tangible links with the past. The **Marine Police HQ** (1884) sits between the modern Omni Hong Kong and YMCA hotels, atop a rocky outcrop that comprises most of the block between Canton Rd. and Kowloon Park Drive overlooking Salisbury Rd. Beside Star Ferry is the electric **clock tower** (1921) of the rail terminal once on this site, demolished in 1978. The tower was saved from the wreckers' ball in one of the conservationists' few victories for preservation against the local authorities.

AFTER WORLD WAR II

The huge refugee influx in the late 1940s and 1950s forced a dramatic transformation of Hong Kong's skyline. Mounting population pressure turned it from a horizontal city of three, four or five stories to a vertical one of 14-20 stories. However, very little of any architectural merit emerged. A change in the law in 1965 allowed for block as well as single-site developments, but this only encouraged a generation of "supertanker" buildings designed to do little more than maximize rental returns. Even the indisputably striking **Jardine's House** (1972), the 52-floor headquarters of Noble House Jardines, was flawed. The building, which boasts 1,748 circular windows, had to be coated from tip to toe with aluminum cladding (1980-82) after tiles falling from its mosaic facing became a hazard to pedestrians.

THE 1980s

The decade just past has seen a change for the better. At the start of the 1980s Hong Kong's financial and related service sector challenged manufacturing as an income generator, and the world's top architects began beating a path to the colony's door.

The **Hong Kong and Shanghai Banking Corporation**, the biggest bank in the territory and the 14th largest in the world, decided it needed a new headquarters that would simultaneously reflect its importance and calm local jitters about the return of the colony to Chinese sovereignty in 1997. The Bank recruited a leading English architect, Norman Foster, to design the new building, and he came up with a revolutionary high-tech structure which, at an estimated cost of a billion US dollars, was thought to be the world's most expensive building.

The 52-floor HQ which opened in 1986 has been likened by critics to a "stainless steel ladder" and a "beached oil rig." But the battleship gray and silver 183m (600-foot) building, with a cathedral-high atrium of 52m (170 feet) lit by natural light, and a helicopter pad on the roof, articulates space in previously unexplored ways. The building, whose floors "hang" from a series of towers on suspension bridge principles, is divided into "sky villages" with wide, open floor spaces linked by slow-moving escalators. Hong Kong opinion is divided into those who loathe it and those who love it, but no one can ignore it.

Interestingly, the Bank too consulted a *fung shui* geomancer on siting, and ensured that the pair of traditional bronze lions from the old building were placed at the entrance of the new one. These lucky lions, first

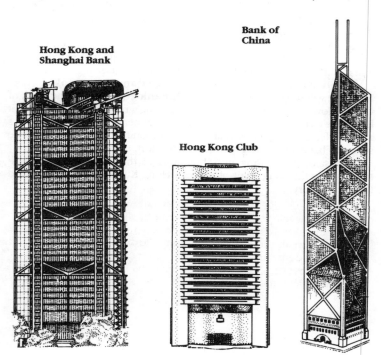

Bank of China

Hong Kong and Shanghai Bank

Hong Kong Club

brought to Hong Kong from the bank's former Shanghai headquarters, still carry bullet scars from the Japanese invasion and were actually salvaged from Osaka after World War II, where they were meant to have been melted down for shell casings.

A daring new addition to the Hong Kong architectural landscape is the replacement building for the 4-story **Hong Kong Club** (1897), which was demolished amid controversy in 1981. The new tower (illustrated on the previous page), which was completed in 1984, was designed by the Australian architect Harry Seidler, a student of Gropius. It has sweeping curves, an irregular roofline, and a monumental base wall oddly broken by a tiny viewing platform which overlooks a small park and war memorial.

Another new Hong Kong landmark is the **Exchange Square** complex. This consists of three towers of elegant pink Italian granite and mirrored glass beside the waterfront. Called a Modernist's Baroque revival, Exchange Square is Asia's first "intelligent" building; its environment is controlled by computers, its elevators talk to passengers, and beneath the floors is a central nervous system which keeps tenants in touch with Hong Kong and the world. The building, designed by resident Swiss architect Remo Riva, has waterfalls, mounts rotating art exhibitions in its rotunda, and encourages the public to use it as a thoroughfare. Its residents include the Hong Kong Stock Exchange and the American Club.

The latest contender for Hong Kong's architectural throne is the **Bank of China building**, designed by the Chinese-American architect I. M. Pei — who also designed the Louvre Museum extension in Paris. Completed in 1989, the Bank (illustrated on the previous page) inhabits a 70-story, 305m (1,000-foot) tower block composed of four triangular glass and metal shafts emerging from a 2-story granite base.

In 1991, a new headquarters for the large **Hang Seng Bank** opened, and 1992 will see completion of two **Citibank Towers** near the Bank of China. However, unless one calls Hang Seng's new building daring (it looks like an oversized Japanese stereo component), the banking sector's appetite for creating modern architectural monuments at great expense seems to have been sated with I.M. Pei's effort.

That said, it is daring new buildings of this kind that have epitomized the thrusting spirit of modern Hong Kong as it moves toward the 21st century.

Art, culture and beliefs

Hong Kong is a grand venue for artistic and cultural expression from elsewhere, but a weak generator of home-grown culture. Only since 1991 has there been a permanent exhibition of Hong Kong with archives of local art and research material — extraordinary in a city of Hong Kong's size and wealth. High rents make studio and workshop space prohibitive to most young artists. Lack of support by all but a tiny sector of the community means that few artists of any kind can make a living by their art alone: most must have other jobs.

Yet despite the impression that little happens outside the ebb and flow of the festival cycle, there is actually a great deal going on most of the time, although it can be difficult to find out about. There is neither a central ticket-clearing office, nor an English publication with comprehensive listings; different groups sell tickets in different places, and they are quite often sold out by mail solicitation in advance of public ticket sales. Good sources of information, however, are the **Arts Centre** in Wanchai, the **City Hall Concert Centre** and the **Tourist Association.**

FESTIVALS

The Urban Council of Hong Kong (the city administration) is the major arts patron. It has built most of the public facilities and created most of the annual festivals to fill them. It also sponsors local performing arts troupes. The four major exceptions to Urban Council patronage are the annual **Hong Kong Arts Festival** (January to February), a world-class event in size and cost, modeled on those in Edinburgh and Adelaide; the **Hong Kong Arts Centre**, a hub of arts activity with an ongoing program of events; the **Hong Kong Philharmonic Orchestra**, which maintains a year-round concert schedule and regularly hosts major conductors and soloists; and the **Academy for Performing Arts (APA)** which is a professional training school but opens its superb performance venues to public uses at various times through the year.

The Urban Council runs all museums in the 11 urban districts of the city and five major performing arts locations (**City Hall, Hong Kong Coliseum, Hong Kong Cultural Centre, Queen Elizabeth Stadium, Ko Shan Theatre**); maintains its own Chinese orchestra, repertory theater and contemporary dance company; and each year organizes the **Hong Kong International Film Festival** (March to April), a world-ranking event, and the biennial **Festival of Asian Arts** (October to November), which is of considerable regional significance.

CHINESE ART

Ink and watercolor painting and calligraphy are the great visual arts; ceramics the great plastic art; playing the Confucian or ancient five- or seven-stringed lute the great musical art; and Peking or provincial (that is, Cantonese) opera the great performing art.

Peking opera tends to be an event staged by the Urban Council, while **Cantonese opera** is a feature of local festivals, staged in great mat-shed amphitheaters over two or three days amid much noise and apparent confusion. For foreign visitors, provincial Cantonese opera at an outdoor festival is much to be preferred. Its closest Western kin is probably the medieval morality play or Shakespearian drama in its 16thC context, with raucous and unruly audiences.

Chinese culture in Hong Kong is derived from that of Guangdong (Canton), and Fujian provinces in South China, plus a rich infusion after the communist victory in 1949 of high Shanghainese culture derived from the literati tradition of Imperial China. During the ten years of the Cultural Revolution (1966-76) Hong Kong was a haven for artists and intellectuals escaping persecution by Red Guards in China. Virtually all the major Chinese painters of this century have spent time in Hong Kong. Elder painters of the **Lingnan School of Guangdong**, famous for colorful bird and flower paintings, migrated to Hong Kong in 1949, as did those of the **Shanghai School**, painters of the classical **Confucian literati movement** inspired by masters of the Sung (920-1280) and Ming (1368-1644) dynasties. A third group are Western-trained or influenced Hong Kong painters who have brought new ideas and materials to the traditional themes of landscape, and who belong to a much broader movement seeking valid modern expression of the ancient painting traditions.

But Hong Kong's role in the **Chinese fine arts world** is more visible in the marketing rather than the creative end of the business. The Chinese government has conducted annual antique sales since 1949, and Hong Kong dealers profited mightily, especially during the Cultural Revolution, by buying up their country's heritage for resale in Hong Kong and abroad. **Sotheby's** has held sales twice a year in Hong Kong since 1973, as has **Christie's** since the early 1980s.

As the economy has prospered, affluent Chinese have turned to Chinese art as an investment, driving prices ever upward. Prices for the best pieces have long since reached the highest international levels — higher than in London and about on a par with New York.

Great buys, however, can be found in lesser artworks of all types: paintings by minor artists or lesser works by major ones; reproductions in porcelain, bronze and jade; and woodblock print reproductions of fine paintings made by art schools in China with such precision that experts have mistaken them for the original brushwork. The city's many art and antique dealers do not cater only to those who can pay millions for a Ming jug. **Chinese Arts and Crafts** shops (see SHOPPING) and related galleries carry both originals and reproductions and an abundance of beautiful things old and new at reasonable prices.

EXPERIMENTS AND TRENDS
The earnest efforts of a small but influential community of young overseas-educated Chinese and Western residents have wrought a number of recent changes in Hong Kong's art scene. They include the launching of the annual **Fringe Festival**, to coincide with the official **Arts Festival**, and a custom-built **Academy for the Performing Arts** opened in 1985 offering training in dance, drama, music and technical skills for talented young locals and providing several state-of-the-art venues. One such, the **Lyric Theatre**, is bigger than London's Covent

Garden. Other recent developments include the opening of the **Fringe Club**, a more informal arts venue in Central District; the work of experimental theater groups; the development of the Lan Kwai Fong area in Central, with its self-consciously "ethnic" Western restaurants, discos and shops; and a Classic Cinema opened in Wanchai's **Great Eagle W.**

CHINESE BELIEFS AND PRACTICES

The Chinese pantheon of gods and system of beliefs is an admixture of **Taoism**, the **Mahayana school of Buddhism**, and ancestor worship associated with **Confucianism**, translated at the popular level into symbols and talismanic power figures which often have little to do with the ethical systems claimed to be their source, and a lot to do with rural animism. **Geomancers**, who judge the good or evil fortune of an office arrangement or building site by interpreting the influence of "wind and water" *(fung shui)*, and trance dancers who chew glass, are performing popular shamanistic rituals, not practicing a formal religion.

For the traveler the blend offers a *potpourri* of more than 300 temples containing an amazing array of deities and architectural detail, a rich festival calendar, and colorful burial rituals which require the burning of paper objects, from models of a Mercedes Benz car to fully furnished split-level houses and wads of $5 million notes drawn on the "Bank of Hell" — everything the departed spirit may need in the netherworld. The ceremony happens outside the home on the sidewalk, where mourners in white, instead of black, burn all this paper wealth in an oversized metal garbage can efficiently provided by the Urban Services Department. "Paper shops" tucked away in all the older Chinese neighborhoods sell Hell Banknotes, paper specie and the full range of funerary trappings, as well as paper effigies of the gods and all their paraphernalia for use on feast days, including many attractive woodcuts. Foreigners are welcome to buy or browse.

Even in their religious rituals southern Chinese are first and foremost materialists (the deity at the popular **Wong tai Sin Temple** gives good horse-racing tips). Their colors of prosperity and power — red and gold — illuminate their three most important institutions: temples, palatial restaurants, and weddings. The bridal shops in Wanchai and elsewhere quite pain the eye with their blazing color. The ever-present dragon and phoenix motifs (man/woman, Yin/Yang) — garish, stylized figures embroidered on bridal blankets or chasing around the eaves of restaurants — are a Hong Kong commonplace found nowhere else in such profusion.

No visitor will fail to notice the bright prints of door guards and assorted immortals, the little wooden altars to the "**kitchen god**" in homes and shops with red lightbulbs aglow beside bowls of oranges and plastic flowers, the red incense burners in hallways, or red altars on sidewalks to appease neighborhood gods. They are so common they have become invisible to Hong Kong residents. Nevertheless, they create a vivid impression of a faery land where spirits, and people who believe in them, have a busy schedule of contractual obligations designed to assure mutual avoidance. An absent spirit is a good spirit in the Chinese scheme of things: when present they are usually malevolent.

Basic information

Before you go

DOCUMENTS REQUIRED

US citizens may stay for up to one month without a **visa**, British citizens for up to six months and British Commonwealth citizens for three months. For further information contact the **Hong Kong Government Office** in your country (see page 32 for US and UK contact details). **Visa applications** take up to six weeks. **Health documents** are only necessary if you have visited an infected country. Check current health requirements when making travel reservations.

Overseas **drivers' licenses** (not provisional) held by visitors are valid in Hong Kong for one year, as are international drivers' licenses. After that, visitors must change to a Hong Kong license. **Third-party insurance** is also required.

TRAVEL AND MEDICAL INSURANCE

Take out travel and medical insurance before you leave. **American Express** provides worldwide comprehensive travel and medical coverage in collaboration with **TransCare International**, who provide on-the-spot emergency assistance worldwide 24 hours a day. Contact **American Express Travel Service** offices for information. **Extrasure** sells a comprehensive package in collaboration with **Medex International**, who operate a 24-hour telephone advice service in Hong Kong. **Blue Cross (Asia Pacific) Insurance** in Hong Kong sells coverage for five days to six months. When buying insurance at home, check whether the company has a reciprocal agreement with companies in Hong Kong for refund of medical expenses.

The **IAMAT** (International Association for Medical Assistance to Travelers) is a nonprofit organization that has a directory of English-speaking doctors who will call, for a fixed fee. There are member hospitals and clinics throughout the world, including several in Hong Kong. Membership is free, and other benefits include information on health risks overseas. For further information write to **IAMAT** headquarters in the US or in Europe *(417 Center St., Lewiston, NY 14092, USA, or 57 Voirets, 1212 Grand-Lancy, Genève, Switzerland).*

MONEY

The unit of currency is the Hong Kong dollar (HK$). It is divided into 100 cents. Since 1983 the HK$ has been pegged to the US$ at the rate of US$1 to HK$7.82, with minor fluctuations. Banks and newspapers provide daily exchange rates. **Travelers checks** issued by American Express, Barclays, Thomas Cook and Citibank, and major charge/credit cards (American Express, Diners Club, MasterCard, Visa) are widely accepted. Stores often add the charge/credit card service charge to goods, and bargaining prices are for cash. Check whether quoted prices refer to HK$ or US$. Confusion often arises because Hong Kong's currency is denominated like American in terms of "dollars" rather than a foreign word.

Carry cash in small amounts only. Travelers checks issued by all major companies are widely recognized. Make sure you read the instructions included with your travelers checks. **It is important to note separately the serial numbers of your checks and the telephone number to call in case of loss.** Specialist travelers check companies such as American Express provide extensive local refund facilities through their own offices or agents.

CUSTOMS
Duty-free allowances for alcoholic drinks, tobacco and perfume conform to international standard limits (details are available on all flights). There are no restrictions on bringing in consumer goods, currency, precious metals or gems. **Airport tax** is HK$150 on departure (no charge for children under 12 years).

GETTING THERE
By air   Most visitors arrive by air, landing on the spectacular harbor runway at Hong Kong International Airport (locally known as Kai Tak), which is just 10-20 minutes from Kowloon city center, depending upon traffic congestion, and 20 to 45 minutes to the Hong Kong Island central business district. More than 30 airlines fly regular scheduled services direct to and from Kai Tak.

By sea   Most visiting cruise liners dock at the Ocean Terminal, which includes a huge upscale agglomeration of interconnected shopping centers with more than 600 individual outlets, as well as three first-class Omni Group hotels, several restaurants, office and apartment blocks. These line the Kowloon waterfront beside the Star Ferry terminal, facing Hong Kong island's Central business district.

By rail   Visitors traveling by train via China arrive at Hung Hom Railway Station in Kowloon. The immigration and customs checkpoint for rail and road is at Lo Wu on the border with China.

CLIMATE AND CLOTHES
Hong Kong is just s of the Tropic of Cancer and has a subtropical monsoon climate. Fall is the most pleasant season. The dry monsoon from late September to late December is characterized by warm temperatures and low humidity, during which medium-weight clothing and sweaters are adequate dress. Winter (January to February) can be uncomfortably cold with a biting N wind, although it never freezes, and heavier winter clothing is advised. Few buildings have central heating

or insulation. Spring (March to May) brings the sw monsoon, with rising temperatures and humidity. Summer (mid-May to September) is hot and wet; temperatures seldom exceed 35°C (95°F), but humidity hovers in the 80s and 90s, without much relief to be found at night.

Shorts, T-shirt, sandals, and a sweater for frosty air conditioning are recommended summer dress. For professionals on business trips, suits are the norm all year round. Dress for dining out varies; if, for example, you are uncertain about whether a jacket and tie are necessary, inquire first. Hong Kong dresses well for work and, often, for evening wear.

US INFORMATION SERVICES

Washington   Hong Kong Government Office, British Embassy, 1233 20th St., NW., 504 Washington, DC 20038, USA ☎(202) 331-8947 [Tx]23-440484 [Fx](415) 421-2612. Information on visas, regulations, advice on living and working in Hong Kong.

New York   Hong Kong Tourist Association, 590 5th Ave., New York, NY 10036, USA ☎(212) 869-5008/9 [Tx]23 425817 [Fx](212) 730-2605.

Los Angeles   Hong Kong Tourist Association, 10940 Wilshire Blvd., Suite 1220, LA 90024, USA ☎(213) 208-4582 [Tx]23-3711534 [Fx](213) 208-1869.

Chicago   Hong Kong Tourist Association, 333 North Michigan Ave., Suite 2400, Chicago, IL 60601, USA ☎(312) 782-3872 [Tx]023 4330404.

UK AND COMMONWEALTH INFORMATION SERVICES

Britain   Hong Kong Government Office, 6 Grafton St., London W1X 3LB ☎(071) 499-9821. Information on visas, regulations, advice on working and living in Hong Kong. The reading room has official public records, departmental annual reports, periodicals, newspapers and cuttings files on cultural, historical and current events.

Hong Kong Tourist Association, 125 Pall Mall, 5th Floor, London SW1Y 5EA ☎(071) 930-4775 [Tx]8950165 [Fx](071) 930-4777. Useful information and publications. If necessary, inquiries are referred to their Hong Kong head office.

Canada   Hong Kong Tourist Association, 347 Bay St., Suite 909, Toronto, ON M5H 2R7, Canada ☎(416) 366-2389 [Fx](416) 366-1098.

Australia   Hong Kong Tourist Association, 55 Harrington St., Level 5, The Rocks, Sydney, NSW 2000, Australia ☎(02) 251-2855.

New Zealand   Hong Kong Tourist Association, PO Box 2120, Auckland, New Zealand ☎(9) 521-3167 [Fx](9) 521-3165.

Getting around

FROM THE AIRPORT TO THE CITY

There are four things to bear in mind once you have cleared immigration at Kai Tak Airport: luggage trolleys are stored at the extreme right and left of the carousels, confusingly out of sight; **free local calls** can be made at the various telephone boxes; the public lavatories (rest rooms) are in the center area near the baggage checking desks; and also in the center area, young women sometimes hand out free packets of useful information from the **Hong Kong Tourist Association (HKTA)**, which is otherwise available for the taking from fixed display stands.

Once through Customs, there is an **information desk** run by the **HKTA**, another by the **Macau Tourism Authority**, and other desks where transportation arrangements can be made before facing the crowds outside. There is also a separate early exit to the **hotel bus pick-up area**, which, unless someone is meeting you, avoids the crush of people waiting outside for arrivals.

The **taxi stand** is near the arrival lounge. All taxis carry yellow labels on inside door panels which show current fares. A yellow notice board shows **taxi fares** to major districts in Hong Kong and Kowloon. There is a **surcharge** for each piece of luggage (HK$3), and another HK$20 is charged for trips through the Cross-Harbour Tunnel to Hong Kong Island, the value of a round trip for the taxi.

The most common error travelers make is thinking the "dollars" on the taxi meter means US$ and sometimes paying accordingly, with drivers obligingly failing to correct them. Rates to Central are typically about HK$65, which can equal an expensive mistake if paid with the wrong currency.

An **airport bus service** (Airbus) operates air-conditioned vehicles on three routes from outside the terminal, stopping at most of the major hotels; the A2 and A3 buses go to Hong Kong Island (HK$12 each) and run every 12 to 20 minutes ; the A1 bus goes to Tsimshatsui tourist district in Kowloon (HK$8) every 10-20 minutes. The ride to Hong Kong takes 20-45 minutes and to Tsimshatsui in Kowloon 10-20 minutes. The A2 goes through the tunnel to Wanchai and Central hotel environs; the A3 goes to Causeway Bay district. No change is given.

The **Regal Airport Hotel** (see WHERE TO STAY), reached by a pedestrian causeway from the terminal, is the place to kill time at the airport. Day-use guest rooms are available. Most luxury items for sale in Hong Kong (apart from cigarettes, liquor and some perfumes) are already duty-free, so shopping in the airport or outer departure Duty Free Shoppers stalls does not save money — and often costs more.

TAXIS

All taxis have meters and are reasonably cheap. They charge for additional luggage and waiting fees. If you cross the harbor, you must also pay the driver's return toll at the Cross-Harbour Tunnel; at Aberdeen Tunnel you pay one-way only. Hong Kongers often think of Kowloon as a foreign city, and vice versa; so taxi drivers unfamiliar with "the other side" may hand you across to a colleague who is. You pay one driver only.

Drivers are often helpful, although their English is likely to be poor-to-nonexistent. To minimize communication difficulties, bring a map, or, before leaving, ask your hotel receptionist to write down your destination in Chinese. Most residents tip only the odd change to the next dollar, if at all. This has led many drivers to develop an annoying habit of assuming the tip when giving change, rather than waiting for you to pass it back. When looking for a taxi avoid restricted areas with a yellow line painted beside the curb.

Taxi habits in Hong Kong can be a source of frustration to tourists. There are few formal taxi lines on public streets, and most residents are accustomed to curbside free-for-alls when taxis are scarce. Besides yellow-line zones where they may not stop, taxi drivers going off-duty or back across the harbor will often cover their meters to indicate they will not pick up passengers. Most travelers don't know this and resent being ignored by drivers. Even when meters are covered, drivers will sometimes pick up passengers going their way, and one often sees local residents calling out their destination in Chinese, in the hope that such drivers will pick them up. Tourists sometimes mistake this interaction for preference by drivers for locals. Taxis can be hard to find during rush hours, when their shifts change between 4 and 5pm, and when it rains.

There are about 15,000 licensed taxis, divided into three types: red in Hong Kong and Kowloon (14,572), green in the New Territories (2,448) and blue on Lantau Island (40). Reds charge HK$9 on flagfall and 90 cents per 250m (275-yard) stretch thereafter; greens and blues are slightly cheaper.

MASS TRANSIT RAILWAY (MTR)

Hong Kong's modern air-conditioned subway system is clean, quick and convenient, despite being reputed to be the busiest subway railway in the world, with a daily passenger load of just under 2 million. Three lines from Central District link most shopping, business and industrial areas in Hong Kong and Kowloon — **see the MTR map at the back of the guide**. Trains run every 5 minutes from 6am-12.45am and are extremely congested at rush hours.

The fare depends on the length of your journey. Ticket machines have maps with prices indicated from HK$3 to $7.50 above them. Buy your ticket from the station vending machines. Exchange silver in the change machines at one of the information desks. Retrieve your ticket at the turnstile going in — you will need it to exit at the other end. **Special tourist tickets** are sold at main stations and by the HKTA; they are only issued within two weeks of arrival and on presentation of a valid **passport** (☎ *750-0170*).

BUSES

The city's double-deckers provide scenic, cheap and efficient travel, but the buses are crowded and rarely air-conditioned. Expect long lines at rush hours. The drivers' nonchalant skill can be breathtaking, especially on mountainous routes (not recommended for those who suffer from motion sickness). The HKTA publishes comprehensive bus route leaflets. Fares, paid on entry, depend on the distance covered, and change is not given.

Bus services are run by two companies, both founded in 1933: **China**

Motor Bus (CMB) on Hong Kong Island and **Kowloon Motor Bus (KMB)** on the peninsula. They jointly operate 26 cross-harbor routes. The smaller CMB operates 87 island routes carrying more than 300 million passengers per year. KMB runs 243 routes and the Airbus system, carrying more than 980 million passengers a year. Both have some schedules running 24 hours a day (☎ *CMB 656-8556; KMB 786-8888).*

New Lantau Bus Co (1973) Ltd has eight routes on Lantau island and a fleet of 60 buses. Weekends the daily passenger numbers swell from the weekday average of 8,200 to more than 20,000 on Sundays and public holidays (☎ *984-7120).*

TRAMS

Hong Kong's electric trams offer an efficient service and the cheapest ride in town — no mean accomplishment for a service that began in 1904. These 160 or so clanking green anachronisms with bells instead of horns have great charm and afford a leisurely view of the theater-of-the-streets for about 13kms (8 miles) from Kennedy Town in the w through Central District (about 30 minutes from Central), Wanchai, Causeway Bay and North Point to Shaukeiwan in the E (about 50 minutes from Central). There is also a route that dog-legs s to Happy Valley.

Avoid rush hours, when trams are packed, and if you can, aim for the best seats, which are upstairs at the front. There are about 30 seats upstairs and 20 below. Smoking is allowed upstairs. On leaving, you pay a flat fare (the princely sum of HK60 cents, 20 cents for children under 12 years), and only exact money is accepted. Not all trams go the full distance, so check the destination board before you get on. There are actually six overlapping routes. The 165 stops are mostly covered islands in the middle of streets, or sometimes just painted yellow street markers. Beware moving vehicles when you exit at the latter. Trams run from 6am to 1am and carry about 350,000 passengers a day.

Ask at your hotel desk for details of organized tram tours for sight-seeing and evening entertainment. The **Hong Kong Tramways Ltd.** (☎ *559-8918)* rents out trams for private tours and parties and has two that have been specially renovated to replicate the 19thC splendor of cars in hardwood, seats in cane and metal parts in gleaming brass. Trams are, more typically, less genteel affairs, used as brightly painted moving billboards for local companies. The HKTA produces a "Tram Travel" fact sheet which includes things to stop and see along the way.

PEAK TRAM

One of the world's steepest funicular railways and in service more than 100 years, the **Peak Tram** (☎ *522-0922, operates 7am to midnight)* runs 1.4km (nearly a mile) from its upper Central station beneath the St John's Building to Victoria Peak and offers superb views of the city and harbor. **Citybus** (☎ *722-4866, operates every 20mins 9am-7pm)* runs a free shuttle service from Star Ferry Hong Kong to the lower Peak Tram terminal on double-decker buses with their upstairs open to the sky. The tram service was completely modernized in August 1989 with new cars and a computerized cable system and carries almost 11,000 passengers daily, more than 90 percent of them tourists.

PUBLIC LIGHT BUS (MINIBUSES)

More than 3,000 comfortable cream and red 14-seaters cover major routes. They are quicker and more convenient than buses, cheaper than taxis, and many have the added attraction of air conditioning. Drivers stop when you shout *"Yau lok!"* Pay the driver as you get off. The fare is determined by the distance traveled.

In addition, there are some 1,300 cream and green 14-seaters which follow fixed routes on fixed fares and timetables. The No. 1 PLB service, which runs every 5 minutes, is the best way of getting from Star Ferry Kowloon to Tsimshatsui East hotel and shopping area. Services also run from Star Ferry Hong Kong for Aberdeen, Ocean Park and beyond, and from City Hall (beside Star Ferry) for Victoria Peak. The fixed fare is payable on boarding the minibus, and change is not provided.

KOWLOON-CANTON RAILWAY (KCR)

Four express trains run daily from Hung Hom Station, Kowloon, to Guangzhou (Canton) in China. One of the world's great train journeys also starts at Hung Hom Station, traveling via Canton, Peking and the Trans-Siberian Railway to Europe — and has been doing so, barring wars and political upheavals, since the KCR began in 1910. Telephone **Hung Hom Station** (☎ 3-646-321) for schedules.

Trains to the China border were electrified in 1983 and now carry more than a half-million passengers daily. Trains have links with the MTR system and run regularly from 5.45am to midnight, and provide quick access to Shatin, the Chinese University, Taipo and the northern New Territories. Trains are crowded at rush hours and on holidays, especially at Chinese New Year and Ching Ming, when large numbers of local people take a traditional trip to China.

KCRC also operates a **Light Rail Transit (LRT)** system along a 23km (14-mile) stretch in the western New Territories, roughly around and between Tuen Mun and Yuen Long, which handles almost 300,000 boardings daily *(service hours: 5.30am-12.30am* ☎ *468-7788)*.

RICKSHAWS

Once a common form of transportation, rickshaws are no longer used by local people. They linger on only as a tourist trap at the Hong Kong terminal of the Star Ferry. If you plan to hire a rickshaw, negotiate the price first — for both the ride and the photographs.

FERRIES

The dramatic growth of Hong Kong around one of Asia's finest harbors has led the territory to develop the largest ferry system in the world.

Star Ferry   Founded in 1898, the famous Star Ferry is still the best way to cross the harbor. It takes 8 minutes from Central to Tsimshatsui. The service is frequent, the fares cheap, the 13 boats immaculate and the views superb. The best seats (first-class) are at either end upstairs.

Another service runs from Central to Hung Hom. The three routes carry about 40 million passengers a year. *(Service hours 6am-11pm)*.

Hong Kong Yaumatei ferries Founded in 1923, this company has altogether some 28 routes, carrying about 200,000 passengers and ferrying 14,000 vehicles daily. These include more than 15 cross-harbor services, including fast hovercraft and three services for vehicles, which link various points on the Island to various points in Kowloon. Some of the 80 HYF ferries can be cheaper and faster than MTR or bus. Call HYF *(☎ 542-3081)* for schedules.

Outlying Island ferries HYF runs three services to Lantau (there is also an independent service to Discovery Bay from Blake's Pier), and two services to Lamma Island, Cheung Chau, Peng Chau and Po Toi. Frequency varies from hourly to twice daily and from a 6am start to 11.30pm final departure time. Air-conditioned deluxe class is available on triple-deckers, with increased fares on weekends *(about HK$20 total one-way)*. The terminal is a short walk to the w of Star Ferry, Hong Kong. The largest boats carry upward of 1,500 people and are extremely crowded and noisy on holiday weekends. A must for those who like mixing with local teenagers fleeing public housing for a bit of island air, but otherwise to be avoided. *(Schedules available from HKTA, or HYF ☎ 542-3081)*. (See EXCURSIONS.)

Hydrofoils and jetfoils Fast hydrofoils and jetfoils make the crossing from Hong Kong to Macau in about one hour, every half hour from 7am to 1.30am. The terminal is at the w end of the Central waterfront sharing the Shun Tak Centre complex with the Victoria Hotel. Weekend trips are more expensive and round-trip fares are cheaper. *(Contact Far East Hydrofoil Co. (☎ 545-7021) or Hong Kong Macau Hydrofoil Co. (☎ 521-8302) for information: boat service hours are 8am-5.30am)*.

Hongkong Hi Speed Ferries Ltd ☎815-3043.

Shun Tak Shipping Co. ☎859-3333 for details of the regular twice-daily ferry service to Macau. The crossing takes 3 hours; cabins can be reserved.

Shun Tak Enterprises Corp/Far East Jetfoils Co Ltd ☎859-3333: boat service hours 6am-4pm.

Junks/sampans Motorized junks and sampans *(gaidos)* run cheap services between the islands and the coastal villages. Some go to remarkably inaccessible places, offering a glimpse of an ancient way of life. (See EXCURSIONS.)

GETTING AROUND BY CAR

Cars drive on the left, traffic rules and signs are standard, and road surfaces are generally good. But in the city a car is usually more of a liability than an asset. Traffic is heavy and parking difficult: the multi-story garages can be expensive and are not always convenient.

A car is more useful for visiting the rural areas in the New Territories. There are several quick exits from the city and some good scenic routes across the mountains and along the coasts. *(Contact the Automobile Association (☎ 739-5273) for details.)*

RENTING A CAR

For chauffeur-driven or self-drive car rentals, contact **Avis Rent-a-Car** (☎ *890-6988 or 576-8831 for international reservations)*, **National** (☎ *525-1365)* or **Hertz** (☎ *774-5776)*. They accept foreign driver's licenses. Insurance is additional. There are altogether about 50 car rental agencies in Hong Kong.

GETTING AROUND ON FOOT

Hong Kong is very compact, and walking is one of the best ways to see the city, despite the crowds. (Details of a number of interesting walks are provided in SIGHTS AND PLACES OF INTEREST.) The HKTA publishes for sale a variety of walking tour booklets with maps and sights routes with helpful hints for visitors. Keep to pedestrian crossings, as jaywalking is illegal and can incur a large fine.

On-the-spot information

PUBLIC HOLIDAYS

Chinese holidays are based on the lunar calendar and vary from year to year. **New Year's Day**, January 1. **Chinese New Year**, first three days of lunar year, excluding Sunday, usually in February. **Good Friday**. **Easter Saturday**. **Easter Monday**. **Ching Ming Festival**, early April. **Dragon Boat Festival**, June. **Queen Elizabeth's Birthday**, June 14, or if a Sunday, following Monday. **August Bank Holiday**, last Saturday and **Liberation Day** (from the Japanese after World War II), last Monday in August. **Mid-Fall Festival** (Moon Festival), late September. **Ch'ung Yeung Festival**, mid-October. **Christmas Day**, December 25. **Boxing Day**, first weekday after Christmas.

TYPHOONS (HURRICANES)

Every summer brings half a dozen typhoon warnings, and every few years Hong Kong takes a direct hit, with torrential rains and sustained wind speeds of 120 knots or more at the height of the storm, which can last between 2 and 15 hours. Everything grinds to a halt, since venturing outdoors during a typhoon can be suicidal.

The danger period for typhoons runs from July to October. Four warning signals are used: Signals 1 and 3 are cautionary and may turn out to be false alarms. However, storm conditions can develop rapidly. Transportation services (especially ferries) may be curtailed at short notice. Signal No. 8 means high winds within hours, and No. 10 is a direct hit. Local radio and television carry regular typhoon bulletins.

TIME ZONE

Hong Kong is 13 hours ahead of Eastern Standard Time all year round with no daylight saving adjustment, so during Daylight Saving, Hong Kong is 12 hours ahead, and 14 to 16 hours ahead of the other time zones in the US. Compared with Europe, Hong Kong is 8 hours ahead of GMT all year round with no daylight saving adjustment. So during British Summer Time Hong Kong is 7 hours ahead of the UK.

Hong Kong Time	9am	5pm
• Sydney	11am	7pm
• Vancouver	5pm ‡	1am
• France	2am	10am
• India	6.30am	2.30pm
• Japan	10am	6pm
• New Zealand	1pm	9pm
• Thailand	8am	4pm
• United Kingdom	1am	9pm
United States		
• New York	8pm ‡	4am
• San Francisco	5pm ‡	1am

‡ Previous day
Where local Summer Time applies, add one hour.

LANGUAGES

All government bodies use English; laws and legislation are in English with translators and translations provided; schoolchildren are taught in English; but the dominant language within the community is Cantonese. Chinese languages have very few basic words, usually fewer than a thousand, but each word can have up to 30 different meanings, depending on context, combination and, chiefly, intonation (Cantonese has nine tones, more than any other dialect). Greetings are complicated — even "thank you" is difficult, for there are two forms of thanks and they are not interchangeable. It is usually possible to get by with English.

BANKS AND CURRENCY EXCHANGE

Banks, money changers and major hotels exchange foreign currency. Most banks are open Monday 9am-4.30pm, Saturday 9am-12.30pm, and are closed on public holidays. The **American Express Bank Office** (One Pacific Place, Flr 35, 88 Queensway ☎ main office 844-0688/customer service 810-8828, map 4 C4) is open Monday 9am-5pm, Saturday 9am-noon; the **Hang Seng Bank** (Hang Seng Bank Building, 83 Des Voeux Rd., Central ☎ 825-5111, map 3 B3) is open Monday 9am-5pm, Saturday 9am-1pm.

Hotels are often willing to change major foreign currencies at any hour. Money changers are private companies that sometimes charge a lower commission than the banks. To save money, avoid using the airport money changer.

American Express also has a **MoneyGram** ® money transfer service that makes it possible to wire money worldwide in just minutes, from any American Express Travel Service Office. This service is available to all customers and is not limited to American Express Card members. Payment can be made in cash, or with an American Express Card with a Centurion Credit Line, an American Express Optima (SM) Card, Visa or

MasterCard. For the location nearest you ☎ **1-800-543-4080** (Canada and US).

SHOPPING HOURS

Most shops and department stores are open on Sunday and public holidays but are closed for the first three days of Chinese New Year. Shops are open 10am-7pm or later, street stalls and night markets until 11pm or later.

RUSH HOURS

Commuters fill streets and public transportation weekdays from 8-9.30am, 12.30-2pm (especially in Central) and 5-6.30pm. On Saturday rush hours are 8-9.30am and noon-2pm. On race meeting days (Wednesday or Saturday during the August to May racing season) heavy traffic builds up from an hour before the start. During holidays and summer weekends Outlying Island ferries and public transportation to amusement parks are very crowded.

POSTAL AND TELEPHONE SERVICES

Two General Post Offices (see USEFUL ADDRESSES) are open Monday to Saturday 8am-6pm, and branch offices (there are more than 100) Monday 9am-5pm, Saturday 9am-1pm. Coin-operated stamp-vending machines are located outside all post offices. Airmail to North America and Europe takes about a week.

Telephones are rented at a flat rate, and local calls are free. Public pay phones are scarce, but shops, offices and restaurants readily oblige if you ask to use the phone. Most major hotels provide International Direct Dialing (IDD) and telex services and charge a flat rate on top of IDD calls, and a 10-25 percent commission on telexes. There are also three cable and wireless offices run by Hong Kong Telecom.

The range of consumer telephone services available is enormous. It includes such things as on-line translators, special overseas calls, charge/credit card services, computer databank links, video-conferencing, *et al.* If you are in Hong Kong on business or for an extended visit, Hong Kong Telephone Co. has booklets for the asking. Facsimile machines and cards in computers have virtually replaced telex use in Hong Kong. For English-language operator assistance ☎1081.

PUBLIC LAVATORIES (REST ROOMS)

Although there are plenty of public WCs, they are not very inviting. In hotels, however, they are usually spotless, and attendants expect a HK$1-2 tip. The WCs in smaller restaurants may not be clean and usually lack paper. Many in the New Territories are squat-style affairs and lack commodes. Mass Transit Railway (MTR) stations do not have public lavatories.

ELECTRIC CURRENT

The current is 220V 50 cycles AC, and plugs are 3-prong and often confusing: there are two peg sizes based on fuse voltage, variously round or square pegs, and differently shaped plug heads and outlet adaptors. The result in most household outlet terminals is an intimidating, unsightly and probably hazardous array of too many electrical connections.

LAWS AND REGULATIONS

Laws follow the British legal system with local variations, such as the HK$2,000 maximum penalty for jaywalking. Morality laws are still Victorian: homosexuality is illegal; "the abominable act of buggery," even between a consenting man and woman, carries a theoretical life sentence. Drug abuse and firearms laws are severe; fireworks are illegal. Although rarely used, extensive police powers still survive from the 1966-67 emergency. For example, more than 2 million people are stopped in the streets of Hong Kong each year to check that they are carrying legally-required identification cards. The ICAC (Independent Commission Against Corruption — or, as some have it, "I Can't Accept Checks") has special investigative powers in both public and private sectors.

NARCOTIC DRUGS

Travelers are warned against carrying drugs in any circumstance. In Hong Kong, the maximum penalty for trafficking is life imprisonment and a fine of $5 million, and the assets of convicted drug traffickers can be confiscated. Even persons found in illegal possession of small quantities of drugs are liable to 3 years' imprisonment and a fine of $10,000.

You are strongly advised:

- **NEVER** to agree to carry any amount of drugs;
- **NEVER** to check in baggage on behalf of someone who claims to have excess baggage;
- **NEVER** to carry packages or baggage for anyone unless you are absolutely sure they don't contain drugs.

Report to the Police (☎ 527 1234) or the Customs (☎ 545 6182) if a possible drug-carrying deal is put to you in Hong Kong. All reports are treated in confidence.

IVORY

The Hong Kong government introduced stringent regulations covering the import and export of ivory in July 1990, in order to comply with the world-wide ban on trade in ivory — imposed because the Convention on International Trade in Endangered Species (CITES) now classifies the African elephant as a highly endangered species.

Visitors who purchase any ivory products in Hong Kong (regardless of the amount) are required to obtain an import license from their country of residence as well as an export license to take the ivory out of Hong Kong. They are otherwise liable to prosecution, resulting in a fine and forfeiture of the ivory in question. Anyone wishing to purchase ivory products is advised to check with the **Hong Kong Agriculture and Fisheries Department** (☎ 733 2144), as well as their own consulate or trade commission.

SOCIAL CUSTOMS AND ETIQUETTE

Hong Kong's generous welcome can easily lull the foreigner into taking the city's people and social customs for granted. Sensitivity to the following cultural differences is advised.

Noise

There's lots of it everywhere — even the countryside is not immune, as camping and vacation crowds rarely travel far without the company of their enormous portable radios and tape decks, blaring "Canto-Pop" songs for the benefit of anyone within earshot. The Cantonese are the Latins of China, loud, voluble and demonstrative when excited. Shops blare music into the street to attract passersby; mahjong players always crack the pieces down with force — the resulting sound is half the fun. Few Cantonese see other people's noise as an invasion of their privacy, nor theirs as an invasion of yours.

Bargaining

Don't be put off — Asians don't just bargain to save money: it's a social convention, and not without its graces. When bargaining is not possible, shops will post a notice saying "fixed price"; everything else is fair game. Most merchants will reduce the original asking price by 10 percent; tough bargainers and large purchases often secure greater discounts.

Crowds

Street crowds can be intimidating, especially if you're in them. They look (and behave) like ants without a queen. It puzzles people that so formally civil and guest-conscious a culture can produce such rude street life. But there is a pattern to it. Westerners demand more personal space in public and react aggressively when it's violated; the Chinese need (and, indeed, have) much less room and simply don't take all the bumping personally. The throngs can be practically navigated if you stay calm and patient, adjust your pace to the conditions and, as you walk, stare fixedly at the sidewalk a few feet ahead, cleaving a path through the oncoming horde.

Encounters

Hong Kong Chinese often smile both when they're embarrassed and happy, and this may confuse the drift of casual conversation. Chinese with poor English can be curt in the effort to escape an awkward situation.

Photographs

In the countryside or even in urban, traditional Chinese districts, tourists are still sometimes chased off by an angry farmer or butcher for trying to steal their spirit essence with their inquisitive cameras. Don't be too obvious, or too intrusive, and take your time. Accept a straightforward "no"; but old people can be coy and open to persuasion. Check the eyes for a smile: when it reaches the mouth you've won. On the tourist trail people might demand a tip; otherwise, never.

Tipping

Most eating establishments include a 10 percent service charge in the bill, but leave more if you enjoyed the meal. Tip hotel rest room attendants HK$1-2. Taxi drivers appreciate small change, or more for longer trips or if the driver has been helpful.

HEALTH AND HYGIENE

Tap water in the urban areas meets World Health Organization standards and is safe to drink. In rural areas it may be polluted and is best avoided; use bottled spring water. The harbor is extremely polluted, and swimming at beaches near the urban areas may be unsafe. Warnings are posted at affected beaches, but independent monitoring suggests official recommendations may not be cautious enough (see SWIMMING, pages 169-170).

DISABLED TRAVELERS

Building codes have only recently required facilities for disabled people, so newer buildings are better equipped. The Hong Kong Arts Centre, Hong Kong Cultural Centre and Museum of Art, City Hall, Queen Elizabeth Stadium and some shopping plazas (notably City Plaza in Tai Koo Shing) have ramps and rest rooms for disabled people. Kai Tak Airport has rest rooms for disabled people next to the women's WC in the departure and arrival lounges. The Kowloon-Canton Railway has manual gates at every station for disabled people, and barrier attendants to help. The MTR network has no special facilities for disabled travelers.

LOCAL NEWSPAPERS AND BOOKSTORES

There are two local English daily newspapers, Rupert Murdoch's pro-establishment *South China Morning Post (SCMP)* and the more independent *Hong Kong Standard;* the *International Herald Tribune* and the *Asian Wall Street Journal* both print editions in Hong Kong. The *Far Eastern Economic Review* and *Asiaweek* are useful weekly regional news magazines; *Time* and *Newsweek* are printed locally.

The SCMP's weekly *TV and Entertainment Times* includes a local entertainment guide, and the monthly *City News*, issued free of charge at the City Hall by the Urban Council of Hong Kong, covers cultural and sporting events. There are also various tourist newspapers and booklets from private publishers and produced commercially by the Hong Kong Tourist Association available at hotels.

International newspapers and magazines are sold at hotels and by the news vendors at Star Ferry, Kowloon and Hong Kong sides. Hong Kong is a regional media center for English-language journalism, and for the Overseas Chinese, who support a total of 65 newspapers in the language, 41 of which are dailies. There are also more than 600 periodicals published in Hong Kong — printing and publishing in both languages is one of the territory's major export industries.

ENGLISH BOOKSTORES

Bookazine Alexandra House, Central/Prince's Building, Central, map **3B3**
Commercial Press Wellington St., Central, map **3B3**
Hong Kong Book Centre 25 Des Voeux Rd., Central, map **3B3**
Kelly & Walsh 100 Ice House St., Central/Pacific Place, map **3C3**
SCMP Family Bookstore Hong Kong Star Ferry Terminal, map **4B4**

Swindons   Ocean Terminal, Tsimshatsui, Kowloon, map **7**F2
Times Books   Hutchison House, Central, map **4**C4
See also SHOPPING, page 153.

Useful addresses

TOURIST INFORMATION
Hong Kong Tourist Association (HKTA)   Head Office, Flr 35 and information center in basement of Jardine's House, Connaught Rd., Central ☎524-4191, map **3**B3. Open Mon-Fri 8am-6pm, Sat 8am-1pm. The Association runs a tourist "hotline" for fast answers in English, Japanese or Mandarin Chinese ☎801-7177.
CAB   For on-the-spot information there is an excellent Community Advice Bureau run by volunteers at St John's Cathedral ☎524-5444.
American Express Travel Service   Grd Flr, New World Tower, 16-18 Queen's Rd., Central ☎843-1888, map **3**C3. Open Mon-Fri 9am-5.30pm, Sat 9am-12.30pm.
Kai Tak International Airport   ☎769-7531 (24 hours), map **2**D5.

IMMIGRATION
Head Office   Gloucester Rd., Wanchai, Hong Kong ☎824-6111, map **5**C6

POST OFFICES
GPO Hong Kong   2 Connaught Pl., Connaught Rd., Central ☎523-1071, map **4**B4
GPO Kowloon   405 Nathan Rd., Tsimshatsui, Kowloon ☎388-4111, map **7**D3

CONSUMER ASSISTANCE
Automobile Association   Marsh Rd., Wanchai ☎827-8394, map **5**C7
Consumer Council   6 Heard St., Wanchai ☎574-8297, map **5**C7

CABLE AND WIRELESS
Hong Kong Telecom Centre   22 Fenwick St., Wanchai ☎829-1111, map **4**C5
Rm 1028   Flr 1, Exchange Sq., Central ☎862-1290, map **3**B3
Ocean Terminal   Tsimshatsui, Kowloon ☎367-6901, map **7**F2

BUS TOURS
Audio Tours   Rm. 1602 Wing On Centre, 111 Connaught Rd., Central ☎545-8388, map **3**A2
Grayline Tours   72 Nathan Rd., Kowloon ☎368-7111, map **7**E3
President Tours   27 Cameron Rd., Kowloon ☎369-4808, map **7**E3
Sightseeing Tours   Lobby, Hong Kong Hotel, Kowloon ☎367-7914, map **7**E2

Winston Tours   Rm. 1512, Lee Wai Commercial Building, 1-3 Hart Ave., Tsimshatsui, Kowloon ☎366-4440, map **7E3**

TRAM TOURS AND OPEN-TOP BUS TOUR
Tourist Enterprises Ltd   Rm. 901, Lee Wai Commercial Building, 1-3 Hart Ave., Tsimshatsui, Kowloon ☎368-0647, map **7E3**

VILLAGE TOUR
Sung Dynasty Village Tour   Lai Chi Kok, Kowloon ☎741-5114, map **2D4**

WATER TOURS
Seaview Harbour Tours   Sincere Building, Central ☎541-6206, map **3A2**. Runs water and land excursions, some of which include the Outlying Islands.
Watertours of Hong Kong Ltd   Boarding points at Blake Pier in Hong Kong and Ocean Terminal promenade in Kowloon ☎525-4808/526-3538 (reservations), 730-3031/367-1970 (information), maps **3B3** and **7E2**. Runs a fleet of six gaily painted motorized junks on about 20 harbor or outlying island tours daily.
  Similar tours also depart from the Hong Kong Hilton *(2 Queen's Rd., Central ☎ 523-3111, map 4 C4)*.

AIRLINES
More than 30 airlines run regularly scheduled flights into and out of Hong Kong. The following is a selection:
Air France   Alexandra House, Central ☎524-8145 (reservations) ☎522-1190 (tickets), map **3B3**
Alitalia   Hutchison House, Central ☎523-7047, map **4C4**
American   Flr 37, Edinburgh Tower, Landmark, Central ☎826-9269, map **3C3**
British Airways   Grd Flr, Alexandra House, Central ☎868-0303, map **3B3**
CAAC   Grd Flr, Edinburgh Tower, Landmark, 17 Queen's Rd., Central ☎521-6416, map **3C3**
Canadian   Swire House, Central ☎868-3123, map **3B3**
Cathay Pacific   Grd Flr, Swire House, Central ☎747-5522 (reservations) ☎747-1888 (flight information) ☎747-1234 (24hrs), map **3B3**
  Note: Cathay Pacific has two CityCheck offices providing a full check-in service for both passengers and luggage. Check-in up to 3 hours before departure or on the day before departure. Offices in China Hong Kong City, Canton Rd., Tsimshatsui, Kowloon and Pacific Place, Level 4, Central. Open 8am-8pm daily.
Japan   Gloucester Tower, Landmark Building, Central ☎847-4567, map **3C3**
Lufthansa   Landmark Building, Central ☎846-6388, map **3C3**
Northwest   Alexandra House, 2 Ice House St., Central ☎810-4288/522-5168, map **3B3**

Qantas   Rm. 1443, Swire House, W Wing, Chater Rd., Central, map **3B3**. For reservations and confirming flights ☎524-2101; for basic flight information ☎525-6206.

Singapore (SIA)   United Centre, Central ☎520-1313, map **4C5**

Swissair   Tower II, Flr 8, Admiralty Centre, 18 Harcourt Rd. ☎529-2193, map **4C4**

Thai International   Shop 124, Flr 1, World Wide House, Central ☎529-5681, map **3B3**

United   Flr 29, Gloucester Tower, Central ☎810-4888, map **3B3**

COMMISSIONS AND CONSULATES
Australia   Flr 23/24, 25 Harbour Rd., Harbour Centre, Wanchai ☎573-1881, map **5C6**

Canada   Flr 12, Exchange Sq., Central ☎810-4321, map **3B3**

China   People's Republic of China Travel Services, China Travel Building, 77 Queen's Rd., Central ☎525-9121, map **3B3**

France   Flr 26, Tower II, Admiralty Centre, Central ☎529-4351/4358, map **4C4**

Germany   Flr 21, United Centre, 95 Queensway ☎529-8855, map **4C4**

Ireland   Flr 8, Prince's Building, Central ☎522-6022, map **3C3**

Italy   Rm. 805-810 Hutchison House, Central ☎322-0037/522-7166, map **4C4**

Netherlands   China Building, Central ☎522-5127, map **3B3**

New Zealand   Rm. 3414 Connaught Centre, Central ☎525-5049, map **3B3**

Switzerland   Rm. 37003, Flr 37, 11 Pedder St., Gloucester Tower, Landmark, Central ☎522-7147, map **3B3**

United Kingdom   Mirror Tower, 61 Mody Rd., Tsimshatsui East, Kowloon ☎733-3111, map **7E3**

United States   26 Garden Rd., Mid-Levels, Central ☎523-9011, map **3C3**

Useful business addresses

HONG KONG GOVERNMENT AND GOVERNMENT-ASSISTED ORGANIZATIONS
Centre of Environmental Technology for Industry (CETI)   City Polytechnic of Hong Kong, 83 Tat Chee Ave., Kowloon Tong, Kowloon ☎788-7097 ☒45531 CPOLY HX ☒788-7090.

HK Consumer Council   China HK City, Tower 6, Flr 19, Tsimshatsui, Kowloon ☎736-3322 ☒736-7700, map **7E2**.

HK Tourist Association   Flr 35, Jardine House, 1 Connaught Place, Central, ☎801-7111 ☒74720 LUYU HX ☒810-4877, map **4B4**. Develops and promotes tourism industry for the benefit of the economy of Hong Kong.

HK Trade Development Council (HKTDC)   Flr 38-39, Office Tower, Convention Plaza, 1 Harbour Rd., Wanchai ☎833-4333 ⓉⓍ73595 CONHK HX ⒻⓍ824-0249, map **5**C6. Promotes and develops Hong Kong's overseas trade. The Council is responsible for exploring new markets for Hong Kong's manufactured goods, promoting Hong Kong products and creating a favorable image of Hong Kong as a trading partner and manufacturing center. It is also one of the territory's biggest publishers of trade journals and organizer of exhibitions.

Trade and Industry Departments   Flr 14, Ocean Centre, 5 Canton Rd., Tsimshatsui, Kowloon ☎737-2573 ⒻⓍ840-1621, map **7**B2. Provides publications, library and consultancy service.

CHAMBERS OF COMMERCE

American Chamber of Commerce   Flr 10, 1030 Swire House, 7 Chater Rd., Central, ☎526-0185 ⒻⓍ810-1289, map **3**B3 (mail to GPO Box 355, Hong Kong)

Australian Chamber of Commerce   701A, Flr 7, Euro Trade Centre, 13-14 Connaught Rd., Central ☎522-5054 ⒻⓍ877-0860, map **3**B3

British Chamber of Commerce in Hong Kong   1712 Shui On Center, 8 Harbour Rd., Central, ☎824-2211 ⒻⓍ824-1333, map **5**C6

Canadian Chamber of Commerce   Flr 13, One Exchange Square, Connaught Place, Central ☎526-3207 ⒻⓍ845-1654, map **3**B3

French Business Association of Hong Kong   Flr 18, Tower 2, Admiralty Center, 18 Harcourt Rd., Central ☎866-1007/523-0818 ⓉⓍ78716 UAPHK HX ⒻⓍ861-0806, map **4**C4

German Business Association of Hong Kong, The Delegate of German Industry and Commerce   Room 701, Euro-Trade Centre, 13-14 Connaught Rd., Central ☎526-5481 ⓉⓍ60128 VDK HX ⒻⓍ810-6093, map **3**B3

Hong Kong General Chamber of Commerce   Flr 22, United Centre, 95 Queensway, Hong Kong ☎529-9229 ⒻⓍ866-2035, map **4**C5

New Zealand Business Association   c/o New Zealand Commission, Rm. 3414, Jardine House, 1 Connaught Place, Central, Hong Kong ☎525-5044 ⓉⓍ73932 KAKA HX ⒻⓍ845 2915, map **3**B3

OTHER BUSINESS ORGANIZATIONS

Diamond Importers Association Ltd   Rm. 1102, Parker House, 72 Queen's Rd., Central, Hong Kong ☎523-5497/526-0581 ⒻⓍ845-9649, map **3**B3

Federation of Hong Kong Industries   Rm.408, Hankow Centre, 5-15 Hankow Rd., Tsimshatsui, Kowloon ☎723-0818 ⓉⓍ30101 FHKI HX ⒻⓍ721-3494, map **7**E3

HK Association of Banks   GPO Box 11391, Hong Kong, Rm. 525, Prince's Building, Central ☎521-1169/60 ⒻⓍ868-5035, map **3**B3

HK Association of Freight Forwarding Agents   Mezz. Flr, AHAFA Cargo Centre, 12 Kai Shun Rd., Kowloon Bay ☎796-3121 ⒻⓍ796-3719

Emergency information

EMERGENCY SERVICES
Police/Fire/Ambulance ☎999
Police Crime hotline ☎527-7177
Police General inquiries ☎528-4284 ext. 231
St John's Ambulance (free service):
- Hong Kong Island ☎576-6555
- Kowloon ☎371-3555
- New Territories ☎043-7543

MEDICAL SERVICES
In an emergency call **999** or your hotel doctor. Hospitals with 24-hour emergency rooms include:
Hong Kong Adventist Hospital　40 Stubbs Rd., Hong Kong ☎574-6211, map **6F8**
Queen Elizabeth Hospital　Wylie Rd., Kowloon ☎710-2111, map **7D3**
Queen Mary Hospital　Pokfulam Rd., Hong Kong ☎819-2111, map **2E4**

LOST PASSPORT
Contact the local police and your consulate immediately.

LOST TRAVELERS CHECKS
Notify the local police immediately, then follow the instructions provided with your travelers checks, or contact the issuing company. Report stolen **American Express** travelers checks and cards at Grd Flr, New World Tower, Central ☎843-1775 (24 hours), map **3C3**.

LOST PROPERTY
Call the police if you have lost something on public transportation or elsewhere.

POLICE ASSISTANCE
English-speaking officers of the uniformed **Royal Hong Kong Police** wear a red shoulder tab, and there are police reporting stations at both Star Ferry Terminals. You can also dial their hotline ☎527-7177 or, in extreme emergencies only, the ☎999 number, which gives operator assistance in reaching the services required.

HK Exporters Association   Rm. 825, Star House, 3 Salisbury Rd., Tsimshatsui, Kowloon ☎730-9851 [Tx]57905 EXASO HX [Fx]730-1869, map **7F2**

HK Hotels Association   508-511 Silvercord, Tower Two, 30 Canton Rd., Tsimshatsui, Kowloon ☎369-9577/375-3838 [Fx]722 7676/375-7676, map **7E2**

North American Medical Association   1138 Swire House, Chater Rd., Central ☎523-2123 [Fx]526-0148, map **3B3**

Retail Management Association   Flr 14, Fairmont House, 8 Cotton Tree Drive, Central ☎526-6516 [Tx]81903 HKMGR HX [Fx]868-4387, map **4C4**

HONG KONG CONVENTION AND EXHIBITION CENTRE

The Hong Kong Convention and Exhibition Centre has established itself as a first-class, flexible meeting facility for business. More than 3,000 events have taken place since the center opened in November 1988, and advance reservations are now being taken for major international events to 1997 and beyond.

A majority of exhibitions, conventions and corporate functions booked in the Centre are international in scope, with Japan developing as a significant player in the incentive market. Local corporate functions such as meetings and banquets are also held at the center.

With Hong Kong's easy accessibility to Asian cities and direct flights to Europe, North America and elsewhere, the Hong Kong Convention and Exhibition Centre is an ideal meeting destination for the international visitor.

For further inquiries, contact Ms Wendy Wong, Public Relations Manager or Ms Flora Lau, Public Relations Officer, Hong Kong Convention and Exhibition Centre ☎864-8888 [Tx]68688 COVEX HX [Fx]866-0000.

Planning

When to go

Although expatriates and some of the local residents may leave the territory to escape the heat and humidity of July and August, business life continues all year round, with a short respite during **Chinese New Year** when many local industries and businesses take their only holidays of the year. The most pleasant time to visit Hong Kong is in the **cool seasons** of spring (April to June) and fall (October to November) when the humidity and temperature drop.

There is no "off season." As a leading international trading, financial and manufacturing center and entrepôt, Hong Kong is always busy and crowded. Some 80 percent of the population lives in a mere 15 square miles of the territory. Even at a 1990 population density of more than 5,400 people per square kilometer *overall* within its 1,075 square kilometers, Hong Kong ranks as one of the world's most densely populated cities. But this averaging of packed urban areas and empty mountain ridges dramatically understates the crowding. The density in the four main urban areas of Hong Kong Island's N shore, Kowloon, New Kowloon and Tsuen Wan was actually *20,300 people* per square kilometer.

Calendar of events

Dates of Chinese festivals are decided by the lunar calendar and vary from year to year according to the Western calendar; check exact dates with the Hong Kong Tourist Association. (See also PUBLIC HOLIDAYS on page 38 and SPORTS AND RECREATION.

JANUARY AND FEBRUARY
‡ Mid-January: **Christie's auction** of Chinese fine arts and porcelain.

‡ Late January to early February: **Chinese New Year**, the most important festival of the Chinese calendar, a time of family celebrations and banquets, new clothes, gifts of red packets containing "lucky money" *(laisee)* to children. The festival period extends across 15 days, but the actual celebrations last for four, starting with a crowded all-night New Year's Eve flower market (peach and plum blossom, kumquat trees, narcissus) and fair at Victoria Park in Causeway Bay and Kowloon Park in Tsimshatsui. An essential Cantonese expression is the ritual New Year

blessing, *Kung hay fat choi!* There's a spectacular annual fireworks display over the harbor on the third evening. Many stores and businesses close for four days or longer.

‡ Late January to mid-February: **Hong Kong Arts Festival**. A wide variety of international artists, orchestras and companies take part; an alternative **Fringe Festival** runs at the same time.

‡ Early to mid-February: **Spring Lantern Festival**. The end of the New Year period, with evening lantern displays in the parks. In Lo Shan Park in Kowloon, there is a charity auction of traditional lanterns made by craftsmen from China.

MARCH

‡ **Hong Kong International Film Festival**. Two weeks of contemporary international film, with a special section for Hong Kong, Chinese and Asian movies.

APRIL

‡ Early April: **Ching Ming Festival** (Grave-sweeping Day), a family festival with visits to ancestral graves to make offerings and burn paper money (drawn on the Bank of Hell). Mountain slopes are favorite spots for graves, and in country areas family groups may be seen struggling through the undergrowth.

‡ Late April: **Tin Hau Festival**, celebrating the birthday of the popular Queen of Heaven and Goddess of the Sea, protectress of fishermen. Tin Hau temples are crowded with worshipers, and hundreds of gaily decorated fishing junks converge on the temple in Joss House Bay in the New Territories.

MAY

‡ Mid-May: **Tam Tung Festival**, birthday of the second patron saint of the fishing community, celebrated with an enthusiastic day-long festival at the Tam Kung Temple of Shaukeiwan.

‡ Late May: **Cheung Chau Bun Festival**, six days of ritual and vegetarianism on Cheung Chau Island to placate ghosts and restless spirits, with Cantonese opera, lion dances, and an extraordinary traditional procession of gods, stilt-walkers, characters of legend, and floats featuring children in splendid traditional costumes who appear to levitate (it's done with wires). Until recently the climax of the festival was a free-for-all in which participants scrambled up three 70-foot towers made of pink buns and erected outside Pak Tai Temple. But now officials collect the buns and distribute them to spectators for good luck that will last a year.

‡ Mid-May: **Sotheby's spring auction** of Chinese ceramics and works of art.

JUNE

‡ Mid-June: **Dragon Boat Festival**, a vivid spectacle with local teams competing in Stanley, Saikung, Aberdeen, Yaumatei, Cheung Chau and Tai O, the cox's drum pounding out the pace as paddles lash the water

51

in unison and the long, slim boats with their rearing dragon heads rush for the finish. The races commemorate the suicide by drowning in 221BC of poet-statesman Chu Yuan in protest against a corrupt government. Local races are followed a week later by the **International Dragon Boat Races**.

JULY
‡ **Summer Fun Festival** organized by the Urban Council of Hong Kong and comprising mostly neighborhood entertainments.

AUGUST
‡ Mid-August: **Festival of the Hungry Ghosts** *(Yue Lan)*, when departed spirits with no descendants to minister to their needs roam the earth and must be placated. In older districts traditional rites are held at the roadsides, with offerings of food and much burning of Hell banknotes and paper replicas of life's (and death's) necessities. Historically the festival honored Chinese insurrectionists executed by the 17thC Manchu invaders who overthrew China's Ming rulers and founded the Ching Dynasty.

SEPTEMBER
‡ Mid-September: Mid-Fall Festival (**Moon Festival** or **Lantern Festival**). Similar to harvest festivals in the West. Crowds gather to admire the moon, with lantern displays all over Hong Kong. The traditional "mooncakes" usually contain one or more egg yolks. Legend has it they were originally used to conceal messages during an uprising against the Mongols in the 14thC.

OCTOBER
‡ Mid-October: **Chung Yeung Festival,** the second annual family remembrance day (equivalent to All Souls Day), with offerings to ancestors, family visits to ancestral graves and a great deal of energetic hill-climbing, which is deemed to bring good fortune.

‡ Late October: **Festival of Asian Arts**. Artists and cultural groups from all over Asia, with the emphasis on Southeast Asia. Classical dancers, singers, musicians and story tellers come from as far afield as Turkey and Australia. It lasts for two weeks at various venues.

NOVEMBER
‡ Mid-November: **Sotheby's autumn auction** (see MAY).

DECEMBER
Early December: **Hong Kong International Salon of Photography Exhibition**.

‡ December 22: **Ta Chiu**, the winter solstice, an important family day celebrated at home, with offerings to nature spirits in rural areas.

‡ December 25: **Christmas** is celebrated with spectacular illuminations in the main streets of Central and Tsimshatsui, and buildings compete to put on the most extravagant displays.

Orientation

Hong Kong's territories lie at the SE tip of mainland China adjoining Guangdong Province just S of the Tropic of Cancer. Hilly countryside covers three-quarters of its 1,075-square-kilometer (412-square-mile) land area. **Victoria Harbour**, one of the best natural harbors in the world, divides **Hong Kong Island** from **Kowloon** and the **New Territories**.

The hilly terrain has resulted in the development of Hong Kong Island in an E-W direction rather than inland toward the S, with the main city and commercial district concentrated along the northern shore facing the harbor and Kowloon. Hong Kong's most westerly tip, **Kennedy Town**, extending into **Western** district, comprises Hong Kong's oldest and most traditional commercial and residential area.

Central is Hong Kong's main business district, where the stock exchange financial centers and Hong Kong's biggest bank, the Hong Kong and Shanghai Banking Corporation, are located. The business quarter has spilled over into **Wanchai**, once the red-light area but now rapidly developing into a major commercial and cultural district where the Hong Kong Arts Centre and Academy of Performing Arts and Convention & Exhibition Centre are located. **Causeway Bay** to the E of Wanchai is the island's most crowded shopping and entertainment center. The residential area of **North Point** leads to the eastern district through **Quarry Bay** and its printing plants to **Shaukeiwan**, a major fishing center at the island's most easterly point.

Hong Kong Island's S shore, although now linked by the four-lane **Aberdeen Tunnel** through the center of the island, is still relatively undeveloped. Here one can find most of the well-known beaches, such as Deep Water Bay, Repulse Bay, Shek O and Stanley. Hong Kong Island's main fishing center, **Aberdeen**, is located on the S shore. So are Ocean Park, Hong Kong's biggest amusement park, and the adjacent Waterworld.

From Victoria Harbour, **Kowloon Peninsula** extends N to Boundary St., which differentiates the area ceded in 1860 as a British Colony from that of the leased New Territories. Kowloon's major tourist/commercial/entertainment center runs from Salisbury Rd. along the harbor to the W on Canton Rd., to the E by the Science Museum Rd. and N to Jordan Rd. This district, bifurcated into **Tsimshatsui** and **Tsimshatsui East**, holds the major concentration of hotels, shopping centers and night spots in the territory. To the W of the peninsula lies **Kwun Tong**, one of the major industrial and residential areas of Kowloon. To the N above Boundary St. lies **Kowloon Tong**, first developed as a residential enclave of some of Hong Kong's wealthiest and oldest families.

Lion Rock Tunnel and **Tate's Cairn Tunnel** connect N Kowloon to **Shatin** and the **New Territories**, where eight new towns, Tsun Wan, Tuen Mun, Tai Po, Fan Ling, Yuen Long, Junk Bay, Shatin and Tin Shui Wan are under development. These new towns are part of a housing and development program launched in the early 1970s to relieve congestion in Hong Kong's urban centers.

In addition to Hong Kong Island, Kowloon and the New Territories, there are 235 outlying islands, of which **Lamma**, **Cheung Chau**, **Peng Chau** and **Lantau** are the most developed. For the visitor these islands may be of particular interest, since many of the fishing villages still maintain a way of life no longer to be seen in the urban centers of Hong Kong. Convenient transport exists by ferry connecting Hong Kong Island to Cheung Chau, Peng Chau, Lamma and Lantau.

The following provides a brief account of Hong Kong's most significant districts, starting with the main city of Hong Kong Island, and encompassing Kowloon Peninsula and the New Territories.

HONG KONG ISLAND
CENTRAL *(maps 3 & 4B-C3-4)*. Hong Kong's financial center. Modern glass and concrete structures, banks, the Stock Exchange and high-fashion designer-label shops. Buildings more than 8 years old are a rare sight. Heavily congested during business hours.

WESTERN *(map 3A-B2-3)*. By no means what its name implies, this traditional Chinese district, with its faded colonial shop fronts lined with rice, herbal medicines and bridal shops, is a stark contrast to modern Central, but developing rapidly with medium-sized office blocks.

WANCHAI *(map 5C6)*. Hong Kong's old red-light district is now gradually being transformed by the spill-over from the business district and the building of the city's major convention center in this area. Multistory constructions by the waterfront tower over little shops and alleys between Johnston and Gloucester Roads.

CAUSEWAY BAY *(maps 5 & 6C7-8)*. Hong Kong's most popular one-stop shopping area among local residents, dominated by restaurants, Japanese and Chinese department stores, fashion, jewelry and electrical appliance outlets. There are many small markets and vendors in its alleys and back streets.

HAPPY VALLEY *(map 5D7)*. Residential high-rises overlook Hong Kong's famous race track of the same name. An area best avoided on Wednesday evenings and Saturdays during the racing season.

ABERDEEN *(map 2E4)*. Gaudily lit floating seafood restaurants in the bay brighten up this fishing village. Its population is sinking as reclamation advances on the s shore of Hong Kong Island.

KOWLOON PENINSULA
TSIMSHATSUI *(map 7E-F2-3)* This is not only a concentration of retail shops, hotels and restaurants but also a famous port of call for international luxury liners. Passengers disembark at Ocean Terminal, which leads into a shopping/entertainment/commercial/residential complex that is the biggest of its kind in Southeast Asia.

TSIMSHATSUI EAST *(map 8E4)*. A concrete square of shops and hotels forming an extension of the Tsimshatsui tourist area and built entirely on reclaimed land in the first half of the 1980s.

HUNG HOM *(map 8D4-5)*. Of interest to the visitor as a point of embarkation for through trains to China and as a factory outlet district best known for its bargain-priced silk wear and jewelry.

YAUMATEI *(map 7 C-D2-3)*. An old Chinese commercial and residential district on the w side of the Kowloon peninsula.

MONG KOK *(map 7B-C2-3)*. Once ranked as the most densely populated area in the world which, in 1976, registered 652,910 people per square mile. Its dilapidated buildings contain shops selling craftwork and small manufactured goods.

NEW TERRITORIES *(maps 1 & 2)*

Comprises Hong Kong's eight satellite new towns, where densely populated housing settlements with populations of up to a half-million people protrude like futuristic implants into Hong Kong's otherwise timeless countryside. Old houses and traditional farming scenes are nevertheless still in evidence.

OUTLYING ISLANDS

LANTAU *(map 1 D-E1-3)*. The largest of Hong Kong's islands, with many beaches and country trails. Pockets of suburban development are beginning to dot this island's landscape. About twice the size of Hong Kong Island, which has more than a million people, Lantau has a population of under 20,000.

CHEUNG CHAU *(map 1 E3)*. Best known for the annual Bun Festival, this is a fishing village of about 25,000 residents, popular with other Hong Kongers on weekends for its beaches and walks (there are no motor vehicles) and on weekday evenings because of its open-air seafood restaurants.

LAMMA ISLAND *(map 2 E-F4)*. A large, relatively unspoiled island, just a 40-minute boat ride sw of Hong Kong. Motor vehicles are forbidden, and the island is popular for its walks, clean, secluded beaches, seafood and pigeon restaurants.

Organizing your time

On a short visit to Hong Kong the visitor may be easily overwhelmed by the *embarras de richesses* that the city offers. Fortunately Hong Kong is linked by an efficient public transportation system that allows for convenient shopping, eating and sightseeing in most districts. If you do not already have an itinerary planned, the following are suggestions for two-day and four-day visits.

TWO-DAY VISIT
Day 1
- Take a breakfast cruise around Hong Kong's harbor and island.
- Disembark on Hong Kong Island side and walk E from CENTRAL DISTRICT along Queens Rd. Central toward Pottinger St. and Hollywood Rd.
- Visit MAN MO TEMPLE and walk down toward Ladder and Cat St. Galleries.

- Try a late *dim-sum* lunch, and in the afternoon take a tram ride E through Wanchai and CAUSEWAY BAY.
- In the evening take the tram to VICTORIA PEAK.

Day 2

- Spend the morning shopping in Tsimshatsui area, especially along the Golden Mile strip off Nathan Rd.
- Take afternoon tea at the PENINSULA HOTEL (see HOTELS), followed by a visit to OCEAN TERMINAL (see SHOPPING) and Harbour City.

FOUR-DAY VISIT
Day 1

- Walk along Jordan Rd. to YAUMATEI. Visit WONG TAI SIN TEMPLE.
- In the afternoon take a bus from Jordan Rd. ferry to New Territories and return by KCR train to Kowloon Tong and MTR.
- Visit Kam Tin walled village or a stop such as Taipo or Shueng Shui for a short break.
- In the evening visit Temple St. and have dinner at one of the many night food stalls.

Day 2

- From Hong Kong Island take a ferry to Cheung Chau. After a stroll through the market have lunch at one of the open-air seafood restaurants.
- Early afternoon: return to Hong Kong Island and take a walk in WESTERN DISTRICT.

Day 3

- Go for a ride on the VICTORIA PEAK tram, then visit the nearby FLAGSTAFF HOUSE MUSEUM OF TEAWARE.
- In the afternoon take a bus to Stanley Market for shopping, returning via Aberdeen, and have dinner at one of the floating seafood restaurants.

Day 4

- Take a breakfast cruise around the harbor and return to Tsimshatsui.
- From Star Ferry visit the shopping center at OCEAN TERMINAL and HARBOUR CITY complex (see SHOPPING).
- Have lunch in Tsimshatsui and spend the afternoon shopping at the New World Centre and Tsimshatsui East.

Sights and places of interest

Introduction

Pedestrian cities are fighting for their lives — especially those whose neighborhoods have developed as haphazardly as Hong Kong's older districts such as Western and Yaumatei. Yet it is the unique atmosphere of these districts that most attracts tourists and holds the sentiments of the people of Hong Kong. As described in this chapter, they are neighborhoods to approach obliquely, on foot, savoring them a few yards at a time.

The appeal of these older districts, and those of Causeway Bay, Central and The Peak, which are also toured in this chapter, can only be absorbed by visiting them. Go there, soak up the atmosphere and observe the marvelous street theater: itinerant barbers, unlicensed hawkers (who will scamper away at the first sign of police), curbside *daipaidongs* at which to eat, tiny shrines on the sidewalks to the neighborhood earth deities of Taoism, people practicing the entranced ballet of *tai chi* exercises in the park or on the rooftops.... Photographs and videos won't do because the marvel exists in the way *you* discover them, like so many small, private revelations.

These neighborhoods are not "places to live," but rather places bubbling over with life that deserve to be visited at least once in a lifetime. Because they are self-contained and indifferent to interlopers, they offer the poetry of place after which every true traveler hungers.

Hong Kong's special wonder is to have evolved into one of the world's greatest modern cities, while remaining blessed with pedestrian neighborhoods that remain resolutely indifferent to their global standing. These determined islands of people are steadfast in their faith in the lesser gods of family, friends, and the very earth from which they and their forebears sprang — even if most of it is covered in concrete.

CENTER OF RELIGIOUS FAITH

Fittingly, it is the temples and churches of these lesser gods or those Western expressions of faith from simpler times that comprise Hong Kong's second most popular attractions. Just over a dozen are included in this chapter, of more than 300 Chinese temples and a spread of religious institutions that range from a Zoroastrian temple in Happy Valley to a Bahai congregation in Kowloon.

While Hong Kong often stands accused of bowing only before the materialist gods of Mammon, it is in fact still the world's major center of traditional Chinese faith — and, as such, can be credited with saving much of its culture's artifacts and many modern intellectuals from the frenzied burnings of Red Guards in the decade of The Great Cultural Revolution in China (1966-76).

Hong Kong also remains a Western missionary outpost to China, where even today a Christian Bible translated into Chinese is considered seditious and liable to be seized by customs authorities as contraband.

DIVERSITY ANCIENT AND MODERN

Selected for this chapter are more than a dozen small museums. They must be savored, like Hong Kong's neighborhoods, for an accrued explanation of what this territory is and has always been about: freedom for diversity of expression and personal or family gain, and "progress" in the Western colonialist sense of the term. From its excavated Han dynasty tomb, older than the whole of Christian history, to the contemporary paintings of its traditional landscapists working in modern Western motifs and materials, Hong Kong's is a story of human adaptation — that quality which everyone agrees sets our species apart from our cousins in the trees.

There is fun to be had too, and not just the shopping. Ocean Park offers an unforgettable array of things to do and see. Its Middle Kingdom, the Sung Dynasty Village and Tiger Balm Gardens offer eccentric explanations of "Chineseness" in theme park form. For the adventurous, there are walled villages, abandoned communities in the hills, hard climbs and walks in the New Territories, and a collection of islands, islets and peninsulas to be discovered by boat. All these too appear in the following pages.

Amazingly, "urban" Hong Kong comprises no more than 15 percent of the territory's land mass, most of that on land reclaimed from the harbor. All around it (save for a half-dozen massive New Town developments) are marshlands, highlands, fish farms and small market gardens, still surprisingly pristine, as yet unaffected by any form of tourism.

Imagine a land where there are people who may still chase a camera-toting tourist off with a hoe, for attempting to steal their "spirit essence" with the suspicious black box. In Hong Kong? ... Yes, in Hong Kong. It still can and does happen on the Outlying Islands and in the New Territories — a refreshing surprise for travelers who are sick to death of beggars, poseurs and touts in virtually every well-trafficked land left of our shrinking global village. Come have a look....

HOW TO USE THIS SECTION

In the following pages, Hong Kong's sights are arranged alphabetically. Look for the ★ symbol against the outstanding, not-to-be-missed sights. Places of special interest for children (✲) and with outstanding views (◀€) are also indicated, as are buildings of architectural interest (血). For a full explanation of symbols, see page 7. A classified list of headings in this chapter appears opposite.

Some lesser sights do not have their own entries but are included within other entries: look these up in the INDEX.

SIGHTS CLASSIFIED BY TYPE

This chart lists all sights and places of interest that appear as headings in this chapter. To locate their entries, simply find the correct alphabetical position. This also provides an at-a-glance list of recommended sights (★), places of special interest for children (♣), Hong Kong's good views (◀€) and buildings of architectural interest (🏛).

ART GALLERIES
Chinese Antiquities Gallery
Chinese Fine Art Gallery
Chinese University Art Gallery
City Hall Exhibition Centre
Contemporary Hong Kong Art
  Gallery
Goethe Institut
Historical Pictures Gallery
Hong Kong Arts Centre

DISTRICTS
Causeway Bay
Central district
Western district ★
Yaumatei ★

GARDENS, PARKS AND THEME PARKS
Hong Kong Park ♣
Hong Kong Zoological and
  Botanical Gardens ★ ♣ ◀€
Kadoorie Experimental Farm and
  Botanic Gardens ◀€
Ocean Park/Water World/ Middle
  Kingdom ★ ♣ ◀€
Sung Dynasty Village ♣
Tiger Balm Gardens

MUSEUMS
Chinese Historical Relics Museum
Flagstaff House Museum of Tea
  Ware ★ 🏛
Hong Kong Museum of Art ★

Hong Kong Science Museum ♣
Lei Cheng Uk Tomb and Museum
Museum of History ★
Police Museum
Space Museum ♣

PLACES OF WORSHIP
Immaculate Conception
  Cathedral
Jamia Mosque
Ohel Leah Synagogue 🏛
Po Lin Monastery ★ 🏛 ◀€
St John's Cathedral 🏛
Sikh Temple

TEMPLES
Ching Chung Koon
Hung Shing Temple
Man Mo Temple ★ 🏛
Temple of 10,000 Buddhas
  ★ 🏛 ◀€
Tin Hau Temple (Joss House Bay)
Tin Hau Temple (Yaumatei)
Wong Tai Sin Temple

OTHER POINTS OF INTEREST
Jade Market ★
Tao Fung Shan Ecumenical
  Centre ◀€
Tram Depot
Victoria Peak ★ ◀€
Walled villages 🏛
Western Market ★ 🏛

Bold type is generally employed to indicate districts, buildings or other highlights. Places mentioned without addresses and opening times are often described more fully elsewhere in this chapter: check whether they are **cross-references**, which are in SMALL CAPITALS.

Hong Kong's sights A to Z

CAUSEWAY BAY
Map 6.

This is Hong Kong's physically smallest district and the island's most intensely developed shopping, dining and entertainment area. The district is centered on the convergence of Yee Woo St. (the eastern extension of Hennessy Rd.) and Great George St. It is where middle-class Hong Kong shops, and its compactness and crowding are reminiscent of parts of Tokyo, which is appropriate since the district's commercial development was led by Japanese investors in 1960.

Today the area is dominated by department stores: **Daimaru, Sogo, Mitsukoshi, Klasse, Matsuzakaya, Pearl City, Lane Crawford** and the island's largest and most modern **China Products** outlet. They are all located around the triangular junction of Paterson St., Great George St. and Yee Woo St. and, in turn, are surrounded by warrens of boutiques and Asian ethnic eating places.

There are also about ten movie theaters in the district, most of which carry English-language films. The oldest is **Lee Theatre** (on the tram line near the junction of Percival St. and Leighton Rd.), built in 1923 as a copy of the Haymarket Theatre in London, but soon to be torn down for redevelopment.

The Japanese department stores offer a wonderful array of exotic processed foods — try dried seaweed snacks, for example. They also love decorating their stationery with curious combinations of English words, such as "I am friend of you," "Banana Moon," or "Beyond Pigs." Such items make hilarious souvenirs for Western visitors.

Household furnishings and kitchen departments offer plastic creations that give new meaning to the word kitsch and show clever ways of adapting to life in small spaces. Lunch in Daimaru or Sogo is highly recommended as a Japanese street food experience.

If you prefer lunch in a restaurant that is not part of a department store, try **Food St.** (see EATING AND DRINKING) and the nearby Paterson St. and Cleveland St. The **Cleveland Sichuan Restaurant** on Cleveland St. has a good reputation for quality fare. There is also a delightful, although noisy, coffeehouse, **Martino's**, on Paterson St., modeled on the Tokyo coffeehouses that specialize in exotic coffees and coffee-flavored products such as cakes and ice cream.

Every day at noon Causeway Bay resounds to the **Noonday Gun**, a reminder of the days when this was a godown (the traditional Eastern term for a warehouse) district for Jardine, Matheson & Co., the long-established trading company that has played such a colorful role in Hong Kong's history. The gun served as a lunch bell for the employees. Noel Coward revived interest in the custom when he mentioned the gun in his song *Mad Dogs and Englishmen,* and since then Jardines has kept the practice going. The gun, a former's ship's weapon, stands on the waterfront in front of the World Trade Centre building (which has in fact not been the exhibition centre its name implies since 1979 but does host the World Trade Centre Club and Palace Theatre).

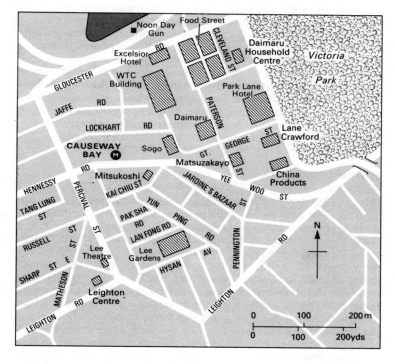

Early risers staying nearby should on no account miss **Victoria Park** just after daybreak, where large *tai-chi* exercise classes take place.

Ideally, the Causeway Bay area s of Yee Wo St. should be the object of a separate expedition, in the evening. Here you will find Jardine's Bazaar and restaurants of many nationalities, offering generally better quality than in the N part of the district.

Jardine's Bazaar, located behind the Klasse department store, is the original Chinese market in the area and still lively. From here, head s to Pennington St., right to Leighton Rd., then sharp right again into Yun Ping Rd. beside the large modern **Sunning Plaza** complex. Alternatively, go via Jardine's Crescent back N to Kai Chiu Rd. and sharp left into Yun Ping Rd. This positions you in the triangle of tiny streets sandwiched between the **Lee Garden Hotel** (see WHERE TO STAY) on Hysan Ave. at the s and **Mitsukoshi** at Yee Woo St. to the N. Boutiques and minute restaurants comprise an odd triangle from Hysan to Yee Woo and Lee Garden Rd. to Yun Ping Rd., crossed by Kai Chiu, Pak Sha and Lan Fong Rds.

The more downscale part of Causeway Bay lies w of Percival St. and below Sharp St. East. Tourist maps issued by The Hong Kong Tourist Association do not identify Matheson St., Tang Lung St. and Russell St. This is a pity, since the area contains a tumbledown world around the tram depot, with hawkers' stalls about a sidewalk's width apart in places, and much streetside manufacturing activity. It contrasts sharply with the manicured world of boutiques and department stores nearby.

Visit the **tram depot**, which at night is a haunting complement to the image of Hogarthian characters around it. At that hour it is virtually deserted save for a few conductors, but the workshops are all well lit — a vision of massive axles and die-cutting tools worthy of an English Industrial Revolution factory. If they are not in use, conductors will show you the marvelously decorated tourist trams, which can be reserved for conducted tours and even for private parties — a popular practice in Hong Kong for people looking for an unusual way to entertain overseas guests or to make a birthday more memorable *(3 tours daily, 2hrs' duration; from MP Tours Ltd ☎ 366-7024/877-2740).*

CENTRAL DISTRICT
Maps 3 & 4.
This business and government district offers many contrasts: colonial buildings and modern skyscrapers, quiet green oases and crowded staircase streets, small stalls and large shopping agglomerations. Traces of old Hong Kong survive in pedestrian areas that are difficult to redevelop. A colorful example is **Pottinger St.** between Hollywood Rd. and Queen's Rd., which is in fact a single narrow staircase or "ladder street," to use a local term, choked with hawker's stalls and the overspill of small shopfronts. The area from Central district w to **Kennedy Town** is laced with similar streets, including an actual Ladder St.

A good point of departure is the **Star Ferry terminal**. The ferry has run between Hong Kong and Kowloon peninsula since 1898 and is still a bargain. As you exit from the terminal turn left to Queen's Pier and the **City Hall complex**. The latter has a high building with a marriage registry and public library halls on two floors, a low building with a concert hall and theater, and a lovely walled garden in between where couples, after their 5-minute civil marriage ceremony, join their families for photographs near a nice little Henry Moore sculpture.

Walk E toward the British Admiralty Garrison complex known as HMS *Tamar* and cross the Murray Rd. pedestrian overpass to the Furama Hotel. Cut back w a block to the **Cenotaph** war memorial faced by the **Hong Kong Club** (illustrated on page 25). The Club's streamlined exterior is more interesting than its interior, which some members are so disgruntled about, they are demanding a complete interior renovation.

Inevitably, tears were shed when the superb colonial-era building housing the club was demolished to make way for a modern high-rise.

Immediately s is the old Supreme Court Building, now preserved and renovated to house Hong Kong's **Legislative Council**. This austere imperial structure has been

Legislative Council

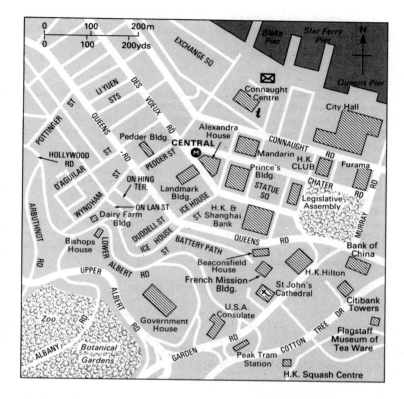

cleaned and is now floodlit at night. Next to the building is **Statue Sq.** (typically for Hong Kong, the statue is of a banker rather than a military hero or government figure). On Sundays this entire district is closed to traffic and becomes packed with Filipinos, many of whom have come to Hong Kong to work as domestic helpers, taking their leisure. Filipinos form Hong Kong's largest single group of expatriates.

Facing the square is the controversial headquarters building of the **Hong Kong and Shanghai Banking Corporation** (illustrated on page 25). Opinions vary as to the beauty of its form and human scale of its function, but all agree it is an awesome building and well worth studying from the benches of Statue Sq.

If you look directly across Queen's Rd. from the Hong Kong Bank plaza, you will see a small staircase cut into the granite retaining wall next to **Beaconsfield House** post office and government building. The staircase brings you to the red-brick **French Mission Building** on top of the bluff above. This building was also once known as Beaconsfield, from an arcade of the same name that stood on the site of the present post office.

The name was chosen by a 19thC businessman, the Hon. E. R. Belilios, to commemorate British Prime Minister **Benjamin Disraeli**, who took the title Earl of Beaconsfield on his retirement. The site is rich in history. It served briefly as headquarters of the provisional Hong Kong government set up in August 1945, after the Japanese occupation of World War II ended, and some believe it was the location of the first Government House, in 1841.

The building has undergone numerous enlargements and transformations since the 19thC, including the addition of a chapel with a cupola built in its NW corner when French Catholic missionaries took it over in 1915. It was sold to the government in 1953, since when it has been occupied, first, by the Supreme Court and now by the Government Information Services office.

Veer left behind the mission building to reach the entrance to ST JOHN'S CATHEDRAL, which faces inward toward a quiet enclave and backs onto busy Garden Rd. Continue up Garden Rd. to the pedestrian overpass, just below Government House, which leads to the entrance of the Botanical Gardens, from which you have the best possible view of **Government House** (illustrated on page 24). One of Central district's most pleasant diversions is a walk through these very well-planned gardens and the adjacent Zoo, especially in the spring when the grounds are ablaze with azaleas.

At the same time of year the Governor's mansion also opens its gardens to the public. The gardens were established and first opened to visitors in 1864 by the then governor, Sir John Bowring, who wanted to spread knowledge of Chinese trees, woods and fibers. The gardens were expanded over the next decade to the current 5.5-hectare ($13\frac{1}{2}$-acre) site at the foot of the Peak. A visitor in 1878 described them as "beautifully laid out, and where all rich and rare forms of foliage, from tropical or temperate climes, combine to produce a garden of delight." The same description holds true today.

In 1979 the gardens and zoo were linked together as the **Hong Kong Zoological and Botanical Gardens** (★ ◀€ ♣). There are separate bird and mammal collections in the zoo, which houses 19 endangered species and is a successful breeding center of rare birds, orangutans and other animals. It supplies and trades with an international network of zoological societies worldwide.

After strolling through the Botanical Gardens look for a pedestrian underpass below Albany Rd. directly into the Zoo. Here cages are still used, rather than the open, moated pens now popular in larger zoos, but most of the animals are small, and the effect is one of intimacy rather than crowding. The bird collection is one of the best in Asia. Everywhere there is luxuriant greenery.

After exploring the Zoo you may wish to end your tour. Alternatively you could proceed out to Arbuthnot Rd., circling up behind the large Caritas building to see IMMACULATE CONCEPTION CATHEDRAL and then back down to Hollywood Rd. Here you will find an exciting array of about 100 antique stores lined along and in the environs of both sides of the street, from its eastern origin at Arbuthnot Rd. to its western limit at Queen's Rd. Hong Kong's "antique mile" runs the full extent of Hollywood Rd. and is as rich a trove of Chinese and other Asian cultural artifacts (especially Japanese and Korean) as you'll find in any museum. From 1993, a public escalator will traverse the hill from Conduit Rd. down to Des Veoux Rd., along the routes of what are now Shelley and Cochrane Sts., making pedestrian access into this steeply pitched upper Central district area considerably easier.

When you have tired of antiques, follow Peel St. down to Queen's Rd. and turn right, back toward the business area. On your left, watch for a large window display at the rear of a shop with a fully armored medieval knight staring out at you, surrounded by the Chinese medicinal herbs of the **Eu Yan Sang Medical Hall**. Inside, elderly men at counters communicate by means of a wire pulley and metal cylinder system reminiscent of photographs from late 19thC department stores. The knight errant, communications system and tellers are the only antique features that remain, as the hall underwent complete renovation in 1989.

The merchandise in this medical cornucopia includes crushed pearls for facial radiance and reindeer horn or ginseng roots for virility. The latter comes mostly from Wisconsin, the US state which enjoys such a booming business in the commodity; there is a ginseng trading exchange in the American city of Wausau. Ginseng was the first American product exported to China in the late 18thC and remains an important staple of trade between the two nations.

Farther on is **Central Market**, the largest of about 65 public markets operated by the Urban Services Department. While the building itself lacks charm, the 300 or so stalls inside fill three floors with seafood and poultry on the ground, meat on the second level, and fruit and vegetables on the third.

Across Queen Victoria St. to the E is a large Communist Chinese Government-owned bookstore, the **Joint Publishing Company Reader's Service Centre**, with many English-language titles about China and Chinese fiction in translation. Across Queen's Rd. to the s is the **Chinese Merchandise Emporium**, with all manner of goods from the mainland, on six floors.

Still continuing, return toward the business center. After crossing Pottinger St., you will come to Central's two most popular bargain alleys: **Li Yuen Sts., West and East**. The former might well be called "bag alley," as it is full of clever imitations of popular designer bags under different labels; the latter deals mainly in clothes. Walk down Li Yuen St. West and up Li Yuen St. East to continue on Queen's Rd. to Pedder St., where you will find the **Pedder Building**, the only remaining prewar business address on this street and now renovated inside to contain a variety of shops selling, among other things, Chinese teas in upscale boutique containers, Japanese household gadgets and high-fashion clothes.

There were once wonderful pharaonic busts jutting out from this building, lacking only the final inscription of Shelley's *Ozymandias* — "Look on my works, ye mighty, and despair" — to write the epitaph of a colonial architectural legacy rendered virtually extinct in Hong Kong's headlong rush to modernity. In 1991, the building was sandblasted and repainted — and the busts were smashed and carted off with other ancient debris. Hong Kong has no truck with epitaphs.

The rest of the route is via the air-conditioned and traffic-free pedestrian overpass network that links the big commercial buildings in the Central district. From the **Landmark Building** you can move across Des Voeux Rd. to **Alexandra House**, then E to **Prince's Building** and from there N to the **Mandarin Hotel**.

These four and **Swire House**, also connected by overpass, comprise the location of most of the district's upscale boutiques, under the names of international designer houses from France, Italy and Japan. Added in 1992 was the **Nine Queen's Road** building, completing a SE link between **Prince's Building** and **Landmark** complex that extends to the new headquarters of Standard Chartered Bank (opened 1991), which has its own overpass to **Battery Path**, the wooded walkway up to the French Mission Building and ST JOHN'S CATHEDRAL.

Alternatively, you can go N from Alexandra House to Swire House, cross Connaught Rd. and cut across to Jardine House, formerly Connaught Centre (where the main office of the **Hong Kong Tourist Association** is to be found on the 35th floor), or veer W to **Exchange Sq.** to see one of the ongoing exhibitions in their rotunda. The square's mezzanine floor has a lovely **Maxim's** restaurant complex, offering Cantonese, Japanese and Western foods, which looks out across running water and flowers flanking escalators in two directions. There is also a pleasant (although noisy) **Brown's Wine Bar**, which looks out across the harbor.

If you prefer a drink at the **Mandarin** hotel, go to the top-floor **Harlequin** bar. This is seldom crowded and has a spectacular view.

All of these buildings belong to the Hong Kong Land Company, and the overpass system begun in the early 1960s continues to grow, most recently beyond Exchange Sq. W to the Macau Ferry terminal and Victoria Hotel. The system also brings you N, beyond the Post Office and out onto Blake Pier upper level for a less expensive outdoor drink and another spectacular harbor view — and finally back E to the Star Ferry terminal where you began.

CHINESE ANTIQUITIES GALLERY   See HONG KONG MUSEUM OF ART.

CHINESE FINE ART GALLERY   See HONG KONG MUSEUM OF ART.

CHINESE HISTORICAL RELICS MUSEUM
China Resources Artlands, Flr 1, Causeway Centre, 28 Harcourt Rd., Wanchai, Hong Kong ☎593-8938. *Map 4C4* 💷 *Open 9.30am-7pm.*
This museum boldly flies the colors of the People's Republic each day to remind its Wanchai neighbors what their flag will look like after 1997.

The museum offers a rare chance to see a slice of life from Beijing's Forbidden City, the home of China's emperors from 1420. On display are imperial artifacts, clothes and *objets d'art,* along with reconstructions of daily imperial life.

CHINESE UNIVERSITY ART GALLERY (The Art Gallery of the Institute of Chinese Studies)

Institute of Chinese Studies, Chinese University, Ma Niu Shui, Sha Tin, New Territories ☎*695-2218. Map 2C5* 📷 📍 *Open Mon-Sat 10am-4.30pm, Sun and hols 12.30-4.30pm. University Station KCR, then taxi or bus, or bus 70 from Jordan Rd. terminus in Kowloon.*

A small gallery, it is distinguished by a major collection of Lingnan School calligraphy and paintings, a Guangdong provincial form that is quite popular in Hong Kong and Taiwan where the elder artists of the genre now reside and teach. It is certainly worth visiting if some of this Jen You-wen collection of 1,300 pieces, ranging from the Ming dynasty (1368-1644) to modern times, is on exhibit. There are also permanent collections of bronze seals (300 pieces from Han dynasty and before), 400 jade-flower carvings and rubbings from stone inscriptions of the Han and Six Dynasties periods in China. The gallery also mounts temporary exhibitions from museums in China and local collectors. A support group, Friends of the Chinese University Art Gallery, holds regular lectures on the arts that are worth inquiring about.

CHING CHUNG KOON ("Green Pine Temple")

Castle Peak, Tuen Mun, New Territories ☎*461-7117. Map 1C2* 📷 📍 *Open 7am-7pm. MTR to Tsuen Wan, then Bus 66M to Tuen Mun terminus, or ferry to Tuen Mun, then LRT to temple station. Opposite Mui Fat Buddhist monastery.*

This Taoist temple is dedicated to Lu Sun Young, one of the Taoist Eight Immortals, patron saint of literati, barbers and the sick. He is said to have been born in AD798 and for 400 years was so successful in spreading Taoism and ridding the earth of evil influences that he was given the title of "Hero of Marvelous Wisdom." His image at the main altar shows him with his devil-slaying saber and his fly-switch, a device for brushing away flies, here denoting the ability to walk on clouds.

Among the temple's many treasures is a library of 3,872 books covering 400 years of Taoist history. Believers meet at the temple every Sunday to read and show visitors around. The temple, completely rebuilt about 20 years ago, is also home to more than 100 destitute old people. Lovely gardens offer a contemplative place to grow older in quiet dignity or ponder the replacement of what once were evergreens in the surrounds — symbols of immortality — with the immutable concrete highrises of the "New Town" that now surrounds them.

A simple vegetarian lunch is available for under HK$50; reserve at the Main Worship Hall.

CITY HALL EXHIBITION CENTRE

Flr 7, High Block, Central, Hong Kong ☎ *522-9511. Map 4B4* 📷 ♿ 🚋 *Open Mon-Fri, Sun 10.30am-7pm. Closed Sat. Star Ferry.*

A general exhibition center open to all comers. Art exhibitions here, which generally last a week at most, embrace a wide variety of work, from paintings by ambitious students to creations by elderly masters. In the Chinese tradition, a master is elderly by definition. A painter of 60 years is considered to be just entering his prime.

CONTEMPORARY HONG KONG ART GALLERY See HONG KONG MUSEUM OF ART.

FLAGSTAFF HOUSE MUSEUM OF TEA WARE ★ ⏏

Cotton Tree Drive, Central, Hong Kong ☎529-9390. *Map* **4C4** ▣ *Open Mon-Tues, Thurs-Sun 10am-5pm. Closed Wed.*

This museum is housed in a two-story building that was formerly the residence of Hong Kong's Commander of British Forces — hence the building's name. Built between 1844 and 1846, it is the oldest extant domestic building of Western style in Hong Kong, and now contains artifacts of the world's oldest tea culture. Nine small galleries house a permanent display from 200 pieces of teaware donated by a single collector, Dr K. S. Lo, who began collecting in the early 1950s and whose donation prompted the preservation of Flagstaff House. The exhibits provide a fascinating insight into the history of teaware and serving practices over the centuries.

The garden around the museum is a delight. The air is filled with the sweet scents of flowering bushes and trees, which hide the din and the ugly traffic congestion below. Above the treetops, the grounds face a phalanx of skyscrapers comprising the city's central business district.

Although only about 10 minutes' walk from the Star Ferry Pier, the museum is hard to reach, as there is no nearby pedestrian crosswalk across or under Cotton Tree Drive. Take a taxi, or walk a long way to a safe crossing up at the Peak Tram station on Garden Rd., or down at Admiralty Centre from whence a pedestrian flyover crosses Queen's Rd. to Pacific Place Mall. There is an entrance to HONG KONG PARK from behind Pacific Place Tower Two.

GOETHE INSTITUT

Flr 14, Hong Kong Arts Centre, 2 Harbour Rd., Hong Kong ☎802-0088. *Map* **5C6** ▣ *Open Mon-Fri 9.30am-5pm. Closed Sat, Sun. Library hours: Mon-Fri noon-7.45pm. Star Ferry and taxi.*

Located in the HONG KONG ARTS CENTRE, this German cultural organization regularly hosts small exhibitions of photography and art in its foyer.

HISTORICAL PICTURES GALLERY See HONG KONG MUSEUM OF ART.

HONG KONG ARTS CENTRE

2 Harbour Rd., Wanchai, Hong Kong ☎582-0230 *(box office),* 582-0200 *(all depts). Map* **5C6** ▣ ═ *Open 10am-8pm.*

This oddly shaped, somewhat triangular building has been the home of innovation in the local arts scene since its foundation in 1977. It remains the most significant private venue for arts activity in Hong Kong, its halls bustling with girls in tutus en route to ballet lessons or residents popping in to purchase tickets for Cantonese theater performances and foreign movies.

The **Pao Sui Loong Gallery** on two floors is an important showcase for local and visiting artists. It has become such a staple location that it must be booked more than two years in advance.

HONG KONG CULTURAL CENTRE   Kowloon's custom-built performance center is illustrated and described in PERFORMING ARTS, pages 131-2.

HONG KONG MUSEUM OF ART ★
Hong Kong Cultural Centre, beside Star Ferry Terminal, Tsimshatsui. Map 7F2 ▨ & *Open Mon-Wed, Fri-Sat 10am-6pm; Sun 1-6pm. Closed Thurs. Star Ferry and taxi.*

Run by the Urban Council of Hong Kong, this museum has since the 1960s enjoyed a generous acquisitions budget and an even older legacy of gifts of complete collections from local connoisseurs. Most of these gifts, however, were seldom seen by the general public until recently because of lack of space at the City Hall, from where the museum moved to its present location in November 1991.

Now the collections occupy a large, bright gallery space in the new Cultural Centre complex in Tsimshatsui, adjacent to the **Space Museum** in Kowloon. Four of the six galleries contain permanent collections.

The **Chinese Antiquities Gallery** is strong on ceramics, with more than 600 pieces (a quarter of the collection). The 2,500 items in total also include textiles, bronzes, snuff bottles, bamboo carvings, jade, lacquer, cloisonné, Canton enamels, paper-cuts, woodblock prints and other artifacts from a legacy of Chinese artistry running from Neolithic to modern times.

The **Chinese Fine Art Gallery** prominently features artists of Guangdong province amongst its 3,200 pictures. Another gallery features the collections of two Hong Kong connoisseurs, Messrs. Low Chuck-tiew and Lau Siu-lui: the former donated his **Xubaizhai Collection** of painting and calligraphy from the 5th to the 20thC to the museum, the latter his **Taiyilou Collection** of 1,100 paintings and calligraphic works by Guangdong and Hong Kong artists.

There is also a **Contemporary Hong Kong Art Gallery** with 1,800 works and an **Historical Pictures Gallery** with so-called "China Coast Painting" in oils (170 of them), watercolors and drawings and prints by the same school. The 1,100 items in this collection were built upon gifts from local businessmen, foreign traders and historians, such as the Chater, Hotung and Law and Sayer Collections. New exhibits have been acquired in recent years from London dealers and auction houses.

There is also a permanent **sculpture court** on the first floor and two special exhibition galleries, which, as examples of their fare, celebrated the opening of the museum by mounting a massive exhibition of contemporary French art, coyly titled *Too French,* sponsored by the Cartier Foundation.

HONG KONG PARK
*Map 4C4 ❋ Entrances: **Cotton Tree Dr.** for Squash Centre, Flagstaff Museum of Tea Ware and Marriage Registry; **Kennedy Rd.** for Children's Playground and Visual Arts Centre; **Pacific Place** Tower Two for artificial lakes, falls and Park Inn restaurant; Youde Aviary and Forsgate Conservatory are within grounds.*

The entire side of a hill between Kennedy Rd., Cotton Tree Dr. and the Pacific Place and Supreme Court complex in Queensway is now a gigantic park containing the FLAGSTAFF HOUSE MUSEUM OF TEA WARE, a squash centre, waterfalls (man-made), a restaurant (overlooking the waterfalls), a 3-level children's playground, a giant walk-through aviary, a large conservatory, a visual arts center featuring photo exhibits, and a viewing tower that looks like something from an M.C. Escher engraving without the optical illusions.

As a park, it is notable only for its peculiar architectural detail — a confusing folly of neo-this and neo-that — which, had it been done with wit, could have been a delight. Even so, as a collection of special-interest sights, it is fun, especially for children. Hang out near the waterfalls and tea ware museum and enjoy the antics of newlyweds fresh from the marriage registry doing their best to turn their surroundings into a stage set for portrait photography.

The **Youde Greenhouse**, named after a recent governor, is Southeast Asia's largest dual-climate hothouse, combining jungle and desert climes. The walk-through **Forsgate Aviary** has some 600 birds of 90 species. Fully-equipped studios for rent for printmakers and practitioners of sculpture, ceramics and the other plastic arts are offered by the visual arts center. Completing the facilities are the large children's playground, on 6 levels, the **Park Inn** restaurant, and trees and greenery speckled among concrete fountains, walkways and artificial lakes.

HONG KONG SCIENCE MUSEUM

Science Museum Rd., bounded by Chatham, Granville and Cheong Wan Rds., Tsimshatsui East ☎ 732-3231. Map 8E4. No.1 Minibus from Kowloon Star Ferry concourse, or hoverferry from E Ferry Pier (Edinburgh Place in front of City Hall) in Central district of Hong Kong (disembarks at floating landing opposite Shangri-La Hotel or Star Ferry from Central to Hung Hom, near Coliseum and KCR station) ☎ ▣ ✦ Open weekdays 1-9pm; Sat, Sun, hols 10am-9pm. Closed Mon, Lunar New Year hols.

About 500 exhibits are housed in this 4-story, custom-built pink and gray extravaganza, 60 percent of them "hands-on" interactive devices that makes science seem like fun, instead of a fatigue-inducing study of things one ought to know. Exhibits are divided by floors into four major themes: Science, Life Science, Technology, and a Children's Area designed especially for those aged 3-7 years.

HONG KONG ZOOLOGICAL AND BOTANICAL GARDENS   See CENTRAL DISTRICT.

HUNG SHING TEMPLE (a.k.a. Tai Wong Temple)

129 Queen's Rd. East, Wanchai, Hong Kong. Map 5D6 ▣ Open 7am-6pm. Wanchai MTR and taxi.

A small Chinese settlement near here predated the British arrival, and this temple, which would have then stood near the shoreline, served local fisherfolk. The deity Hung Shing's reputation for saving seamen from peril has been overshadowed by the popular sea goddess Tin Hau, but he still has a following. There are temples dedicated to him on the islands of Ap Lei Chau (c.1888) and Cheung Chau (c.1813), at

Sheung Shui (c.1860), and near Yuen Long at Ping Shan and the walled town of Kam Tin (both dating from the 18thC).

This temple, which backs onto a huge boulder, was built in its present form in the 1860s. A shrine inside is dated 1847-48. The roof sports fine examples of Shek Wan pottery from the locally renowned Guangdong province kilns in the town of Shek Wan, which specializes in detailed ceramic figurines rendered with great skill and handpainted. These are thought to have been added early in this century.

This area of Wanchai was originally developed as a European enclave but by the 1860s had already reverted to use by Chinese residents.

IMMACULATE CONCEPTION CATHEDRAL
16 Caine Rd., Hong Kong ☎*524-0681. Map 3C3.*
The first permanent Catholic church in Hong Kong was built in 1842 and burned down in 1860, when a fire started in a nearby saloon. The present cathedral is an Italianate structure, dating from 1888, and is hidden away behind a gigantic building occupied by the Catholic charitable organization, Caritas.

The altars, three of which date from the earlier church, were made in Italy. One, devoted to St Joseph, was presented by King Victor Emmanuel II and bears the heraldic arms of the House of Savoy.

JADE MARKET   See YAUMATEI.

JAMIAH MOSQUE
30 Shelley St. at Mosque St. (below Robinson Rd.), Hong Kong. Map 3C2.
First built in 1890, for Lascar seamen from the South Philippines who lived in the Lower Lascar Row area near Cat St., this lovely little mosque is set in its own spacious walled compound, forming a quiet corner of the Islamic world amid the bustle of Hong Kong. It is located in a tiny residential district of dead-end pedestrian terraces such as Chico, Prince's and Rednaxela (an anagram for Alexander), in a quiet, intimate area. Across the street from the mosque are little workshops where craftsmen create carved wooden and painted ceramic curios on special order for major American department stores such as Bloomingdale's in New York. It can be visited in conjunction with a walk in either Central or Western district.

Muslims from the Punjab of India came later as soldiers, prison guards, police and watchmen, and others, from Bombay, became prominent businessmen and philanthropists. Essack Elias was one such, and he underwrote construction of the mosque in 1915. Today, there are more than 50,000 Muslims of many nationalities in Hong Kong, about half of whom are Chinese.

KADOORIE EXPERIMENTAL FARM AND BOTANIC GARDENS
Lam Kam Rd., Tai Po, New Territories ☎*488-1317. Map 2B4* 🖼 《€ *Open Mon-Thurs, Sat 9.30am-4pm. Closed Fri, Sun, hols. Call at Farm Administration office before proceeding on your tour. Apply 2 days in advance. MTR to Kowloon Tong station, then KCR to Taipo and take KCB bus 64K, 65K.*

It was not just perversity that impelled Horace Kadoorie to build a farm on the side of a mountain. A large proportion of Hong Kong's land area is mountainous, and Kadoorie wanted to prove that the slopes could be opened up for fruit, vegetable and livestock production, as in earlier times they had been used to grow tea.

The result is spectacular. The 145ha (360-acre) farm, begun in 1961, ascends the steep slope in a succession of massive, stone-buttressed terraces built around a hairpin road leading to the summit of **Goddess of Mercy Mountain** at 549m (1,809 feet); the terraces continue up an adjacent slope to a height of 762m (2,500 feet). There are orchards, vegetable gardens, nursery areas and different types of pig and poultry units at various altitudes, with superb views along the way, especially from the summit.

Although the vast botanical collection is scattered throughout the farm, several sections are devoted to gardens of indigenous and exotic flora, including special collections of camellias, bougainvilleas, hibiscus and orchids. Paths meander among terraces, streams, waterfalls and ponds, rock gardens and boulders, shady groves, shrubs and flowerbeds, with the tranquil, intimate charm of the classical Chinese garden, and everywhere there is a profusion of blooms. One of the ponds (near the Rest House at Cascade Falls) is big enough for a dip, so take bathing suits if the weather is hot.

The mountain itself is charged with myth. A sort of geological honeycomb, it takes in warm air from the valley below and emits it, still warm, from two natural air vents that can be seen at the summit. These vents are surrounded by stone circles of great antiquity and are still venerated by local villagers, for, while every Chinese mountain is believed to house a dragon, not many actually breathe!

Since the farm was built, the mountain has certainly sent forth abundant good fortune to the farming villages in the valleys and has played a pivotal role in the little-known success story of Hong Kong's agricultural development in the past 35 years.

It is advisable to bring food and drink with you, as the food stalls on the farm keep unpredictable hours. There are plenty of benches in shady spots where you can picnic, and there are playgrounds for children.

LEI CHENG UK TOMB AND MUSEUM

41 Tonkin St., Lei Cheng Uk Resettlement Estate, Sham Shui Po, Kowloon
☎ *386-2863. Map 2D4* 🚇 ♿ *Open Mon-Wed, Fri, Sat 10am-1pm, 2-6pm; Sun and hols 1-6pm. Closed Thurs. MTR to Cheung Sha Wan and 5mins' walk, or KMB bus 2 from Kowloon Star Ferry, alighting at Tonkin St.*

This small tomb was found by accident in 1955 during the ground preparations for building the government resettlement estate that surrounds it. It is precisely that accident of location that makes it a major Hong Kong sight for those who pay homage to the architecture of human habitation. The small barrel-vaulted brickwork chambers of the tomb are reminiscent of Chinese "dragon kilns" in which ceramics were fired; they establish that Hong Kong was part of Pan-yu County under the Eastern Han Dynasty (AD25-220), which makes it about as old as the existence of Christianity in the West. The tomb artifacts in the adjacent gallery provide architectural interest, specifically the clay models of houses and barns. There is an audiovisual display.

MAN MO TEMPLE ★ ⌂

126 Hollywood Rd. at Ladder St. junction ☎540-0350. *Map 3B2* ◎ *Open 7am-5pm. Bus 26 from in front of HongkongBank headquarters, second stop on Hollywood Rd.*

This is among the most popular of Hong Kong temples for visitors. Its name refers to two traditional qualities or virtues: that of the statesman *(man)* and that of the soldier *(mo)*. Representing these qualities are the two deities to whom the temple is dedicated: **Man Cheong**, the god of literature and patron of civil servants, and **Kwan Tung**, god of war and patron of curio dealers and pawnbrokers. The latter dedication is particularly apt in view of the profusion of antique and curio stores in the vicinity.

The temple, dating from the 19thC, is built along traditional lines, with bell tower, smoke tower and main palace. It has a fine collection of brassware, pewter and altars made in China, and a fine example of a *dong chung,* a screen door for the exclusive use of VIPs. The temple also possesses three antique sedan chairs made of teak, two of them intricately carved and fashioned like small temples. There are three splendid altars carved in wood, each about 15 feet high. On the main altar sit the two gods, black-faced and black-bearded. Man Cheong is in red robes. Kwan Tung is in green and wears the imperial headdress, an allusion to the fact that when he became a god he was also posthumously given the title of Emperor. Kwan Tung is worshiped by Buddhists and Taoists alike, and there is a shrine to him in every police station. The other two altars in the temple are dedicated to Pau Kung, the god of justice, and Shing Wong, the city god.

MIDDLE KINGDOM   See OCEAN PARK.

MUSEUM OF HISTORY ★

Kowloon Park, Haiphong Rd., Tsimshatsui, Kowloon ☎367-1124. *Map 7E3* ◎ *Open Mon-Thurs, Sat 10am-6pm; Sun and hols 1-6pm. Closed Fri. Tsimshatsui MTR.*

This small but intriguing museum is an eye-opener for those who believe Hong Kong's history began with the arrival of the British in 1841. It houses collections in four categories: archeology, local history, ethnographic records, and natural history of the region. Most of the permanent collection consists of objects donated by local missionaries, civil servants and amateur enthusiasts. The museum also holds historical photographs and newspapers from the 1860s onward and has published two books of photographs on local history: *Hong Kong 100 Years Ago* and *The Hong Kong Album.*

There are also superb models of local fishing junks and of ships related to the China trade, such as the historic junk, *Keying,* which sailed from Hong Kong to New York and then to London in 1846 (according to the legend, sailors who had jumped ship founded New York's now famous Chinatown district).

The museum is housed in the former Whitfield Barracks buildings of the British army, which vacated what is now Kowloon Park in the early 1970s. Both museum and park have been extensively renovated, the latter hosting as many as 60,000 people on a weekend day. Hong Kong's largest mosque is at the SE corner of the park on Nathan Rd., and there is a pleasant **sculpture garden** of mostly local and some international artists' works.

OCEAN PARK/WATER WORLD/MIDDLE KINGDOM ★

Wong Chuk Hang Rd., Aberdeen, Hong Kong ☎ *873-8888 (Ocean Park and Middle Kingdom), 555-6055 (Water World). Map 2E4* ▨ ═▪ ♣ ◀€ *Open at all times. Dolphin and high-dive show 12.30pm daily. Tai Shue Wan escalator entrance open only on weekends. Shuttle by double-decker bus from Star Ferry, or Citibus from Admiralty Centre bus depot (half-hourly) — included in $148 adult ticket price, purchased at bus stop ($74 for children).*

This startling complex of 73ha (180 acres) sprawling up the side of a mountain in Aberdeen was opened in 1977, since when it has expanded continuously. Among its multiplicity of attractions for young and old, it claims the largest oceanarium (marine mammal tank) in the world and one of the largest aquariums. The **Water World** annexe, which has a separate admission fee, was added in 1984, with all manner of water slides down which to splash.

Cable cars convey 4,000 visitors an hour up to the site on the Aberdeen side. Alternatively, the new Tai Shue Wan entrance is reached by what must be the world's longest escalator, in four sections totaling 225m (738 feet) and offering superb views of the harbor and the nearby Lamma Island. At its foot is the Middle Kingdom theme park, a walk-through aviary and bird show theater.

Among the park's most popular attractions are the **Atoll Reef**, a microcosm of the living undersea world containing 5,000 creatures from 400 species, and the **Wave Cove**, a habitat for seals and sea lions. There is also a daily show featuring dolphins and a killer whale, which carries the trainer around the pool on its back. Another show features the American Eagles high-diving team. In 1991, a **Shark Aquarium** was opened, featuring a plastic tunnel which allows visitors to walk under water amid those frenetic eating machines. A **Japanese Garden** was added, along with a 70m (230-foot) **Sky Tower**, which offers panoramic views of Lamma Channel, Aberdeen and the s shore from almost 200m (650 feet) above sea level.

For those looking for action, the park also offers thrilling swings and roller-coaster rides designed to put hearts in mouths and leave stomachs behind. These attractions are especially popular with children. *Top Spin* is the newest of these, added in 1992.

Middle Kingdom offers a walk through the 13 dynasties of 5,000 years of continuously recorded Chinese history, in the form of architectural replicas, craft workshops and historical galleries. Adjacent to the escalator entrance at Tai Shue Wan, this theme park offers opportunities to do one's own stone rubbings, polish jade or just watch the ancient crafts of paper-making and lacquerware in progress. There is an outdoor theater with acrobats, archers and opera staged 3-4 times a day (45 minutes per show) and even a replica of one of the ships sailed by China's greatest navigator, Admiral Zheng He (Cheng Ho). His fleet reached as far as East Africa in the early Ming dynasty's great age of Asian exploration and even once kidnapped the king of Sri Lanka for refusing to pay tribute.

These are only some of the reasons for visiting this intriguing place. The lower section of Ocean Park, reached from the escalator side of the mountain by a spectacular cable car ride, features a children's zoo, Chinese goldfish collection and other attractions. Allow plenty of time if you are going to get the best out of it.

OHEL LEAH SYNAGOGUE ⋔

70 Robinson Rd., Hong Kong ☎*559-4872. Map 3B2* 📷 *Open Mon-Sat 6am-9pm. Closed Sun. Services: Fri 6.30-7pm; Sat 9am-noon.*

Tucked slightly below Robinson Rd. is the lovely little Ohel Leah Synagogue, built in a style thought to be derived from Dutch colonial architecture. The land and building were a donation from the Sassoons, the famous Sephardic Jewish family who were active as entrepreneurs in Shanghai and Hong Kong in the late 19thC. The name means "Tent of Leah," and an inscription at the entrance, dated 1902, explains that the building was "erected by Jacob Elias David Sassoon at his sole expense on the land given jointly by his brothers and himself in memory of their mother Leah."

The Jewish community has a long involvement with Hong Kong, and this synagogue is its main center of worship.

POLICE MUSEUM

27 Coombe Rd., Wanchai (site of former Wan Chai Gap Police Station) ☎*849-6018. Map 4E5* 📷 *Open Wed-Sun 9am-5pm, Tues 2-5pm. Closed Mon, hols. CMB bus 15 from Central; alight at junction of Stubbs and Peak Rds.*

The Royal Hong Kong Police Force was formed in 1844 and has as interesting a history as any such organization in the world, being at once a national and municipal police force born in a multiracial pirates' lair. Opened in 1988, the museum is divided into four exhibits: an Orientation Gallery, Narcotics Gallery, Triad Societies Gallery and one used for current exhibitions. It also has the mounted head of the first tiger known for certain to have been shot in Hong Kong, in 1915, after killing one policeman and wounding another.

PO LIN MONASTERY ★ ⋔

Ngong Ping, Lantau Peak, Lantau Island ☎*985-5113/985-7268. Map 1E1* 📷
𝄇 ⟊ ◖ *Open at all times. Silver Mine Bay ferry and bus to monastery.*

Lantau Island, twice the size of Hong Kong Island, is sometimes called the Island of Prayer in recognition of the 500 monks who dwell in 135 or so Buddhist monasteries there. Chief of these is Po Lin (Precious Lotus) Monastery, a site revered by Buddhists throughout the Far East for holding the triennial Hoi Gai ceremony during which hundreds of

monks and nuns from the region converge to complete their training and be formally initiated as servants of their faith. They spend two months in prayer, meditation, fasting and sutra recitations of Lord Buddha Sakyamuni's doctrines. This event can be conducted only at important temples, which makes Po Lin something akin to a Christian cathedral in its influence.

The monastery (illustrated on page 23) is perched on **Ngon Ping**, a large plateau about half way up Lantau Peak (a.k.a. Phoenix Mountain), at about 762m (2,500 feet) above sea level. Originally a modest meditation center in stone huts, founded by three reclusive monks in 1905, it had by 1927 developed into a well-known Buddhist religious community with a two-story main temple, a sub-temple and two pavilions — the fruit of 2 million Hong Kong dollars raised in pledges. In 1990, the monks and their benefactors unveiled the world's tallest bronze figure of Buddha, constructed by engineers brought from the People's Republic of China. The figure, which is 34m (111 feet) high and mounted on a platformed altar, weighs well over 250 tons and is visible from Macau, some 40 miles away on the other side of China's great Pearl River.

Despite being dedicated to Sakyamumi, whose name means "one who lives in seclusion and silence," this is a busy, noisy place. At holiday times, up to 2,000 visitors come every day, and up to 10,000 for Sakyamuni's birthday on the eighth day of the fourth moon (around mid-May). Many visitors spend the night in somewhat spartan accommodations for a very modest daily charge, which includes three vegetarian meals prepared and served by nuns. They are often pilgrims who rise before dawn the next morning to climb the peak and see a magnificent sunrise.

Po Lin is, in its way, an expression of Buddhism's great paradox: a religion that aspires to an other-worldly Nirvana, yet so often concerns itself with practical efforts to alleviate worldly problems and help human beings still living lives dictated by desire.

ST JOHN'S CATHEDRAL (Anglican) 🏛
Garden Rd. (behind Hilton Hotel), Hong Kong ☎523-4157. *Map 4C4.*
An attractive neo-Gothic structure built on a high and wooded site, this church is one of Hong Kong's best-known landmarks, the full name of which is Cathedral Church of St John the Evangelist. Begun in 1847 and completed in 1849, it was made a cathedral upon the establishment of the Anglican bishopric of Victoria in that year. The first Anglican ser-

vice in Hong Kong was held in 1842 in a shed built on what was then the Murray Barracks parade ground down the hill from St John's on a site where the Hilton Hotel now stands.

Lunchtime recitals, often by high-caliber musicians, are given here on Wednesday from 1.20-1.55pm. A simple lunch is served, or you can bring your own.

SIKH TEMPLE
371 Queen's Rd. East, Hong Kong ☎ *572-4459. Map* **5D7** ⬛ *Open 8am-9pm.*
The Sikhs are an Indian warrior caste who came to Hong Kong and elsewhere in Asia with the British armed forces in the 19thC. They are from the Punjab region of northern India and are generally tall and of strong physique, which led to their comprising a large part of the Royal Hong Kong Police Force before World War II. Men wear their hair unshorn and wound in a topknot under a distinctive style of turban. Surnames all end with Singh. Nowadays Sikhs are commonly seen standing guard with pump-action shotguns outside jewelry shops.

The temple sits on a small open site at the junction of Queen's Rd. and Stubbs Rd. across the street from Queen Elizabeth Stadium, near Happy Valley Race Track's entrance. It was established in 1901, and traditionally one of its special features is the provision of free meals and short-term accommodations for overseas visitors of any faith. Services, held every Sunday morning, include readings from the Sikh Holy Book *(Guru Granth)*, a sermon and singing. The temple library is reputed to have a good collection of books on the Sikh religion and culture. There is a starters' school for Indian children aged 4-6 to prepare them for English-stream primary schools in Hong Kong.

SPACE MUSEUM (Planetarium)
10 Salisbury Rd., Tsimshatsui, Kowloon ☎ *734-2722. Map* **7F3** ⬛ *(separate charges for Space Theatre and Exhibition Hall)* ♿ ♣ *Open Mon-Fri 1-9pm; Sat-Sun 10am-9pm. Space Theatre closed Tues. Sky Show and Exhibition Hall schedules available at the museum. Tsimshatsui MTR or Star Ferry.*
This giant igloo of a building, opened in 1980, was the first development on a former rail station site, which now also houses the HONG KONG CULTURAL CENTRE and HONG KONG MUSEUM OF ART.

The museum's *Sky Show* in the **Space Theatre** is popular with both visitors and school groups. An Omnimax 70mm film projector and hundreds of special-effects projectors create a breathtaking image of Hong Kong's night sky. Special-effects films, mostly from the United States, projected onto the inside of the dome, are watched by 300 people at a time. Each seat is equipped with simultaneous translation headphones offering Mandarin, English or Japanese narration, with public narration in Cantonese.

The films deal with such subjects as Einstein's theories, the origin of volcanoes and history of cosmic exploration. Arrive and line up early: shows are popular, and the best seats are behind the giant Zeiss projector, which emerges from a central pit like some alien satellite from a science fiction movie. Highly recommended.

The hallways around the dome's two stories were reworked over a 3-year renovation from 1988-91, into a **Hall of Space Science** on the ground floor and **Hall of Astronomy** on the first. There are 55 groups of mostly interactive exhibits in all, from models of Stonehenge and ancient Chinese astronomy to artifacts donated from astronaut Scott Carpenter's *Mercury* space shot in 1982, which include the space capsule itself. There is a space suit and moon rocks, and story boards explaining man's quest in space. You can experience a simulated moonwalk and the rigors of space travel in a multi-axis chair. There are also small lecture rooms, and what must be the noisiest hallway in Hong Kong, wherein the voices of up to 400 people lining up for shows bounce about in a domed acoustical nightmare. About 400,000 visitors attend per year.

SUNG DYNASTY VILLAGE

Kau Wa Keng, Lai Chi Kok, Kowloon ☎ *741-5114. Map 2D4* 🔳 *except Sat 12.30-5pm* 🍴 ✗ ✿ *Open 10am-8.30pm. Lai Chi Kok MTR.*

This theme park, the creation of Hong Kong businessman Deacon Chiu, celebrates one of China's greatest epochs, the Sung dynasty (AD960-1279). The genesis of the venture is described by Mr Chiu as follows:

> The Sung Dynasty Village represents a dream into reality for myself. Many years ago, after seeing a print of the *Spring Festival by the River,* a painting depicting a scene in a village during the Sung Dynasty, an idea grew in me to re-create a replica of such a village here in Hong Kong. The idea was to provide not only a unique tourist attraction to Hong Kong but a monument to remind Hong Kong people of their ethnic background, of a history filled with color, the arts and culture.

So there it is: Sung Dynasty Village, a rich man's re-creation of life as he envisions it was lived 1,000 years ago — complete with acrobats and jugglers, musicians, bakers of honey biscuits, wax museum, teahouse musical performances, and a rich man's villa housing items such as a jade pagoda with a golden Buddha on each floor from the personal collection of Deacon Chiu.

TAO FUNG SHAN ECUMENICAL CENTRE

Shatin, New Territories ☎ *605-0839. Map 2C4* 🔳 ✦ *Open Mon-Fri 9am-5pm; Sat 9am-1pm; Sun for Mass: Chinese 10am, English 4pm. MTR to Shatin, then walk or taxi.*

It is easy to mistake this lovely building, nestling among the trees on top of a hill overlooking Shatin, for a Buddhist temple. Indeed, this is the intention, for the design and construction of the buildings were meant to fool even Buddhist monks. Tao Fung Shan is a Christian mission founded by a Norwegian evangelist, the late Karl Reichelt, who had dedicated his life to converting Buddhist monks to the Christian faith. The mission was built in 1931 under the guidance of a Danish architect, Prip-Moller, who had made a deep study of Chinese Buddhist architectural forms.

At that time many thousands of itinerant Buddhist monks wandered the roads of China, seeking shelter when they needed it at any of the myriad Buddhist sanctuaries that were then scattered throughout the land. Tao Fung Shan — translated as "The Mountain of the Christ Wind" — was built in the semblance of a Buddhist haven where these wandering monks would not think twice about seeking shelter. Some of them stayed on to learn more and eventually became Christian evangelists themselves.

For 10 years Tao Fung Shan prospered in its strange role, until Hong Kong fell to the invading Japanese forces in 1941; the temple never fully recovered after the Japanese left in 1945.

Soon after the war a team of former monks set up a library at the mission and began a literary program, producing Christian material specially adapted to appeal to Buddhists and issuing a proselytizing magazine for distribution to Buddhist centers. Another group of ex-monks with a more artistic bent set up a porcelain-decorating workshop, using the classic styles of Chinese watercolors to depict Christian scenes in order to "propagate the Gospel through art."

The institute still serves as the headquarters of a Southeast Asian mission to Buddhists and hosts regular regional conferences on the subject. Porcelain is still decorated and sold here, although only about half of it now has a religious message.

Access is by car, or on foot up a steep winding road from the valley. Descend via the TEMPLE OF 10,000 BUDDHAS.

TEMPLE OF 10,000 BUDDHAS ★ 血

Tai Po Rd., Shatin, New Territories ☎691-1067. Map 2C4 ⊡ ⫷ Open 9am-5pm. MTR and KCR to Sha Tin station, then 20-25mins' walk 400 steps uphill.

Built on a terrace out into the hillside overlooking Shatin Valley and its new town, this temple was founded by the monk Yuet Kai. The temple's name refers to the vast array of black and gold Buddhas (in fact 12,800 of them), arrayed on shelves reaching to the ceiling, a height of 13.5m (45 feet). These were all donated by worshipers.

The center of the temple is dominated by three gilded Buddhas about 2.5m (8 feet) high. At the end of the terrace in front of the main temple is a 9-story, 6-sided pagoda with a spiral stone stairway leading to the top. At every level and on every side an image of a Buddha looks out from an archway.

In the grounds are three smaller temples; one of them contains Yuet Kai's body in a glass case.

TIGER BALM GARDENS (a.k.a. Aw Boon Haw Gardens)

Aw Boon Haw Villa, Tai Hang Rd., above Causeway Bay ☎576-0467. *Map* **6**D10 ☒ *Open 10am-4pm. CMB Bus 11 from Vehicular Ferry Pier.*

Built in 1935, these gardens, with their pagodas, grottoes and colorful painted plaster statues, are intended to evoke the special hells awaiting those who fail in filial loyalty or patriotism. Burma-born Mr. Aw made his fortune selling the now world-famous Tiger Balm mentholated ointment (a more potent version of Vicks Vapo-rub) — and later in Chinese-language newspaper publishing for overseas Chinese and banking. He built a pair of gardens in Hong Kong and Singapore in the grounds of his estates, with the aim of offering a kind of moral theme park, whose evocation of inspirational fables might have a salutary effect on public behavior. His balm seems to have worked better than the allegorical bite of his often grotesque tableaux. Somewhat run to seed, but worth a visit if you are in the vicinity.

TIN HAU TEMPLE (JOSS HOUSE BAY)

Joss House Bay, Fat Tong Mun, Clearwater Bay Peninsula, New Territories, about 40km (25 miles) from Tsimshatsui, Kowloon ☎719-9257. *Map* **2**F5 ☒ *Open 6am-6pm.*

This is one of the oldest temples in Hong Kong. It dates originally from 1266, and has been rebuilt an unknown number of times. It is one of at least 24 temples in Hong Kong dedicated to the sea goddess Tin Hau, Queen of Heaven, protectress of seafarers and patroness of sports groups, *kaifongs* (family clan groups for mutual welfare) and other community organizations.

Tin Hau's birthday (late April/early May) sees thousands of fisherfolk arrive offshore, masts ablaze in colorful banners. A large mat-shed amphitheater is built for days of continuous performances of Chinese operas, and the floating world of Hong Kong gets together for its most important annual carnival *(HKTA organizes bus tours; Watertours also offers cruises).*

This beautiful building, the most popular of Tin Hau's temples, is built along traditional lines with bell tower and smoke tower and elaborate woodcarving under the eaves. Within the temple, two circular doorways lead to side halls. On one side are the keeper's quarters, on the other a hall dedicated to the Laughing Buddha. Between these two halls is Tin Hau's bedchamber containing two dragon beds. The altar has two statues of Tin Hau, along with various guards and attendants.

Another temple to Tin Hau is in **Ma Han Village** *(map* **2**E5), just beyond Stanley market, dating from 1767. Inside hangs what is thought to be the last living tiger shot on Hong Kong island, supposedly by militiamen in 1942 during the Japanese Occupation. There is an interesting temple to Tin Hau in **Aberdeen** *(Aberdeen Main Rd., map* **2**E4), built in 1851, and one in YAUMATEI (see page 86), which is one of five temples in a shaded courtyard near the famous **Jade Market** (see SHOPPING).

All of the large outlying islands also have temples to Tin Hau, perhaps the most interesting being that on **Peng Chau**, which is two centuries old and has an ancient whale bone on display.

TIN HAU TEMPLE (YAUMATEI)   See YAUMATEI.

TRAM DEPOT   See CAUSEWAY BAY.

VICTORIA PEAK ★
The Peak, Hong Kong. Map 3D2 🚻 *to garden* 🚋 ◀◀ *Peak Tram, bus 15 or free-excursion open-top double-decker bus from Star Ferry (20-minute intervals daily from 9am-7pm).*

No trip to Hong Kong would be complete without a visit to the Peak, preferably by means of the famous Peak Tramway. The trip takes about 8 minutes from St John's building on Garden Rd. (across the street from the American Consulate) to the incongruous viewing tower complex set in the saddle of Victoria Gap 398m (1,305 feet) above sea level.

Until 1990, the tramcars were tugged up and eased down on a motorized pulley system, with up to 72 people at a time sitting in chairs angled back as if for a moonshot, listening to brakesmen communicate in bell signals with the control room on top of the mountain. Bells have now given way to computer buttons, but the ride is still magical and the views at the end simply unmatched anywhere. Perhaps the best proof of this is that 90 percent of the tram's passengers are tourists. The cars run every 10-15 minutes between 7am and midnight.

The view from the top is one of the world's legendary vistas: the breathtaking expanse of Hong Kong, Kowloon, the harbor and the hills beyond. On a clear day you can see as far as Macau. To get the best variety of views walk around the Peak's circular road system (Lugard Rd. and Harlech Rd.), a journey that is all on the level and takes from 45 minutes to 2 hours. This allows panoramic views of Hong Kong Island's southern exposures as well as an urban overview. Then return to the Peak Tower for dinner, or just watch the sunset from its rooftop garden or viewing platform. The view of Hong Kong after dark is also spectacular.

The building houses both Chinese- and Western-style restaurants and a crafts shopping center with 32 stalls, called the Peak Tower Village. Part of the path outside the building is strung with tourist junk outlets, and there are self-consciously "quaint" pagoda-style viewing platforms for photography a bit farther on.

A lovely cottage restaurant, the **Peak Cafe**, opposite the upper terminus, dates from 1901 and was constructed as a shelter for sedan chair bearers. From 1947 to 1989 it was a simple and inexpensive affair. Then it was taken over by California celebrity chef, Jeremiah Tower. His specialty is a blend of light West Coast cuisine with savory Asian ingredients. The structure was kept intact, the interior made more comfortable. With quality came high cost. Still, there is no prettier place to sit and sip a cappuccino before or after a brisk walk around the Peak.

WALLED VILLAGES 🏛
Chai Wan, Hong Kong Island; Tsuen Wan and Kam Tin Valley, New Territories.
The fertile valleys of the New Territories were settled by Hakka farmers as early as the Ming dynasty (1368-1644). They also developed kilns for

brickmaking around the area's limestone deposits. Villages and even family compounds were walled for defense against assaults by disputing neighbors, bandits on land and pirates from the sea.

KAM TIN WALLED VILLAGE
Map 1C3.

Kat Hing Wai in the Kam Tin valley, much visited by tourist buses, has an outer wall, corner towers and moat still intact. Tour guides generally over-simplify by failing to explain that this is only *one* of some half-dozen ancient walled villages or family compounds in Hong Kong, one third of which can with equal accuracy be called "Kam Tin Walled Villages." Much of the inside of this one has been rebuilt without very much sensitivity, and its resident elderly folk have become little more than abrasive tourist touts for cheap souvenirs and photo opportunities involving them wearing their black pajamas and broad straw hats.

Like the villages of Kat Hung Wai, Wing Lung Wai and Tai Hong Wai, which are also in this valley, this is a walled village built by the Tang family clan. In Lung Yeuk Tai district, near Fanling golf course, are five more walled villages of the Tangs and a sixth belonging to the Hau clan. They were among the "five great clans" who settled the New Territories between 200 and 500 years ago.

SAM TUNG UK FOLK MUSEUM
Kwu Uk Ln, near Tsuen Wan MTR station ☎*411-2001. Map 1C3* ◙ *Open Wed-Mon 9am-4pm. Closed Tues.*

A walled Hakka village set in the dead center of urban Tsuen Wan, one of the new towns of the New Territories, with a population approaching a million people. Here, in 1786, Mr. Chan Yam-shing and family members migrated from Fujian province to the NE. In 1981, the village was declared a monument and bought from the Chans by the government, which opened it as a museum in 1987.

LAW UK FOLK MUSEUM
14 Kut Shing St., Chai Wan, 5mins' walk from Chai Wan MTR station. Map 2E5 ◙ *Open Tues-Sat 10am-1pm, 2-6pm; Sun, hols 1-6pm. Closed Mon.*

This museum is a single Hakka village house of the same 18thC vintage and likewise mired among massive blocks of modern flats — in this case located in Hong Kong island's easternmost district, Chai Wan.

SHEUNG YIU FOLK MUSEUM
Sheung Yiu, along Pak Tam Chung Nature Trail ☎*792-6365* ◙ *Open Wed-Mon 9am-4pm. Closed Tues, Lunar New Year hols.*

This 19thC village was deserted by Wong family descendants in the 1960s, apparently after the young men had gone off to England to open Chinese restaurants. It was built beside a lime kiln.

WATER WORLD See OCEAN PARK.

WESTERN DISTRICT (Sheung Wan)
Map 3.

This area includes Hong Kong's oldest business district, the Nam-Pak-Hong, which specializes in wholesale traditional Chinese goods such as medicines and rice from foreign lands. It also includes an area renowned for curios and antiques in the environs of W Hollywood Rd.

Sheung Wan or Western district is surrounded roughly by the harbor on the N, Caine Rd. to the S, the Tung Wa hospital to the W and the Central Market area to the E. From Caine Rd., in Upper Sheung Wan, you can enter the district by half a dozen or so staircase streets from Elgin St. to Hospital Rd.

Lower Sheung Wan is best seen by way of a route that allows time to explore the blocks between Queen's Rd. and Des Voeux Rd.

Start at Wing On St. and move W sweeping up and down the short blocks between the main thoroughfares.

Wing On St., also informally known as **Cloth Alley**, is a small thoroughfare with the feel of an Arab *souk*. It is lined by about 40 shops filled with colorful bolts of fabric. In the next block is Wing Kut St. and an even smaller cloth bazaar.

Jervois St., farther on, is reached by veering right off Queen's Rd. into Bonham Strand East. It is also a traditional silk merchants' center, although greatly diminished in recent years. Jervois St. was also the center of the legal opium trade, at least until the Hong Kong Government created a monopoly to control it in 1909, and it was the site of the first Chinese bazaar in the area. This was the birthplace of Hong Kong's textile industry and its premier business district for more than a hundred years.

Wing Lok St. was once a center of rice merchants and is still sometimes referred to as Mi Kai, or "**Rice Street**." The trade has generally moved W toward Wing Lok wharf, and the best place to see the magnificent wooden barrels of rice is in the shoreline shops of Connaught Rd. Wing Sing, or "**Egg Street**," is still a good place to watch the egg dealers, with their colorful produce in all varieties from large goose eggs to tiny speckled quail eggs. Apart from fresh eggs, the dealers also sell preserved and salted ones, considered great delicacies by the Chinese.

Nearby Man Wah Lane is the center for craftsmen who carve the seals that have been used in China for the past 3,000 years or more for marking documents and works of art — known locally as "chops." A chop will usually bear between two and four characters indicating the owner's name or office, and can be made in a variety of materials including porcelain, wood and soapstone. It will take an hour or so for one of the craftsmen to carve your own personal chop, bearing a set of characters representing your name and presented to you with a small pot of red ink — a charming souvenir to take home.

Hillier St., which runs between Queen's and Bonham Strand East, has a remarkable assortment of goods from frozen foods to plastic colorants. Watch for specialists in navigation lamps.

Bonham Strand, from Queen's to Cleverly St. is an area developed to house gold dealers and Chinese banks, but in the fall, this street does a bustling business in snakes. These are viewed as an invigorating winter food and an aphrodisiac.

Bonham Strand is also a good street for studying the clever adaptations of rattan to furniture and household items. WESTERN MARKET is at the intersection of Bonham Strand and Wing Lok St. and was similar in scope and size to Central Market (see CENTRAL DISTRICT) until its transformation in December 1991 into a Covent Garden-style showpiece of boutiques and Chinese eating designed to introduce tourists to Chinese hawkers' foods in genteel and sanitary surrroundings. One floor is devoted to some of "Cloth Alley's" former denizens, who were relocated to make way for redevelopment. It offers a pleasant offstreet place to snack while exploring the area.

Bonham Strand West puts you in Nam-Pak-Hong proper. Although its buildings are unexciting, the goods carried by its traders are interesting. Here herbs, ginseng roots, reindeer horns, twigs, seeds, shells, fruits, grasses, flowers and numerous other items are supplied to traditional pharmacies and to doctors who practice traditional medicine.

Medicinal supplies merge into foods where Des Voeux Rd. West is met by Bonham Strand West. Salted fish and other preserved foods will be found hanging from the rafters of shops, as will pressed ducks, sausages of pork and liver and lots of fat. There are restaurants in the area with *dim sum* if it's afternoon and you're hungry.

Ko Shing St. continues the medicinal theme. Follow it round to Sutherland St. to see some of Hong Kong's remaining **street barbers**.

Queen's Rd. West should not be ignored. Watch for the **tea shops**. The older ones have wonderful, large copper cauldrons that act as samovars. Their inviting interiors are lined with wood and mirrors adorned with calligraphy. See at least one of these before leaving the district. There are also shops selling wedding gowns, and others selling paper offerings. These latter carry notes from the Bank of Hell, colorful slips of paper with calligraphic messages, paper door guardians, paper clothing, rough squares of Chinese-style toilet paper in stacks, and amazing paper constructions of Mercedes Benz cars, houses and furnishings — all intended to accompany the spirit of the dead to the nether world.

It is not uncommon to see these items being burned in annual ceremonies of remembrance or to stumble upon an actual funeral. All present will be in white, the color of mourning in the Chinese spectrum. During the Mid-Fall Festival these shops carry magnificently elaborate lanterns shaped as butterflies, symbolizing hope of longevity, or lobsters, for mirth, or goldfish, for wealth and knowledge.

Upper Lascar Row used to be a great place for buying antiques at rock-bottom prices, but the quality antiques have moved to Hollywood Rd., and Upper Lascar Row has become a flea market selling everything from copper kettles to old sewing machines. In Lok Ku Rd., however, is the **Cat St. Centre**, an exhibition complex with art galleries, antique dealers and craft stores. Here you will find a good selection of Oriental and Western antiques and crafts products.

The shops continue back into the Central district sector of Hollywood Rd., gaining in price and prestige *en route*.

Veer left down Lyndhurst Terrace, once a street of flower vendors and European or American prostitutes. When you reach Wellington St. cross over to the stairs of Pottinger St. and continue down one block to Stanley St. Complete your journey with a proper Chinese tea-break at the **Luk Yu Teahouse** (see WHERE TO EAT), about midway down Stanley St.

between Pottinger St. and D'Aguilar St. Try the upstairs if it's not crowded. The small cubicled rooms with brass spittoons and wooden swinging half-doors represent the style of both office and restaurant interiors before World War II.

WESTERN MARKET ★ 🏛

323 Des Veoux Rd. (entrance also on Connaught Rd., block square building at the junction with Morrison St., where the tram turns N from Des Veoux onto Connaught Rd W, Sheung Wan ☎ *815-3586. Map 3A2* 🚋 *Open 10am-7pm. Tram or 5mins' walk from Sheung Wan MTR station of Macau ferry pier.*

This is Hong Kong's most successful restoration and the crowning achievement of local conservationists to date. Redesigned by the locally renowned architect Tao Ho (who also designed and won awards for the HONG KONG ARTS CENTRE), the exterior of this stone and wrought-iron neo-Gothic colonial structure has been preserved intact, as has much of the interior detail. Inside, instead of the former wet fish market, you will find four floors of shops, places to eat, and occasional evening recitals, mime shows or comedy cabarets.

Over 30 boutiques offering Chinese crafts and souvenirs line the ground floor, including a paper goods outlet for the legendary Kwong Sang Hong facial cream company (see SHOPPING). The first floor is dedicated to cloth merchants relocated due to partial redevelopment on Wing On St (a.k.a. Cloth Alley) — see WESTERN DISTRICT — and the top two floors offer delightful *dim sum* specialties and a bilingual menu with such Chinese delicacies as eggs with barnacles and black mushrooms (most of which taste better than they sound).

WONG TAI SIN TEMPLE

Lung Cheong Rd., Wong Tai Sin, Kowloon ☎ *3-211-444. Map 2D4. Open 7am-5.30pm. Wong Tai Sin MTR.*

Wong Tai Sin is the god of healing, originally a shepherd boy who at 15 learned from one of the immortals the art of refining cinnabar into a drug to confer eternal life. He is also sometimes known as the Red Pine Fairy (from the area called Red Pine Hill in Zhejiang province), not to be confused with another Taoist deity of the same name. It is believed that water from his temple can cure sickness, and many worshipers go there to drink or to fill bottles to take home to the sick. The temple was originally built in 1921, pulled down in the 1960s and then rebuilt in the early 1970s.

Before reaching the temple you pass up a flight of steps and through an imposing granite gateway 9m (30 feet) high. Worshipers are not generally allowed into the main part of the temple itself, but the altar, with its portrait of Wong Tai Sin, can be seen through open windows and doors all around the building, as can the sumptuous decorations of the interior.

The sanctuary has a ceiling of paneled pinewood from Burma, with bright red pillars supporting the roof and ceiling. Beneath the ceiling is a frieze of large paintings on silk depicting Taoist, Confucian and Buddhist teachings.

YAUMATEI ★
Map 7.

This is Kowloon's most authentic older Chinese commercial and residential area. In 1860, it was the first area chosen for development by the British government, and more than half the area between Nathan Rd. and the sea is on reclaimed land. It was here that the millions of male "sojourners" were gathered before shipping off to labor camps around the world, and this can arguably be considered the first "Chinatown" of the modern world.

In **Shanghai St.** (Kowloon's main thoroughfare before Governor Nathan developed the "golden mile" road which now carries his name) you will find a variety of colorful retail businesses. Chinese herbalists jostle with textile and jewelry shops. Wedding costume and bedding shops offer lessons in Chinese symbology. You can rent or buy embroidered dresses decorated with dragons and phoenixes (standing for male and female or *Yin* and *Yang*), similarly treated bedspreads and even car hood ornaments for the procession from church to banquet hall. Note the hard pillows and the woven bamboo bed cooler mats for summer use.

A crush of *daipaidongs* (street stalls selling cooked food) dominate the cross streets between Kansu and Jordan Rd. — Saigon, Pak Hoi, Ning Po and Nanking. Such stalls have been a typical feature of Chinese cities and towns at least since the 19thC, and are thought to have always formed part of the Hong Kong scene.

Under the overpass that overhangs Kansu St. there is both a food market and the famous Canton Rd. **Jade Market (★)**, which was moved here to accommodate Harbour City expansion and lies a block E of Canton Rd. There are 450 registered stallholders clustered under the overpass in a triangle where Kansu meets Battery St. and Reclamation St. The market, open from 10am-4pm, has jades in every color and style of carving in the Chinese idiom. Be aware that only jadeite and nephrite are truly jade in the gem sense, and that there is much "new jade" or serpentine from Taiwan that is *not* the real thing. There is also much glass and an enormous amount of junk masquerading as good value. Bargaining is quite acceptable.

From the Jade Market walk N to Market St. and right for a short block to the **Tin Hau Temple** complex *(Public Square St., 2 blocks S of Yau Ma Tei MTR station, map 7 C3)*,, which actually contains four temples and usually a hundred or so lugubrious-looking men gathered about gambling in its courtyards. It can be intimidating, but the natives are indifferent, although seldom friendly, toward your presence. The complex is more than 100 years old. The main temple goddess, Tin Hau, is most popular with boat people (when built, the temples would have been near the shoreline) and is the Taoist Queen of Heaven.

To the right of her temple as you face it is the **Shing Wong**, the City God who reports on urbanites' behavior to both heaven and the underworld. Beyond his temple is that of Fook Tak, the Earth God. To the left of the Tin Hau temple is the **Shea Tan Temple**, dedicated to local community deities.

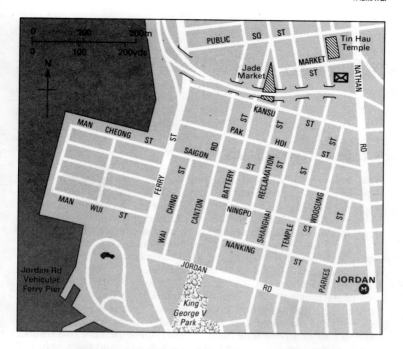

It is worth making a separate evening visit to this district to see the **Temple St. night market**. On any night of the week a couple of thousand people may be seen strolling past Temple Street's 450 or so merchandise stalls and around 100 cooked-food stalls for a third of a mile. Upwards of 20,000 people may pass through the market on a single evening, which is known locally as Yong Shue Tau, meaning "foot of the banyan tree." This may refer to its original location marker: a large banyan tree actually remains in the temple complex nearby. These night markets are often referred to as "poor man's nightclubs."

From about 8-10pm on each evening Yaumatei is also Hong Kong's home to street theater. It throngs with fortune tellers, street singers, medicine men and anyone else with a flair for performance. All very colorful — but beware of pickpockets.

Where to stay

A tale of two cities

There was a time when Hong Kong was so easy to traverse that it mattered little in which hotel you stayed. Traffic congestion and spiraling property values put paid to that halcyon era. As in North America, Europe and Japan, centralized urbanity has been replaced by atomized urban sprawl: megalopolis with all of its incumbent mega-headaches.

Over the past decade, Hong Kong has sprawled, as have its hotels. One of its most famous attributes, local transportation convenience, is fast disappearing. More than 100,000 new vehicle licenses were issued in the five years between 1987 and 1991. To keep all the cars of private commuters moving, transportation planners have transformed urban districts into a maze of yellow-lined, one-way streets where neither cars, taxis nor minibuses may stop. Once the urban areas were a cozy two-some, set about a busy little bowl of water; there are now two distinct cities separated by a common harbor — Kowloon and the N shore of Hong Kong Island.

MOVING AROUND
Taxi drivers no longer know street plans or addresses on the "other side" and fear being caught up in unexpected traffic jams so much that they rush back to their own turf as quickly as they can find a return fare. Tunnels below the harbor running s to Hong Kong and below the Kowloon mountain ridge running N to the New Territories are jammed at rush hours and lunch hour. Luckily, both a clean and safe subway system and the famous Star ferries remain efficient people-movers — though even these are best avoided at rush hours.

The final end to Hong Kong's convenience of scale will come when Kai Tak airport is replaced by the new Chek Lap Kok facility on Lantau Island — which is expected to occur in 1997. The end of the inner-city airport will close the chapter on Hong Kong's post-World War II past as dramatically, in fact, as the resumption of Chinese sovereignty the same year will do in theory. Without air traffic overhead, Kowloon's building height restrictions will be lifted and without doubt so will its skyline. The city's center of gravity will shift westward toward the massive new developments linking Lantau, the western New Territories, and the urban shoreline of western Hong Kong Island between Kennedy Town and Sheung Wan. In future, travelers will need to select their hotel from the city area within which they anticipate spending the most time.

SELECTING YOUR AREA

Even today, before this massive shift in Hong Kong's center of gravity, visitors need to select the location of their hotel with the utmost care. Tourists must plan visits to special sights keeping traffic flows and time constraints in mind. And these constraints are even more pressing for business travelers, who once needed only to make a simple choice between **Tsimshatsui, Kowloon** or **Central, Hong Kong**.

The former is favored by manufacturers who can more easily get to factories in the **New Territories**, the latter by bankers and other service industry people more likely to visit company headquarters' offices. High rental costs for office and industrial space have driven new cleavages into older business centers. Thus in Hong Kong, **Causeway Bay** has become home to most advertising agencies and publishers, **Sheung Wan** has the most firms of accountants, and traders have moved to **Wanchai**. All were once in **Central** district, which today largely houses financial services and regional headquarters of multinational companies — and even they have moved most back-of-house operations such as computer services into cheaper rental districts like **North Point** and **Quarry Bay**.

There are five major hotel areas in Hong Kong: **Central**, **Wanchai**, **Causeway Bay**, **Kowloon** and **Tsimshatsui East**. Each of these has several smaller clusters on its fringes, and each is examined in the following area-by-area survey.

CENTRAL

Despite being a major hotel district since the early 1960s, Central has only three hotels, the **Mandarin Oriental**, **Hongkong Hilton** and **Furama Kempinski**. A fourth, the **Ritz Carlton**, is en route.

On Central's w fringe, in Sheung Wan District, is the **Victoria**, which is attached to the Shun Tak Macau ferry terminal complex. To the E in the Queensway area, opposite Admiralty Centre, is the massive Pacific Place complex, with three grand-luxe hotels: the **Conrad**, **Marriott** and **Island Shangri-La**.

WANCHAI

Since the completion of the Hong Kong Convention & Exhibition Centre in 1989, Wanchai has come into its own with a full range of accommodations. At the top of the scale, **Grand Hyatt** and **New World Harbour View** are physically linked to the Centre. They are thus very close to its adjacent islands of business office blocks, among the largest of which are the Sun Hung Kai Centre, Great Eagle Centre, Shui On Centre and China Exhibition Centre.

Popular business accommodations around the district are **Luk Kwok**, **Harbour** and **New Harbour**, the Taiwanese-owned **Evergreen**, the **Wharney** (formerly Ramada Inn), the **Harbour** and the **Harbour View International House (YMCA)**, all within 5 minutes' walk of the Centre.

CAUSEWAY BAY

Causeway Bay has a long tradition of Japanese and other Asian clientele, but mainly accommodates tourist groups on short shopping sprees. This is reflected in the absence of any grand-luxe property in the district. Its three major hotels, the **Excelsior**, **Park Lane** and **Lee Gardens**, are 2- to 3-star properties and very group-oriented. From here, the drop is steep to the strictly functional likes of the **Cathay**.

KOWLOON

On Kowloon side, the "Golden Mile" district along and about Nathan Rd. is the granddaddy of all tourism development. It began with the **Peninsula**, built in 1929. Circa 1959, it was joined by the **Miramar**. Of late 1960s/early 1970s vintage are the **Sheraton**, **Holiday Inn Golden Mile** and **Hyatt Regency**. The **Ramada Renaissance** enriched the area at the top end of the scale in the 1980s, and a **Ramada Inn** enlarged the budget end.

At the s end of Nathan Rd., Tsimshatsui has long been home to the budget-conscious, from backpackers hanging out at **Chung King Mansion**, to Asian regional businessmen with cash-limited expense accounts, who frequent hotels such as the **Grand**, **Astor**, **Imperial**, **Nathan**, **Fortuna** and **Ambassador**.

At the N end of Canton Rd., the **Royal Pacific Hotel & Towers** opened in 1990. It is set in the China Hong Kong City pier and commercial complex of five bronzed-glass, curtain-wall buildings from whence all China-bound commuter boats now embark. Their coloration and peculiarly shaped key-fret window configurations, individually incised into the upper floors of each building, have made of the complex a rather cryptic new harborfront landmark. This is Kowloon's answer to the Victoria hotel in Central Hong Kong's Shun Tak Macau ferry terminal (see above), and it is likewise situated at the western fringe of the main tourist district.

To the SE of Nathan Rd., New World Development's hotel/shopping/office/residential complex of distinctive red-brick buildings prefigured the surge of creation of such commercial "islands" throughout the 1980s. Set across the six lanes of Salisbury Rd. from Isetan Department Store and the **Sheraton**, this self-contained city at the E end of the HONG KONG CULTURAL CENTRE grounds (which also contain the SPACE MUSEUM and HONG KONG MUSEUM OF ART) holds the top-scale **Regent** and mid-range **New World**.

TSIMSHATSUI EAST

Tsimshatsui East, s of Chatham Rd. along the Salisbury Rd. harborfront, took the "reclaimed island" concept one step beyond into the creation of an entire district that had not existed before 1980. Now there are five huge hotels and more than a dozen commercial/retail space complexes, and the Hong Kong SCIENCE MUSEUM, all in their own self-contained, high-standing and curtain-walled neighborhood of the city — like a downtown district without a hinterland.

Hotels here include the **Shangri-La** at the grand-luxe end and four others of roughly the same 4- to 5-star standard: **Regal Meridien** (owned by Air France), **Regal Kowloon**, **Royal Garden**, **Holiday Inn Harbour View** and **Nikko** (owned by Japan Air Lines).

HOTELS CLASSIFIED BY PRICE

HONG KONG ISLAND

INEXPENSIVE ▯▭
Harbour View International
    House (YMCA) ♣
Helena May ♣
New Cathay ▰ ♣
YWCA ♣

MODERATELY PRICED ▱▭
City Garden
Grand Plaza ♣
Harbour ♣
Luk Kwok ♣
New Harbour
Wharney

EXPENSIVE ▯▭
Eastin Valley
Excelsior ♣
Furama Kempinski
Hongkong Hilton
Lee Gardens
New World Harbour View
Park Lane
Victoria ♣

VERY EXPENSIVE ▱▭
Conrad ▰
Grand Hyatt ▰ ♣
Island Shangri-la ▰
Mandarin Oriental ▰ ♣
Marriott ▰

KOWLOON

CHEAP ▭
Chung King Mansion ▰ ♣
YMCA ♣

INEXPENSIVE ▯▭
Concourse
Fortuna ▰ ♣
Imperial ▰ ♣
Metropole
Nathan ▰ ♣
Ritz ▰ ♣

MODERATELY PRICED ▱▭
Empress ♣
Grand ♣
Grand Tower
Guangdong ▰
New World
Omni Marco Polo
Omni Prince
Ramada Inn ♣
Royal Pacific Hotel & Towers

EXPENSIVE ▯▭
Ambassador
Eaton
Holiday Inn Golden Mile
Holiday Inn Harbour View
Hyatt Regency
Kowloon ♣
Miramar
Omni Hongkong
Regal Airport Hotel ♣
Regal Kowloon ♣
Royal Garden
Sheraton

VERY EXPENSIVE ▱▭
Nikko ▰
Peninsula ▰
Ramada Renaissance ▰
Regent ▰ ♣
Shangri-la ▰ ♣

NEW TERRITORIES

MODERATELY PRICED ▱▭
Regal Riverside

HOTEL RESTAURANTS

Unlike many parts of the world, Asia is a region where hotels are preferred venues for fine dining. Some of the world's best chefs have set up kitchens here, and restaurants such as **La Plume** (Regent), **Gaddi's** (Peninsula), **Pierrot** (Mandarin) and **Le Restaurant de France** (Regal Meridien) are among about a dozen world-class French, Northern Italian or Continental European restaurants located in Hong Kong hotels.

Likewise, leading hotels have appointed some of Hong Kong's best Chinese chefs to create landmark Cantonese restaurants such as the **Eagle's Nest** (Hilton), **Lai Ching Heen** (Regent), **Man Wah** (Mandarin), **Loong Yuen** (Holiday Inn Golden Mile), **Shang Palace** (Shangri-La) and the *nouvelle Chinois* creations and ambience of the **Chinese Restaurant** (Hyatt Regency).

Holiday Inn and **Sheraton** are also notable for having created cuisines specially for their own groups. Hybrid East-West menus available in all of their outlets cater to the health conscious, with an emphasis on light dishes with low salt and cholesterol, which still (now comes the tricky part) taste, look and satisfy like *haute cuisine*.

ENTERTAINMENT

Hotel entertainment can range from a pianist or trio in the lobby to a discotheque in the basement or penthouse. Some hotels, such as the Hilton and Miramar, also offer dinner theater.

In recent years, valiant experiments have been essayed. Live-music "blues" and "jazz" bars with American singers were attempted: notable examples include **Gripp's** at the Omni Hong Kong, **Oasis** at the New World Harbour View and **Cyrano** at the Island Shangri-La. Another new idea was the creation of theme decor and party bars, pioneered at the Sheraton by **Someplace Else** and now led by **JJ's** in the Grand Hyatt. (See NIGHTLIFE for most of these.)

FACILITIES AND TERMS

All hotels of any reasonable standard in Hong Kong have air conditioning, television, facsimile lines (at the desk, business center or in-room), telephones (most often with International Direct Dialing), elevators, private bath/shower, accept most or all major international charge and credit cards, and have at the very least a Chinese restaurant and Western-style coffee shop.

From the moderate price range upward, they also all have discotheques and/or bars, and mini-bars with small refrigerators in rooms. None accepts dogs or other animals, but Hong Kong's stiff quarantine laws preclude the need in any case. Some hotels offer "family plan" rates wherein children under 12 to 14 years stay free.

RESERVATIONS

All but the lowest-end hotels are linked into major international reservations networks. You can also contact the **Hong Kong Tourist Association** (☎ *801-7111* 🆀 *74720 HX* 🅵 *810-4877*) or **Hong Kong**

Hotels Association *(☎ 369-9577/375-3838 [Fx] 722-7676/375-7676).*
HKTA has offices in 11 countries: Australia, Britain, Canada, France,
Germany, Italy, Japan, New Zealand, Singapore, Spain and the US.

ABOUT THIS CHAPTER

Our selection leads with a feature on the **Peninsula**, the prince of
Hong Kong's hotels, and is followed by an entry on the only hotel of
international standard in the New Territories. The remainder of the
chapter is divided into two alphabetical lists, covering recommended
accommodations on Hong Kong Island and Kowloon respectively.

Addresses, telephone, telex and fax numbers are given, and symbols
show hotels that represent good value in their class (❂), or are particularly
luxurious (▥) or simple in style (▰). Other symbols show price
categories, and give a résumé of the available facilities. See KEY TO SYMBOLS
on page 7 for the full list of symbols.

A list of all hotels featured in this chapter, classified alphabetically into
our five price categories, can be found on page 91.

HONG KONG'S LANDMARK HOTEL — THE PENINSULA ▥

Salisbury Rd., Tsimshatsui, Kowloon ☎ *366-6251* [T] *43821* [Fx] *722-4170. Map*
7F3 ▥ *156 rms* ≡ ▰ AE ⊙ ⊙ VISA ⊀ ⚎ ▣
Location: Close to the s tip of the Kowloon peninsula. Asia has a long
and glorious hotel tradition, and some hotels have attained such dis-
tinction that they transcend commercial concerns and have become
important cultural and historical sights. In Hong Kong, the Peninsula,
dating from 1929, is one such hotel.

This elegant hotel was built in a Mediterranean-inspired architectural style, at what was then the terminus of the Kowloon-Canton
Railway and the destination of the *Orient Express,* perhaps the world's
most romantic railway train, traversing China, Central Asia and Continental Europe to Paris.

The hotel's legendary lobby has imposing Neoclassical off-white
columns, studded with gold heraldic emblems, from which satyrs' faces
impishly survey passing events below — such occasions as the expansive
Eggnog and Black Velvet receptions held every Western New Year's Day
to the music of the Royal Regiment of Wales, or the full, traditional high
tea offered every afternoon. An eclectic and Victorian array of interior
detail — such as the dancing maidens incised into key-fretted wall
emblems — provides guests with a constant source of unexpected visual
delight.

The Peninsula was occupied and used as the Japanese military headquarters during the wartime occupation of Hong Kong. Its pre-eminence
continued after the war, and the hotel remained at the center of colonial
social life just as it had since its earliest days. Even with the fading of the
colonial lifestyle, the Peninsula had no peer on the Kowloon peninsula
until the early 1980s, when the REGENT opened. As for Hong Kong Island,
its competitors there of the same vintage and architectural grandeur are
long gone.

More recently, the grand-luxe developments in Tsimshatsui East and the RAMADA RENAISSANCE on the next block have started to contend for its top-scale clientele. What the "Pen" has going for it, in this struggle, is the measureless value of its history and tradition. But its former view of the harbor has been obstructed by the Space Museum and other buildings in the Cultural Centre complex, and its standards, although high, are not noticeably better than a half-dozen competitors located within walking distance. And, unlike the upstarts, the Peninsula has no business, health or recreation facilities — although it does have a shopping annex.

A new tower block behind it is underway to avert the destruction of the original structure — a commendable act of conservation by its management, led by Lord Kadoorie. (This is fitting, for he was twice denounced in the Hong Kong press for rapacious redevelopments of historically important buildings: once for the destruction of the much-loved Repulse Bay Hotel, and later for the attempted destruction of the OHEL LEAH SYNAGOGUE on Robinson Rd. The latter was saved by a determined alliance of conservationists and congregation members.)

Crucially, the Peninsula's food and beverage outlets continue to hold their own: **Gaddi's** for fine Continental dining, CHESA for Swiss fondues (see EATING AND DRINKING), the **Spring Moon** for Chinese cuisine, and even the lobby for those legendary New Year's eggnog parties when the *hoi polloi* hobnob with the high and mighty over news of the latest joint resolutions from London and Beijing.

NEW TERRITORIES' HOTEL — THE REGAL RIVERSIDE

Tai Chung Kiu Rd., Shatin, New Territories ☎649-7878 ⊠30013 ℻637-4748 ▥□
820 rms ⊟ ⌨ ▣ ▣ ▣ ▣ ⌂ ⅙ ⧉ ⌁ ♨ ♿/nearby ♠nearby ●nearby ❦ ⅏
▣ ⌁ ⚓ ▣ ▱
Location: On the bank of the Shing Mun River, in the foothills opposite Kowloon's "Nine Dragon" mountain ridge. This is the only hotel of international standard in the New Territories and is deservedly popular with local companies for short conferences. The key to its success is its strategic location, only 15 minutes from the airport, and just 20 minutes from Tsimshatsui (Lion Rock tunnel traffic permitting). Extensive recreation facilities lie nearby.

Hong Kong Island's hotels A to Z

CITY GARDEN

231 Electric Rd., North Point ☎887-2888 ⊠69128 ℻887-1111. Map **6A9** ▥□ 617 rms ⊟ ⌨ ▣ ▣ ▣ ▣ ⅙ ⌁ ❦ ⅏ ⌁ ▣ ▱

Location: Several blocks from Fortress Hill MTR station in an industrial/residential district. Managed by the same group who operate ROYAL PACIFIC HOTEL & TOWERS in the China Hong Kong City complex and two hotels in Singapore, this is an example of the "business hotel" breed in the district. It has an outdoor pool and Jacuzzi.

CONRAD ⌂

88 Queensway, Pacific Place ☎521-3838 ⊠69678 ℻521-3888. Map **4C4** ▥▥ 513 rms ⊟ ▣ ▣ ▣ ▣ ▣ ⌂ ⅙ ⅏ ⧉ ⌁ ❦ ⅏ ⌁ ⚓ ▣ ▱

Location: One of three hotels in the large Pacific Place commercial center, set between Central and Wanchai. Like many others in Hong Kong, this is a top-rank hotel. It opened in 1990 as this US group's flagship, the first of 12 properties planned to be completed in Asia before the end of 1992. The 61-story building is a distinctive dual-elliptic shape, more reminiscent of compass curves on sailors' charts than any known architectural tradition. A delightful sculpture in the lobby, by American artist Kirk Newman, takes the form of a tableau depicting 16 *Hong Kong People* — not in the straw Hakka hats and slit *cheong sam* skirts pictured in tourist guides, but the truer picture of harried commuters in suits, schoolgirls in jumper uniforms, a 3-generation family group, a bargain hunter, a bird walker, and even a tourist (that troublesome tribe whose numbers virtually double Hong Kong's population each year). Apart from all that, there are executive floors, a business center and a heated outdoor pool. The location within the Pacific Place centre gives immediate access to 185 retail shops and various entertainments including a United Artists quad cinema.

EASTIN VALLEY

1A Wang Tak St., Happy Valley
☎574-9922 ☒84323 ☒838-1622. Map
6E8 ▥ 111 rms ☵ ☚ ▣ ◉ ▣ ▦
▤ & ⟨⟨ ☄ ♈ ⟶ ▤
Location: In the downtown section of a mid- to upper-market residential district. One of the new "business class" hotels in Hong Kong's different neighborhoods, this is handy for shopping in Causeway Bay and for the race track. But there are no nearby MTR stops. The Hong Kong tramway cuts through the area; otherwise, taxis and buses are the main modes of access.

EXCELSIOR ♣

Causeway Bay ☎894-8888 ☒74550
☒895-6459. Map 6B8 ▥ 948 rms ☵
▣ ◉ ▣ ▦ & ⟨⟨ ♈ ☄ ▣ ▤
Location: At the heart of Causeway Bay, facing the harbor, adjacent to the World Trade Centre and Palace Theatre cinema. The Excelsior was

erected on the first plot of land bought by Jardine for their godowns (warehouses) after the establishment of the colony. It is successful more because of its location and service than anything else, and is able to command high room rates despite the lack of flashy facilities. The **Talk of the Town** cocktail lounge, 34 floors up, affords a spectacular view of the harbor at night. The **Dickens Bar** in the basement is a popular pub, featuring Dixieland jazz on Sunday afternoons. Completing the picture are a business center, three executive floors and five nonsmoking rooms.

FURAMA KEMPINSKI

1 Connaught Rd., Central ☎525-5111
☒73801 ☒845-9339. Map 4C4 ▥ 466
rms ☵ ▣ ◉ ▣ ▦ & ⟨⟨ ☄ ☄ ⟶
▲ ▤ ▮
Location: At the E corner of Central District, on the waterfront, a short walk to the shops, the MTR and the Star Ferry. All rooms have a view of either the harbor or Victoria Peak. A spectacular panorama can also be enjoyed from the revolving LA RONDA restaurant on the roof (see EATING AND DRINKING). The Furama was among the first hotels to cater to business travelers, with a business center and business studios and suites. The health center has a sauna, steam bath and Jacuzzi. The **Lau Ling** lobby bar features a Filipino band, and the **Rotisserie** French grill room is an intimate local favorite which hosts periodic *Soirée Classique* dinner sessions with classical music. The German Kempinski group took over management of the hotel from the US Inter-Continental group in 1990.

GRAND HYATT ♣ ▦ ▥

1 Harbour Rd., Wanchai ☎861-1234
☒68434 ☒861-1677. Map 5C6 ▥ 575
rms ☵ ▣ ▣ ◉ ▣ ▦ & ⟨⟨ ⟨⟨ ☄
⟲ ⟲ ☄ ☄ ⟶ ▲ ▤ ▮
Location: One of two hotels within the massive waterfront Hong Kong Conference & Exhibition Centre complex. Opened in 1989, this hotel aspires to a grand European style of architecture, with 50-foot black marble columns and

a domed ceiling. Walls throughout the hotel are in lavish parquetry of dappled cherry and other distinctively textured blond woods. The interior decor strains to evoke the Roaring 20s in sleek outlets like the **Champagne Bar**. This 31-story evocation of excess is Hyatt's pride in Asia, and small wonder. Note, for example, the cunning use of interior architectural details to evoke a bygone interwar era of luxury, tapping into the collective imagination of Europe and America that draws dimly on movies and F. Scott Fitzgerald novels: a fuzzy, halcyon time, when Neoclassicism, Art Nouveau and Art Deco collided, spawning Classical marble columns, parquetry furniture finishes applied to walls, and hard-edged functional household objects in primary colors intended also to double as *objets d'art*. What Steven Spielberg's *Star Wars* is to the original *Flash Gordon* movies, this hotel is to hotels of that style actually built in the 1920s: a kind of literary allusion brought about and heightened for effect with today's technology. (For the *real* thing, see the PENINSULA.)

Naturally, the Grand Hyatt provides all the pampering you would expect from a hotel with its haughty pretensions. Facilities include a business center with offices to rent, rooftop pool, tennis, and a golf driving range and putting green. The hotel boasts one of Hong Kong's most elegant function rooms, with genuine antiques and two fake fireplaces in a drawing-room setting worth of a French château.

GRAND PLAZA ♣
2 Kornhill Rd., Quarry Bay ☎886-0011
67645 886-1738 □ 498 rms
🖾 🖾 🖾 🖾 🖾 ♨ ♨ ♨ ♨ ♨ ♨ ♨
🖾
Location: Directly over Tai Koo MTR station, and part of the massive mid-market apartment complexes at Tai-koosbing and adjacent Kornbill. Unlike its spartan sister hotels in the Grand Group, this large facility boasts a pool, putting green, squash courts, health club, 9th-floor terrace garden and extensive business meeting fa-

cilities. Long-staying guests are served by two private elevators to 150 rooms on its 18th to 22nd floors. It is close to a total of 8 MTR exits from Central or Tsimshatsui districts, which are within 20 minutes' reach.

HARBOUR ♣
116-22 Gloucester Rd., Wanchai
☎574-8211 73947 572-2185. Map
5C6 □ 201 rms 🖾 🖾 🖾 🖾 🖾 ♨
Location: On the Wanchai waterfront, halfway between Causeway Bay and Central. Within 5 minutes' walk of the HONG KONG ARTS CENTRE, the Convention Centre and Wanchai MTR station, this is one of a number of hotels taken over by China Travel Services. It was recently renovated to cater to businessmen drawn to Wanchai by events at the Hong Kong Convention & Exhibition Centre. If you want a visa for China, the staff can assist.

HARBOUR VIEW INTERNATIONAL HOUSE (YMCA) ♣
4 Harbour Rd., Wanchai ☎520-1111
61073 865-6063. Map 5C6 □ 320
rms 🖾 🖾 🖾 🖾 🖾 🖾 🖾 ♨ ♨ ♨ 🖾
Location: On the Wanchai waterfront, next door to the Arts Centre. Untypically upscale for the YMCA, with its marble-lined lobby and all. Despite that, this is excellent value, with all the usual hotel services. Most rooms overlook the harbor. It is adjacent to the HONG KONG ARTS CENTRE and the Academy for Performing Arts, and within 5 minutes' walk from the Hong Kong Convention & Exhibition Centre. Across a pedestrian overpass (flyover) are a small park and the GRAND HYATT hotel.

HELENA MAY ♣ ⌂
35 Garden Rd., Mid-Levels ☎522-6766.
Map 4C4 □ 30 rms 🖾
Location: Above Queen's Rd., Central District. Accommodations in this lovely 3-story, Edwardian-revival building are for women with overseas passports who are working in Hong Kong. It was opened in 1916 under the sponsorship of a former colonial governor's wife, Lady Helena May, and paid for as an act of

philanthropy by two patriarchs of leading business families, Sir Ellis Kadoorie and Ho Kam-ton. It is very conveniently located: within 5 minutes' walk of CENTRAL DISTRICT and the Botanical Gardens and Zoo; adjacent to the Peak Tram station; across Garden Rd. from the US Consulate General; and across Cotton Tree Dr. from the Hong Kong Squash Centre, the FLAGSTAFF MUSEUM OF TEAWARE and HONG KONG PARK. It has a library, and occasionally stages small chamber music concerts.

HONGKONG HILTON

2 Queen's Rd., Central ☎523-3111
✆73355 ✉845-2590/868-1444. Map
4C4 ▥ 743 rms ⬛ ▣ ▣ ▣ ▣ ▥ ⬛
⬛ ⬛ ⬛ ⬛ ⬛

Location: At the corner of Garden Rd., surrounded by big banks; a block from the Landmark complex and a short walk from the Admiralty/Pacific Place complexes. The Hilton was opened in 1963 and has been periodically renovated, most recently adding three executive floors. An outdoor heated pool and 3 outdoor tennis courts are up on the roof of an adjacent parking garage. The Hilton's 33.5m (110-foot) brigantine, *Wan Fu*, takes guests for daily cruises and private charters. The **Eagle's Nest** supper club features plays and entertainers from London's West End several times a year. In the 2-story shopping arcade are no fewer than 64 shops. The Hilton International Group pioneered US-style luxury hotels in the region and is responsible for training up an entire generation of Asian hoteliers. Originally an American spin-off of the US Hilton chain (which now goes by the name **Conrad** overseas), the group was bought by London interests in the late 1980s.

ISLAND SHANGRI-LA ▥

Pacific Place, Supreme Court Rd.
☎877-3838 ✆70373 ✉521-8742. Map
4C4 ▥ 565 rms ⬛ ▣ ▣ ▣ ▣ ▥
⬛ ⬛ ⬛ ⬛ ⬛ ⬛ ⬛ ⬛

Location: One of three deluxe hotels in the Pacific Place complex, in the Queensway area, between Central and Wanchai districts. Opened in 1991, this Hong Kong Island sister hotel to Kowloon's Shangri-La contains a 14-story Chinese landscape mural in its atrium, painted on 250 silk and paper panels by more than 40 artists brought over from Beijing. The ballroom boosted imports to Hong Kong of Carrara marble and Viennese crystal chandeliers. London's art gallery owners must forever love this hotel for hiring a Hong Kong-based consultant to arrange the purchase of more than 500 original works of art in Britain for the restaurants and public areas. English artist Kate Lovegrove has also painted 16 murals in the ballroom, which seek to evoke the mood of *Lost Horizon*, the best-selling novel in which writer James Hilton created the legendary mountain paradise of "Shangri-La" from which the hotel takes its name. Four American artists who work under the name "The Emmerling Studios" were also commissioned for various decorative domes and a 47-foot mural meant to suggest the Art Deco era of the 1930s. The overall effect is a bit like paint-by-numbers, but still worth a look. Perhaps because it takes its name from a book, the hotel has reintroduced literacy to travel in the form of a lending library for guests, with a range of books there just for the joy of reading (if that doesn't beat all!).

LEE GARDENS

Hysan Ave., Causeway Bay ☎895-3311
✆75601 ✉576-9775. Map 6C8 ▥ 720
rms ⬛ ▣ ▣ ▣ ▥ ⬛ ⬛ ⬛ ⬛ ⬛
Location: Close to shopping in the extreme s of the Causeway Bay district; 10 minutes' walk to the MTR. A comfortable hotel, more Oriental than most, with neither business nor health centers, but with shops on the 2nd floor. A good Japanese restaurant in the basement (the **Shosen**) is complemented by another more modest one across the street, plus fine Asian restaurants nearby. The surrounding streets are chock-a-block full of bargain boutiques, good for strolling and shopping. Nearby are Jardine's Crescent Street Market and the "Little Tokyo" district of

Japanese department stores around Yee Wo and Paterson Sts. This hotel, with the EXCELSIOR at the N waterfront extreme and the PARK LANE at the E edge of Victoria Park, comprise the sum of upscale hotels in Causeway Bay. They also define three of the district's geographic perimeters.

LUK KWOK ♦

72 Gloucester Rd., Wanchai ☎*866-2166* [TX]*69628* [Fx]*866-2622.* Map **5***C6* ▥ *198 rms* ═ ▦ ▣ ▥ ▦
Location: Near corner of Luard Rd., 5 minutes' walk from the Hong Kong Convention & Exhibition Centre or from Wanchai nightlife. This old hotel is reputed to be the location used in the filming of the movie *The World of Suzie Wong* — an attribution its former management never took as a compliment. Now part of the China Travel Services group of hotels, it was completely renovated in 1990. Suzie would stand agog to see her simple hostelry reclad in black and gray marble, all cool and sleek in its new heart of stone.

MANDARIN ORIENTAL ▥ ♦

5 Connaught Rd., Central ☎*522-0111* [TX]*73653* [Fx]*810-6190.* Map **3***B3* ▥ *541 rms* ═ ▦ ▦ ▣ ▥ ▦ 《 ⋙ ⩩ ⩗ ♔ ♠ ▤ ▢
Location: Opposite the Star Ferry, near the MTR, in the center of the business district and connected by a glassed-in air-conditioned walkway to Prince's Building, and from there the Landmark shopping complex. This superb hotel was opened in 1963 as a showpiece for Hong Kong's major property developers. Since 1982 it has frequently been voted "the best hotel in the world" or ranked among the top three by the financial and travel press. Small wonder. Its lavish interior is the work of film-set designer Don Ashton (the sculpture of a ship's figurehead in the mezzanine **Clipper Lounge** is a stage prop left over from the movie *Billy Budd*). The hotel is renowned for its impeccable attention to detail. In the days long before computerized systems were invented, the Mandarin's staff would stun its guests by remembering their names, favorite drinks, flowers, foods — whatever — during the course of their stay and on subsequent visits. In its almost 30-year history, the hotel has aged into an elegant institution: the parting shot "Meet me at the Mandarin" equates to what "Meet me under the clock at the Biltmore" once meant in New York City. In other words, it serves locally as an expensive but memorable transit lounge, lunch venue or happy-hour cocktail spot. Each of its many aspects is immaculate: the unimpeachable service, top-quality restaurants, fine shops, a well-equipped rooftop fitness center, a 2-story indoor pool area modeled on Roman baths, and a business center. Each of its 58 luxurious suites is equipped with private facsimile machines; others can be rented upon request. (See PIERROT, MAN WAH and MANDARIN GRILL in WHERE TO EAT, and CAPTAIN'S BAR in NIGHTLIFE.)

MARRIOTT ▥

88 Queensway, Pacific Place ☎*810-8366* [TX]*66899* [Fx]*845-0737.* Map **4***C5* ▥ *609 rms* ═ ▦ ▦ ▣ ▥ ▦ 《 ⋙ ⩗ ♠ ♔ ▤
Location: One of three hotels in the Pacific Place commercial complex, between Central and Wanchai districts. This was the first of the three grand-luxe hotels in the Pacific Place complex, and it suffers somewhat by a confusion of floor levels when you enter from the shopping mall. The management has made an ingenious effort to create a *cordon sanitaire* between the hotel function rooms and the shopping center by dropping between the two a massive 2-story stage prop worthy of a Busby Berkeley 1930s film-set. There, sits a man at a baby grand piano afloat an artificial island of salmon-pink marble, surrounded by gently tumbling waters poured evenly by hidden pumps down a mirrored staircase ascending behind him. Above this surreal scene is a 2-story glass panel through which one can stare at the most exotic commodity in Hong Kong: absolutely empty space in an open sky.

NEW CATHAY 🏨 ♣
17 Tung Lo Wan Rd., Causeway Bay
☎577-8211 ᵀˣ72089. Map **6C8** ▥ 142
rms ≕ ᴀᴇ 🅞 🅒 ᴹᴵ

Location: At the edge of the Causeway Bay shopping area, 5 minutes' walk to Causeway Bay MTR Station beneath Daimaru and Sogo department stores. An old-style Asian business hotel with basic facilities. Although very convenient during midweek, this is the virtual epicenter of where the crowds gather for weekend shopping. Thus, it's a favorite with tourists from Southeast Asia.

NEW HARBOUR
41-49 Hennessy Rd., Wanchai ☎861-1166
ᵀˣ65641 ᶠˣ865-6111. Map **5C5** ▥
173 rms ≕ ᴀᴇ 🅞 🅒 ᴹᴵ

Location: 5 minutes' walk from the MTR at the corner of Luard Rd. A touch of old Hong Kong is to be found s of here around Wanchai and Johnston Rds., a bustling district of many little shops. Previously called the Hotel Singapore, it was taken over by China Travel Service and refurbished, as well as renamed. There is no harbor view, despite the new name, but the rates are reasonable. The **Perfume River** (Vietnamese) and CINTA (Filipino/Malay) restaurants flank the hotel (see WHERE TO EAT for the latter), and the Lockhart Rd. bar strip starts a block N behind it and runs E to Tonnochy Rd.

NEW WORLD HARBOUR VIEW
1 Harbour Rd., Wanchai ☎866-2288
ᵀˣ68967 ᶠˣ866-3388. Map **5C6** ▥ 852
rms ≕ ▰ ᴀᴇ 🅞 🅒 ᴹᴵ ⌂ & ♣ ◄
≋ ♪ ✓ ♈ ♨ ⛵ ♠ ▣

Location: One of two hotels forming part of the Hong Kong Convention & Exhibition Centre complex on the Wanchai waterfront, 5 minutes' walk from Wanchai ferry pier. Although overshadowed by the glamorous GRAND HYATT at the opposite end of the complex, this is a very fine, well-equipped hotel. It is connected by a pedestrian overpass (flyover) to the Great Eagle Centre commercial complex and the Hong Kong Exhibition Centre. Good restaurants include the **Scala**, which

serves *nouvelle cuisine* from North Italy. The **Oasis** "blues" bar is well known.

PARK LANE
310 Gloucester Rd., Causeway Bay
☎890-3355 ᵀˣ75343 ᶠˣ576-7853. Map
6C8 ▥ 850 rms ᴀᴇ 🅞 🅒 ᴹᴵ ⌂ ◄
♈ ♨ ♠ ▣

Location: Overlooking the 50-acre Victoria Park. A large, spacious hotel with a low-key decor in wood and marble by Dale Keller, the celebrated designer of Asian hotel interiors. Facilities include business and fitness centers, the Premier Club business lounge, a nonsmoking floor, four shops, a public swimming pool, tennis courts, and convenient access to a jogging track in Victoria Park, Hong Kong's answer to New York's Central Park and its largest urban playground (rise early to see or join *tai chi* classes held there). Formerly owned by Japan Airlines, the hotel is set one block E of the "Little Tokyo" department stores district favored by Japanese tourists, who come to Hong Kong to buy Japanese goods for less than they can buy them at home.

VICTORIA ♣
Shun Tak Centre, Connaught Rd., Central
☎540-7228 ᵀˣ86608 ᶠˣ858-3398. Map
3A2 ▥ 536 rms ≕ ▰ ᴀᴇ 🅞 🅒 ᴹᴵ
◄ ≋ ♪ ♈ ♨ ▣ ♨

Location: Shun Tak Centre is the vast Macau Ferry terminal complex to the w of the Central waterfront, at the edge of Sheung Wan district. Access to Sheung Wan MTR station is through the basement; there is an elevated, covered walkway from the 2nd floor along the waterfront to Central District; and the hotel has its own separate elevator to the 160-plus shops and restaurants in the Shun Tak Centre. Furnished apartments and hotel rooms are on the 26th to 40th floors, and most have a spectacular view of the harbor. Also here: a business center, swimming pool, outdoor tennis courts, luxury accommodations at the exclusive **Victoria Club**, and seven suites, each with a rooftop garden, up on the 40th floor — and a star attraction: one of Hong Kong's best grill rooms (see BOCARINOS GRILL in WHERE TO EAT).

WHARNEY

57-73 Lockhart Rd., Wanchai ☎861-1000 ☒82590 ☒865-1010. Map 5C6 ⅢⅢ 335 rms ☴ ⌂ Ⓐ Ⓒ Ⓓ ☒ ⇗ ⍦ ⚓
Location: On the Lockhart Rd. nightlife strip, 5 minutes' walk from the new Hong Kong Convention and Exhibition Centre. Built by the Ramada group in the mid-1980s and sold to the Guangdong Travel group in late 1991, when it was renamed. A pool and health club were added in 1991.

YWCA ♣

1 MacDonnell Rd., Central ☎522-3101 ☒845-6263. Map 3C3 ⅢⅢ 130 rms ☴ Ⓐ Ⓒ Ⓓ ☒ ⇗ ⍦
Location: Near the first Peak Tram stop above Central district, at the corner of Cotton Tree Dr. and a short but steep 5 minutes' walk s of Queen's Rd. Like the Salisbury Rd. hotel across the harbor, this facility was completely demolished, rebuilt and reopened in late 1990. With the exception of HELENA MAY nearby, Central district has no better value for money for accommodations than this. Unusually, there is a badminton court.

Kowloon's hotels A to Z

AMBASSADOR

26 Nathan Rd. (at corner with Middle Rd.), Tsimshatsui, Kowloon ☎366-6321 ☒43840 ☒369-0663. Map 7E3 ⅢⅢ 315 rms ☴ Ⓐ Ⓒ Ⓓ ☒ ⌇ ⚓ ♩ ⬒
Location: On the Golden Mile strip, beside the Sheraton hotel and opposite the Peninsula Hotel on Nathan Rd. The nondescript **Charlotte's** Continental restaurant and **Point After Laser Lounge** nightclub confirm that this hotel's appeal is strictly its convenient location.

CHUNG KING MANSION ▄ ♣

40 Nathan Rd., Kowloon ☎366-5362 ☒51463. Map 7E3 ⅢⅢ 82 rms ☴
Location: In a good position on the Golden Mile. This is a basic hotel with no frills. The mansion is a legendary center of unlicensed Indian restaurants and downscale clientele. Many Westerners who have "made it" in Hong Kong on pluck and a prayer first stayed here. It has the kind of ambience most people prefer to find in novels.

CONCOURSE

20-46 Lai Chi Kok Rd., Mongkok, Kowloon ☎397-6683 ☒46841 ☒381-3768. Map 7B2 ⅢⅢ 372 rms ☴ ⌂ Ⓐ Ⓒ Ⓓ ☒ ⚓ ⬒

Location: Near Prince Edward Rd. MTR Station, just off Nathan Rd. at the N edge of Kowloon (just below the appropriately named Boundary St. divide). One of many hotels in the China Travel Service group spread throughout Hong Kong, this one is unusual in featuring a Korean restaurant, the **Daewongak**. The district was for decades ranked by *The Guinness Book of Records* as the most densely populated in the world — so for those who want an "authentic" Hong Kong experience, this is where to come: crowded, dirty, rough, and probably more fun for day-tripping than for spending the night. Golden Arcade, the city's most notorious computer knockoffs shopping center, is nearby.

EATON

380 Nathan Rd., Yaumatei, Kowloon ☎782-1818 ☒42862 ☒385-8132. Map 7D3 ⅢⅢ 93 rms ☴ Ⓒ Ⓓ ☒
Location: In the Jordan Rd. area of the Golden Mile. Less hubbub than in the Golden Mile, less shopping too, but the main strip is one stop away by MTR, and the Shanghai St. and Temple St. areas w of it are a major attraction for visitors. A pleasant, clean hotel formerly known as Chung Hing has undergone renovation and was relaunched in 1990 as a "bou-

tique" all-suites hotel. To glimpse the old breed, visit the **Bangkok Royal Hotel** nearby, the home of Hong Kong's oldest and, until the early 1980s, only Thai restaurant.

EMPRESS ♥

17-19 Chatham Rd., Tsimshatsui, Kowloon
☎366-0211 ⊞44871 ℻721-8168. Map **7E3** ⅢⅢ 189 rms ≡⊒ AE ⊡ ⊡ ⊞ & ⊀⊑ ⊟

Location: On the corner of Mody Rd., at the edge of both the Golden Mile and Tsimshatsui East. A "continental-style" hotel, small but made especially pleasant by having balconies outside most rooms: the higher rooms have harbor views. Its **Mayfair Coffee Shop** is above average and a fine place to people-watch at street level on a busy intersection. Close to everything in Tsimshatsui.

FORTUNA ⌂ ♥

355 Nathan Rd., Yaumatei, Kowloon
☎385-1011 ⊞44897 ℻780-0011. Map **7D3** ⅢⅢ 300 rms ≡⊒ AE ⊡ ⊡ ⊞

Location: In the Jordan Rd. area N of the Golden Mile, near the Temple St. market. A friendly hotel with a pleasant atmosphere and helpful staff. No business services.

GRAND ♥

14 Carnarvon Rd., Tsimshatsui, Kowloon
☎366-9331 ⊞44838 ℻723-7840. Map **7E3** ⅢⅢ 194 rms ≡⊒ AE ⊡ ⊡ ⊞

Location: Off Nathan Rd., in the Golden Mile area. Reasonably priced, good service and in a very convenient area. No business services. Use of Club Grand recreation facilities in Grand Plaza is permitted, but they are a 20-minute MTR ride away in Quarry Bay, over on Hong Kong Island.

GRAND TOWER

627-641 Nathan Rd., Mongkok, Kowloon
☎789-0011 ⊞31602 ℻789-0945. Map **7B2** ⅢⅢ 549 rms ≡⊒ AE ⊡ ⊡ ⊞ & ≛ ⊟ ⊒

Location: Sits atop the Mongkok MTR Station near Argyle St. One of the new "business class" hotels and one of the

Grand hotel group. Business center, but no health or recreation facilities.

GUANGDONG ⌂

18 Prat Ave., Tsimshatsui, Kowloon
☎739-3311 ⊞49067 ℻721-1137. Map **7E3** ⅢⅢ 245 rms ≡⊒ AE ⊡ ⊡ ⊞ ≛ ⊟ ⊒

Location: Well located E of Nathan Rd., near Chatham Rd., in a major tourist area. A luxury penthouse on the 17th floor with terraces goes for about the standard room rate of luxury hotels across Chatham Rd., in Tsimshatsui East. The same group also manages the NEW CATHAY hotel and a third hotel in Thailand.

HOLIDAY INN GOLDEN MILE

50 Nathan Rd., Tsimshatsui, Kowloon
☎369-3111 ⊞56332 ℻369-8016. Map **7E3** ⅢⅢ 600 rms ≡⊒ ⌂ AE ⊡ ⊡ ⊞ & ≈ ⊻ ≛ ⊶ ⊟ ⊒

Location: Hard to beat for shopping in the heart of the Golden Mile. Holiday Inns in Asia are more upscale than their US counterparts. Standards are exceptionally high and service is excellent. Holiday Inns have made a marketing virtue of their health and fitness facilities, with gyms, jogging maps, healthy menus and nonsmoking floors. This one has a rooftop pool and health club. They also make much ado of their German and Austrian wines and cuisine, featuring bakery-delicatessens and gourmet game foods, such as venison, here at the BARON'S TABLE (see EATING AND DRINKING). The lobby is something of a thoroughfare (although with discreet security), but it provides a lively passing show of local life, with 54 shops featuring in its arcade.

HOLIDAY INN HARBOUR VIEW

70 Mody Rd., Tsimshatsui East, Kowloon
☎721-5161 ⊞38670 ℻369-5672. Map **8E4** ⅢⅢ 600 rms ≡⊒ AE ⊡ ⊡ ⊞ & ⊀⊑ ≈ ⊻ ≛ ⊶ ⊟ ⊒

Location: Facing the Tsimshatsui East waterfront parade. The company's regional flagship caters to business travelers, with a business center and executive floor with 38 rooms. The waterfront promenade is part of the hotel's recommended jogging route, and its view of the harbor is superb. Its restaurants are innovative, with gourmet health menus at all outlets and memorable Mediterranean cuisine at **The Mistral**. Holiday Inns also bake by far the most nourishing bread in town, which is sold at their **Corner Delicatessen** outlets in both hotels and at a bakery arm on the mezzanine floor of Hutchison House in Central district. Nonsmoking rooms.

HYATT REGENCY

67 Nathan Rd., Tsimshatsui, Kowloon
☎311-1234 ᵀˣ43127 Ⅸ739-8701. Map
7E3 ░░░ 723 rms ≈ ⌧ ⊙ ⊠ ⬚ & ⛟
⬛

Location: One of the best Golden Mile locations, with an MTR station entrance right in front, and just 5 minutes' walk from Harbour City and the big arcades. The Hyatt group pioneered the concept of special "business class" floors, complete with separate concierge, private elevator, and, as in this example, the exclusive **Regency Club**, with its own facsimile network. Opened in 1969, the hotel was strikingly transformed into an elegant property by a HK$120-million renovation completed in early 1988. Extensive use of Asian arts and antiques and museum lighting techniques shrewdly distract from, and compensate for, low ceilings by creating pockets of intimacy and discrete spaces. There are three stories of shops, with the Nathan Rd. street-front boasting an array of upscale European designer boutiques. Two guestrooms and public rest rooms are provided specifically for disabled visitors. There are no health or recreation facilities. (For a near-legendary hotel restaurant, see HUGO'S in EATING AND DRINKING.)

IMPERIAL ⬛ ♨

30-34 Nathan Rd., Tsimshatsui, Kowloon
☎366-2201 ᵀˣ55893 Ⅸ311-2360. Map
7E3 ░░░ 219 rms ≈ ⌧ ⊙ ⊠ ⬚ ⛟ ⬛
Location: At the center of Tsimshatsui, near the Holiday Inn Golden Mile and

across the street from the Hyatt Regency. A good-value hotel with rates that are half to two-thirds below the deluxe properties around it: ideally placed for the premiere Kowloon shopping locations, but without the usual high accommodation costs. A limited range of business services is available. The group also manages the Pousada de Sao Tiago in Macau.

KOWLOON ♨

19-21 Nathan Rd., Tsimshatsui, Kowloon
☎369-8698 ᵀˣ47604 Ⅸ369-8698. Map
7E3 ░░░ 707 rms ≈ ⌧ ⊙ ⊠ ⬚ ⬛ ⛟
Location: At the waterfront end of the Golden Mile, behind the Peninsula Hotel; MTR and Star Ferry are within 5 minutes' walk. Built in the mid-1980s by the Peninsula Group, this is a business traveler's hotel with hi-tech frills: each room has a TV with videotext access to a database as well as messages, bills, etc. The business center in particular boasts state-of-the-art computer gear. A basement arcade features local designer boutiques.

METROPOLE

75 Waterloo Rd., Kowloon ☎761-1711
ᵀˣ45063 Ⅸ761-0769. Map 8B4 ░░ 487
rms ≈ ➡ ⌧ ⊙ ⊠ ⬚ ⌂ & ♨ ⛟
⬛ ⬛
Location: w edge of Mongkok district. A bit out-of-the-way, but a shuttle bus circles Kowloon half-hourly from 8am-7.30pm and stops at Yaumatei MTR station. One of the China Travel Services group of urban district "business-class" hotels, with two executive floors, a business center, a rooftop pool and a karaoke bar. Distinctive for its size if not its artistry, a mural 50m (165 feet) long featuring scenes from China fronts the building.

MIRAMAR

130 Nathan Rd., Tsimshatsui, Kowloon
☎368-1111 ᵀˣ44661. Ⅸ369-1788.
Map 7E3 ░░░ 713 rms ≈ ⌧ ⊙ ⊠ ⬚
& ♨ ⛟ ⛟
Location: In the Golden Mile, a short walk to the MTR, not far from the Jordan Rd. area. The Miramar was built in

the late 1950s, the first "international-style" hotel in Hong Kong, and was quite the thing in its day. It boasts four floors of shopping arcade and a conference center refurbished in 1991.

NATHAN 🏨 ♨
378 Nathan Rd., Yaumatei, Kowloon
☎388-5141 📠31037 📠770-4262. Map
7D3 🛏 *150 rms* ≈ 🎹 📺 🎮 📻 ≈ ⚑
Location: One of the group of inexpensive hotels N of the Golden Mile near the Jordan Rd. area. Clean and convenient, and a good choice for visitors on a modest budget.

NEW WORLD
22 Salisbury Rd., Tsimshatsui, Kowloon
☎369-4111 📠35860 📠369-9387. Map
7F3 🛏 *550 rms* ≈ 🚗 🎹 📺 🎮 📻 ♿
♨ ⚑ ≈ ♥ ⚑ ⚓ 🍴 🍷 🛗
Location: On the waterfront between Nathan Rd. and Tsimshatsui East. The New World Centre plaza just below the hotel boasts some 400 shops, anchored by the Tokyu Japanese department store. Within, there are executive suites with business services on three **Dynasty Club** floors, a nonsmoking floor, six rooms designed for disabled travelers, and specially appointed rooms for female executives. A HK$200 million renovation to the 12-year-old property was completed in early 1991. The large swimming pool is set in a lush, 40,000-square-foot roof garden. All suites have their own fax machines, E-mail, teletext messaging and laser disc players. Relax in the **Catwalk Karaoke** lounge.

NIKKO 🏨
72 Mody Rd., Tsimshatsui East, Kowloon
☎739-1111 📠31302 📠311-3122. Map
8E4 🛏 *461 rms* ≈ 🚗 🎹 📺 🎮 📻
🍷 ≈ ♥ ⚑ ⚓ 🍴 🛗
Location: At the N end of the district, across from the Holiday Inn Harbour View, and farthest E from the Chatham Rd. intersection that joins Tsimshatsui East with the main tourist area. Connected to Japan Air Lines and one of a group of nearly 20 Nikko hotels, this 15-story deluxe accommodation, with a

heated rooftop pool and topping two "Nikko Floors" for business travelers, opened in early 1988.

OMNI HONGKONG
3 Canton Rd., Tsimshatsui, Kowloon
☎736-0088 📠43838 📠736-0011. Map
7F2 🛏 *710 rms* ≈ 🚗 🎹 📺 🎮 📻 ♿
♨ ⚑ ≈ ⚑ 🍴 🛗
Location: A few steps from the Star Ferry, and part of the amazing Ocean Terminal/Ocean Centre/Harbour City complex. The lobby bar or coffee shop are convenient bases for forays into the 600 or so shops of the three adjoining shopping malls. For almost 25 years this has been a favorite rendezvous and landmark location. You can't get much closer to the harbor, and the view from rooms facing N over Kowloon's Golden Mile is also superb. All 117 rooms on the 17th-18th **Continental Floors** are devoted to business travelers. Other rooms overlook the hotel's tropical roof garden and unusual outdoor (heated) swimming pool, which is surrounded by sculpted walls, elaborate staircases and shrubbery, all designed to create a "Roman bath" environment. A nonsmoking floor and a good "blues" bar (see GRIPP'S in NIGHTLIFE) complete the picture.

OMNI MARCO POLO
Harbour City, Canton Rd., Tsimshatsui,
Kowloon ☎736-0888 📠40077
📠736-0022. Map *7E2* 🛏 *440 rms* ≈
🏠 🎹 📺 🎮 📻 ⚑ 🍴 🛗
Location: In the center of the main shopping malls. All three of the hotels in the Ocean Terminal/Ocean Centre/ Harbour City shopping complex share facilities: the Marco Polo has no swimming pool or health center, but guests have access to those at the OMNI HONGKONG, just down the mall. A reference library is a thoughtful touch, but expect no harbor views from this hotel.

OMNI PRINCE
Harbour City, Canton Rd., Tsimshatsui,
Kowloon ☎736-1888 📠50950
📠736-0066. Map *7E2* 🛏 *400 rms* ≈
🚗 🎹 📺 🎮 📻 ♨ ⚑ 🏠

Location: The third of the three Omni hotels set into the enormous Harbour City complex, which sprawls along Canton Rd., Kowloon, NW of the Star Ferry terminal. For guests who don't mind the proximity of their rooms to the corridors of an enormous shopping center, these three Omni hotels are clean, reliably serviced and rank as 3- to 4-star accommodation centers. Facilities used and chits acquired in any one of the hotels (the **Hong Kong Pool** is open to guests from all three) can be charged directly to your room bill. The Omni Prince caters mostly to tour groups, members of which can sometimes be seen wandering the halls searching for the lobby entrance among the shops. The mammoth shopping complex was built more than 25 years ago to service cruise ships that dock at the pier outside. Although there are no harbor views, the higher rooms look out across Kowloon Park.

PENINSULA   See page 93.

RAMADA INN ♨

73-75 Chatham Rd. S, Tsimshatsui, Kowloon ☎311-1100 ✉44582
☏311-6000. Map **7E3** ▥ 205 rms ⚐
▨ ⚏ ⊙ ⊠ ▥ ≛

Location: Well-placed for walking tours. A pioneer of the "business class" hotel developments now popular in Hong Kong, built in the mid-1980s with that brief specifically in mind, and far earlier into the field than most others of its type. The limited amenities are compensated for by location and low price.

RAMADA RENAISSANCE ▦

Sun Plaza, 8 Peking Rd., Tsimshatsui, Kowloon ☎311-3311 ✉81252
☏861-0958. Map **7E3** ▥ 501 rms ⚐
⚊ ⚏ ⊙ ⊠ ▥ ⚑ ⟨≪ ⚐ ≛ ⚐ ⊟ ⚏

Location: At the intersection with Kowloon Park Dr., one block from Star Ferry and two from Nathan Rd. MTR station. The Ramada hotel group, bought by Hong Kong's New World Development Group in 1990, is the third-largest in the world, and this hotel is the best they've got. Somewhat over-shadowed by other 5-star hotels in the vicinity, it is an unexpectedly pleasant surprise for those who can afford luxury hotels. Opened in late 1988, the 19-story hotel has excellent restaurants and is 5 minutes from everything in Tsim-shatsui. There is a nonsmoking floor, and five rooms for disabled guests. Many of the rooms have their own fac-simile machines, and all have full-sized work desks. Other facilities are legion: for example, the **Renaissance Club** for business travelers on the 11th and 12th floors; the business center, which has offices to rent; the rooftop pool and health club, with stunning views; the squash court; and the shopping arcade in the basement.

REGAL AIRPORT HOTEL ♨

Sa Po Rd., Kowloon ☎718-0333
✉40950 ☏799-2503. Map **2D5** ▥ 380 rms ⚐ ⚊ ⚏ ⊙ ⊠ ▥ ⚐ ≛ ⚐ ⊟ ⚏

Location: Connected by an air-conditioned walkway to the Kai Tak Airport terminal. Designed for businessmen on a short stopover, this is often fully reserved, although day reservations for transit passengers will be taken providing space is available. A business association recently rated it the best airport hotel in the world. The hotel's business center specializes in the China trade, with translations, assistance with China travel and a China-oriented reference library. Temporary offices can be rented on the first floor, and portable computers and room facsimile machines are available. Computerized flight information is displayed on monitors spread throughout public areas and shown on room TVs. All rooms are sound-proofed against the roar of the jets. The **Five Continents** restaurant serves good "country French" food and has a spectacular view of the airport runway. Although there are no in-house recreation facilities, public tennis courts and swimming pool are at hand nearby. The hotel also offers guests access to the **Clearwater Bay Golf & Country Club**, which is some distance away (see SPORTS), where there are golf and full recreation facilities.

REGAL KOWLOON ✿

71 Mody Rd., Tsimshatsui East, Kowloon
☎722-1818 ⊠40955 ⊠369-6950. Map
8E4 ⫿ 600 rms ⊟ ━ 🆎 ⊙ 🔳 📼
✿ ✓ 🏋 ☂ 🖃 🎱

Location: In the middle of the new shopping city of Tsimshatsui East. Formerly an Air France Meridien group hotel, where the airline's flight crews still stay, the hotel blends France and China in its atmosphere and decoration. The **Le Restaurant de France** features the *haute cuisine* of consulting chefs such as Outhier and Bocuse. The **RMH Shopping Arcade** has 30 shops. "Super-saver" rooms are especially good value.

REGENT 🏨 ✿ ⏲

Salisbury Rd., Tsimshatsui, Kowloon
☎721-1211 ⊠37134 ⊠739-4546. Map
7F3 ⫿ 602 rms ⊟ ━ 🆎 ⊙ 🔳 📼
✿ 《 ≈ 🎺 🏋 ☂ ⚓ 🖃

Location: Attached to the New World Centre. A kind of latter-day Mandarin, this caters to the American rag trade rather than to the wealthy *taipans* of colonial-era companies (the *hongs*). Almost half its trade comes from visiting business people associated with the enormous Hong Kong apparel industry and its most important market, the United States.

The Regent, brainchild of an American hotelier, Robert H. Burns, offers Hong Kong's best banqueting facilities, and a self-consciously grand Carrara marble staircase that leads to the ballroom and is used both in its normal capacity and for fashion photography. The lobby bar has a magnificent view of Hong Kong harbor, and a lower-level coffee shop looks out across the water through three stories of high glass panels. Externally, the hotel is part of a massive architectural island of red brick, which also includes the NEW WORLD hotel, the New World shopping, office and apartment complex, and the Japanese Tokyu department store. The terrace of the Regent has the best panoramic views of the Chinese New Year fireworks, if you happen to be there at the time.

RITZ 🏨 ✿

122 Austin Rd., Tsimshatsui, Kowloon
☎369-2282 ⊠49794 ⊠845-3910. Map
7D3 ⫿ 60 rms ⊟ 🆎 ⊙ 🔳 📼 🖃

Location: At the N edge of the Golden Mile area, near Yaumatei and Jordan Rd. Pleasant surroundings and good value for money complement decent room service, laundry and dry-cleaning facilities, and baby-sitting services.

ROYAL GARDEN

69 Mody Rd., Tsimshatsui East, Kowloon
☎721-5215 ⊠39539 ⊠369-9976. Map
8E4 ⫿ 433 rms ⊟ ━ 🆎 ⊙ 🔳 📼
🎺 🏋 ☂ ⚓ 🖃 🎱

Location: In the heart of Kowloon at Tsimshatsui East. Unique in Hong Kong, this hotel is effectively a huge indoor garden surrounded by terraced rooms overlooked by balconies. All rooms open onto a lofty, 110-foot-high air-conditioned atrium, designed as a garden, with trees, masses of greenery and ornamental pools. Rooms contain original paintings, and Chinese desks by world-ranked interior designers Howard Hirsch & Associates. The hotel's 4-story shopping arcade is linked by two air-conditioned walkways to other commercial buildings with shopping arcades, so you need neither get wet in the rain nor sweaty in the sun to spend your money. Fine restaurants include the **Tomowa Kyokuhin** (Japanese) and **Lalique** (French), and there is a popular disco, **The Falcon**. Nonsmoking rooms, now widespread in Hong Kong hotels, are available.

The Royal Garden is owned by the large, diversified Sun Hung Kai group, which also operate the **Royal Park Hotel** in Hong Kong.

ROYAL PACIFIC HOTEL & TOWERS

33 Canton Rd., China Hong Kong City, Tsimshatsui, Kowloon ☎736-1188
⊠44111 ⊠736-1212. Map 7E2 ⫿ 626
rms ⊟ 🖪 🆎 ⊙ 🔳 📼 ✿ 《 ≈ 🎺
🏋 ☂ ⚓ 🖃

Location: On the waterfront at the N edge of Tsimshatsui, near Austin Ave. in Yaumatei district. More like an airport hotel than its OMNI group neighbors to the s along Canton Rd. in the Harbour and Ocean City complexes, this caters to commuters to China and, to a lesser extent, Macau. China Hong Kong City is now the terminus for virtually all hovercraft and Chinese-owned cruise ships to destinations in mainland China. Like Shun Tak Centre across the harbor, which caters to Macau traffic, this complex combines boat quays, shopping, offices and a hotel into a center comprising several curtain-walled buildings in bronzed-glass cladding.

SHANGRI-LA 🏨 ♣

64 Mody Rd., Tsimshatsui East, Kowloon
☎721-2111 📠36718 📠723-8686. Map
7E3 ▥ 719 rms ⬛ 🖃 🔼 ⊙ 🔘 ▦
🖂 ♿ ◁€ ≋ ♈ ⛴ ⇪ ⚓ 🖃 ⬛
Location: Close to the waterfront and the New World Centre. Built by the Kuok group, who manage more than two dozen hotels and whose flagship is the sister hotel of the same name in Singapore, this is an exceptionally luxurious hotel. It has several times been ranked amongst the world's top ten hotels by business and travel press surveys.

Although a fine hotel, the Shangri-La loses some of its luster by being located in a city sated with deluxe hotels. Its sumptuous interiors are by movie-set designer Don Ashton, who also designed the **Mandarin Oriental** across the harbor. Chinoiserie murals in the 2-story lobby area are by British artist Malcolm Golding. The marble is from Carrara, Italy, and the crystal chandeliers from Vienna. The overall effect is one of opulence, at the expense of intimacy. A nonsmoking floor, the **Club 21** business floor, business and health centers, and a rooftop lounge are among the facilities.

SHERATON

20 Nathan Rd., Tsimshatsui, Kowloon
☎369-1111 📠45813 📠739-8707. Map
7F3 ▥ 842 rms ⬛ 🖃 🔼 ⊙ 🔘 ▦
◁€ ≋ ♈ ♈ ⛴ 🖃 ⬛
Location: At the waterfront end of the Golden Mile. "A hotel within a hotel" is the concept underlying the stepped-up luxury and service found in the **Sheraton Towers**, on the upper floors. A unique bubble-elevator mounted outside the building makes for an exciting ride up to the **Sky Suite** supper club on the 18th floor, which stages theme nights and costume parties and by night has superb views of the city and harbor. Reuter's World Report is channeled to room Tvs. SOMEPLACE ELSE is a popular nightspot (see NIGHTLIFE), and **Bukhara** serves excellent North Indian tandoori cuisine. There is a well-equipped gym, and the arcade has about 65 shops.

YMCA ♣

41 Salisbury Rd., Tsimshatsui, Kowloon
☎369-2211 📠739-9315. Map 7F3 ▢
400 rms ⬛ 🔼 ⊙ 🔘 ▦ ◁€ ≋ ♈ ♈
Location: Facing s toward the waterfront on one of the best sites in town, next door to the Peninsula Hotel. Until 1991, this was the best accommodations deal in Hong Kong: an old hotel at hostel rates right next to the PENINSULA, with terraces overlooking one of the world's most beautiful harbors. It's still inexpensive and good value, but the rambling old facility has been demolished — a pity, that — and replaced by a 400-room, block-square building, *sans* terraces.

As before, there is an Olympic-sized indoor swimming pool and generally good sports facilities. YMCA members are given priority.

Eating and drinking

The restaurant and teahouse tradition

Hong Kong is one of the world's great centers of Chinese food and *the* capital of Cantonese food, arguably its most subtle regional cuisine. One of the major tour packages offered in overseas Chinese enclaves such as Singapore or Penang is a dining excursion to Hong Kong.

Given the city's 8,000 licensed restaurants and at least as many more unlicensed ones, masquerading as "clubs," its culinary status is hardly surprising. Hong Kong has inherited a restaurant and teahouse tradition believed to have begun in the 12th century during the Southern Sung Dynasty, when scholar gourmets first codified the principles of imperial cuisine and thereby also identified its regional variations.

Since the Communist revolution in China in 1949, Hong Kong has also been the center of Chinese capitalism, intellectual freedom and hedonism, providing a haven and an affluent, appreciative clientele for the finest regional chefs. The city now offers authentic cuisine that spans the range of China's widely varying regional styles.

SCIENCE OF YIN/YANG

As well as satisfying appetite and senses, Chinese food provides a solid base for a healthy diet. As with other traditional cultures, cooking and medicine are closely tied. Underlying all Chinese cooking is the *Yin/Yang* theory of food science, which divides all food into three groups: *Yin* for cooling, *Yang* for heating and *Yin/Yang* for neutral. This grading has nothing to do with the food's actual spiciness or means of preparation, but is instead based on maintaining the balance of the body and its energies, which are likewise explicable in *Yin/Yang* terms. Thus, while certain piquant herbs are deemed "cooling" in effect, other food, such as lychee, is labeled "hot" even when chilled.

Vegetables, herbs, fungi and meats all have relative health-promoting values and are combined and prepared according to long traditions of encouraging balanced health and vigor. For example, ginger, taken by most Chinese every day, is not only delicious but also promotes respiration and digestion.

WINTER FOODS

Also following *Yin/Yang* principles are the winter foods restaurants, which are frequented in the fall and serve "tonic" ("heating") foods. They are usually identifiable by the word "Park" in their name. Sample the warming game soups with herbs, seeds and roots to judge for yourself the effectiveness of ancient Chinese wisdom.

Few Westerners, however, will enthusiastically embrace the most popular Cantonese winter tonic, dog soup, which is illegal in Hong Kong but widely available in Guangdong province. Many other dishes savor of sympathetic magic. Owl soup is prescribed to alleviate night blindness, eagle soup to reduce dizzy spells, snakes to regenerate the reproductive organs. Turtles, pangolins, civets, bear paws, monkey brains, as well as many other species of wild birds and beasts, are also often necessary ingredients for traditional cures — although for the squeamish Westerner, an insider's knowledge of the means of preparation might understandably sabotage the potion's desired remedial effect.

JUNK FOODS

Such culinary idiosyncracies aside, the Chinese diet is generally healthy and well balanced. Although there always seems to be plenty of it about, less meat is consumed in Hong Kong than in the West, and digestive ailments attendant on a Western low-fiber diet are virtually unknown here. However, the onset of packaged and junk foods and the heavy-handed use of monosodium glutamate in the Chinese kitchen in recent years are ominous trends.

The incidence of breast cancer in younger women, associated with a high-fat diet, has risen sharply; local salted fish *(baam yu)* has been linked with cancer; certain freshwater crustaceans carry dangerous parasites; local oysters are often contaminated; and most local shellfish are probably best treated with suspicion, or eaten only in superior restaurants.

CHINESE REGIONAL CUISINES

The many variations in Chinese culinary styles can be broadly divided into four main regional cuisines associated with the cities of **Guangzhou** (Canton) in South China, **Beijing** (Peking) in the north, **Shanghai** in the northeast, and **Szechuan**, China's largest province bordering Tibet, to the northwest.

Other distinctive styles include the cuisines of **Swatow (Chaozhou/Chiuchow)**, a port city to the east of Guangzhou, and that of the **Kejia (Hakka)**, a northern dialect group now spread throughout Guangdong province and believed to have migrated to the south centuries ago. Most recently, **Hunan** cuisine has come to Hong Kong by way of American overseas Chinese communities from Mao's home province in mainland China. These communities have made it an American "discovery" of the 1980s, close to Szechuan cuisine in its fondness for chilies, but without the heavy-handed use of garlic.

Common to all Chinese cuisine is a preference for fresh produce. The south, with its lengthy coastline and year-round growing season, is one of China's most intensive rice- and vegetable-producing regions. Cantonese cuisine consequently has the largest range of fresh vegetable, rice and seafood dishes. The harsh climate of the north limits the range of fresh vegetables available. Out of season, northerners rely on preserved produce and the dried flavor-enhancing ingredients for which their cuisine has become famous. Extensive wheat, corn and sorghum farming is concentrated in the north, and the use of grains, other than rice, as a staple, often in the form of noodles and bread, is a distinctive feature of northern cuisine.

CANTONESE CUISINE

This is by far the best-represented regional cuisine in Hong Kong, Cantonese cooking is known for its imagination and culinary versatility, evident in anything from a quick snack to an elaborate banquet. The freshest ingredients are blended with basic herbs and spices and usually flavored with soy, hoisin or oyster sauce.

Dim sum, a vast array of tasty bite-sized morsels, is part of *yum cha* (which literally means "drinking tea" — an important daily social event) and is served from early morning to noon, at lunch and, in many restaurants, until 5pm.

Between sips of tea one eats an exotic and seemingly endless assortment of seafood and meat dumplings, fried or steamed buns, glutinous savory rice in lotus leaves, savory chicken rice and spring rolls, all usually followed by a wide variety of *dim sum* desserts. The food is wheeled among the tables and served on request. Although portions are small, you can down a terrific variety at one sitting, especially if in a group. Despite the noise, it's a delightful and cheap way to eat.

A good Cantonese dinner is based on a balanced presentation: vegetable, meat and a large variety of seafood dishes are simply prepared by steaming, blanching or poaching, and often served with a subtle sauce of light vinegar, minced ginger and scallions.

CHAOZHOU (CHIUCHOW) CUISINE

Famed for its excellent seafood dishes, specialties of this style of cooking include thick shark's-fin soup, steamed eel and sautéed whelk, as well as duck-and-lemon soup and braised goose. Although desserts do not generally feature in Chinese cuisine (fresh fruit traditionally finishes a Chinese meal), bird's nest with coconut milk is a superb exception. To stimulate the appetite before a Chiuchow meal, the strong astringent Iron Goddess of Mercy tea from Fujian Province is served in miniature teacups.

SHANGHAI CUISINE

For two months each fall, hairy freshwater crabs, sent from Shanghai — China's largest city and greatest port — are the highlight of Chinese dining in Hong Kong. Steamed, and served with ginger tea and vinegar sauce, these crabs and their roe have a passionate following among Hong Kong's Cantonese as well as Shanghainese residents. Shanghai cuisine uses a great range of fresh produce as well as many preserved vegetables and pickles.

The most prevalent cooking techniques are steaming and stir-frying in sesame oil and soy sauce; the result tends to be heavier and richer than Cantonese fare.

SZECHUAN CUISINE

The spicy and fiery food typical of this regional style is strongly flavored with chili, peppercorns, onions and garlic and is usually served with bread and noodles. Smoked dishes are rare in China, but Szechuan smoked duck or pigeon in camphor and tea is a dish of note. Other specialties include braised eggplant, pork dumplings and dry-fried string beans — all accompanied with spicy sauces.

BEIJING (PEKING) CUISINE

Beijing was once the base of the Imperial Court of China, and its influence is visible in many of the region's impressive dishes such as the famous Peking Duck. The cuisine uses more meat, particularly mutton, than most southern dishes, and places greater emphasis on bread and dumplings. A distinctive feature of Beijing-style eating is the hot pot (often advertised as a "Mongolian hot-pot" in winter), a type of fondue that uses boiling stock instead of oil. It is served in a big chafing dish, its contents shared by all at the table. Substantial, strongly flavored meals as well as sizzling and often spectacular platters are characteristic of northern cuisine.

HAKKA CUISINE

Perhaps the least well known — although the famous salted baked chicken often thought to be Cantonese is in fact a Hakka dish — this cuisine is noted for its bean curd and use of salted vegetables, and its black herb soup is greatly favored locally. However, Hong Kong does not have a wide selection of Hakka restaurants.

Where to eat

There are five styles of Chinese restaurants that, once experienced, are everlastingly remembered:
- banquet halls-cum-*dim sum* parlors
- teahouses
- Cantonese seafood restaurants
- *daipaidong* side stalls
- and noodle and *congee* shops

To guide you through the maze of possible dishes, the Hong Kong Tourist Association publishes several useful, well-illustrated and bilingual booklets on Chinese cuisine.

A good place to start is **Food St.** in Causeway Bay. The street — more an arcade — has 20 restaurants offering a range of choices from Nanjing beef noodles to Japanese, Taiwanese and Vietnamese food, all at moderate prices.

BANQUET HALLS

Usually occupying several floors, these important social centers serve morning, afternoon and Sunday *dim sum* — this last often a half-day excursion for the entire extended family, which may total 10 to 20 people or more. They are also the place for one of the great occasions in Chinese life: wedding ceremonies.

Their decor reflects their function. Restaurateurs will spend upward of a million Hong Kong dollars to create an opulent secular temple of reds and golds for their patrons, with gigantic relief sculptures of dragons and phoenixes — the central symbols of Chinese culture, symbols of *Yin/Yang* balance, and of man and woman. Giantism and garish colors are intentional, appropriate to the scale of events hosted by these populist palaces, and should be enjoyed for their colorful exuberance.

TEAHOUSES

That great modern Chinese drama, Lao She's *Teahouse,* offers a memorable image of this institution, which in China has traditionally been a man's preserve. Historically, Confucian *literati* -would gather in tea pavilions to read and write poems over wine, and they have traditionally immortalized in their work these centers of creative activity.

Hong Kong's teahouses, which are more akin to the local bar in the US or the pub in Britain, remain close to the spirit of the 19th century. They are where "Coolie-brokers" congregated to recruit the thousands of people who emigrated from South China a century ago. In 1876 a witness from Singapore said there were 20 or 30 such teahouses in Swatow (Chaozhou) alone.

A magnificent example of an upscale teahouse is **Luk Yu** in Stanley St., which has retained its marvelous wooden booths and fittings from the 1930s. Today, it caters to local gold and stockmarket brokers. Other teahouses are famous for the bird enthusiasts who congregate for tea and wagers on singing contests in the early mornings, after "walking" their caged songbirds.

SEAFOOD CENTERS

These eating places have enormous, and usually rather slimy, glass-walled seawater tanks of fish and crustaceans — a source of endless fascination to visiting children, as well as of one's dinner. English-speaking managers or waiters are generally happy, in slack periods, to expound the virtues of the various fish swimming in their tanks, and advise you on what to order.

DAIPAIDONGS

These assemblages of street stalls are effectively outdoor versions of noodle and *congee* shops — Hong Kong's answer to the street café. Sociability among regulars can be combined with a quick snack from early morning to late at night, the latter being the more leisurely time. The food is generally good, although occasionally slightly greasy.

Their indoor equivalents are usually narrow-fronted shops with the chef in the window and his rack of barbecued meat and fowl hanging at the ready for an entering customer's inspection. Inside or out, the *daipaidong* bellows steam, sizzles with stir-frying, and offers absorbing opportunities to watch Chinese-style fast-food preparation in action.

HOTEL RESTAURANTS

Under the guidance of such master chefs as the Frenchmen Bocuse and Outhier, the best restaurants in the grand hotels offer some of the world's finest European *haute cuisine*. Some hotels run year-long programs in which master chefs of Continental and other cuisines demonstrate their culinary skills in two-week food fairs: these are worth inquiring about.

In the endless quest for culinary one-upmanship, three newer hotels have brought northern Italian *haute cuisine* to Hong Kong at **Capriccio** (Ramada Renaissance), **Grassini's** (Grand Hyatt) and **Nicholini's** (Conrad). Two older hotels, **Sheraton** and **Holiday Inn**, have researched and developed their own light cuisines for those concerned with salt, fats and carbohydrates. "Sheraton Cuisine," for instance, now features in 25 percent of the entrées in all of their restaurant outlets.

NON-CHINESE RESTAURANTS

Outside the hotels, non-Chinese restaurants are seldom outstanding, although this pattern is changing as local Chinese diners explore foreign cuisines more freely and the expatriate business population grows to create a more diverse demand. Two above-average newcomers are **Il Mercato**, an Italian restaurant with locations in Lan Kwai Fong, Central and in Stanley, founded by former international newsweekly journalist Barry Kalb (who studied with Roman chefs while based in Italy), and **Mozart Stub'n** on Glenealy St., Central, which features very fine Austrian cuisine.

"HAUTE CHINOIS"

The international competition has also affected Chinese cuisine. It has led to the creation of self-consciously *haute Chinois* restaurants, which adopt the French *nouvelle cuisine* concern for presentation and experiment. Examples are the **House of Canton Restaurant** in D'Aguilar House, Central, and **The Chinese Restaurant** in the Hyatt Regency.

OTHER ETHNIC CUISINES

Little eating places offering other ethnic cuisines are scattered throughout the main shopping areas on Hong Kong Island, especially in Causeway Bay and Central, and in a 10-block area flanking the last "Golden Mile" of Nathan Rd. to the harbor. With exceptions, they are uniformly mediocre.

Most common are Indian curry restaurants, followed by Vietnamese, Japanese, Korean and Malay. *Nouvelle Américaine* restaurants feature upscale hamburgers, Jewish delicatessen snacks (a New York and Los Angeles influence) and "Tex-Mex" dishes. British or Australian pub-style fare, several undistinguished Italian eateries, as well as some German, French and other kinds of European restaurant can also be found in the area.

The best recent news on the ethnic eating scene is the opening of Thai restaurants of a reasonably high standard such as **Chili Club**, in Wanchai, **Sawadee** in Tsimshatsui, and **Silks** and **Supatra's** in Central. There are

RESTAURANTS CLASSIFIED BY PRICE

HONG KONG ISLAND

INEXPENSIVE 🔲
Andy's Kitchen 🍲 ♣
Chili Club ♣
Cinta
Indonesian Restaurant 🍲 ♣
Koreana 🍲
Vegi Food Kitchen 🍲 ♣

MODERATELY PRICED 🔲
Al's Diner
American Restaurant 🍲
Brown's Wine Bar
Galley and Pier One ♣
Landau's ♣
Rainbow Room ♣
La Ronda ♣
Le Tire Bouchon ♣

EXPENSIVE 🔲
Amigo 🔺
Bentley's
Bocarinos Grill 🔺 ♣
Central Park
Cleveland Szechuan Restaurant
Luk Yu Teahouse (🔲 to 🔲)
North Park Restaurant
Pep'n Chili ♣
Sun Tung Lok Shark's Fin

VERY EXPENSIVE 🔲
Fook Lam Moon
Grassini ♣
Man Wah 🔺
Mandarin Grill
The Pierrot 🔺 ♣

KOWLOON

MODERATELY PRICED 🔲
Sawadee Thai Restaurant ♣
Spring Deer 🍲

EXPENSIVE 🔲
Au Trou Normand ♣
Baron's Table
Golden Island
Great Shanghai

Hugo's
Nadaman
Shang Palace 🔺 ♣
Tien Heung Lau

VERY EXPENSIVE 🔲
Chesa 🔺
La Plume 🔺

now more than two dozen scattered about the territory. Numerous Japanese fast-food outlets have also opened — but beware their heavy-handed use of monosodium glutamate.

VEGETARIAN EATING
The most consistently reliable ethnic minority cuisine offered outside the hotels is found in vegetarian restaurants, which cater primarily for Chinese Buddhists, such as **Choi Kun Heung** *(219E Nathan Rd., Tsimshatsui)*. As a quirky way of getting the best of both worlds, wheat-gluten-based entrées are prepared to imitate convincingly the look and taste of various Chinese meat dishes. Even this cuisine has been recently franchised by a local fast-food group.

STREET FOOD

A network of *daipaidongs* (street food stalls) covers the city, and you are seldom far from one of their encampments — a cluster of stalls in a side street, or an alleyway between main streets, usually in a busy, crowded area.

In the morning they serve a quick breakfast of *congee* (rice porridge, *jook*) with pork or fish, Chinese pastries *(yao tieo)* and Chinese cannelloni *(cheung fun)*. Lunch is also quick and simple: barbecued pork *(chai siu fun)* and rice, *won ton* and noodles. Nights are for *siu yeah*, leisurely late snacks, or a more serious meal. The following *daipaidongs* serve night food from about 7pm to midnight or later.

Hong Kong Island   The *daipaidong* stalls at the corner of King Kwong St. and Sing Woot Rd. in **Happy Valley** serve Chiuchow-style fast-food dishes such as braised goose, fish, prawn or crab balls with noodles; they close around midnight. The **Poor Man's Nightclub** in Connaught Rd., Central, opposite Cleverly St. where the tram turns near the Macau Ferry Pier, specializes in a broad range of seafood dishes: clams, crabs, prawns, fish. It shares a daytime parking lot with a thriving night market. The **Western** *daipaidong* in Queen St., between Queen's Rd. West and Des Voeux Rd. West, has a good local atmosphere and is well known for Chiuchow food and winter hot pots.

Kowloon   The **Tsimshatsui** *daipaidong*, tucked beneath an overpass (flyover), is easily missed. You can enter it from Haiphong Rd. (between Nos. 24-41) or from Ashley Rd. It is good for Cantonese fried dishes, such as fried beef with vegetables, and famous for its meatballs. The **Temple St.** *daipaidong* adjoins the lively Temple St. Market and serves seafood of every kind, beautifully displayed.

EATING AFLOAT

For a totally different kind of dinner, ask the doorman at the Excelsior Hotel for directions to the tunnel under Gloucester Rd. to the **Causeway Bay Typhoon Shelter**; the exit is near the famous Noonday Gun at the quayside, where you will be assailed by women with sampans for hire. For a moderate fee they will row you around the shelter; food sampans will surround you, taking orders for seafood, noodles, vegetables, beer or a full Chinese dinner, returning about $\frac{1}{2}$ hour later with the food prepared. You eat under Chinese lanterns. There's even a boat with a Chinese orchestra that plays the world's worst Western music and has to be bribed to go away.

Aberdeen's famous floating restaurants, **Jumbo**, **Tai Pak** and **Sea Palace**, are palatial 2 or 3-story banquet halls, blazing with light after dark. Inside they are the usual incredibly ornate and opulent banquet-hall style, especially the *Jumbo,* with its million-dollar chandeliers. Naturally they specialize in seafood. Shuttle launches leave regularly from Aberdeen Main Pier.

Secrets of the Chinese kitchen

There are eight common cooking methods, most of which use the ubiquitous *wok*. This large, shallow cooking-dish and a razor-sharp cleaver are virtually the only steel tools a Chinese cook needs. With the addition of bamboo steaming racks, fitted baskets or wire strainers, the versatile *wok* can be used to stir-fry, deep-fry or pan-fry, as well as to simmer, steam, boil, double-boil (protracted steaming), and even to roast its contents. To produce such a diversity of food with so few tools is culinary art in action, and a visit to a Chinese kitchen is highly recommended.

Besides deft strokes of the cleaver and virtuoso *wok*manship, the Chinese cook depends on certain basic combinations of spices, herbs and sauces fundamental to Chinese cuisine. Ginger is considered essential for eliminating strong animal odors from meat and excessive fishiness from seafood. Sweet soya pastes are used to season roast pork. Oyster sauce enhances seafood. Tart plum sauce cuts the grease and fat of roast goose. Sweet plum sauce complements roast duck, quail or pigeon, and light soy sauce always replaces salt.

TABLE ETIQUETTE

Chinese diners eat in groups, from a shared array of mixed entrées. Except for rice and noodles, which are served generously, single portions are smaller than in the West, although the variety is greater.

When, in Canton 150 years ago, the high Manchu mandarin, Viceroy Lu, and some noble friends visited the British merchants' wharfside factory, they were offered tea, with the best English silver laid out in all its formality. Lu remarked that it was typical of the Barbarians to eat with kitchen utensils. Yet, despite the variety of dishes that pass across it, the Chinese table is as simple as the Chinese kitchen (and probably more untidy afterwards): basic equipment includes teacups, sauce dishes and bottles, bowls, chopsticks and a ladle-like porcelain spoon.

Chopsticks need skill, but local etiquette is generally relaxed: "As long as you get the food into your mouth," an old hand coaches. As for the Chinese soup spoon, a Chinese gourmet claims it was designed for slurping. The "tablecloth" is not meant to survive the occasion and is thus available as a dumping area. Don't hurry, leave time to savor the food, and watch how your neighbors deal with it. If invited out to dinner by a Chinese, he may honor you by placing choice delicacies (a fish eye, a chicken's foot, a piece of bright orange intestine) on your plate: hearty appreciation is your only option. Tap on the table if you want something someone offers you: tap again when served enough.

EXPLORING THE MENU

Most major restaurants will now offer set dinners that are good value and provide a fairly representative sample of the cuisine's distinctive style. The Chinese/English *à la carte* menu is divided into meats and poultry, seafood, soups, rice dishes, noodles and vegetables. Recommendations can also be requested from the Chinese menu. In small local restaurants where there may not be an English menu, point to what you want among the barbecued meats on display; your choice will be accompanied with rice *(fon)* or noodles *(mein)*.

When planning a formal banquet or a special meal it is advisable to consult the restaurant manager and his head chef the day before. They perform best for people who show an interest, and will probably offer invaluable advice on how to balance and complement different dishes, as well as what is in season and what isn't — a central consideration in fine Chinese dining.

WHAT TO DRINK
Oolong green tea — or others teas delicately scented with jasmine, chrysanthemum or rose petals — is an integral part of any Chinese meal and is usually served without charge in tumblers whether ordered or not, as is water in American eating places. Indicate that an empty pot needs filling by cocking its lid half open. Taken straight, never with milk or sugar, tea ideally complements highly flavored Chinese dishes both as a palate cleanser and as an aid to digestion. Alcohol less commonly accompanies Chinese meals: beer is most common, as the wine selection is limited in most restaurants. Many restaurants allow diners to bring their own alcohol — feel free to ask to do so.

White wines, comparable to very sweet riesling, have been exported from China in joint ventures with French firms. Locals, however, are inclined to favor brandy, cognac or the light but satisfying Tsingtao beer from China.

ABOUT THIS CHAPTER
The restaurant selection that now follows starts with two alphabetical lists, covering recommendations for Hong Kong Island and Kowloon respectively, and ending with a general compendium of ideas for eating out. Restaurant names, type of cuisine, addresses, telephone numbers and map references are given. Symbols show which restaurants are particularly luxurious (▲) or simple (▬), and which represent particularly good value in their class (♣). Other symbols show price categories, charge/credit cards and other noteworthy points. See KEY TO SYMBOLS on page 7 for the full list of symbols.

A list of all restaurants featured in the Hong Kong Island and Kowloon listings, classified alphabetically into our five price categories, appears on page 113.

Hong Kong Island's restaurants A to Z

AL'S DINER American
Shop F, Grd Flr, 27-39 D'Aguilar St., Central
☎869-1869. Map 3C3 ▢ ▥ ▤ ▦
This adds an American diner to the self-consciously "ethnic" cluster of Western eating places in Lan Kwai Fong district. A Wurlitzer juke box forms the centerpiece, with tabletop versions at each booth. If you love large US-style prime beef hamburgers or Elvis's favorite, a sandwich of peanut butter and banana slices, you're home free "Jimmy Dean, Jimmy Dean...."

AMERICAN RESTAURANT ◗ Chinese
20 Lockhart Rd., Wanchai ☎527-1000.
Map 4C5 ▢ ▤ ▦
Named to welcome Suzie Wong's generation of sailors, this and the New American Restaurant on Johnston Rd. and Manhattan Restaurant on Hennessy Rd. are all that's really left of their era in Wanchai. Neither food nor decor has changed for decades. Sizzling prawns on a hot metal plate, roasted Peking Duck, shark's fin and chicken soup in earthenware, and Beggar's Chicken baked in clay have, since the place opened in 1946, provided the exotic entrées of the East in these homey surroundings.

AMIGO ⌂ French
Amigo Mansion, 79A Wong Nai Chung Rd., Happy Valley ☎577-2204/8993. Map 6D8 ▢ ▤ ▥ ▦
All pomp and circumstance, vintage wines and very fine French provincial food set in a cozy, intimate atmosphere of wooden beams and soft lights. Dishes with long French names are dressed as well as the customers — men must wear white jacket and tie. Waiters in white gloves and romantic live music distract from the pain in one's wallet that will follow dinner. Popular with the horse-racing crowd that spills across from Happy Valley racecourse across the road. One of the "Sixties Generation" of freestanding restaurants in Hong Kong (it was established in 1967), which also include San Francisco

Steak House (opened the same year), Au Trou Normand (1964), and La Taverna (1968), an Italian eatery of the hanging straw-clad Chianti bottles school of decor, now on Ice House St.

ANDY'S KITCHEN ◗ ♣ Chinese
25 Tung Lo Wan Rd., Causeway Bay
☎890-8137. Map 6C9 ▢
Good home-style Shanghai food, very local with simple décor, unremarkable service, but great food. Try the spare ribs and vegetables with New Year's cake, or the fried flat bean cake. The staff's English is patchy, so either take a Chinese friend or the Tourist Association's bilingual booklet on Shanghai cuisine.

BENTLEY'S English
B4 Prince's Bldg.(Statue Sq. entrance), Central ☎868-0881. Map 4B4 ▢ ▤ ▦ ▥ ▦
A branch of the Bentley's seafood and oyster bar in London, which has transformed a commercial center's basement into a world of Victorian prints, cozy bar and banquettes and English seafood specialties, such as Dover sole and fish pie. A large selection of the world's oysters is flown in fresh daily.

BOCARINOS GRILL ⌂ ♣ Continental European
Hotel Victoria, Shun Tak Centre, 200 Connaught Rd., Sheung Wan ☎540-7228 ext. 7421/2. Map 3A2 ▢ ▤ ▦ ▥ ▦
A first-rank restaurant in a second-rank hotel. Spacious and lush with high pile carpet, high windows with swagged drapes, and overstuffed chairs well-spaced for private conversation at table. Notable is the clever use of silently gliding food trolleys with which they spoil their customers for choice. All hotels come round with roasts and desserts on wheels, but here grilled foods arrive followed by trollies: one with a choice of 12 sauces; another brings a half-dozen breads, from sourdough to darkest ryes, to clear the palate; the salad sauce trolley boasts four oils, 26 differ-

ent vinegars and a dozen mustards; and the cheeseboard trolley will bring tears to a Frenchman's eyes, with 50-odd choices ordered weekly and changed daily as they mature.

BROWN'S WINE BAR Western
104 and 206 Two Exchange Tower, Connaught Rd., Central ☎523-7003. *Map 3B3* ▥ ▣ ▦ *Closed Sun.*

Hong Kong's only real wine bar boasts eight house wines and a fine selection of rare vintages. The food is average and European in style. Fresh asparagus shoots are a house specialty. There's a good view of half the harbor, and the atmosphere is relaxed — as is the service, which can be slow. Popular with the building's stockbrokers and packed at lunchtime, so reserve ahead.

CENTRAL PARK Japanese/Western
15 Lan Kwai Fong, Central ☎845-4332 *Map 3C3* ▥ ▣ ▣ ▣ ▦ *Lunch: noon-3pm, Dinner: 6pm-midnight. Closed Sun.*

Rather cold the "Upper East Side" decor may be, with its stiff chairs, linen tablecloths starched and folded to military standard, and spindly constructions of halogen spotlights, but this outfit is unique in its marriage of Japanese and Western cuisines. This leads to dishes such as stuffed chicken marinated in Japan's sinus-searing *wasabi* mustard, and other hybrids, as well as a menu mix that runs from *sashimi* to Louisiana "Cajun." It's modeled on a Tokyo restaurant with the same culinary miscegenation. Like the English non sequiturs on Japanese T-shirts, the dishes do not always translate successfully, but they are always inventive.

CHILI CLUB ♣ Thai
Flr 1, 88 Lockhart Rd., Wanchai ☎527-2872. *Map 5C6* ▥ ▣ ▣ ▦ *Lunch: 11am-3pm. Dinner: 6-10pm.*

Opened in 1986, this little gem of a Thai restaurant has been packed ever since, and is consistently ranked best or among them by local lovers of hot foods — largely because there are more than chilies in this club's cuisine. Even dishes

as simple as *satay* (marinated and barbecued meat or seafood on a skewer, common to all Southeast Asian countries) are delightfully aromatic and spiced. A feature is Thailand's very good Singha beer; but the best liquid antidote to a chili bite is their fresh young coconut milk served in the shell. Reservations a must.

CINTA Filipino/Thai/Indonesian/Malaysian
41 Hennessy Rd., Wanchai ☎529-0330. *Map 4C5* ▥ ▣ ▣ ▦

The entrance is on Fenwick St., around the corner from and in the basement of the New Harbour Hotel building. This is a large restaurant by Hong Kong standards and very popular for birthday parties, reunions and the like. It is one of only a handful of Filipino restaurants in Hong Kong, which is ironic since Filipinos comprise the largest foreign minority here, at about 70,000 residents. This and another in the Tsimshatsui district of Kowloon, **Mabuhay**, are the oldest and best known. Cinta is unique in adding Thai and Malay (both Indonesian and Malaysian) foods to its extensive, if somewhat uninspired, menu. It's a popular spot for American sailors to dine out with Filipina friends — the restaurant posts a board which lists all ships in port in its upstairs foyer as a welcome (and perhaps an aid to girls looking for long-lost "Johnnies" to come marching home). Live music after 8pm.

CLEVELAND SZECHUAN RESTAURANT Chinese
6 Cleveland St., Causeway Bay ☎576-3876. *Map 6B8* ▥ � ▣ ▣ ▣ ▦

Some say that the Cleveland serves the best Szechuan food in Hong Kong: spicy eggplant (aubergine) in garlic and chilies, smoked duck, and also the less common pigeon, prepared in the same way, with tea and camphor. But beware the unmarked "market" prices, which can be orders of magnitude higher than other menu entrées. This is a busy restaurant, so reserve ahead.

FOOK LAM MOON *Chinese*

35-45 Johnston Rd., Wanchai ☎*866-0663.*
Map 5C6 ▨ ▦ ▣ ▤

An expensive, popular Cantonese restaurant famed for its seafood. The chef is an abalone virtuoso who began as a caterer to Hong Kong's high society and is often invited to mainland China to teach his secrets. There is probably no better place to brave the four most prized Cantonese delicacies: abalone (often derided as "Chinese chewing gum"), *beche de mer* (a.k.a. sea slug or sea cucumber — ugh!), shark's fin and fish maw. Try the abalone, as well as shark's fin and crab dishes. The other two are only for the stoutest gastronomes. Service is friendly.

GALLEY AND PIER ONE ♣ *English*

Basement, Jardine House, off Connaught Rd., Central ☎*526-3061. Map 3B3* ▨
▦ ▣ ▤ *Closed Sun.*

Near Blake's Pier and so a long-time watering hole for the Discovery Bay (Lantau Island) commuter set, whose boats embark from there. This pub and restaurant recently expanded to open a sandwich bar and bakery, providing extra seating in what was an outsized hallway. Opened in 1975, the interior decor remains a replica of the below-decks world of 18thC pirate ships: lots of coarse wooden benches, beams and booths, a rather kitsch menu full of precious nautical names and blarney about the nautical origins of dishes, walls bedecked in monochrome enlargements of scenes from Errol Flynn movies, and reproductions of 18th and 19thC posters advertising for sailors or expedition investors and the like. Even Long John Silver would get a belly-full on their pirate-sized portions of food. Rated by one local poll to have Hong Kong's best fish and chips. Obligatory pub dart board, and ales on tap.

GRASSINI ♣ *Italian*

Flr 2, Grand Hyatt Hotel, 1 Harbour Rd., Wanchai ☎*861-1234 ext. 7313. Map 5C6*
▨ ▦ ▣ ▤ ▥

Nouvelle cuisine with a Tuscan accent, eaten over a stunning harbor view.

Grassini's cellar boasts a serious introduction to the full range of Italian wines. Those accustomed to Italo-American street food and low-to-mid-range Italian family restaurants will be disoriented by its high prices, but stunned by the presentation, imaginative range and exquisite taste of this food from northern Italy.

Capriccio in the Ramada Renaissance was the first to bring this still quite new level of northern Italian cuisine to Hong Kong in 1989; a later example, in 1991, was the Conrad Hotel's **Nicholini's**. These restaurants' peers are high-end French and Continental outlets, and it is against restaurants such as LA PLUME, CHESA and THE PIERROT that these Italian stallions bear favorable comparison.

INDONESIAN RESTAURANT ▥ ♣ *Indonesian*

26 Leighton Rd., Causeway Bay
☎*577-9981. Map 6C8* ▥ ▦

The number of Indonesian and Malaysian Chinese émigrés among the clientele is sound testimony to the food served in this simply decorated restaurant, very near to the Indonesian consulate. Specialties include the *sambals* (spicy sauces eaten as condiments with meat and seafood). Also recommended are the excellent prawn and eggplant dishes, as well as *rijsttafel*(rice served with a variety of small side dishes).

KOREANA ▥ *Korean*

Grd Flr, Vienna Mansion, 55 Paterson St., Causeway Bay ☎*577-5145/1784. Map 6C8* ▥ ▦ ▤

This reliable little eatery has been located at the epicenter of Causeway Bay's "Little Tokyo" shopping district since 1966. Each table has its own grill and stovepipe exhaust system for the personal barbecue that has become a trademark of Korean cuisine. Entrées are simple: beef, chicken, cuttlefish, accompanied by a half-dozen condiments in side dishes — where all the flavors are found. Add rice and soup and it's a meal.

LANDAU'S ♣ Western

Flr 2, Sun Hung Kai Centre, 30 Harbour Rd., Wanchai N ☎*893- 5867/891-2901. Map 5C6* ▥ ▣ ▣ ▣ ▨

A pleasant and popular place, serving reliably good European cuisine and a broad selection of wines. The spaciousness, calm colors, dark wooden paneling, thick carpets and upholstered chairs give it the feel of a London club. Service is excellent, the waiters attentive, and there are fresh flowers at each table. First established in 1975, this is one of a quintet of such eating places led by flagship **Jimmy's Kitchen**, in two locations (the original was opened by Jimmy Landau in Wanchai, in 1928, and family-run until the late 1980s — a business story that's now become part of Hong Kong's expatriate folklore), the more recently opened **JW's On The Peak** (1988), and **Tivoli Terrace** at the Taikooshing apartments-and-shopping complex in North Point.

LUK YU TEAHOUSE ▥ Chinese

24-26 Stanley St., Central ☎*523-5463/5. Map 3B3* ▥ *to* ▥ *Closed Chinese New Year.*

Open from 7am-10pm, the Luk Yu prides itself on maintaining a teahouse tradition that's all but vanished in Hong Kong. The building is a 3-story cultural relic of South China teahouses of the 1920s and '30s era, comprising semiprivate rooms behind swinging wooden doors, with straight-backed wooden booths, latticed wall mirrors and fine Chinese paintings on the walls, and brass spittoons at each table. In keeping with tradition, the *dim sum* selection is limited but is changed weekly. It's the leisurely social chat over tea that matters; the snacks are secondary, and usually sparingly eaten. The opinionated waiters are not known for their graciousness to strangers, and foreigners may have to rely on their own wits to find an "unreserved" table or to decipher the Chinese menu; regulars, however, are treated with great deference and ushered to "their" table. Although it may seem like a club of

which you are not a member, don't be put off: go early — around 11am on weekdays and 10am on weekends. Ignore the potentially frosty reception: the tea and snacks are tasty, for the Luk Yu is renowned for using only the best ingredients.

MAN WAH ⌂ Chinese

Mandarin Hotel, 5 Connaught Rd., Central ☎*522-0111. Map 3B3* ▥ ◀€ ☰ ▣ ▣ ▣ ▨

Like THE PIERROT, with which it shares the penthouse of the Mandarin Hotel, the Man Wah offers spectacular views across Hong Kong, and spectacular food to match. Chef Fok Kam Tong regularly rewrites the menu to take advantage of seasonal ingredients. The food is Cantonese, of the highest quality, with selections from China's imperial past. Try the Dragon King's offering (braised bird's nest with diced prawn, crab coral and night blossom) or the Rousing of the Rooster by the Deer (fried boneless chicken with minced carp and prawns).

MANDARIN GRILL Western

Flr 1, Mandarin Hotel, Connaught Rd., Central ☎*522-0111 ext. 4020. Map 3B3* ▥ ☰ ▣ ▣ ▣ ▨

Food here is impeccably presented and served, the high-quality fare including the standard grill-room offerings of beef, game and seafood. This is a favorite "power lunch" location and, for Americans, "power breakfasts" as well — partly because the MANDARIN hotel's function rooms for business meetings are on the same floor; partly because the Mandarin is a much-favored rendezvous point in Central; but mostly because the food and service are so very good.

NORTH PARK RESTAURANT Chinese

Grd Flr, Lockhart House, 440 Jaffe Rd., Causeway Bay ☎*891-2940. Map 5C7* ▥ ▣ ▣ ▣ ▨

Well-known locally for Cantonese seafoods and "winter tonic" game such as civet cat, snake and venison, this restaurant also serves excellent shark's fin soup and *geoduck*. The last named is a suggestively-shaped type of giant clam (it looks like human genitalia), which is an ostentatiously expensive local favorite, imported from the cold Pacific waters around Vancouver. The giant clams are a modern addition to the Cantonese pantheon of foods revered for reasons other than nutrition, in this case aphrodisiac powers and a price that bespeaks an ability to indulge in conspicuous consumption. Reserve ahead.

PEP'N CHILI ♣ Chinese
12 Blue Pool Rd., Happy Valley ☎573-8251/4. Map 6E8 ▥ ▆ ▣ ▣ ▣ ▩

Serves excellent but expensive Szechuan cuisine. Try the smoked duck or sesame chicken. The service is friendly, the seating spacious by Chinese restaurant standards, and the decor contemporary "Chinoiserie" rather than Chinese.

THE PIERROT ▵ ♣ French
Flr 25, Mandarin Hotel, 5 Connaught Rd., Central ☎522-0111. Map 3B3 ▥ ▆ ▣ ▣ ▣ ▩ *Closed Sat, Sun lunch.*

This is one of Hong Kong's finest restaurants. It is named after Picasso's painting *Pierrot with Flowers,* and the decor is modeled around circus themes, albeit an opulent circus with red velvet wall coverings and crystal chandeliers. There is a choice of three menus: *nouvelle cuisine,* French traditional and a daily five-course *gastronomie légère.* Top French chefs are regularly flown in for guest appearances in the kitchen. More than 300 wines are held in the cellar, with 40 on the rare and old vintage list. Happily, there is a HK$520 per head evening menu for gourmands of modest means — about half the price of full 5-course fare.

RAINBOW ROOM ♣ Chinese
Flr 22, Lee Garden Hotel, Hysan Ave., Causeway Bay ☎576-7211 ext. 2439. Map 6C8 ▥ ▆ ▆ ▣ ▣ ▣ ▩

Open noon-3pm for excellent *dim sum*, which are highly esteemed by local Chinese. Go early, as reservations are not taken.

LA RONDA ♣ Western/Chinese
Flr 30, Hotel Furama Kempinski, 1 Connaught Rd., Central ☎525-5111 ext. 50213. Map 4C4 ▥ ▆ ◀ ▆ ▣ ▣ ▣ ▩

This revolving restaurant 30 stories above Central has stunning views and live music while you dine. The food is a multinational buffet spanning East and West, including Chinese and Japanese. Very popular, so reserve ahead. (See FURAMA KEMPINSKI in WHERE TO STAY.)

SUN TUNG LOK SHARK'S FIN Chinese
137 Connaught Rd. W, Sheung Wan ☎546-2718, map 3A2, and 376 Lockhart Rd., Wanchai ☎574-8261, map 5C7 ▥ ▣ ▣ ▣ ▩

Famed for its shark's fin and a pioneer among seafood restaurants, Sun Tung Lok was also responsible for introducing *geoduck* clams (imported from Vancouver) to Hong Kong. Shark's fin is usually prepared in one of three ways: braised (a costly dish but worth splurging on, which requires the finest shark's fin, known as *bow chi*); as a thick soup (a dish at which Chiuchow cuisine excels, although it is also served in Cantonese restaurants); or Cantonese-style (as a thin soup, with the fin cooked in chicken stock with vegetables). Better still is the Peking version, in which the shark's fin is simmered whole along with an entire chicken. These and many other kinds of shark's-fin dish are available for sampling here.

LE TIRE BOUCHON ♣ French
Grd Flr, 9 Old Bailey St., Central ☎523-5459. Map 3B2 ▥ ▣ ▣ ▣ ▩

The location of this wine bar/bistro, at the upper reaches of Central and hence requiring a steep hike or roundabout taxi ride, has probably helped keep prices down and service congenial, if a bit sleepy at times. Its French provincial menu has won consistent praise since this tiny bistro opened in 1987. New management in 1991 retained the French kitchen staff and the cozy layout, which features a mezzanine that seems custom-built for intimate assignations. If you are alone, sit downstairs and bring a book to start your stay in Hong Kong with a lunch that moves at the same leisurely pace as in southern France; it could hardly be more unlike the frenzied haste of Hong Kong just outside.

VEGI FOOD KITCHEN ⚓ ♣ *Vegetarian*
Grd Flr, Block B, 8 Cleveland St., Causeway Bay ☎ *890-6660. Map 6B8* 🖰 🎫 🔲 🔳 🌃

This Chinese vegetarian restaurant offers a wide variety of imaginative dishes, including the famed meat substitutes made from wheat gluten. Rec-

ommended are the stuffed eggplant with bitter cucumber, green chili and black bean sauce, or Buddha's Cushion, a tasty steamed mushroom and black fungus dish. Another vegetarian "meat" dish worth trying is the fried vegetable rib steak with chili in sweet and sour sauce. A chain of these meat-imitators has been launched under the name **Bodhi Vegetarian Restaurant** *(60 Leighton Rd., Causeway Bay* ☎ *895-2505, map 6C8; 384 Lockhart Rd., Wanchai* ☎ *573-2155, map 5C7; 56 Cameron Rd., Tsimshatsui, Kowloon* ☎ *721-3561, map 7E3).*

Kowloon's restaurants A to Z

AU TROU NORMAND ♣ *French*
Grd Flr, 6 Carnarvon Rd., Tsimshatsui, Kowloon ☎ *366-8754. Map 7E3* 🖰 ➡ 🎫 🔲 🔳

Founder Bernard Vigneau has gone, having sold his "Norman Hole" to his senior staff in 1990. But Calvados still flows, and this has been one of the best Provençal French restaurants in Asia since it opened in 1964. The decor is northern French farmhouse and the atmosphere one of boisterous enjoyment. The fish dishes — especially the *bouillabaisse* (served only on Friday: you must order ahead) and skate fried in black butter — are a joy. Also recommended are fish and herb terrine, roast rack of lamb and, of course, apple pancakes flambéed with Calvados.

BARON'S TABLE *German*
Flr 1, Holiday Inn Golden Mile, 50 Nathan Rd., Tsimshatsui, Kowloon ☎ *369-3111 ext. 291. Map 7E3* 🖰 🎫 🔲 🔳 🌃

Perhaps the highest accolade is that this is the regular eating place for homesick Germans and Austrians on the road in Asia. In fickle Hong Kong, for a hotel restaurant to disdain renovation since its opening in 1975, save for a minor reupholstering and new carpet in 1991, suggests the food must be good. *Matjes* herring, duck and cabbage, dumplings, venison in gingerbread sauce, and pig's

knuckles in split pea sauce and sauerkraut need only good German grog and Black Forest cake to lend weight to thoughts of Deutschland and your physique.

CHESA ⌂ *Swiss*
Flr 1, Peninsula Hotel, Salisbury Rd., Tsimshatsui, Kowloon ☎ *366-6251 ext. 1187. Map 7F3* 🖰 ➡ 🎫 🔲 🔳 🌃

Fine Swiss cuisine served in a rustic Swiss Inn-style room in the *grande dame* of Hong Kong hotels. Monthly highlights feature traditional dishes from different Swiss regions: a wide selection of entrées, high-quality meats, especially veal, and an excellent cheese fondue are all regularly available. (See page 93.)

GOLDEN ISLAND *Chinese*
25 Carnarvon Rd., Tsimshatsui, Kowloon ☎ *369-5211. Map 7E3* 🖰 🎫 🌃

A well-known Chiuchow restaurant, highly regarded by local Chinese. The lobster dishes are memorable — meaty chunks served with the shell, sautéed with ginger and scallions, or steamed and served with a tangerine sauce.

GREAT SHANGHAI *Chinese*
26 Prat Ave., Tsimshatsui, Kowloon ☎ *366-8158/366-2693. Map 7E3* 🖰 🔳 🌃

Often the locals' choice for good Shanghainese food, this huge restaurant seats 500 and has an experienced staff to offer suggestions if needed. The menu is extensive, but house specialties are Beggar's Chicken and Peking Duck. (Although both Shanghai and Peking restaurants serve Beggar's Chicken, neither can stake territorial claim to the dish, which originated in Hangzhou in Chekiang Province.)

HUGO'S Continental European

Hyatt Regency, 67 Nathan Rd., Tsimshatsui, Kowloon ☎ *311-1234 ext. 877. Map 7E3* ▦ ▣ ▣ ▣ ▣

Hugo's is as much a literary as a culinary invention, which has remained the realm of Herr Hugo for more than 20 years. This imaginary Bavarian host is described in 3-stanza doggerel on the menu as the man after whom the restaurant is named: "...Hugo's portrait we found/On the banks of the Rhine,/And welcomes you still/As you come to dine —/With Hugo Ludwig von Gluckenstein." Portrayed as a knight errant outfitted in a *melange* of Alexandrian sandals, Saracen sword, Roman body armor and heavily feathered visor of the medieval joust, Herr Hugo's attire is matched by a castle-hall decor set in the hotel's basement, which is remarkable for somehow retaining a sense of intimacy. This is a grill room, dressed up as a Teutonic lodge. In fact, the menu is less inventive than the jester who conjured up Hugo, but it is solidly satisfying. The quality is as steady as the neighborhood clientele of businessmen who, when polled, insisted that no changes be made to Herr Hugo's lodge hall when the hotel underwent a major renovation in the late 1980s.

NADAMAN Japanese

2nd Basement, Shangri-La Hotel, 64 Mody Rd., Tsimshatsui East, Kowloon ☎ *721-2111. Map 7E3* ▦ ▣ ▣ ▣ ▣ ▣

This small, traditional-style restaurant serves fine Japanese food. The name comes from a master of the Shijo style of cooking, Mansuke Nadaya, who founded a restaurant chain in Osaka

more than 150 years ago. Have *sushi* for starters, with side orders of *tempura,* followed by thin slices of the famous Kobe beef prepared and served at your table. Set lunches are the best value. Service is attentive and the waitresses helpful. Reserve ahead.

LA PLUME ⌂ Continental European

Flr 2, Regent Hotel, Salisbury Rd., Tsimshatsui, Kowloon ☎ *721-1211 ext. 2256. Map 7F3* ▦ ◄ ▬ ▣ ▣ ▣ ▣ *Closed lunch.*

Perhaps the most imaginative Continental cuisine available in Hong Kong. The food is served on two floors linked by glass elevators, with a panoramic view of the city as a backdrop. On being seated, diners are offered a champagne cocktail with hot Indian *nan* bread baked in a *tandoori* brick oven, which is visible behind a glass partition. The food is excellent (the menu changes regularly), and the wine list extensive. The prestigious **Lai Ching Heen** Cantonese restaurant is also here. (See REGENT in WHERE TO STAY.)

SAWADEE THAI RESTAURANT ♣ *Thai*

Grd Flr, 1 Hillwood Rd., Kowloon ☎ *722-5577. Map 7D3* ▦ ▣ ▣ ▣ ▣

Good Thai food at reasonable prices has been the house specialty since this restaurant first opened in 1984, the vanguard of what became a wave of more than two dozen Thai restaurants by the end of the decade. The cuisine is less explosive than that of the CHILI CLUB across the harbor, but satisfying nevertheless. Try the sour prawn soup, chicken appetizer wrapped in pandanus leaves, Thai vermicelli salad, or rice served in a pineapple.

SHANG PALACE ♣ ⌂ Chinese

Basement, Shangri-La Hotel, 64 Mody Rd., Tsimshatsui East, Kowloon ☎ *721-2111. Map 7E3* ▦ ▬ ▣ ▣ ▣ ▣

First-rate Cantonese cuisine, from seafood to meat dishes. Specialties include the shark's fin soup with pigeon and the ginseng drunken prawns, and, although not Cantonese, the Peking duck is also good. A popular place for *yum cha* and *dim sum,* it is often crowded at lunch. Reservations for *dim sum* are not accepted, so go early.

SPRING DEER 🍴 *Chinese*
42 Mody Rd., Tsimshatsui, Kowloon
☎723-3673. Map 7E3 ▥ ▤
For long a popular restaurant serving good Peking food; its specialty is a memorable Peking duck. The service is good, the ambience pleasant, and private rooms can be reserved for parties. This is a major stop for inbound tour groups and can get extremely crowded in the tourism high seasons (fall and winter — the best seasons to eat North China's hearty foods).

TIEN HEUNG LAU *Chinese*
18C, Austin Ave., Kowloon ☎366-2414.
Map 7E3 ▥
Local food writers have on occasion gone so far as to rate this tiny restaurant above all others in Hong Kong. The cuisine is from Hangzhou — and the robust flavors of that southwestern city were enough to impress even that worldly-wise old traveler, Marco Polo. Its most famous dish is Beggar's Chicken, a whole chicken baked in a wrapping of lotus leaves and mud. Try also the smoked cold duck, and Tien Hung Lau's specialty, *wonton* soup. Reservations are essential, and it's advisable to pre-order the menu.

Other notable restaurants

There will be freewheeling days when your movements around the Territory do not focus around a preplanned restaurant selection. Any of the restaurants described in the closing pages of this chapter are well worth trying if you find yourself nearby.

THE MAXIM'S GROUP
Most restaurants that have "Garden" in their name are part of the Maxim's chain ("Jade" in the name indicates that the cuisine is Cantonese), and serve regional Chinese cuisines with balanced set menus for both residents and tourists. The food is reliable and is well-liked by the local Chinese.

Maxim's Caterers Ltd, often called "Hong Kong's *de facto* national restaurateurs," operate 222 restaurants, bakeries, fast-food shops and bars. The chain includes Chinese, Japanese and Western restaurants and serves about 200,000 customers a day — about one in every 28 Hong Kong residents. This generates annual revenues approaching the staggering sum of HK$25 billion.

The following represent a well-tried personal selection, most of them in Central district:

Chiuchow Garden ♣ Basement, Jardine House, Central ☎525-8246. Map 3B3 ▥ 🍴 ▣ ◉ ◎ ▨ A wide selection of Chiuchow dishes.

Hunan Garden The Forum, Exchange Square, Central ☎868-2880. Map 3B3 ▥ ▣ ◉ ◎ ▨ Well worth trying.

Jade Garden Flr 1, Swire House, Central ☎523-9666. Map 3B3 ▥ ▣ ◉ ◎ ▨ Closed Chinese New Year. A wide and imaginative range of Cantonese food.

Jade Garden 25-31 Carnarvon Rd., Tsimshatsui ☎366-0788. Map 7E3 ▥ ▣ ◉ ◎ ▨ Serves interesting *dim sum.*

Jade Garden   Flr 4, Star House, Tsimshatsui ☎372-2688. Map **7**F2
▥ AE ⊙ ⊡ ⟦VISA⟧ Inviting *dim sum* is on offer.
Peking Garden   ♣ Basement, Alexandra House, Des Voeux Rd.,
Central ☎525-5688. Map **3**B3 ▥ ☞ AE ⊙ ⊡ ⟦VISA⟧ Serves delicious
Peking cuisine, an excellent Beggar's Chicken, and features an amaz-
ing noodle-making demonstration.
Sichuan Garden   Flr 3, Gloucester Tower, Landmark, Central
☎521-4433. Map **3**C3 ▥ AE ⊙ ⊡ ⟦VISA⟧ Closed Chinese New Year.
Well worth trying.

THE LAN KWAI FONG AREA

A clutch of restaurants in this area of Central are as much a cultural as a
culinary expression of contemporary Hong Kong's hybrid society. They
may be home to Hong Kong's Yuppies, Chuppies (Chinese Yuppies),
Preppies and any stray Sloane Rangers in town after dark, but their
preening rituals are colorful, and the ambience of the restaurants
congenial and the food good. Two distinguished representatives of the
genre in our main listings for Hong Kong Island are AL'S DINER and
CENTRAL PARK.

Also typical in its way is **Post 97** *(Cosmos Building, Flr 1, 8-11 Lan
Kwai Fong, D'Aguilar St., Central* ☎810-9333, *map* **3**C3 ▥ ☞ AE ⊙
⊡ ⟦VISA⟧ *closed Sun lunch)*. The name refers to the date when China
resumes sovereignty of Hong Kong (it was formerly called Nineteen 97).
This popular upstairs spot, which usually hosts an art exhibition, serves
undistinguished food, but offers an interesting environment full of people
trying hard to look interesting to one another. The clientele is youngish
and Western, and there's a **Nation 97** disco downstairs with a street-level
entrance that looks like the side of a ship (with porthole), with theme
nights such as "Eurasians get groovy" and "Flare with 70s Vibe."

An associated street-level restaurant in the same building has had four
identities in about as many years. Now known as **Mecca 97**, it boasts
Middle Eastern decor and fare. In 1991, a street-level bar opened next
door with yet another identi-kit, this time dark, hardwood pillars and
lintel frame: a small pub named **1998**. It's all a bit of a bizarre architectural
bazaar, where food follows ambience for quality.

Nearby is **The California** *(Grd Flr, 30-32 D'Aguilar St., Central*
☎521-1345, *map* **3**C3 ▥ AE ⊙ ⊡ ⟦VISA⟧), which offers *nouvelle
Américaine* cuisine and a varied salad bar. The interior has been innova-
tively decorated with murals depicting a 1960s *American Graffiti*-style
drive-in restaurant; a wall-mounted Vespa scooter doing duty as a piece
of contemporary sculpture blinks its headlight in the foyer. Multiple
videos and disco-dancing after dinner make this popular with singles.
Dick Kaufman, its American founder (along with the four original European partners at Nineteen 97), created the concept of a Lan Kwai Fong
nightlife "neighborhood," with an annual street festival and other cooperative promotions.

Disco Disco, a controversial dance hall run by an American around
the corner and just up D'Aguilar St., was the third major area outlet when
it all began in the early 1980s. Kaufman has since moved on (to market

a Singapore department store), as have most of the original European group. Memory of the once notoriously gay and "high" dance hall has all but faded away under police pressure and changing fashions. It is now (what else?) the **DDII** *karaoke* bar. (As with nightlife centers everywhere, the area remains a magnet for drug abuse and was recently featured on a local television documentary about heroin addiction among locally-raised foreign teenagers.)

The **Beverly Hills Deli** (♣ *2-3 Lan Kwai Fong, Central* ☎ *801-5123, map 3 C3* Ⅲ 🖭 💽 🖸 🖾) offers ample servings of American Jewish deli food: pastrami sandwiches, bagels and cream cheese, kosher products and pasta are all served by a friendly and competent staff. It's crowded at lunch, so reserve ahead.

These days, besides the pillars of the area mentioned above, one is spoiled for choice in the two square blocks that comprise greater and lesser Lan Kwai Fong.

GREATER LKF: The square block boasts the following:
A Thai restaurant:
- **Supatra's Thai Gourmet**   50 D'Aguilar St. ☎521-8027. Map 3B3.

A total of 4 Japanese restaurants:
- **Kiyotaki**   19 D'Aguilar St ☎877-1772/1803. Map 3B3.
- **Hanaguchi Yakitori**   Flr 1, California Entertainment Building, 34-36 D'Aguilar St ☎521-0868. Map 3C3.
- **Nambantei of Tokyo**   52 D'Aguilar St ☎526-7678. Map 3C3.
- **Yorohachi**   Grd Flr, 5-6 Lan Kwai Fong ☎524-1251. Map 3C3.

Two German pubs with food:
- **Schnurrbart**   Winner Building, 8 D'Aguilar St ☎523-4700. Map 3B3.
- **Bit Pointe**   Winner Building, 8 D'Aguilar St. ☎523-7436. Map 3B3.

One American pizza/sandwich/salad bar where you're given crayons and invited to decorate the paper tablecloth:
- **Graffiti**   17 Lan Kwai Fong St ☎521-2202. Map 3C3.

One French restaurant run on personality by Maurice Gardette, a former French radio entertainer, genuine World War II "Resistance" hero, and caterer to the American navy in South Korea:
- **Cafe de Paris**   California Tower, D'Aguilar St ☎524-7251. Map 3C3.

One Italian restaurant:
- **Il Mercato**   California Entertainment Building, 34-36 D'Aguilar St ☎868-3068. Map 3C3.

And several bars or pubs with food: examples are **Jazz Club** (see NIGHTLIFE), which features live top-rank performers such as Jimmy Witherspoon flown in from the States, **Scotty's** for the brogue and kilts club, and **Hardy's** folk music bar.

LESSER LKF: On two small, dead-end lanes that run w from D'Aguilar St. are the following:

Two Vietnamese restaurants, **Bon Appetit** *(Grd Flr, 14/B D'Aguilar St., Win Wah Lane* ☎ *525-3553/525-2605, map 3 B3)* and **Overseas Vietnamese Association** *(Flr 2, 14 Wo On Lane* ☎ *522-4270/523-5105, map 3 B3).*

One French restaurant, **La Rose Noire** *(8-13 Wo On Lane* ☎ *526-5965, map 3 B3).*

One Japanese restaurant, **Jo Gichi** *(Grd Flr, 5 Wo On Lane* ☎ *521-8818, map 3 B3).*

One Indian restaurant, **India Curry Club** *(Flr 3, Winner Building* ☎ *523-2203, map 3 B3).*

ON THE FRINGE OF LAN KWAI FONG: A block above it on Wyndham St. are **La Bodega Tapas Bar** and the **Mad Dogs** English pub (see NIGHTLIFE). Around the corner on Wellington St. is **Yung Kee Restaurant** (see below).

THE MALL, PACIFIC PLACE
Construction in 1990-91 of a new commercial island in the Queensway area, which separates Central and Wanchai districts, has created some outstanding eating places. Besides those contained within the three hotels of the complex, MARRIOTT, CONRAD and ISLAND SHANGRI-LA, The Mall's most notable examples (all on map 4C5) are:

Zen ☎845-4555. A *haute Chinois* restaurant despite the Japanese name.

Spice Islands ☎845-4798. Features Southeast Asian cuisines and good-value buffets.

Dan Ryan's Express ☎845-4600. Also in Kowloon at Ocean Terminal ☎735-6111. A theme bar and American food restaurant serving very large portions. Its topic is the history of the city of Chicago, with what seems every souvenir or poster ever produced up there on the walls, period music from *My kind o' town* in the aisles, and old "Windy City" mayoral speeches piped into the comfort rooms. The rack of barbecued ribs is unbeatable.

Grappa's Restaurant Toscana ☎868-0086. An excellent northern Italian restaurant, featuring fresh bread and a dish of olive oil instead of butter for starters, and superb pastas.

Seibu Food Hall In the basement of The Mall's main department store: a cafeteria-style cornucopia of cuisines at low prices.

There's also a **MacDonald's** (one of almost 50 in Hong Kong), two Japanese restaurants, and the **Park Inn** *(Cotton Tree Dr., Hong Kong Park* ☎ *522-6333),* this last being within HONG KONG PARK. This abuts the rear of The Mall, is a short walk away, and can be considered one of the center's dining options.

OTHER FAVORITES
To close this chapter, here is an assortment of establishments whose cuisine, style and ambience range freely around the continents.

Ashoka Grd Flr, 57 Wyndham St. Central ☎524-9623. Map 4C3 ▥▢

AE **⊕** **CD** **VISA** Closed Sun lunch. An Indian restaurant with a good tandoori selection.

Spice Island Gourmet Club   Mezzanine, 63-67 Wellington St., Central ☎524-7926/522-8706. Map **4**B3 **AE** **CD** **VISA** South Indian specialties prepared by the wife of a local Hong Kong business-magazine editor who hails from Kerala State. Great buffet dinner bargain at HK$60. Memberships can be purchased at the door.

Rigoletto   14-16 Fenwick St. Wanchai ☎527-7144. Map **5**C5 **III** **AE** **⊕** **CD** **VISA** Average Italian food in an above-average ambience.

San Francisco Steakhouse   ♣ 101 Barnton Court, Harbour City, Canton Rd., Kowloon ☎735-7576. Map **8**C2 **III** **AE** **⊕** **CD** **VISA** Closed Sun lunch. Excellent prime US beefsteaks and "Surf and Turf" (steak and lobster) specials.

SMI   ☕ ♣ Flr 1, 81-85 Lockhart Rd., Wanchai ☎861-1024. Map **6**C6 **II** **AE** **⊕** **CD** **VISA** A colorful Southeast Asian potpourri of curries from Singapore, Malaysia, Indonesia (hence the restaurant's name); also from India, Pakistan and virtually everywhere else where curries are a staple diet.

Unicorn Restaurant   ♣ 11 Kingston St., Causeway Bay ☎577-9117. Map **7**B8 **III** **AE** **⊕** **CD** **VISA** A wide variety of Cantonese cuisine, especially seafood (the famous "drunken prawns" dish was invented here). It is the original of what is soon to be a sextet: **The Sunning Unicorn** *(1, Sunning Rd., Causeway Bay* ☎ *577-6620, map* **6** *C8);* **The Golden Unicorn** *(Omni Hong Kong Hotel* ☎ *736-0088, map* **7** *F2);* **Unicorn Szechuen** *(Sunning Plaza, Causeway Bay* ☎ *576-8026, map* **6** *C8, and in Lei Shun Ct., Mei Foo Sun Chuen apartment complex, Kowloon* ☎ *890-8079, map* **8** *C5);* and an as yet unnamed Unicorn in Central's new Ritz Carlton Hotel.

Yung Kee Restaurant   ♣ 32-40 Wellington St., Central ☎523-1562. Map **3**B3 **III** **AE** **VISA** Excellent Cantonese cuisine — it is famed for its roast goose — and one of the few restaurants that serves you "one-thousand-year-old eggs" with ginger when you sit down (green, fermented for months, not years, and an acquired taste). Founded in 1942, it was chosen in the mid-1960s by a *Fortune* magazine correspondent (thanks perhaps to its Wellington St. location, then Hong Kong's answer to "Fleet Street") as one of the world's 10 best restaurants. Its chefs still win accolades and medals in the Food Festival Culinary Awards sponsored annually by the Hong Kong Tourist Association.

Nightlife and entertainment

Hong Kong by night

Just 20 years ago the image of Hong Kong's nightlife was Suzie Wong in a *cheongsam* slit to the thigh, the universal clatter of mahjong tiles and the occasional high-pitched arias of Cantonese opera. No longer. In recent years a more affluent and well-educated population has demanded a greening of the cultural landscape — and both government and private enterprise have responded.

Necessarily, with a population that is 97 percent Cantonese, much of what's on offer, from nightclubs to theatrical performances, is targeted toward the local population. But Hong Kong has always been a cultural melting pot; there's something for every taste, and unrivaled scope for interface and exchange between Chinese and Western artistic traditions and innovations. It is one of perhaps only a dozen truly 24-hour cities in the world, with a vitality matched by few cities in Asia or elsewhere. Equally intriguing is that nowhere else offers better access to currents from the post-Maoist mainland Chinese arts scene.

WHAT'S ON
The English-language dailies run entertainment sections, and there is a weekly *TV & Entertainment Times* magazine sold at newsstands and supermarkets. A free monthly guide to entertainment, *City News,* is published by the Urban Council and available at their venues. An "alternative" guide, *HK Magazine,* is available at counters of about 50 restaurants, nightspots and arts venues around town. In December 1991, its publishers launched a "talking magazine" called *HK Line,* which carries a menu of entertainment listings at HK$4 a minute: reach it from any IDD telephone on ☎173-000-500.

Performing arts

The Urban Council of Hong Kong is financed by taxes on real estate. Besides carrying out mundane tasks such as picking up some 3,000 metric tons of garbage a day, chasing unlicensed hawkers off the streets and doing a rather poor job of keeping more than 300 public lavatories clean, the Urban Council is the major arts patron. It has built most of the city's largest performance venues and all the satellite venues in various urban districts, such as the **Sheung Wan Civic Centre**, which is one of a trio, with more underway.

In a given year the council organizes more than 400 performance events by local and overseas artistes and almost 300 entertainment programs such as street carnivals and seasonal festivals. It underwrites a Chinese orchestra, professional theater and dance companies, and an annual two-week international film festival in springtime, which runs from March to April. Other arts groups are partially funded by government directly through an appointed body, The Council for the Performing Arts of Hong Kong.

TICKET RESERVATIONS

The Urban Council operates a ticketing system through its URBTIX outlets. Reservations can be made up to one hour before performances (☎ 734-9009).

FESTIVALS

The main high spots of the performance arts year are the month-long **Hong Kong Arts Festival** (January to February), during which a dazzling range of international talent offers a veritable Aladdin's cave of performances — everything from symphony orchestras and classical ballet to fire-eaters and belly dancers — and the biennial **Festival of Asian Arts** (October to November), in which the emphasis is on regional performers and genres. Be aware that during both festivals performances by star turns are often fully reserved weeks beforehand.

THE MAJOR PERFORMANCE CENTERS

CITY HALL (LOW BUILDING)

7 Edinburgh Place, Central ☎522-9928 *(information). Map 4B4. Box office open 10am-10pm* ⛴ *Star Ferry terminal.*

Hong Kong's oldest public home to performing arts and exhibitions, built in the early 1960s, stages regular classical music concerts and recitals by visiting and local musicians, plus less frequent ballet and dramatic performances. About 750 performances every year are hosted in its three auditoria, which comprise a concert hall, theater and recital hall.

FRINGE CLUB ⅲ

2 Lower Albert Rd., Central ☎521-7251. *Map 3C3. Open Mon-Thurs 5pm-1am; Fri, Sat 5pm-2am. Box office open 5-11pm.*

Conceived primarily as a hangout for local artists, the Fringe Club is now the center for experimental and avant-garde events, including drama, music, mime, poetry readings, films and workshops. It is set in one of two historic buildings on the site (the second houses the Foreign Correspondents' Club), first built in 1892, but rebuilt in 1913 and 1917 respectively. They comprised the first main depot of the Dairy Farm Company at the sharply triangular junction of Wyndham St., Lower Albert Rd. and what becomes Hollywood Rd. Leased to the present tenants in 1981, the Fringe Club sublets spaces to **M at the Fringe** restaurant and the POTTERY WORKSHOP (see SHOPPING, page 149).

HILTON HOTEL DINNER THEATRE

2 Queen's Rd., Central ☎523-3111. *Map 4C4. Check with hotel for times of performances.*

Light comedy of the Noel Coward variety from visiting British companies of West End stars, flown out several times a year. Very popular, and tickets are hard to come by. Contact the hotel's information desk for the performance schedule and for reservations.

HONG KONG ACADEMY FOR THE PERFORMING ARTS
1 Gloucester Rd., Wanchai ☎823-1500. Map 4C5. Box office open 10am-8pm.

Built with money from the Royal Hong Kong Jockey Club, this provides a training ground for homegrown talent in dance, drama, music and related arts. Since its opening in 1985, its lavish custom-built facilities have made it Hong Kong's premier performance center. The 1,188-seat **Lyric Theatre**, one of four state-of-the-art theaters in the complex, compares with the best in the world in terms of acoustics and technical facilities. It stands across the road from the HONG KONG ARTS CENTRE and Grand Hyatt Hotel.

HONG KONG ARTS CENTRE
2 Harbour Rd., Wanchai ☎823-0200. Map 5C6 ⚌ Box office open 10am-8pm.

Opened in 1977, the center has three small theaters and two even smaller galleries, as well as workshops. Many groups associated with the arts such as the GOETHE INSTITUT (see page 68) and local dance or music schools rent space in the building. Nightly concerts, recitals, movies, poetry readings, plays etc. are staged here, from local dramatic works in Cantonese to foreign movies.

Internationally-known Chinese artists exhibit in the **Pao Sui Loong Gallery** (see page 68), but this is mostly a community-owned and operated facility for nurturing and appreciating the output of local talent. Details of forthcoming events can be seen in the lobby and in the local newspapers. It houses small but thoughtfully stocked crafts, music and art book shops.

HONG KONG COLISEUM
9 Cheong Wan Rd., Hunghom, Kowloon ☎765-9215. Map 8E4. Box office open 10am-6.30pm. Beside rail terminus.

One of Asia's largest multipurpose indoor stadia, this 12,000-seat mega-venue looks like a truncated pyramid set on its head. Since opening in 1983, it has been home to world sports spectaculars and pop music concerts by international and local superstars. Most prominent among the latter are Alan Tam and Leslie Cheung, who each recently staged more than 30 sellout concerts there within the same year. The Coliseum hosts more than 250 events, entertaining more than 1.6 million people annually.

HONG KONG CONVENTION & EXHIBITION CENTRE
Harbour Rd., Wanchai ☎833-4333. Map 5C6. Between Grand Hyatt and New World Harbour View hotels on the waterfront.

Although this center was built primarily for trade shows, since its opening in 1990, it has been used for entertainment events as diverse as a road show performance of *My Fair Lady* by an American troupe, and a live concert by US songstress Randy Crawford.

HONG KONG CULTURAL CENTRE Ⅲ
10 Salisbury Rd., Tsimshatsui ☎734-2009. Map 7F3. Box office open 10am-9pm.

Opened in late 1989, this custom-built facility, illustrated overleaf, is a virtually windowless, wing-swept structure next to the Star Ferry terminal on the Kowloon waterfront. It looks the odd couple set behind the preserved colonial-style clock tower, built in 1915, and equally incongruous against the igloo-shaped SPACE MUSEUM next door. The new HONG KONG MUSEUM OF ART, opened in late 1991, is in the same

131

**Hong Kong
Cultural Centre**

complex. Despite the lukewarm-to-hostile public response to the design of this new harborfront edifice — which looks less an architect's "statement" than a tongue-tied environmental sculpture of the New York School — its interior acoustics and technical facilities for the performing arts are superb. The center has three auditoria: a 2,100-seat concert hall, a 1,750-seat Grand Theatre, and a studio theater which seats up to 500 people.

KO SHAN THEATRE
Ko Shan Rd. Park, Ko Shan Rd., HungHom, Kowloon ☎334-2331. Map 8C5.
Home to Cantonese opera and pop music concerts in a semi-open atmosphere, with covered seating for 1,000 and open-air seating for another 2,000 spectators. About 130 performances a year are held here.

QUEEN ELIZABETH ("QE") STADIUM
18 Oi Kwan Rd. (back faces Queen's Rd. East), Wanchai ☎575-6793. Map 5D7. Across from Happy Valley Race Track at E perimeter of Wanchai district. Box office open 10am-6.30pm.
This 3,500-seat multipurpose venue is properly built for sports events. Despite the use of portable staging, which had the Royal Ballet's birds of *Swan Lake* sounding like a cattle stampede, and the acoustics of a basketball court, the stadium's great size and accessible position in Wanchai have made it a major venue for artistic events.

It has been the location for memorable performances by Roberta Flack, the late Miles Davis and other jazz greats in the annual "Select Live Under the Sky" concert brought across from Tokyo each August, and for that annual ballroom dancing extravaganza, the International Dance Festival (November to December). In all, it hosts some 140 events a year, ranging from Billy Graham's revivalist religious crusade through hairdressers' conventions to Sesame Street road shows, which, between them, attract about a quarter-million people. That is in addition to those who use the stadium for the purpose for which it was really built and is best suited: championship sporting events.

ST JOHN'S (ANGLICAN) CATHEDRAL
Garden Rd., Central ☎523-4157. Map 4C4. Music recitals Wed 1.30-2pm.
A haven of tranquility amid the bustle of Central district, the cathedral hosts short lunchtime classical recitals on Wednesdays. Entry is free.

THE PERFORMERS

There is plenty of year-round activity, what with two full-time orchestras (a Chinese one and a Western symphonic one), three professional dance companies, half a dozen theater groups, amateur musical comedy presentations and, more often than not, a wide choice of visiting performers from mainland China and overseas. Almost every night of the year, something is offered at one or another of the major performance centers. One week it might be Fujianese String Puppets, the next a Gilbert and Sullivan operetta or an international festival of dance academies.

The outstanding musical and theatrical performance ensembles in Hong Kong are listed below.

ACTORS' REP
A professional theater troupe that performs mostly light English-language drama, usually at the CITY HALL.

CHUNG YING THEATRE COMPANY
A brainchild of the British Council, the company provides a bridge between Western and Chinese theater, performing in English and Cantonese throughout Hong Kong.

CITY CONTEMPORARY DANCE COMPANY
Grd Flr, 110 Shatin Pass Rd., Wong Tai Sin, Kowloon ☎ *326-8597 (information), 322-9616 (reservations). Map 2D4.*
Specializes in contemporary dance and works by local choreographers (e.g., *Wanderings in the Cosmos,* inspired by lyrics from the earliest Chinese poetry, *The Book of Poetry,* c.700BC). Details of its small hall for performances are given above, but the company is seen to best advantage at the CITY HALL or HONG KONG ARTS CENTRE.

HONG KONG CHINESE ORCHESTRA
☎ *721-3283.*
Formed in 1977 to perform Chinese and reworked Western classical music on traditional instruments, the orchestra does not have a regular concert hall but gives weekly performances around Hong Kong.

HONG KONG PHILHARMONIC ORCHESTRA
☎ *832-7121.*
A hundred resident musicians from Hong Kong, Europe and North America, and guest appearances from world-renowned conductors and soloists. Regular concerts are given at the CITY HALL.

SUN KWONG THEATRE
423 King's Rd., North Point ☎ *563-2959. Map 2D5.*
To the uninitiated, a 3-4 hour Chinese opera can be deeply mysterious. It is highly stylized and its characters are invariably stereotypes. Thus an evil character has a white face, a heroic but foolish character has a red face, green costume indicates high rank, etc. Sword fights and acrobatics, slapstick and mime alternate with shrill singing. Nonetheless, there is a story, usually grounded in history or legend. It is not to everyone's taste, but the costumes and makeup alone are delicious. At various venues: check local newspapers.

ZUNI ICOSAHEDRON
26 Leighton Rd., Causeway Bay ☎ *577-2303. Map 6C8.*
An avant-garde mime-and-movement theater/opera company, performing in Cantonese and more often in the stiff, geometric body-language choreography their name implies.

LECTURES

ROYAL ASIATIC SOCIETY
P.O. Box 3864, Hong Kong ☎819-1061.

This extraordinary organization dates from the 18thC and followed the pink path on the map of the British Empire from India throughout the Asian colonies. A child of the Enlightenment, it provided a platform for the recording of primary observations from amateur naturalists, cultural observers and government field officers.

It was members of organizations such as this and the Royal Geographical Society who made possible the explorations of Charles Darwin and other adventuring archeologists. To our information-sated age, their lectures and field trips may appear a predominantly male alternative to colonial ladies' tea parties. But for the authors of those thousands of prosaic monographs in RAS journals, the world was still new and unexplained, and they were doing their bit to add to the composite understanding of an age. There are few overseas chapters of the RAS left in the world where such people still determinedly carry on with this work; most prominent are one in Hong Kong and another in India.

The society has no regular location for events, but it organizes monthly lectures, seminars and trips for those interested in Asian arts, literature and science. It also publishes books and an annual journal. Its expeditions to out-of-the-way Hong Kong places, such as the waterfall in Pokfulam, which first attracted British sailors looking for potable water to Hong Kong, or to the Bogue forts spread about Chinese waters in the mouth of the Pearl River, which were once occupied by European traders and invaders of Canton further upriver, are a history buff's delight. They are well worth inquiring about before you travel to Hong Kong.

The HK$150 annual overseas membership fee is so low that it's worth joining just to stay on their mailing list for upcoming events and copies of the annual journal. Back copies of the journal going back to the early 1960s are on sale to the general public.

CINEMA

If there is a black spot in Hong Kong's entertainment scene, it is cinema. Government censors appear to have inherited their guidelines from the Victorian era (no limits on violence, but any glimpse of pubic hairs is sinful, as are certain expletives, which get blipped), and local distributors can be ruthless and insensitive in editing movies to fit in with their tight screening schedules.

A handful of cinema clubs and Western cultural missions such as the **British Council** *(Easey Commercial Bldg., 255 Hennessy Rd., Wanchai* ☎*831-5138, map 5 C6)*, the **Goethe Institut** *(Fl.14, Hong Kong Arts Centre, 2 Harbour Rd., Wanchai* ☎ *527-0088, map 5 C6)* and the **Alliance Française** *(123 Hennessy Rd., Wanchai* ☎ *527-7825, box office open 10am-8pm, map 5 C6)* do better, but their venues are small and shows are frequently sold out.

There *are* bright spots. You can see a wide range of mainland Chinese movies with English subtitles. And, each spring (March to April), you can squeak into viewings during the **International Film Festival**, which screens nearly 200 films all day long, all across the city, for two solid weeks. A pain in the eye sockets, but salvation for serious film buffs.

Hong Kong is the world's second-largest exporter of films, cranking out Chinese-language movies from its two home-grown studios, Shaw

Brothers and Golden Harvest, and a few English-language efforts each year. Golden Harvest has, for instance, hit it big with their *Ninja Turtles* movies. Canto-comedies, ghost stories, second-rate Cantonese remakes of Western first-run movies, and endless reels of *kung-fu* period pieces set in the dynastic history of China are always on offer at most of the city's 152 movie theaters and on television. With the new "Nicam" technology, these often have sound tracks already dubbed for multilingual, Chinese-English-Japanese television broadcasts in the better hotels. Fewer than two dozen movie theaters carry English-language films at all and, of those, only a half-dozen have sound systems that are reasonably audible.

Hong Kong movie-goers are perhaps the strangest in the world. Tickets can be and often are reserved up to a day in advance and, in any case, all tickets are for assigned seats. This, however, does not deter a mad rush up escalators and into elevators so as to reach the loge or other seating first. The popcorn is served British-style — that is, sweet rather than salted and buttered as Americans have it. There are normally four showings a day: a 3.30pm matinee, and 5.30, 7.30 and 9.30pm. See the local newspapers for what's on offer.

COLUMBIA CLASSIC
Great Eagle Centre, 23 Harbour Rd., Wanchai ☎573-8291. *Map* **5C6**. *Great Eagle Centre complex is in front of Wanchai Ferry Pier and across the road from the Hong Kong Convention & Exhibition Centre complex and its two hotels.*

Intimate, comfortable, European-style arts cinema with good acoustics. Runs intelligent Western, Japanese and Chinese movies that the bigger chain theaters ignore or rotate within a week — and will hold a single film for many weeks if interest is keen.

NAN YANG THEATRE
23 Morrison Hill Rd., Wanchai ☎573-7388. *Map* **5C7**.

Movies from mainland China, in Chinese with English subtitles or vice versa. Stages an annual festival of mainland films.

OCEAN THEATRE
3 Canton Rd., Kowloon ☎724-5444. *Map* **7F2**. *Star Ferry*.

Major theater for first-run English-language movies, set beside Omni Hong Kong Hotel and Ocean Terminal and 5 minutes' walk from Star Ferry.

PALACE THEATRE
280 Gloucester Rd., Causeway Bay ☎795-1500. *Map* **6B8**.

Hong Kong's biggest, with the most comfortable seats and more leg-room than any other movie theater in town. Beside the Excelsior Hotel, inside the World Trade Centre building, this specializes in Hollywood blockbusters and romances. It's the place to catch periodic revivals of *Somewhere in Time* and *Gone With The Wind*. The former touched a chord here which local pundits have yet to understand, and it holds the record as Hong Kong's longest-running English-language movie, at more than two months — and this in a city of movie distributors who spare no sentiment about shortening a showing schedule or chopping arbitrary bits from a movie to make it fit the schedules of four showings a day.

UA (UNITED ARTISTS) THEATRES
Pacific Place Mall, Queensway ☎869-0322. *Map* **4C4**.

This Quad cinema carries four first-run movies simultaneously, but not for long. Popular movies are sold out early.

Nightlife

BARS

Hong Kong is sated in bars of every type and price category. They range from cozy to clever, from cool and sleek to downright sleazy. Virtually all hotels have lobby lounges, such as the Captain's Bar or Dragon's Bar in the Mandarin Oriental and Hilton. Some have self-styled party bars like JJ's or Someplace Else in the Grand Hyatt and Sheraton. Still others have music bars like Gripp's in the Omni Hong Kong.

The Japanese-style *karaoke* singalong bar is all the rage here. There are sociable pubs like Mad Dogs or Bull and Bear, those for ogling bare-breasted bartenders, or for rubbing up against lithe young women paid to be interested by the drink or by the hour. Some in Lan Kwai Fong are darkened for effect and trendy; others in the back streets off Nathan Rd. are just dimly lit and dirty.

Virtually without exception bars are friendly places where the worst that may happen to a stranger is to be ignored by people too busy partying among themselves to take notice. Following is a sampler from a cast of thousands.

LA BODEGA TAPAS BAR & NIGHTSPOT

Grd Flr, 31 Wyndham St., Central ☎877-5472. *Map 3C3* 🟦 🟦 🟦 *Open noon to 2am daily.*

Hong Kong discovers Spanish bar snacks in this tiny, 2-story bar and restaurant club, with a metal staircase so tightly spiraled it would be safer descending a fireman's pole after drinks upstairs. An annual membership fee (HK$120) is required unless you arrive with a member or they forget to ask. Comedy workshop on Tuesdays, live commercial radio broadcast on Wednesdays and live music every night.

BOTTOMS UP

Basement, 14-16 Hankow Rd., Tsimshatsui, Kowloon ☎721-4509. *Map 7E3* 🟦 🟦 🟦 🟦 *Open 4pm-3am. 5mins' walk from Tsimshatsui MTR.*

The only topless bar where men and women customers really seem to enjoy themselves, perhaps because it's one of only a handful that are not clip-joints. Scenes for the James Bond movie *The Man with the Golden Gun* were shot here. Plush "bordello" decor, cosmopolitan line-up of barmaids, and friendly management.

BULL AND BEAR

Hutchison House, Central ☎525-7436.

Map 4C4 🟦 🟦 🟦 *Open 11am-2.30am.*
One of Hong Kong's ersatz British pubs, with European staff. Attracts resident British businessmen, lawyers, government types and single females. Imported British beers.

CAPTAIN'S BAR

Mandarin Hotel, Connaught Rd., Central ☎522-0111. *Map 3B3* 🟦 🟦 🟦 🟦 *Open 11am-2am.*

As you would expect from the MANDARIN (see WHERE TO STAY), impeccable service in elegant and relaxed surroundings is the order of the day here. A resident Filipino band plays soothing music for listening and easy dancing on a floor that fits perhaps three couples without unintended jostling. This, the **Chinnery Bar** on the mezzanine and **Harlequin** bar nestled on the top floor between the Pierrot and Man Wah restaurants, are all extremely popular places to rendezvous on business or after it. The Harlequin has magnificent views across the harbor and Chater Gardens, facing the Hong Kong Club.

DRAGON BOAT BAR

Hilton Hotel, 2A Queen's Rd., Central ☎523-3111 ext. 748. *Map 4C4* 🟦 🟦 🟦 🟦 *Open 11am-1am.*

One of the best hotel bars in Hong

Kong. The bar itself is shaped like a dragon boat, and the waitresses wear those famous slinky silk *cheongsams* slit to the thigh, inside of which, it seems, only a Chinese woman's figure can be flattered. Elegant, comfortable and crowded, especially around the cocktail hour.

GRIPP'S

Flr 6, Omni Hongkong Hotel, Harbour City, Tsimshatsui, Kowloon ☎736-0088. *Map 7E2* 🆎 📀 📀 📼

Opened in January 1990, at a cost of HK$5 million, as a jazz bar, Gripp's takes its name from a legendary bar in the former Hongkong Hotel (1868-1954) in Central district across the harbor. The center of the room is a large island bar, fitted out in granite, brass and teakwood. Internationally ranked blues and jazz singers such as Almeta Speaks and Mildred Jones play here.

JJ's

Grand Hyatt Hotel, 1 Harbour Rd., Wanchai ☎861-1234. *Map 5C6* 🆎 📀 📀 📼 *Open Sun-Thurs 6pm-2am; Fri, Sat, public holidays to 3am.*

Once upon a time the hotels had lost dominance of nightlife to freestanding areas such as Lan Kwai Fong and the Canton Rd. discos. Since its opening in 1989, JJ's has led the charge to take it back with its 2-story "entertainment center" concept, which offers six completely different "environments," some loud and live, some quiet and intimate. These include a discotheque with the C.C. Ryders American rhythm and blues group as house band, a billiards room, a dartboard and even a pizzeria lounge.

JOE BANANAS

Grd Flr, Shiu Lam Bldg., 23 Luard Rd., Wanchai ☎529-1811. *Map 5C6* 📀 📼 *Open Mon-Thurs 11.30am-5am; Fri-Sat to 6am; Sun and public holidays to 2am. 5mins' walk from Wanchai MTR.*

Run by the people who own MAD DOGS, this is an American-style bar filled with 1950s memorabilia, neon and young expatriates. Good live music, but awful acoustics and an eccentric, unfriendly door policy — no sneakers, no hats etc.

MAD DOGS

33 Wyndham St., Central ☎525-2383, *map 3C3, and 32 Nathan Rd., Tsimshatsui, Kowloon* ☎301-2222, *map 7E3.* Both 📀 📼 *Open Sun-Thurs 11am-4am; Fri-Sat to 5am.*

A British pub run by a long-time resident Scotsman, Andy Neilson. The decor very carefully evokes Britain's imperial heyday with prints, posters and other ephemera of empire. The owner is a former soldier, a cartoonist and history buff who has also created a successful business in the export of precision-modeled toy soldiers, called "God And Country," recalling Her Britannic Majesty's many regiments through their long history. The Central Hong Kong location above Lan Kwai Fong is chock-a-block full on weekends, when an exclusively young expatriate clientele is served up its Bass beer and Scotch malt whiskies by a bevy of British barmaids. All part of keeping up the side, old boy.

RED LIPS BAR

1a Lock Rd., Tsimshatsui, Kowloon ☎368-4511. *Map 7E3. Open 11am-4am. Tsimshatsui MTR.*

One of Hong Kong's oldest "girly" bars, with possibly the oldest "girls" in town — you might meet Suzie Wong's grandmother here. Still, the hole-in-the-wall bar has a seedy, antique charm, and the staff is friendlier, less predatory than most.

SOMEPLACE ELSE

Sheraton Hong Kong Hotel & Towers, 20 Nathan Rd., Tsimshatsui, Kowloon ☎369-1111 ext. 5. *Map 7F3* 🆎 📀 📀 📼 *Open Sun-Thurs 11am-1am; Fri-Sat to 2am. 5mins' walk from Tsimshatsui MTR.*

Decor is an eclectic American turn-of-the-century theme on two floors in dark wood booths with tables. The trim is offset by funky reproductions of signboards and imitation stained glass. A very popular singles bar to which come stunningly dressed Chinese females either accompanied by or to meet less stunning but well-employed Western males.

LIVE JAZZ, DISCO AND POP

For live jazz and popular music fans, there is a wide choice of performances at major hotels, discos, restaurants, bars and nightclubs. They can be old-world elegant, hi-tech chic, or basic and boisterous, but the mix of Oriental and Western ambience and clientele is unique. Occasionally they feature world-class acts who are passing through, but more usually there are resident Filipino or European expatriate musicians performing.

The Chinese community has its own home-grown "Canto-pop" stars, but they usually perform in huge auditoria to sellout houses.

CANTON

Phase IV, Harbour City, Tsimshatsui, Kowloon ☎721-0209. *Map 7E2. Open 9.30pm-2.30am.*

This is the biggest, slickest disco in town, with an excellent sound system, choice of bars, dance floors and discreet cubbyholes, which can accommodate 1,200 people on two floors. It often features visiting Western bands and cult stars such as "Divine" for a young and chic clientele of Chinese and expatriates.

DICKENS BAR

Excelsior Hotel, 281 Gloucester Rd., Causeway Bay ☎894-8888. *Map 6B8* 🆎 🔲 🔲 🔲 *Open Sun-Thurs 11am-2am; Fri-Sat to 3am.*

An English-style pub, adorned in wood paneling, brass horse fittings and Dickensian prints, with live performances by big-band jazz outfits every Sunday afternoon from 3pm and visiting acts (Caribbean steel band, Dixieland) some evenings. Draft beer from England, pub food, and a lunchtime buffet. Liveliest late at night.

THE GODOWN

Grd Flr, Admiralty Centre, Tower II, 18 Harcourt Rd., Central ☎866-1166. *Map 4C4* 🔲 🆎 🔲 🔲 🔲 *Open 9am-2am.*

A restaurant-cum-disco, with jazz on Wednesday at 9pm. The food is mediocre, but the atmosphere is lively.

HOT GOSSIP

160 Ocean Galleries, Harbour City, Canton Rd., Tsimshatsui ☎730-6884. *Map 7E2* 🆎 🔲 🔲 🔲 *Open Sun-Thurs noon-2.30am; Fri-Sat to 3.30am.*

An outpost of London's Juliana chain of discos boasting the latest in laser shows and video magic. A favorite with swinging singles.

THE JAZZ CLUB ★

California Entertainment Bldg., 34-36 D'Aguilar St. ☎845-8477. *Map 3C3* 🔲 🆎 🔲 🔲 🔲

The real thing, featuring international stars such as Anita O'Day, Joe Henderson and James Moody. It's not unusual for the likes of Chick Corea and Pat Metheny to join a jam when in town. The house band, Encounters, led by Hong Kong's premier jazzman Rick Halstead, is excellent, whether playing alone or backing-up the likes of Jimmy Witherspoon, with whom they've recorded.

NED KELLY'S LAST STAND

11A Ashley Rd., Tsimshatsui, Kowloon ☎366-0562. *Map 7E3. Open 11.30pm-2am. Tsimshatsui MTR.*

This lively, sometimes raucous Australian "Goodtime Dixieland Fun Pub," featuring live folk, Dixieland and rock music, has been honoring the memory of the Outback's most famous outlaw, Ned Kelly, for almost 20 years. Decor is coarse-wood benches and photographs of old Ned in his stovepipe helmet or his "Wanted" posters. A good place for a knee-slappin' good time, mate.

RICK'S CAFÉ

Enterprise Centre, 4 Hart Ave., Tsimshatsui, Kowloon ☎367-2939. *Map 7E3* 🔲 🔲 🔲 *Open 3pm-3am. 5mins' walk from Tsimshatsui MTR.*

It may not be as atmospheric or exciting

as its original namesake, but this one serves fair Mexican food, and there's good music to be enjoyed when the resident jazz-fusion band plays. It is a venue for visiting artists such as Chick Corea.

NIGHTCLUBS

There are five major nightclub districts in Hong Kong. They cater to differing tastes, spanning the range from upscale chic through low-down but funky to just plain low-down.

Lan Kwai Fong

This 2-square-block area in Central district is popular with upscale expatriates, their teenage children and Westernized Chinese looking to mingle in the exotic world of Western ethnicity.

Lockhart Road

Running E from Fenwick St. to Tonnochy Rd., this strip is sustained, between visits from foreign navies, by both tourists and residents. It consists of ersatz British or Australian pubs, "topless" bars, "hostess" bars and disco bars. These last are singles' pick-up bars populated by Filipinas. Only four of them remain: Pussycat, Neptune, New Makati and New Popeye. There are numerous "short-time" hotels in the upper floors of the street's older buildings as well.

West of Nathan Road

Similarly, the area to the w of Nathan Rd. around Peking Rd., Haiphong Rd. and Hanoi Rd., is a warren of streets providing the same fare for the same reasons — for what is now Kowloon Park was formerly a British military base. Soldiers still filter down from the New Territories, but mostly tourists make up the clientele these days.

Canton Road

Newest of the nightlife strips, this built its party reputation on two racy discotheques, Canton and Hot Gossip, in different basements of the Ocean Terminal complex. Being upscale singles bars, these are more akin to those in Lan Kwai Fong than to their equivalents in the more downscale environs of the other two nightlife areas.

Tsimshatsui East

The fifth area for nighttime entertainment is Tsimshatsui East, the home of budget-busting hostess nightclubs. Catering to Japanese business-men on unlimited expense accounts, these gigantic clubs feature live music and multinational hostesses whose time is measured by the minute. Although extremely expensive escort services are available, these clubs are really designed to assuage egos with extravagant decor (one has a vintage Rolls Royce on rails in the basement to take people to their tables), expensive brandy, opportunities for rubbing up against exotic females from faraway places, and enormous bar bills with which to brag about conquests back home.

Hostesses, escorts and their ilk

Suzie Wong, of course, is alive and well — although these days she's unlikely to have a heart of gold and might even be a moonlighting domestic maid from the Philippines. In her old Wanchai haunts and in the Tsimshatsui area of Kowloon the choice ranges from elegant and expensive Japanese-style "hostess" clubs to sleazy topless bars. Scores of "escort" agencies and massage services advertise in the yellow pages.

But for value for money and fun-loving companionship, most people would choose to catch a flight to Bangkok or Manila. The price differential for a night on the town with a professional "escort" in either of those cities might well cover the cost of an air ticket.

Useful to know

Some nightspots charge an entrance fee, others set a cover charge, and some charge neither. Almost all have early-evening "happy hours" (from 5 to 8pm) when drinks are half-price or, more commonly, you can buy two for the price of one.

People in Hong Kong work long hours, so it can be late in the evening before things liven up. As many people work on Saturday mornings as well, it is Saturday night, rather than Friday, that is the busiest.

CALIFORNIA

Grd Flr, California Tower, 24 Lan Kwai Fong, Central ☎521-1345. Map 3C3 🞔 🞔 🞔 🞔 🞔 Open Mon-Sat noon-1am (dancing Wed, Fri, Sat); Sun 5pm-1am.

A trendy cocktail bar, with West Coast cuisine and dancing till dawn. It's very popular with fashion-conscious yuppies, models and gays, gets very crowded late at night, and can be difficult to get into. The disco is a private club, although membership can be paid for at the door. Sometimes it stages risqué floor shows such as *Chippendales*, an all-male American striptease revue.

CHINA CITY

Flr 4, Peninsula Centre, 67 Mody Rd., Tsimshatsui East, Kowloon ☎723-3278. Map 7E3. Open 9pm-4am.

It's a classic example of bad taste: 4,650sq.m (50,000 square feet) with hi-tech decor, state-of-the-art electronics, fountains and light show beneath a glass dance floor. Some 800 girls are available to dance or chat. Charges for companionship and drinks are high. It's worth a visit only for the anecdotes.

CLUB BBOSS

Lower Grd Flr, Mandarin Plaza, 14 Science Museum Rd., Tsimshatsui East, Kowloon ☎369-2883. Map 8E4 🞔 🞔 🞔 🞔 Open 3pm-4am. Also operates next door **Club Metropolitan**, Lower Grd Flr,

Chinachem Golden Plaza, 77 Mody Rd., Tsimshatsui East ☎311-1111. Map 8E4.

The 400 Asian and European hostesses dress in flashy pink evening gowns and fur shawls and carry walkie-talkies. A Rolls Royce ferries guests to their table or private room, and a giant digital timer keeps track of what's owed. Live music, a dance floor, and a rich male clientele. Forced to give up its "Club Volvo" moniker in 1991 under threat of a lawsuit by the Swedish car company of the same name. The fracas might have been avoided had the ferry been something safer and less flashy than a Rolls: say a....

MEZZANINE LOUNGE

Regent Hotel, Salisbury Rd., Tsimshatsui, Kowloon ☎721-1211. Map 7F3. Open 11pm-1am.

Very elegant, with a resident band and smooth service. The main attraction is the breathtaking view of HK Island seen through 3-story-high glass walls. Only the view from the Peak can compete.

NEW TONNOCHY NIGHT CLUB

1-5 Tonnochy Rd., Wanchai ☎575-4376. Map 5C7 🞔 🞔 🞔 🞔 Open 1pm-4am.

Bands, singers and scores of paid-by-the-hour hostesses in elegant gowns perform for a largely Asian male clientele. Expensive, and not everyone's cup of tea, this nevertheless has some amusement value.

Shopping

Where to go

Of the 6 million or so tourists who visit Hong Kong each year, a good many are lured by the city's world-renowned shopping facilities. These range from mammoth malls to busy side streets crammed with small shops selling everything from jewelry, electronic gadgets, audio and camera equipment to boutique clothes, antiques, and sports equipment and clothing.

In 1990, for instance, 5.9 million visitors spent almost HK$40 billion in Hong Kong, and half of that was on shopping.

The premier shopping district is **Tsimshatsui** *(map 7E3)*, which is at the toe of Kowloon peninsula and has three parts:

- the famous "**Golden Mile**," the traditional center around Nathan Rd., stretching from Kowloon Park s to the waterfront
- **Ocean Terminal** and its adjacent shopping malls
- the newer shopping/hotel/business district of **Tsimshatsui East**.

Each of these is a small city in itself; as a shopping area, any one of the three would do most cities more than proud. In the following pages we look at this trio, and its opposite numbers across the harbor, to provide a snapshot of the astonishing scope for shopping in Kowloon and Hong Kong Island. Occasional map references provide an anchor as our survey ranges across the city. Otherwise, for pinpoint locations you should look to the shop listings, which are treated alphabetically subject by subject under the following headings:

- ANTIQUES, ARTS AND CRAFTS, page 145
- AUDIO, VIDEO, PHOTOGRAPHIC AND ELECTRONIC EQUIPMENT, page 150
- BOOKS, page 153
- CLOTHES, page 154
- COMPUTERS, page 157
- FABRICS, page 157
- GENERAL AND DEPARTMENT STORES, page 158
- JEWELRY, page 160
- MARKETS, page 162

OCEAN TERMINAL
Developed in three stages since 1966, the Ocean Terminal shopping complex *(map 7F2)* is enormous. Starting right at the Kowloon Star Ferry terminal, it is really three centers in one: **Ocean Terminal** (which opened in 1966), **Ocean Centre** (1977) and **Harbour City** (1984), all interconnected and merging into one another, with 600-odd

shops, the three **Omni group hotels** *(map 7E2),* three cinemas, office buildings and upscale apartment blocks — 15 big buildings in all. The warehouse of the Marine Deck was transformed, in the late 1980s, into a branch of **Toys "R" Us**, which claims to be the world's biggest toy store, with more than one million items in stock.

It's easy to lose yourself among the endless air-conditioned malls. Find an Information Desk and pick up their map brochure and also the center's magazine *Harbour Citizen*. Ocean Terminal has a slick touch-screen computer directory and guide; the other two centers have orientation maps and wall-mounted directories, but these are hard to find. It's best to approach the desk just inside the main entrance from Star Ferry.

If the sheer scale of shopping here seems a bit overwhelming, the style makes up for it. You are seldom confronted by more than a dozen shops at a time, and they are always a good variety, with strategically positioned cafés and restaurants along the way. The shops are chic and upscale, the displays attractive and excellent for window-shopping.

NATHAN ROAD

For those who prefer a less synthetic environment, the Golden Mile of Nathan Rd. and its surrounding streets *(map 7E3)* is at least out in the open air — and, as often as not, crowded, hot, dusty and noisy with it. The Golden Mile is in fact only $\frac{5}{8}$ mile from the waterfront to its northern limit at Austin Rd., but don't feel short-changed: it probably has more shops than any other $\frac{5}{8}$ mile in the world. Unlike the shops in Ocean Terminal and Tsimshatsui East, they cover the full spectrum of quality and value. The PENINSULA, the district's most expensive hotel, is only a block away from the cheapest, CHUNG KING MANSION (see WHERE TO STAY for both). Each has a shopping arcade: the Peninsula's with top-class jewelers, designer boutiques and pricey antiques, the Chung King arcade containing a very serviceable curry restaurant, tailors and music tape shops.

The keynote of the Golden Mile district is its variety. Snooty boutiques with a Nathan Rd. frontage hold their noses against the alleyway next door where stallkeepers peddle a decidedly *risqué* line of sealed adult books. Modern shops and storefronts mingle with the more traditional, and there's a fantastic range of restaurants: a concentrated variety that indoor arcades cannot match. Tsimshatsui MTR station has six entrances in and around Nathan Rd., and one at the Hyatt Regency Hotel.

TSIMSHATSUI EAST

To the E of Nathan Rd. is Chatham Rd., which divides Tsimshatsui from Tsimshatsui East *(map 7E3-4),* a curtain-walled city built from scratch in 1980 on landfill, with the tourist very much in mind. It contains half a dozen 5-star hotels, and the shopping style can best be described as upscale international, concentrated into highrise commercial malls, with the same canned air and canned music as that found at Ocean Terminal, although here the shopping centers are not interconnected. In fact, no fewer than 13 big shopping plazas stand side by side, inconveniently separated by streets, which you have to cross.

Many Hong Kong factory outlets have opened shops lining Chatham Rd. opposite the Inter-Continental Plaza, as a sort of annex to their main hive at Kaiser Estate *(map 8 D5)* in nearby Hunghom. A promenade half a mile long runs the length of the Tsimshatsui East waterfront ending at the New World Centre, a pleasant walk with a fine, unobstructed view of the harbor and Causeway Bay.

CAUSEWAY BAY
Tsimshatsui East is adjacent to the Cross Harbour Tunnel. Cross the harbor and you are in **Causeway Bay** *(around the top center of maps 5 and 6)*, known in early times as East Point. As a sample of what you will find there, consider the following:

- two big **China Products** department stores
- five major Japanese department stores
- a branch of **Lane Crawford's** upscale department store
- a British **Marks & Spencer** department store
- five shopping malls
- the **Yee Tung Village Craft Centre**
- a good street market for clothing at **Jardine's Bazaar**
- and a dozen excellent shopping streets, most of them modern in style, some more traditional.

The Chinese shops are samplers of China, in the style and variety of their goods and in the way they do things. They are rather like the Friendship Stores found N of the border in the People's Republic. The goods are certainly very Chinese, and you can find some attractive things, although the staff is sometimes offhand.

Similarly, the Japanese shops are samplers of Japan: Japanese-owned showcases of mostly Japanese goods. They have a large clientele in the resident Japanese population and an even larger one in the tour groups from Japan on shopping sprees, many coming for Japanese products that they can buy more cheaply in Hong Kong's Japanese department stores than in their own. **Mitsukoshi** in Hennessy Rd., not far from **Daimaru** and **Matsuzakaya**, has an art gallery that exhibits only originals, usually French lithographs (Bernard Buffet, Brassillier) — very much to Japanese tastes and sold mostly to Japanese.

The Japanese shops offer not only Japanese products but also a reasonable selection of Western goods. In fashion, for example, all the shops have a range of collections from European designers and Europe-based Japanese designers. There are fashions for all styles and all age groups. Goods are not cheap, but the shops hold frequent sales where you can often pick up terrific buys.

CENTRAL AND WANCHAI
To continue this intercultural shopping tour — if you have the strength — take a taxi to **Central district** *(around the top center of maps 3 and 4)*. Here, the **Landmark**, and sister structures connected by covered pedestrian overpasses (**Prince's Building**; **Alexandra House**; **Swire House**; **Nine Queen's Road**; and **Mandarin Hotel Arcade**), contain a bevy of chic European and Japanese designer-label boutiques.

Or stop at the newest shopping island, **Pacific Place Mall** *(map 4 C4-5)* in Queensway, just between Central and Wanchai districts. **Seibu's** first department store outside Japan anchors this Hong Kong-side challenger to the dominance of Tsimshatsui's shopping centers. Besides many unique shops, the Mall has a similar variety of eating places to the Ocean Terminal group (meaning about a half dozen cuisines ranging from Southeast Asian to Northern Italian) and a **UA Quad cinema** (see CINEMA in NIGHTLIFE AND ENTERTAINMENT), which screens four first-run movies at a time.

Less expensive shops can be found in the **Admiralty Centre** complex, which houses five commercial buildings with different names, including the two architecturally striking towers of the **Bond Centre**; they are across a pedestrian overpass and above the MTR station of the same name.

HUNGHOM AND YAUMATEI

If what you seek is fashion apparel, go to the rag-trade factory outlets of **Kaiser Estate** in **Hunghom** *(map 8 D5)* to purchase silks and satins of Martini-set wear at rock-bottom prices. These outlets are supplied by the factories that sell the very same apparel to virtually every famous-name US department store, from Bloomingdale's in New York, through Marshall Field's in Chicago, to I. Magnin in San Francisco. The only differences are the price and the absence of a store label.

Computers populate the labyrinthine and surreal **Golden Arcade** in **Yaumatei**, a hotbed of pirated technology — judging by the rate of Hong Kong Customs officials' raids — but a hacker's heaven. The **Asia Computer Plaza** in Silvercord is the major center of strictly legal outlets, and there are smaller centers in Wanchai on Hong Kong Island.

SHOPPING STRATEGIES

Street shoppers can purchase a designer T-shirt in Nathan Rd. boutiques for HK$500-$1,000, or wend round the corner into the warren of discount houses and buy a "second" with a small fault or an imitation of the same shirt for HK$10-$50 (especially in Granville Rd. and Kimberley St.). It is all a matter of budget, energy and preference. These roughly 40 square blocks offer maybe the widest selection of goods in every price range to be found anywhere on earth. There are fabulous bargains to be had — if you are willing to:

- compare prices across the ten blocks running N-S from Austin Rd. to Salisbury Rd.(at the top of Kowloon Park), crisscrossed by streets that run 3-4 blocks E-W from Nathan Rd. to Chatham Rd. *(map 7 D-F3);*
- bargain like your children's education depended upon it;
- ignore brusque clerks who see hundreds of shoppers by the busload each week and are not in the least interested in a hard sell;
- carefully inspect anything you purchase before paying for it;
- and, unless the shop has the red "junk" boat logo of the Hong Kong Tourist Association, live with the risk of finding one trouser leg shorter than the other when it's too late to go back and complain.

Here is a small but telling example: the local Consumer Council has estimated that of about 250 camera shops in Hong Kong, 40-50 are regularly complained about for cheating customers or uncalled-for rudeness, most of them in the Golden Mile district. This is tiger country and, unless you've the teeth for it, stick with the shops endorsed by HKTA, which publishes lists of its members in its several free shopping guides, and will mediate disagreements between you and shopkeepers.

ANTIQUES, ARTS AND CRAFTS

Hong Kong is the premier trading center for Chinese antiquities. Some of the Hollywood Rd. dealers have supplied the world's major museums, as well as those wealthy individuals who buy at the spring and fall auctions held here by Christie's and Sotheby's. The highest prices ever paid for Chinese arts have been fetched at these auctions. So beware: there are no "bargains" for objects of great antiquity here.

Hong Kong's cultural pride means that people pay more, not less, here for the best pieces. High-end antiquities are traded in a seller's market, and what makes the free and freewheeling port of Hong Kong so precious is that the pieces are here to purchase — via a clutch of rich collectors trading, through dealers and auctions, the spoils from the break-up of noble estates in the faraway homelands of 19thC "gunboat diplomatists" in Great Britain, North America and continental Europe (and smuggling rings operating out of mainland China). That's the wonder of it. As to bargains, it's a bit like the old Rolls Royce adage which holds, "If you have to ask the price, dearie, you can't afford one."

What is here at street-level, a blessing to middle-class collectors of oddities and artifacts, is a trove of minor arts objects of genuine age but little significance, heavily restored pieces that wouldn't pass muster with collectors of museum-pieces but look perfect to the layman's unpracticed eye, and brilliant reproductions which, when not mistakenly purchased as the real thing, offer good value for fine craftsmanship.

Hollywood Rd. runs 2.5km (1½ miles) W from Central Police Station at Arbuthnot Rd. to Queen's Rd. in Western district, just beyond MAN MO TEMPLE. This "Antique Mile" is as "golden" to lovers of Chinese, Korean and Japanese decorative arts as Nathan Rd. is to less specialized shoppers in Kowloon, with about 100 shops within its immediate environs. The entire street shuts down on Sunday, and some shops close on Saturday after lunch. Shops generally open Monday to Saturday from 10am-6pm.

In many countries, including the US, Customs duties are waived on art objects and antiquities certified to be 100 years old or more. All the shops that claim to carry genuine antique objects will provide certificates and, conveniently, you will be hard put to find anything less than a century old in the shop. Your "early 19thC" Korean chest may, in fact, have only a small section of its back or center shelf left that is authentic — but it will likely cost little more than a comparable contemporary piece, be a beautiful addition to your home, and come certified as "authentic" and therefore Customs-free.

The best dealers on the street will tell you about such anomalies and will be frank about extensive restorations to porcelains and so on — but only if you ask. Likewise, they will not trot out their high-end treasures unless you first establish — with the right questions — that you know enough to be indulged. Many of them come from families that have been handling rare pieces for three or four generations. This is a specialists' world, to be entered with a stubborn faith in your own sense of beauty, the humility of an apprentice, and the guile of a moneychanger. Allow time to shop around and return for purchasing, rather than relying only on your wits for impulse buying.

Do not buy solely as an investment. Choose, instead, what you want to live with for years to come. You will know far less than the dealers do, and you will not get below-market rates. But if you truly love a piece, your life will be as enriched by its presence in your home for a lifetime as it was when you first cast eyes upon it. Let your heirs fret over any gain in relative worth.

Besides Hollywood Rd., there are antiques, arts, curios and crafts dealers sprinkled about in all the major shopping complexes. The following selection should set you off in the right direction.

ALISAN FINE ARTS LTD.
315 Prince's Bldg., 10 Chater Rd., Central
☎*526-1091. Map 3B3.*
Easily the leading gallery for modern Chinese painting using traditional materials, from both Overseas Chinese artists and those from the mainland. Exhibitions change monthly, but a large stock is kept on hand and is worth asking to see. Wucius Wong and Hon Chi Fun are probably the two most locally renowned contemporary landscapists, whose works come about as close to Abstract Expressionism as one can get and still reside within a recognizable landscape. There are altogether perhaps half a dozen Hong Kong painters who have made the international art market charts. All of them can be seen here. Alice King is proprietress.

ALTFIELD GALLERY
45 Graham St. (above Hollywood Rd.)
☎*524-4867. Map 3B2.*
Fine reproductions of Ming and Ching dynasty Chinese furniture, small Chinese and Tibetan altar carpets and China trade prints. Also the sole agent for Jim Thompson pure Thai silks and Jack Lenor Larsen fabrics. This is the chief of three branches. The others are at **Prince's Building** *(☎524-7526)* and **31 Lyndhurst Terrace** *(☎542-*

2098). The Altfield Gallery has been run by an American attorney, David Halperin, with British partner, Amanda Lack, since 1982.

BUTT ORIENTAL CARPETS
Grd Flr, 44 Hollywood Rd., Central
☎*850-6900. Map 3B2.*
There are several so-called Persian Carpet shops in and around Hollywood Rd., notable for their perpetual "clearance sale" signs in the windows. Don't be lured by the signs, but do have a look at their magnificent hand-knotted carpets from Afghanistan, Iran, India, Turkey, the former Soviet Central Asia (Bukhara and Samarkand in Uzbekistan) and Pakistan. The Butt family operates out of Kashmir in North India and is perhaps the best organized of such dealers, with outlets seemingly everywhere and prices to match. They operate their own factories in Kashmir as well as dealing, and have a wide selection.

CAT STREET GALLERIES
38 Lok Ku Rd., Western ☎*543-1609. Map 3B2.*
A traditional antique and curio market, consolidated from the original street stalls that stood on or near the site into this modern complex in the early 1980s: six floors of antiques, curios, and arts

and crafts shops. Access is from Lok Ku Rd. or Upper Lascar Row.

CHARLOTTE HORSTMANN & GERALD GODFREY

Shop 2104, Ocean Terminal, Harbour City ☎367-7167. *Map 7F2.*

Founded and run by Mrs Horstmann for decades and taken over upon her retirement in the early 1980s by Mr Godfrey. Many a home on Hong Kong's Peak has been decorated by this pair, and it has been their specialty to combine decorators' instincts with solid knowledge of Asian antiques. Their prices reflect the affluence of their clientele.

CHINA RESOURCES ARTLAND CENTRE AND DEPARTMENT STORE

Low Block (ground to 2nd floors), China Resources Building, 26 Harbour Rd., Wanchai ☎834-4567. *Map 5C6.*

Two floors of well-displayed Chinese art products, from knick-knacks to very expensive, finely crafted works. For fine quality pieces, this is probably the best shop of a group of mainland China-controlled "arts and crafts" outlets that have operated in the territory for more than 30 years. They also stock some fine antiques. The **Museum of Chinese Historical Relics** is in the same block.

There are five other **China Arts & Crafts** shops: in Central, Hong Kong *(Shell House, Wyndham St. entrance, just above Queen's Rd.* ☎522-3621, *map 3B3),* in Tsimshatsui, Kowloon *(Star House, Grd Flr, 3 Salisbury Rd.* ☎735-4061, *map 7F2; Silvercord, 30 Canton Rd.* ☎722-6655, *map 7E2; New World Centre, Shop G34-35, Salisbury Rd.* ☎369-7760, *map 7F3)* and Yaumatei *(233-239 Nathan Rd.* ☎730-0061, *map 7D3).* All these are also excellent outlets for contemporary crafts products and some antiques.

Unless you want it only for decoration, beware the heavily painted chinaware from China. It has been found by Hong Kong's Consumer Council to contain unacceptably high levels of toxic lead. Stick with the simple, underglazed blue-and-whites for use in the kitchen or dining room.

EASTERN DREAMS

47A Hollywood Rd., Central ☎544-2804. *Map 3B2.*

Set nicely at the junction of Hollywood Rd. and Lyndhurst Terr. on two floors of a building which curves round the intersection. A good shop for browsing around *chinoiserie* decorator items, such as boldly painted and lacquered jewelry boxes, and footlockers awash in lotus leaves and flowers. Just beside it sprawls a delightful curbside junk shop that does not pretend to be anything else, where you can find everything from Mao buttons through lewd photographs of nubile Chinese lasses circa 1920s to battered old trombones.

FLAGSTAFF MUSEUM OF TEAWARE

Cotton Tree Drive (or via Hong Kong Park), Central ☎529-9390. *Map 4C4.*

The shop in this Urban Council museum (see SIGHTS) offers excellent reproductions of teaware from the same periods as those covered in the collection, at very fair prices.

FOOK SING ARTS CO.

26 Middle Rd., Tsimshatsui, Kowloon ☎366-7502. *Map 7E3.*

A highly-regarded antique arts dealer specializing in archeological pieces. Legendary among European dealers for their faultless porcelain restorations.

FOOK TSU TONG GOURMET SHOP/FOOK MING TONG TEA SHOP

Grd Flr, Pedder Bldg., Theatre Lane, Central ☎521-0337/845-1633. *Map 3B3.*

Here is an upscale twist on a gift item long exploited by the supermarkets of the China Products shops in Hong Kong. Artistically packaged tea is the specialty of this lovely shop, which has an adjacent tea parlor, ideal for taste-testing. They are set in the rear of Pedder Building, which fronts the street of the same name. Sets include things like tins with reproductions of 19thC China Trade rice-paper paintings depicting the picking, packing and trading of tea, or the shapes of traditional Chinese teapots. Versions in supermarkets of mainland-controlled department stores range from intricate bamboo constructions to very kitsch tins painted with flamboyant Chinese faeries. Prices range from pocket change to serious investments in curative teas.

GAMMON ART GALLERY LTD.
Grd Flr, 53 Wellington St., Central ☎*522-0501/522-0648. Map 3B3.*
This shop, run by the Lee family, is reputed to have access to rare private collections in Japan. Whatever their sources, they are well known for very ancient, high-quality pieces of ceramics, such as 3-color glazed dishes and figurines from the Tang dynasty (AD618-906). Very little is on display in their shop, as they seldom deal in anything less than museum-quality goods. That makes what *is* on display always worth seeing.

HANART 2 GALLERY
Basement 28, 30 Braga Circuit, Kadoorie Ave., Kowloon ☎*713-9266. Map 7B3.*
Hong Kong's most adventuresome dealer in contemporary Chinese paintings by mainland, Hong Kong and Taiwanese artists. Only the most ardent enthusiasts are likely to venture a trip so far out of the way in N Kowloon, however. New exhibitions monthly.

HONEYCHURCH ANTIQUES
29 Hollywood Rd., Central ☎*543-2433. Map 3B2.*
Oriental furniture, porcelain, old silver (Oriental and English), Asian jewelry, old Asian books and prints. Operated for almost 20 years in Hong Kong by an American couple, Glenn and Lucille Vessa, whose daughter also runs a sister shop in Seattle, Washington. Popular with foreign buyers for their integrity and patient explanations of pieces.

HONG KONG TOURIST ASSOCIATION
Star Ferry Concourse, Tsimshatsui, Kowloon, map 7F2; Shop 8, Basement, Jardine House, 1 Connaught Place, Central, map 4B4; and Shop G2, Grd Flr, Royal Garden Hotel, 69 Mody Rd., Tsimshatsui, Kowloon, map 8E4.
In true *laissez faire* fashion, the HKTA must work to be self-supporting, while being helped by the government. Part of their efforts have gone into producing their own line of souvenirs, of good quality and at fair prices. These run from postcard packs to backpacks, snappy umbrellas and much in between. Don't overlook them as a source of clever, well-made mementos.

IAN MCLEAN ANTIQUES
73 Wyndham St., Central ☎*524-4542. Map 3C3.*
A lovely shop, selling 18th-19thC Chinese furniture and associated scholar's accouterments (such as brush pots and ink stands), scroll paintings, and other works of art. Especially well-known for a fine selection of Chinese desks and chests: the proprietor, Alan Fung, was a pioneer in marketing stripped-down furniture to show the beauty of the wood grain for Western tastes, in the early 1980s. The Chinese typically coated their furniture in heavy lamp-black finishes or rosewood stains. The stripped-down and polished look has become *de rigueur* among the many furniture dealers that have since opened on Hollywood Rd. Common woods are elm and the harder, rarer and twice as expensive *huang hua li*. All other Chinese hardwoods, except rosewood, are so denuded and rare that they are beyond the pale price wise.

KWONG SANG HONG
122-124 Connaught Rd., Central ☎*544-5233, map 3B2; 271 Shanghai St., Yaumatei, Kowloon, map 7D3; and Grd Flr, Western Market, Sheung Wan, map 3A2.*
Established about 90 years ago, when most Chinese women wore Chinese-made hair lotions and brilliantines, looking much like they still do on the company's packaging of its legendary "Two Girls" label product line. It has resolutely kept to its advertising theme of cherubic maidens in Chinese gardens so long that, like the pocket packs of Tiger Balm, its aged packaging has itself become a modern collector's item — and a great souvenir. The "Two Girls" face cream, *sut fa-go* (literally "snow

cream"), can be had for about two US dollars. **China Products** stores offer the mainland's line of balms and toiletries, equally exotic. Try "Ballet" pearl cream, made by the mashing of pure Taihu pearls, for facial radiance or, for the bath, "Florida Water," the smell of which lingers like Everglades swamp gas — but happily smells a lot better. There's also "Fang Fang" vanishing cream (just the ticket for Transylvanian counts), "Royal Concubine" jelly, "Fely Jilin" ginseng hair lotion, and lots more where those came from, ladies.

L&E COMPANY

Grd Flr, 188 Hollywood Rd. ☎546-9886 ⊠858-2435. *Map 3B2.*

Reproductions, contemporary *chinoiserie* lacquer furniture, carvings, bamboo bird cages and occasionally actual antiques are made or traded by this large exporter, whose 60,000-square-foot Hong Lok Yuen wholesale showroom is in Tai Po, New Territories *(map 2B4)*. A good outlet for people who like the shapes of China's chinaware but not the decorations, as they sell porcelain blanks, which can be decorated to taste or just left a glazed china-white.

MING PEI

Grd Flr, Wilson House, 19-27 Wyndham St., Central ☎521-3566 ⊠845-2052, *map 3C3, and Shop 131 Ocean Terminal, Harbour City, Kowloon* ☎736-3736, *map 7F2.*

These two shops have eliminated the issue of age from their fine Chinese ceramics by specializing only in very high-quality reproductions of pots in classical shapes and colors. The selection is superb.

MOUNTAIN FOLKCRAFT

12 Wo On Lane, Grd Flr, Central ☎523-2817. *Map 3B3.*

Hard to find, this little shop is in a dead-end lane near Lan Kwai Fong St., off D'Aguilar St., but it's well worth the search. It carries a wonderful array of mainland Chinese crafts items, embroidered and tie-dyed clothing and sil-

ver costume jewelry, all cramped into a small shop. The selection is eclectic and even includes incongruous additions such as framed Japanese prints, but there is something for every purse and much that you won't found elsewhere. Note the small shrine at the street's end as you leave.

NISHIKI GALLERY

Shop 304, Podium Area, Tower One, Exchange Square, Central ☎845-2551. *Map 3B3.*

A good shop for Japanese dolls, fans, paintings, kimonos and other traditional arts and crafts products. Next door is a decently laid out gallery for Chinese painters, **Plum Blossoms** *(Shop 305-307* ☎521-2189), which also carries a nice selection of exhibition catalogs for sale.

P.C. LU AND SONS LTD.

Grd Flr, 26 Hollywood Rd., Central ☎522-2038, *map 3B2, and Omni Hongkong Hotel, Kowloon* ☎736-6009, *map 7F2.*

One of the first families of Hong Kong dealers and among the most respected Chinese antiques dealers in Asia. Particularly strong in Imperial wares.

POK ART HOUSE

Grd Flr, Chong Tak Bldg., 18 Granville Rd., Tsimshatsui, Kowloon ☎368-5930. *Map 7E3.*

Long the leading China-controlled paintings and stone rubbings gallery in Hong Kong. Its wares include contemporary Chinese ink and watercolor paintings and a good selection of rubbings of ancient Chinese carvings.

POTTERY WORKSHOP

Grd Flr, Wyndham St. (or via Fringe Club on 2 Lower Albert Rd.) ☎525-7634. *Map 3C3.*

Serious contemporary ceramicists in Hong Kong find an outlet for their creations here. Prominent among them is Mak Yee-fun, whose works have been widely exhibited locally over the past decade, but many equally fine potters sell their works here. These are hand-thrown or individually molded art objects, as well as bowls, flower pots and coffee mugs. Prices vary widely.

SHUANGLE GALLERY

Flr 5, On Lan Centre, 11-15 On Lan St., Central ☎840-0112. Map 3C3.

Founded in 1990, this small gallery is set in converted office space. It features modern paintings by mainland and overseas Chinese artists in traditional media and ceramics.

TERESA COLEMAN FINE ARTS

Grd Flr, 37 Wyndham St., Central ☎526-2450/521-6125 ⌷525-7159. Map 3C3.

Ms. Coleman is best known for imperial robes and embroideries, such as "Mandarin patches" and magnificent Chinese men's and women's coats: one is usually displayed in her shop window.

TRIO PEARL CO. LTD.

Peninsula Hotel Arcade, Tsimshatsui, Kowloon ☎367-9171. Map 7F3.

A jewelry store, as its name implies. But the Chow family members who run it are also well-known and reputable dealers in antique jade sculptures.

VINCENT SUM COLLECTION

15 Lyndhurst Terr., Central ☎542-2610, map 3B3, and 348-349, Flr 3, Omni Hong Kong Hotel, Tsimshatsui, Kowloon ☎736-1762, map 7E2.

If Indonesia is not on your travel itinerary, this shop offers a fine selection of Malay crafts such as masks and woodcarvings, reproductions of 17thC Dutch colonial furniture and hanging hurricane lamps, Balinese peasant paintings, batik cloth and pillow covers (made with a unique wax-resistant dyeing-and-painting method), and carved wooden Asmat warrior's shields from Irian Jaya (formerly part of New Guinea). Prices are considerably higher than they would be in Jakarta or Bali, but the mark-up is still far less than an air ticket.

WELFARE HANDICRAFTS SHOP

Basement, Jardine House, Connaught Rd., Central ☎524-3356, map 4B4, and Salisbury Rd. (between Canton Rd. and Kowloon Park Dr.) ☎366-6979, map 7F3.

All proceeds from sales go to various charities, for which these two outlets act as a clearing house. Everything from the Community Chest to Friends of the Earth have crafts products on sale, and the prices are very competitive for most items. Another such outlet is run by **Caritas** (2 Caine Rd., beside the Botanical Gardens exit ☎524-2071, map 3 C3).

AUDIO, VIDEO, PHOTOGRAPHIC AND ELECTRONIC EQUIPMENT

HKTA's free *Shopping* booklet and its special *Shopping Guide to Video Products* booklet are essential references before you buy. The former explains the peculiar forms of camera "guarantees" of which you must be aware (not all are honored outside Hong Kong). The latter explains the technical niceties of the world's three major television broadcasting systems (Pal, NTSC and Secam), which are mutually incompatible for reasons incomprehensible to most laymen, and all of which are sold here. This explains the latest craze in multisystems equipment, along with stereo TVs. The booklets list recommended shops.

They also list contact information for the exclusive import agents of major brand-name products. This is extremely important to know and cannot be found elsewhere. For example, there is no Sony Co. listed in Hong Kong's phone book. There are, however, Fook Yuen Electronic Co. and Chung Yuen Electronic Co., the two official agents and service representatives. They can tell you the current Hong Kong "list" price of products, and that will tell you just how much below list a shopkeeper is truly prepared to go.

Hong Kong is not the bargain basement for electronic goods that it once was. In some cases, you will find little difference in price from discount houses in the United States, for instance. If you do find an appreciable difference, make certain that you have all the parts listed on the box plus the proper international guarantee before you conclude you have found a bargain.

Think of this as a "spot" market, based almost entirely on trading concerns like foreign-exchange rates, or luxury goods and retail sales taxes in other countries, all of which are absent in Hong Kong. Unlike clothes, jewelry, toys, watches, computers or little LCD games, where Hong Kong is a major manufacturing center and exporter of finished goods, cameras and audio goods are largely imports controlled by traders. Most final manufacturing is centered elsewhere, although many parts and supplies are made here. There are no "factory outlets" for these goods in Hong Kong; there is no dumping of unbranded overruns or seconds into the local market. But there are several hundred small shops, probably controlled by a cartel of just a few Chinese families, playing on Hong Kong's historical renown as a bargain center, earning small margins on what they must then sell in great volume, paying extortionate rents to be in tourist districts, and willing to make easy prey of the uninformed.

Good places to see new electronic products in town are the **Fortress Premium Shop** (*Shops G6/G7, Grd Flr, China Bldg., 29 Queen's Rd., Central* ☎*868-3428, map 3B3*), **System One** (*United Chinese Bank Bldg., 31-37 Des Voeux Rd., Central* ☎*868-1611, map 3 B3*) or **Radio City** in Causeway Bay (*505-511 Hennessy Rd., map 6 C8*). The first is owned by Hong Kong Electric, which has outlets all across Hong Kong and which carries most brands of electronic items and audio-video goods. The second is owned by Dai-Ichi Kaden, a huge Japanese firm, has eleven Hong Kong outlets and also stocks most brands. Neither will have the lowest prices, but they will back up their sales with proper guarantees and service. Radio City opened as a single-purpose shopping, showroom and office complex for consumer electronics companies in 1991. There are 4 floors of shopping.

PHOTOGRAPHIC EQUIPMENT

Brand	Sole Agent	Phone No.
Agfa-Gevaert †	Agfa-Gevaert HK Ltd	☎555 9420
Arrifles †	Jebsen & Co. Ltd	☎873 7878
Asahi Pentax †	Jebsen & Co. Ltd	☎873 7878
Bolex	J.H. Trachsler (HK) Ltd	☎563 1223
Bronica/Hoya †	Fuji Photo Products Co. Ltd	☎499 8168
Bushnell †	Wood's Photo Supplies	☎736 8128
Canon †	Jardine Photo Systems	☎565 2001
	Canon Camera Centre	☎724 3255
	Canon Camera Service Centre	☎564 0263
Carl Zeiss (binoculars)	Carl Zeiss Far East Co. Ltd	☎333 9201

Chinon	WIDEX Import & Export Ltd	☎416 3585
Contax Camera †	Wing On Cheong Emporium Ltd	☎544 6171
Elmo †	Kingstone Development Co	☎730 5663
Enna	China Sales Corporation	☎543 3922
Fuji/Fujinon †	Fuji Photo Products Co. Ltd	☎499 8168
Goko †	Jebsen & Co. Ltd	☎873 7878
Gossen	Schmidt & Co. (HK) Ltd	☎833 0330
(light meters)		
Hanimex †	Hanimex (HK) Ltd	☎363 6313
Hasselblad †	Shriro (HK) Ltd	☎524 5031
Kodak †	Kodak (Far East) Ltd	☎564 9333
Konica	Konica HK Ltd	☎575 7288
Leica	Schmidt & Co. (HK) Ltd	☎833 0222
Mamiya	Narwood Ltd	☎344 9381
Metz †	Jebsen & Co. Ltd	☎873 7878
Minolta †	Minolta HK Ltd	☎565 8181
Minox	Colorprint Ltd	☎873 7934
Nikon †	Shriro (HK) Ltd	☎524 5031
Nissin †	Jebsen & Co. Ltd	☎873 7878
Olympus	Kingstone Development Co	☎730 5663
Ozeck (lens)	China Sales Corporation	☎543 3922
		☎543 7272
Paximat †	Melchers (HK) Ltd	☎546 9069
Polaroid	Polaroid Far East Ltd	☎895 1725
Praktica Co. Ltd	Hong Kong China Mercantile	☎545 2286

† HKTA Member

AUDIO/ELECTRICAL/ELECTRONIC EQUIPMENT

Brand	**Sole Agent**	**Phone No**
Aiwa	Aiwa/Dransfield & Co. Ltd	☎787 0838
Akai	Y.S. Tso Ltd	☎723 5252
B & W	Wing Fung Audio Trading Co	☎790 8903
Bang & Olufsen	Bang & Olufsen (HK) Ltd	☎526 8800
Bose	Pacific Audio Supplies Ltd	☎760 7818
Hitachi	Hitachi (HK) Ltd	☎780 4351
JVC	Shun Hing JVC Ltd	☎722 0320
Kenwood	Kenwood & Lee Electronic Ltd	☎525 1204
Marantz Corporation Ltd	Forward International	☎521 0883
Nagra	J.H. Trachsler (HK) Ltd	☎563 1223
Nakamichi	TRP Consumer Electronics Ltd	☎887 2008
National †	Shun Hing Electronic Trading	☎733 3833
Ortofon Co. Ltd †	Dah Ghong Hong Ltd	☎846 8190
Pentax	Jebsen & Co. Ltd	☎873 7921
Philips †	Philips (HK) Ltd	☎524 9566
Pioneer	Shinwa Engineering Co. Ltd	☎854 2053

Proton †	Elephant Radio Co. Ltd	☎520 2330
Quad	Radio People Ltd	☎877 2008
Sansui †	Wo Kee Hong Ltd	☎523 1036/5
Sanyo Co. Ltd	Tatt Sing Sanyo Electric	☎524 5114
Sharp	Sharp-Roxy (HK) Ltd	☎822 9311
Sony †	Chung Yuen Electrical Co. Ltd	☎543 1227
		☎780 0311
Teac †	Dah Chong Hong Ltd	☎846 8190
Technics Co. Ltd †	Shun Hing Electronic Trading	☎733 3833
Thorens	Edward Keller Ltd	☎895 0888
Toshiba	Man On Toshiba Ltd	☎730 6461
Yamaha †	Tom Lee Music Co. Ltd	☎723 9932, ext.115

† HKTA Member

BOOKS

Most shops in tourist areas are members of four large groups: **Swindon's**, **SCMP Family Bookstores**, **Bookazine** and **Jumbo Grade A**. All carry reasonably good selections of travel titles and current books on Hong Kong, China and the rest of Asia. Mainland China controls a number of bookstores, which are worth visiting for their translations.

The best book values in Hong Kong are to be had at the **government bookstore** in the Hong Kong General Post Office near Star Ferry, and at **Urban Council** museums or entertainment center bookstalls. Books published by both are subsidized and so extremely cheap. URBCO's exhibition catalogs in full color are especially good finds.

Unless locally published, books are expensive — up to 16 per cent over the list price of foreign publishers. This is disguised by the use of an artificial exchange rate to translate US dollars or sterling into Hong Kong dollars, and has traditionally been justified by dealers as a way to cover shipping costs.

This is an incongruous explanation, given that Hong Kong is the world's fifth-largest exporter of English-language books and that many, if not most, of those marked-up books are printed here.

CHUNG HWA BOOK CO.

Main Store, 450-452 Nathan Rd., Kowloon ☎*385-6588/385-1811/385-7238. Map 7C3.*

There are three floors here, with books from China on most subjects, as well as a Taiwan section. The 3rd floor has an English book section and a gallery that sells superb and expensive reproductions of classical paintings from the national museums. A second shop is at **760A Nathan Rd.** (☎*394-6375, map 7B2).*

COMMERCIAL PRESS LTD.

9-15 Yee Wo St., Causeway Bay ☎*790-8028. Map 6C8.*

The basement has a good selection of stamps and stationery; the 1st floor features English and foreign-language books, and a good selection of children's books; the 3rd floor is the art section, with a gallery exhibiting mainland painters and lots of art books in English and Chinese. A second shop is the **Stamps and Art Centre** *(28 Wellington St., Hong Kong* ☎ *522-6503, map*

153

3 B3), with a wide selection of stamps and albums. Commercial Press also publishes its own English-language titles, mostly textbooks and some general-subject works. Pick up their catalog if you visit.

JOINT PUBLISHING CO. READER'S SERVICE CENTRE

9 Queen Victoria St., Central ☎*525-0102. Map 3B3.*

Good selections of books on offer here; also stamps. Also tapes and records — Western classical as well as Chinese.

PARENTHESES (CONTINENTAL BOOKS LTD.)

Flr 4, Duke of Wellington House, 14 Wellington St., Central ☎*526-9215. Open 10am-7pm. Map 3B3.*

A French-language bookstore and video club which, judging by its address, has clearly forgiven the British for Waterloo. It publishes a magazine, *Parentheses,* which is what most people

have come to call this shop, tucked into a converted office space. This is a good place to buy French-language music for those with a Jacques Brel or Edith Piaf bent and, being a French bookstore, *vins de France* are thoughtfully provided for purchase from racks near the entranceway. *Très bon!*

WANDERLUST

Flr 1, 30 Hollywood Rd. (entrance on Shelley St.) ☎*523-2042. Map 3B2.*

This unique bookstore, built around the theme of travel, is by far the best place for travel guides in Hong Kong and possibly in all of Asia. It was founded by two Americans, one formerly the editor of a travel magazine and the other a financial journalist. The selection is very well presented, with travel interpreted in its broadest and best senses to include culturally relevant novels, essays and historical monographs as well as pocket guides, maps and coffee-table photo surveys.

CLOTHES

Hong Kong has become the world's 11th-largest trading nation built largely on the back of clothing exports, which still comprise more than a third of all the territory's exports, although electronics and other categories are nibbling at its lead. There is virtually nothing made to fit the body or to be carried as an accessory by it that you cannot buy here.

Every major American, British, French, Italian, German, Spanish and Japanese signature design house quietly manufactures here and in China and loudly lets its presence be known in the chic shopping centers or hotel arcades: **Alfred Dunhill**, **Bally**, **Bennetton**, **Burberry's**, **Celine**, **Daks**, **Giorgio Armani**, **Issey Miyaki**, **Calvin Klein**, **Gucci**, **Givenchy**, **Hermès**, **Loewe**, **Louis Vuitton**, **Kenzo**, **Valentino**, **Nina Ricci**, **D'Urban** *et al.* Hong Kong's duty-free port status and absence of luxury retail sales taxes mean savings of up to 25 percent over New York or Tokyo or Paris. Southeast Asians who are heavily taxed at home for such goods are regular customers, as are the travelers from these labels' home countries.

There is a significant indigenous design industry as well. Hong Kong designers such as Diane Freis and Eddie Lau have made their reputations for ready-to-wear creations at the Paris *Pret-à-Porter* show and others.

The HKTA's free *Factory Outlets* guide lists more than 50 ready-to-wear shops, covering every known clothes fabric from lace to lizard skin. For more than a decade, American author Dana Goetz has published a

Complete Guide to Factory Bargains, which she updates annually. Excess stock, overruns and quality-control rejects in Western sizes, originally intended for export, abound in Hong Kong.

Tailored clothes

There are more than 2,500 tailors in Hong Kong whose skills are legendary. Bring them a picture, pick your desired cloth and they will replicate it, or just select from their existing catalog. In some windows you will see pictures of them standing proudly with people such as George Bush, Ronald Reagan and Prince Charles, for whom they've made clothes. Virtually every office building with a shopping arcade has at least one tailor within. Those tailors and the ones in major hotel arcades are best attuned to Western tastes and sizes, and are more expensive. Tailors will keep your measurements on file for 3 years, and can fulfill mail orders with them. A 50 percent deposit with an order is usually required unless they already know you.

Furs and leather

The Siberian Fur Store has been here for almost 60 years, indicating the territory's well-established position as a fur center. In the past decade, however, Hong Kong has become the world's 5th-largest fur exporter.

Where there's fur there's leather, and the bags and jackets of all the big names of Germany, Italy and Spain are here, as are good selections without designer labels in various outlets and at the **China Products** clothing departments.

Where to look

The HKTA's free *Shopping* booklet offers a full selection of clothiers, but in the following list a representative few that are always worth a visit are described briefly.

A-MAN HING CHEONG CO.

M4, Mandarin Arcade, Mandarin Hotel, Central ☎ *522-3336. Map 3B3.*
Men's tailors. Pure cotton shirts and good-quality suits at fair prices.

H. BAROMAN

Swire House, Central ☎ *523-6845. Map 3B3.*
Top-quality workmanship — with top prices to match.

BLUE ANGEL FUR CO.

Shop 221, Edinburgh Tower, The Landmark, Central ☎ *525-2339. Map 3B3.*
A wide selection with good-quality furs. Another shop is at **48 Mody Rd.**, Tsimshatsui *(map 7E3).*

BOUTIQUE PARKLAND (a.k.a. LA-WINS CO.)

Rm 133-134, Melbourne Plaza, Queen's Rd., Central ☎ *524-1316/522-6285. Map 3B3*

A dependable tailor with a good selection of quality suit and shirt materials. Prices are a bit better for their being in a building with mostly local business traffic, rather than tourists.

CAMBERLEY ENTERPRISES LTD.

Grd Flr, Kaiser Estate Phase II, 51 Man Yue St., Hunghom, Kowloon ☎ *333-7038. Map 8D5.*
Anne Klein II classic-style clothes, leatherwear, cashmere, knits, silks, from about HK$200 and up. There's another shop at **813 Swire House**, Central *(* ☎ *524-6264, map 3B3),* one of the best-known factory outlets.

DAVID'S SHIRTS

Grd Flr, Wing Lee Building, 33 Kimberley Rd., Kowloon ☎ *367-9556. Map 7E3.*
Good-value shirts for both men and women. Other branches are at the **Royal Garden Hotel** *(Tsimshatsui East, Kowloon, map 7E3* ☎ *366-7092)*

and the **Mandarin Hotel** (*Central* ☎ 524-2979, *map 3 B3*).

FOUR SEASONS ARTS AND CRAFTS LTD
Grd Flr, Phase II, Kaiser Estate, 22 Man Lok St., Hunghom, Kowloon ☎ 365-2526. *Map 8D5.*

Despite the name, the only "arts and crafts" found here are silk combination sets, which are overruns from shipments sent off to fill order books from virtually every major American department store. If you like silk and expensive fashions and you don't tell anyone wearing the same outfit from Macy's or Gimbel's the name on your collar label, you can save so much money buying things here that it hurts (but only when you pay the bill).

HIMALAYA LEATHER GOODS
130A Cheung Chau Gallery, Ocean Terminal Deck 1, Tsimshatsui, Kowloon ☎ 367-4617. *Map 7F2.*

A wide selection of leather goods, most imported, but not designer labels; also Hong Kong-made leather goods.

ISETAN
Sheraton Hotel Arcade, 20 Nathan Rd., Tsimshatsui, Kowloon ☎ 369-0111. *Map 7F3.*

The least expensive of the Japanese clothing stores, fairly mass-market.

JINDO FUR SALON
308-309 World Finance Centre, Harbour City, Tsimshatsui, Kowloon ☎ 730-9208, *map 7E2, and Grd Flr, 17-19 Percival St., Causeway Bay* ☎ 572-9577, *map 6C8.*

One of the larger fur shops, with a big display area, carrying Saga, Emba and Blackgama.

KID-BIZ
Shop 39, B2, New World Centre, Tsimshatsui East, Kowloon ☎ 369-0497. *Map 7F3.*

A wide selection of children's wear from Japan. Other branches are located in **Sogo Department Store,** Causeway Bay (☎ 833-8338, *map 6 C8*) and **Tokyu Department Store** (*New World Centre* ☎ 721-7450, *map 7 F3*).

LAFAYETTE
Shop 21, Central Building, Queen's Rd., Central ☎ 523-8088. *Map 3B3.*
Italian shoes at reasonable prices. There is another shop at **Causeway Bay Mansions**, Causeway Bay (☎ 790-6886, *map 6 C8*).

LANCEL BOUTIQUE
Mitsukoshi, Hennessy Centre, Causeway Bay ☎ 795-6597. *Map 6C8.*
Lancel's designer handbags, leather goods. Another branch is at the **Peninsula Hotel** (☎ 368-3313, *map 7 F3*).

MISS O
Room 801, Sands Building, 17 Hankow Rd., Tsimshatsui, Kowloon ☎ 367-2575. *Map 7E3.*
A good selection of silk dresses, both day and evening wear, with better designs and lower prices than some outlets. Another branch is at **Room 404, D'Aguilar Place** (*1-5 D'Aguilar St., Central* ☎ 526-0731, *map 3 B3*).

MITSUKOSHI
500 Hennessy Rd., Causeway Bay ☎ 576-5222. *Map 6C8.*
Four floors with a wide selection of men's, women's and children's clothing, and an art gallery selling fine lithographs, porcelain and ceramics.

MOTHERCARE
Shop 338-340, Flr 3, Prince's Bldg., 10 Chater Rd., Central ☎ 5223-5704, *map 5C4, and Shop 2137, Ocean Terminal, Harbour City, Canton Rd., Tsimshatsui, Kowloon* ☎ 735-5738, *map 7F2.*
The well-known British infants' and children's accessories and clothing store. Excellent quality, with the emphasis on child safety, but prices are far higher in their class than almost anywhere else in the city.

ORIENTAL PACIFIC
Room 602, Sands Building, 17 Hankow Rd., Tsimshatsui, Kowloon ☎ 724-2633. *Map 7E3.*
For men, women and children, this is one of the best outlets in the territory for knitwear. Another outlet is at **Room**

612, Star House *(Tsimshatsui* ☎ *724-2633, map 7 F2).*

SIBERIAN FUR STORES
29 Des Voeux Rd., Central ☎*522-1380, map 3B3, and 21 Chatham Rd., Tsimshatsui, Kowloon* ☎*366-7039, map 7E3.*
Established since 1935, Siberian has been decking out ladies of means in furs from Siberia and elsewhere for more than half a century. Never mind that in Hong Kong's climate one can only hope to wear such a coat about 2 weeks a year: after all, there are grand European and American tours to be made in fall and winter. Besides, Chinese restaurants obligingly keep their air conditioning cranked up to full throttle all year round.

SPLENDID DUESSELDORF PRODUCTION LTD.
Unit A, Flr 7, Sun Ping Industrial Bldg., 912-922 Cheung Sha Wan Rd., Cheung Sha Wan ☎*742-2832.*
Germans are extremely active in leather apparel manufacturing, as is proudly reflected in this factory outlet's moniker. **GoldPfiel**, a German bag-and-luggage company at the high end of the price scale, is also represented through its own boutiques in Central and Ocean Terminal, and **Porsche Design** is carried by several department stores.

COMPUTERS

Hong Kong actively discourages the pirating of intellectual property with frequent raids and cooperative involvement with international agencies to break up smuggling rings that specialize in illegal computer clones and unlicensed copies of software disks and manuals. *Caveat emptor:* ensure that what you buy is compatible with your electric current at home, with your television broadcast system if it's a game, and with your home country's Customs officers' guidelines for what may be legally imported. With those warnings in mind, you are bound to want to look at both the following renowned computer centers.

ASIA COMPUTER PLAZA
Lower Grd Flr, Silvercord, 30 Canton Rd., Tsimshatsui, Kowloon ☎*734-6111. Map 7E2.*
Two floors of a shopping mall devoted entirely to computers (more than 30 makes, all name brands, no counterfeits), peripherals, software, games, books.

GOLDEN SHOPPING ARCADE
156 Fuk Wah St., Shamshuipo, Kowloon.
Trade fluctuates, not for want of custom but because of frequent raids as Hong Kong cracks down on computer pirates. Cheap IBM and Apple compatibles, terrific peripherals, software treasures — but visitors may have problems taking them home, so check first.

FABRICS

As you would expect in such a great garment center, all manner of fabrics can be found here. Silks from the people who first unwound that mile of thread from around the worm's cocoon are available at all the **China Products** shops, along with some very interesting tie-dyed blue-and-white cottons.

Ironically, in perhaps the world's archetypal clothes-making center, few people apart from those who do piecework for garment factories can sew — so there aren't many clothing fabric shops *per se*. Most fabric shops are for curtains and couch covers. Besides silks and country cottons from China, there are some fine fabrics from India and Japan at specialty shops. Wellington St., between D'Aguilar St. heading w to the junction at Lyndhurst Terrace, has become a center of such shops.

ÇA VA
Grd Flr, 34 Man Yue St., Hunghom, Kowloon
☎ 362-9303. Map *8D5*.
A wide selection of quality silks. Other shops are at **1522 Central Building** *(Pedder St., Central, Hong Kong* ☎ *525-7524, map 3B3)* and **1726 Star House** *(Tsimshatsui* ☎ *723-1922, map 7E2)*.

DESIGN SELECTION
Grd Flr, 39 Wyndham St., Central
☎ 525-8339/525-8330 ☒ 521-7980. Map *3C3*.
Striking Asian cottons in textures are a specialty here. They make beautiful and durable couch and accessory covers. Note especially the heavily textured Indian cottons, which make very striking furniture covers.

EASTERN FABRIC
Upper Grd Flr, Ivy House, 18 Wyndham St., Central ☎ 524-4003. Map *3C3*.
British proprietor Jacky Andrews op-ened here in 1980 and has made excellent use of a very small shop space in converted office quarters. The stock rotates regularly, but there is always a fine supply of *futon* fabrics, *kimonos* and *obi*, books about things Japanese, odds and ends such as lacquerware, fans, *shoji*-paper hanging lampshades, wooden lamps and room dividers, folding kimono racks, etc. As things from the land of the rising Yen go, prices are kept quite fair.

WING ON STREET (a.k.a. CLOTH ALLEY)
Between Des Veoux and Queen's Rds., Sheung Wan. Map 3B3.
No serious student of fabric should leave Hong Kong without a stroll through the shops along both sides of this tiny pedestrian lane — the area where what is now Hong Kong's and, arguably, the world's most mammoth garment industry was born during the Korean War.

GENERAL AND DEPARTMENT STORES
There are three types of department stores: mainland Chinese, Japanese and home-grown Hong Kong. Those of the last group are least interesting, in that they generally have poorer selections and higher prices for things imported from Western Europe and the United States than can be found overseas (these include **Sincere, Wing On, Dragon Seed** and **Lane Crawford**). The British group, **Marks & Spencer**, now has five stores.

The Japanese are clear leaders, with some 40 percent of total department store sales. They are moving in on the local stores: Seiyu now owns 40 percent of **Wing On**, and Tokyu recently took control of **Dragon Seed**. Their most bizarre contribution so far has been the building of a Hunghom district shopping center in the shape of a luxury cruise ship.

Cityplaza in the Taikoo Shing housing complex (atop Tai Koo MTR station in North Point; buses 2, 20 and 21 from Central) is a mammoth shopping and entertainment center, with its own ice skating rink, periodic Chinese cultural shows for free, and ongoing exhibitions or *divertissements* to keep up interest.

Mammoth "Ginza-style" shopping/entertainment islands (meaning simply without commercial office spaces) are planned for the New Towns in the New Territories (Shatin, Tuen Mun *et al*), where the Japanese **Yaohan** is a big name. One such has already begun at Site 12 of the Whampoa Garden housing estate in Hunghom, East Kowloon, with the opening of **Hong Kong Place**, billed as "the largest tourist shopping arcade in Southeast Asia" when it opened in August 1991.

Meanwhile, Wharf Properties, the corporation behind Hong Kong Ocean Terminal, is busy building **Times Square** in Causeway Bay, expected to have the greatest number of shops and restaurants under one roof in Hong Kong, with 14 shopping floors and 2 basement shop levels, upon its completion in 1993.

CHINA PRODUCTS

19-31 Yee Wo St., Causeway Bay
☎*890-8321. Map 6C8.*
Perhaps the most representative of the People's Republic stores, and the biggest downscale shop, along with **Chinese Merchandise Emporium**. A terrific jumble of goods in fantastic variety and quantity. A second branch a few blocks away (*488 Hennessy Rd., Causeway Bay* ☎*577-0222, map 6C8*) is smaller than the main shop, but great for bargains.

CHINESE ARTS AND CRAFTS

Central Branch, Shell House, 24 Queen's Rd., Central ☎*522-6758. Map 3C3.*
A good selection of arts and crafts. Other items include sequinned clothes and bags, silk pajamas and underwear, and some designer wear by Hong Kong designers such as Eddie Lau (silks) and jewelry designer Kai Yin Lo. The shop holds good sales. There are four other branches of Chinese Arts and Crafts that between them sell a variety of things from cameras to herbal medicines. Addresses are: **Star House** (*Tsimshatsui* ☎*735-4061, map 7F2*), **30 Canton Rd.** (*Tsimshatsui* ☎*731-1333, map 7E2*), **New World Centre** (*Tsimshatsui* ☎*369-7760, map 7F3*) and **Nathan Rd.** (*Yaumatei* ☎*730-0061, map 7D3*).

CHINESE MERCHANDISE EMPORIUM

92-104 Queen's Rd., Central ☎*524-1051. Map 3B3.*
Seven floors altogether, with goods piled up everywhere, and a large supermarket. Everything is here, from clothing to sporting goods and stationery to toys.

CHUNG KIU CHINESE PRODUCTS EMPORIUM

Main Store, 17 Hankow Rd., Tsimshatsui, Kowloon ☎*723-3211. Map 7E3.*
The usual selection of arts and crafts, mass-produced and not always top quality. This is a good place to buy silk quilts, down quilts and winter woolen underwear. There's a good selection of woolen material for men's suits, and a fine choice of bead curtains. The Nathan Rd. branch (*528 Nathan Rd.* ☎*780-2351, map 7C3*) is a smaller version of the main shop — again, bargain prices in quilts, embroidered garments and winter underwear. A third branch (*47-51 Shandong St* ☎*780-2331, map 7B3*) caters to locals, and the products are far more downscale: cheap luggage, Chinese medicine, and bargain prices for small arts and crafts gifts.

DAIMARU (HOUSEHOLD SQ.)

Kingston St., Causeway Bay ☎*576-7321. Map 6B8.*
Daimaru has two stores. **Household Square** (at the address above) has three floors exclusively for houseware. On the ground floor is The Food Paradise, one of the biggest Japanese food displays in Hong Kong.

Fashion Square (*Paterson St., Causeway Bay* ☎*576-7970, map 6C8*) has two big floors, mainly devoted to fashion (designers and other ranks), with a good selection of shoes and of costume jewelry, and the only Japanese Extra Large dress shop (for extra large Japanese, that is). In fact, there is something here for all the family, plus a good sporting goods and sports wear section, cameras, watches, and a café.

DESIGN GALLERY, HONG KONG TRADE DEVELOPMENT COUNCIL

Upper Grd Flr, Hong Kong Convention & Exhibition Centre, 1 Harbour Rd., Wanchai ☎833-4333. Open Mon-Fri 8.30am-5pm; Sat 8.30am-12.30pm. Closed Sun. Map 5C6.

A showcase for Hong Kong-designed products, from Sesame Street toys done under license to handheld calculators and clocks in exotic shapes. There are featured product lines which rotate about every 6 weeks and a variety of items on permanent display. All are available for purchase at fair prices. In broad terms the product lines include garments and accessories, household and decorative items, electrical and electronic products, hardware and general goods.

MATSUZAKAYA

6 Paterson St., Causeway Bay ☎890-6622. Map 6C8.

Typical of the big Japanese stores — four big floors, modern and chic, with everything from fashions to cosmetics, keenly priced bags and shoes to electrical goods, and luggage to stationery. This is a very good store. The **Admiralty** branch *(Queensway Plaza, Admiralty Centre* ☎5-295-671, *map 4C4)* has one floor only, with constant price-cutting sales of hosiery and underwear.

SEIBU

Pacific Place Mall, Tower Two, Queensway ☎868-0111. Map 4C5.

This is the first store opened by this large, upscale department store group outside Japan. It anchors one of the two Pacific Place Mall towers; the other is anchored by a branch of **Lane Crawford**. Seibu's hallmarks are very inventive displays and a remarkable selection of gift items at the ground-floor level beside **Grappa's Restaurant Toscana** (see EATING AND DRINKING, page 127) — from a selection of recycled paper stationery to neon-lit clocks and telephones.

SOGO

East Point Centre, 555 Hennessy Rd., Causeway Bay ☎833-8338. Map 6C8.

Ten floors of Japanese goods, with the widest selections of European and Japanese designer-wear and much else besides. Sits atop the Causeway Bay MTR station.

YAOHAN

New Town Plaza, 18 Shatin Centre St., Shatin, New Territories ☎697-9338. Map 2C4.

The biggest Hong Kong department store, with a staggering 180,000 square feet of floor space on four levels. They recently made headlines by moving their regional headquarters here from Japan and buying a group of ten fast-food restaurants.

YUE HWA CHINESE PRODUCTS EMPORIUM

301-309 Nathan Rd., Kowloon ☎571-2621. Map 7D3.

This is really a sophisticated version of the **China Products** and **Chung Kiu** shops. There are great bargains and sales, with goods displayed in an orderly fashion.

JEWELRY

There are about a half-dozen product ranges in which Hong Kong excels as a shopping center, but clothing and jewelry are the most memorable. This is the world's third-largest diamond trading center; the world's leading center for the cutting and polishing of opals; among the world's top gold trading centers; the largest jade jewelry center; and one of the major regional outlets for cultured pearls and colored precious and semiprecious stones, especially rubies and sapphires, vying with Thailand and Singapore for prominence.

Hong Kong law protects buyers of gold and platinum by requiring it to be sold with the content stamped on the metal. HKTDC goes further and requires its members to stamp the shop's seal inside as well. They also publish the very useful (and free) *Shopping Guide to Jewellery*. The **Gemmological Association of Hong Kong** (☎ *366-6006*) will provide callers with a list of qualified gem testers, and the **Diamond Importers Association Ltd** (DIA) (☎ *523-5497)* will assist curious diamond buyers with tips on quality and recommended outlets.

All shops have their own factories or connections with factories and will copy from a photo any design you request — but watch closely the quality of stones used and the workmanship. It is not uncommon for the stone in that freshly pressed earring or pendant to fall out quickly due to sloppy mounting.

Asians like higher gold content in their jewelry than Westerners, and even hard-use items such as gold bands will usually be no less than 14K (fineness not less than 585, which is the number that will be stamped on the ring) and often 18K. A traditional Chinese shop's gold, called *Chuk Kam,* looks very reddish and bright, is malleable and almost pure (990 will be the minimum fineness; 24K is 999.9), because here gold remains the refugees' flight capital.

They also prefer jade to virtually any other stone, save perhaps diamonds. There are only two substances considered gemstone jade: jadeite or Burmese jade, and nephrite or Old Jade (it originally came from NW China but was played out there centuries ago), or, variously, Taiwan jade, New Zealand jade, Canadian jade. Unless you are deeply taken by it, don't even try to understand the Chinese lexicon of quality in jade. There are pieces of nephrite that look literally like a lump of "mutton fat" (which is what their Chinese name means) over which a devotee may go wild. Buy some for its color and/or carving quality and rest assured that most of what you see that isn't extremely expensive is not true jade, but one of its five simulants — variations on serpentine, soapstone or the quartz family.

CASEY DIAMONDS
Shop 106, Gloucester Tower, The Landmark, Central ☎ *522-0189. Map 3B3.*
Recommended. The designs are modern and are regularly seen at diamond design shows.

DABERA LTD.
Flr 28, Tower I, Admiralty Centre, 18 Harcourt Rd., Central ☎ *527-7722. Map 4C4.*
This shop has been a consistent winner of international diamond jewelry design contests for more than a decade.

An excellent place to see Hong Kong designers at their best.

JADE MARKET
Under the Kansu St. traffic overpass, Yaumatei. Map 7D2. Open 10am-4pm daily.
Morning is the best time to visit the 400 or so stalls licensed to operate here, after being pushed out of the way for redevelopment of the waterfront a decade ago (this used to be called the **Canton Jade Market**, referring to its former location on Canton Rd.). Vendors actually start leaving right after lunch hour (1-2pm). To Chinese, jade is

lucky; it protects against evil and disease — which is why even infants have jade bracelets and lucky ring pendants. It represents beauty, nobility and purity of spirit. HKTA has a free "Factsheet" on the area and the market, which describes five ways to define jade quality. But to a touring Occidental, the best advice is to buy for your own sense of beauty and to bargain hard. The "treasure" of this market is in the pleasure of seeing how much a corner of mankind has done with a single stone material, how wonderfully confused they seem to be about defining quality in something they so highly esteem, and, maybe, in taking home a favored personal memento that will for all time say "China" to you alone.

KAI-YIN & CO.

Flr 2, 4-6 On Lan St., Central ☎*524-8238. Map 3C3.*

Hong Kong designer Kai Yin Lo's costume jewelry is also available at **Chinese Arts and Crafts**, as well as at Bloomingdale's and Saks in the US and Issey Miyake's in Tokyo.

KING FOOK GOLD & JEWELRY

30-32 Des Voeux Rd., Central ☎*523-5111. Map 3B3.*

Well known for its gold jewelry as well as diamonds and other precious stones. The prices are reasonable, and they often have sales.

LARRY JEWELRY

Shops 49-50, Gloucester Tower, The Landmark, Central ☎*521-1268. Map 3B3.*

You will find here a good selection of diamonds, rubies, precious stones and jewelry, and exclusive antique-style jeweled watches.

MIKIMOTO SHOP

Matsuzakaya Department Store, 6 Paterson St., Causeway Bay ☎*576-8319. Map 6C8.*

Cultured pearls, from the people who invented them.

THE OPAL MINE LTD.

Burlington House Arcade, Grd Flr, 92 Nathan Rd. (between Cameron and Granville Rds., opposite the mosque), Tsimshatsui, Kowloon ☎*721-9933. Map 7E3.*

Adds an education and a bit of fun to opal shopping by replicating an Australian mine environment to illustrate the stone's origins. There are uncut opals on the walls and thousands of cut, polished and mounted ones to purchase.

THE SHOWROOM

1203 Central Building, Pedder St., Central ☎*525-7085/522-1573. Map 3B3.*

The Showroom offers a large selection of moderately priced 14K and 18K fashion accessories. Items range from under US$60 to just more than $1,000 — but most are under $500. Proprietor Clare Wadsworth has also been a fine arts dealer in modern Western drawings and prints. She has a reputation for good taste in just about everything and a Peak Rd. clientele who appreciate it, which makes her collection worth a look if you are in the Central business district.

TRIO PEARLS

Peninsula Hotel, Salisbury Rd., Tsimshatsui, Kowloon ☎*367-9171. Map 7F3.*

One of the few Hong Kong jewelers still dealing in precious South Sea pearls. This is also an important antique jade dealer.

MARKETS

Itinerant street markets are an important part of pedestrian life in Hong Kong, where the rate of issue of hawkers' licenses has been one of local government's traditional devices to offset pressure for jobs in time of recession. Even in these days of virtually full employment in Hong Kong, there has been no visible decline in the number or size of street-market districts, nor in their popularity with residents or tourists.

Our selection includes the best known, but there are hundreds more tucked into side streets and areas near housing estates all over Hong Kong.

The rules are simple: bargain hard but cheerfully, and check what you intend to buy carefully for defects before you bother. Prices are so low it may seem mean to do so, but bargaining is a social convention in these markets, where only a fool or a *gweilo* (foreigner) would ever pay the asking price. Since it's likely that a "*gweilo* tax" will have been tacked onto the price in any case, bargaining tends just to get you back down to the local asking price.

JADE MARKET   See JEWELRY, above.

JARDINE'S BAZAAR
Beside Hennessy Centre, Causeway Bay. Map 6C8.
Market stalls packed into narrow lanes: mainly women's casual wear and accessories, also T-shirts, jeans, sportswear. Sizes tend to be small. There are bargain prices, but check the goods.

LADDER STREET
From Man Mo Temple on Hollywood Rd. to Queen's Rd., Central. Map 3B2.
Trash and treasure, side by side. A street stall antique market selling jade carvings and knick-knacks, old watches, reproductions, jewelry, rings, chains — you name it.

LI YUEN STREETS, EAST AND WEST
Pedestrian alleys between Queen's Rd. and Des Voeux Rd., Central. Map 3B3.
Stalls cluttered with copied and faked designer-label bags, casual wear, underwear, children's wear, and great junk jewelry.

MARBLE ST.
At North Point MTR station. Map 2D5.
One of the smaller street markets and not crowded; good for teenage clothes.

POOR MAN'S NIGHTCLUB
Opposite Victoria Hotel at the Macau ferry pier, Central/Western. Map 3A2.
A great variety of goods, but with an emphasis on clothes. There is a fortune-teller whose tame bird chooses your fate. Good seafood *daipaidongs* are everywhere.

STANLEY MARKET
Stanley Town, s Hong Kong. Bus 6 or 260 from Central bus terminal (30-45mins' ride). Open 10am-7pm. Map 2E5.
This is a bargain paradise, open seven days a week. It is the best market for brand-name casual wear, winter sweaters and jackets, and curios in Western sizes.

TEMPLE ST.
Jordan Station to Yaumatei Station, Kowloon. Map 7D3.
One of the best street markets, especially for clothes.

WING ON ST. (CLOTH ALLEY)
Between Queen's Rd. and Des Voeux Rd., Central. Map 3B3.
This is the place for bargains in materials. All the shops sell fabrics: linens, silks, cottons, wool. Quality varies, and haggling produces results.

Sports and recreation

Although many Hong Kong residents are sports enthusiasts, space in the territory is at a premium and sports facilities are not widespread. Many facilities are housed in multipurpose indoor sports complexes and recreational grounds, and applications for their use must be made well in advance. Some sports, such as badminton and tennis, are very popular and allocation is often done by ballot. Sports complexes and recreational grounds in Hong Kong and Kowloon are managed by the Urban Council, which is responsible for the provision of municipal services to Hong Kong residents.

Private clubs offer an alternative to public sports facilities, but usually have limited facilities and are open to members only. With a popular sport such as golf, the waiting period for membership can often be several years. However, most golf and some yachting clubs issue overseas visitors' passes.

Visitors interested in sporting events in and around Hong Kong will find a detailed monthly "Sports Diary" in the Urban Council paper, *City News*, and in a monthly sports calendar published by the Sports Promotion Programme. Both paper and calendar are available at the **City Hall** and the **Government Book Shop** *(in the GPO near the Hong Kong Star Ferry concourse, map 4 B4)*. Another useful publication, *A Guide to the Booking of Urban Council Recreational Facilities,* listing facilities in each district, is available from the Urban Council and the **Sports Promotion Programme** office at Queen Elizabeth Stadium *(18 Oi Kwan Rd., Wanchai ☎ 575-6793, map 5 D7).*

Hong Kong is a participant in the international Olympiad, where its sports people have won medals in archery and bowling, as well as the Asian Games. A Festival of Sport is organized each March as the culmination of the annual build-up to identify talent of international class. It has its own professional soccer teams and is a major venue on various international and regional circuits for most major spectator sports, including badminton, golf, rugby, lawn bowls and tennis.

These are the main locations for sporting events:

Hong Kong Coliseum   9 Cheong Wan Rd., near Hung Hom Ferry, Hung Hom, Kowloon ☎765-9215, map **8**D4

Hong Kong Stadium   So Kong Po, Wanchai ☎576-8828, map **6**D8

Jubilee Sports Centre   Shatin, New Territories ☎605-1212, map **2**C4

Queen Elizabeth Stadium   18 Oi Kwan Rd., Wanchai ☎575-6793, map **5**D7

Victoria Park   Causeway Bay ☎890-5824, map **6**B8-9

Unlike other sports centers in Hong Kong, the Jubilee Sports Centre is an independent organization and not open to the public. Applications must be made for use of the centre's facilities.

Various sporting and recreational activities are discussed in the following pages, arranged alphabetically by subject.

AUTO RACING AND CAR RALLIES

The **Macau Grand Prix** is the auto racing event of the year. International entrants and sponsors arrive in Hong Kong for the races, which are held in November on the Guia Circuit — one of the few places in the world where cars speed around street circuits. The Grand Prix was started in 1954 and is an annual event. Races include Formula Three cars and motorcycles, as well as a go-kart competition and a vintage-car race. It is sponsored by the Leal Senado (Loyal Senate) of Macau, but any Hong Kong driver can participate, and the Hong Kong Automobile Association helps to organize it. For more information on the Grand Prix, call the **Macau Tourist Information Bureau** *(Rm. 305, Shun Tak Centre, 200 Connaught Rd., Central* ☎*540-8180* Fx *559-6513, map 3 A2).*

A major race first run in 1985 is the **555 Rally, Hong Kong-to-Beijing**. Scheduled around September, it covers approximately 3,400km (2,125 miles), with international rally drivers and teams participating. There is also an annual Go-Kart rally held in Victoria Park. For more information on both events, call the **Hong Kong Automobile Association** *(Marsh Road, Wanchai, Hong Kong* ☎*827-8394, map 5 B7).*

BADMINTON

Popular among young people, with major local competitions held annually, this is a major competitive sport in Asia and is followed very seriously. Indonesians have dominated the international competitions in recent years. For details of facilities and events call the **Sports Promotion Programme** *(* ☎*575-6793)* or the **Hong Kong Badminton Association** at Queen Elizabeth Stadium *(* ☎*836-4066).*

BOWLING

A popular sport among local people, this produced an Olympic gold medalist in Ms. Cha Kuk Hung. The major bowling alleys are the following:
Brunswick Bowling Centre   Middle Road (behind YMCA), Kowloon ☎723-8404, map **7**E3
Fourseas Bowling Centre   City Plaza, Taikooshing ☎567-0813
New Town Bowling Centre   New Town Plaza, Shatin, New Territories ☎699-5992, map **2**C4

CHINESE MARTIAL ARTS

The famous Shaolin School form, *taekwando,* traveled with Buddhism to Korea and Japan. It is the most elegant of the North Asian *kung fu* forms, which all derive from Chinese models. (It was once televised *ad*

165

nauseam in an American series starring David Carradine.) The most memorable link here is less with grunts, kicks and lightning punches and more with dance and the elegant *tai chi* exercises (the full name of which translates from the Chinese as the "great ultimate fist" or some such euphemism).

The most interesting aspect of the endless reels of violent *kung fu* epics on the Chinese television channels and at movie theaters is the way that different directors choreograph their fight scenes. Those who are most traditional almost invariably transform the body language into something much closer to ballet than boxing.

A Chinese Martial Arts Invitation Tournament is held each year. Call **Sports Promotion Programme** (☎ *575-6793)* for further information. For inquiries regarding martial arts call the **Hong Kong Chinese Martial Arts Association** (☎ *394-4803).*

GOLF

Late February features the **Cathay Pacific Hong Kong Open** at the Royal Hong Kong Golf Club, with a very large purse and many golfers of international rank participating. Golf is extremely popular among business executives and political leaders in Asia, most of all in Hong Kong, where it was founded by Scots (who, after all, created the game). It is not unusual for Japanese men to arrive on strictly golf tours, while their wives shop in the Japanese department stores and European boutiques in town.

Enthusiasts should contact the following golf clubs for reservations as early as possible:

Royal Hong Kong Golf Club   Deep Water Bay ☎812-7070, map 2E4; Fanling, New Territories ☎670-1211, map 2B4. This celebrated its centenary in 1989 and actually includes four courses in two locations, both of which began operations in 1911: Deepwater Bay Golf Club, with a 9-hole course on Hong Kong Island, and Fanling Golf Club in the New Territories, with three 18-hole championship courses, the "Old," the "New" and the "Eden." This last was designed in the early 1970s by Peter Thomson and Michael Wolveridge. All open to visitors only on weekdays, excluding public holidays.

Clearwater Bay Golf and Country Club   Saikung Peninsula, New Territories ☎719-1595. The Hong Kong Tourist Association offers a sports and recreation tour for golfers at this club. It is rumored that the number of balls its distracting beauty causes golfers to lose each month currently approaches 5,000! Designed by Japanese architects T. Sawai and A. Furukawa, the first nine holes opened in 1982 and the second in 1987. It is approximately 45 minutes' drive from Tsimshatsui. For inquiries call HKTA's Tour Development Department (☎ *801-7111).*

Discovery Bay Golf Course   Lantau ☎987-7271, map 1D3. Reservations for this course can be made one week in advance. Designed by Robert Trent Jones Jr., it is terraced into a mountainside, from which there are spectacular views of Hong Kong's harbor.

New Town Plaza   Shatin, New Territories ☎699-5992, map 2C4. 18-hole mini golf course and practice range on the roof terrace.

HORSE RACING

By far the most popular spectator sport in Hong Kong, with the world's richest purses: total bets in 1989 were nearly US$5.6 billion. Races regularly attract crowds of almost 50,000 people at each of the two race tracks, and the current one-day betting record stands at US$114 million.

The horse-racing season runs from September to June. Races are run on Wednesdays and Saturdays and sometimes on Sundays, at **Happy Valley Race Track**, Hong Kong Island *(map 5 D7)* or at **Shatin Race Track** in the New Territories *(map 2 C5)*. Happy Valley has also featured night racing since 1973.

About 130 off-track betting centers are dotted throughout Hong Kong and the territories. For those aged 18 and over, the Hong Kong Tourist Association offers a "Come Horse Racing" tour package, which includes transfers, guide service, lunch or dinner, and a ticket to the members' enclosure (☎ *801-1711 for details)*. For those who wish to go alone, the Royal Hong Kong Jockey Club offices adjacent to the racecourse in Happy Valley will give visitors a badge on presentation of a passport containing a Hong Kong entry date. The badge must be purchased by 5pm on the day preceding the race meet.

Racing is operated exclusively by the Royal Hong Kong Jockey Club, a government-sanctioned and protected monopoly which must distribute a portion of its enormous annual profits to good works and public recreation projects as quid pro quo for the privilege of official patronage.

ICE-SKATING

City Plaza *(Taikooshing* ☎ *567-0813, map 2 D5)* has one ice-skating rink, at which classes are available. There is also a rink in **Lai Chi Kok Amusement Park** *(Lai Chi Kok, Kowloon* ☎ *744-2960, map 7 B2)*. Why ice-skating in Hong Kong's tropical heat? Perhaps as an antidote, but more likely as an exoticism.

RUGBY

Every Easter, Hong Kong plays host to the annual "Invitation Sevens" competition, with more than 24 international teams from abroad competing in two days of matches organized by the **Hong Kong Rugby Football Union** *(Block A, Rm 1401, Sea View Estate, North Point* ☎ *566-0719)*. Almost 30,000 tickets for this event are normally sold out well in advance.

Seven-a-side is a faster-paced variation of the Rugby Union game, which normally has 15 players per team. Both games bear some resemblance to American football — but are close only in the way that Tokyo is closer to Los Angeles than is Vladivostok.

For those interested in joining a team, this union is very helpful.

RUNNING

There are races and runs almost every weekend of the year. The **Hong Kong International Marathon** is in January; in March, there is the **Coast of China Marathon**; in December, the **Shum Chun** (a.k.a. Shenzhen) marathon takes place just over the China border.

Five different companies sponsor running events. Adidas have a "King of the Road" series over 10-20 kilometers; Brooks sponsor 10-kilometer races from September to February; Nike sponsor a half-marathon in November, a Ladies Race in December and a 15-kilometer run in March; HongkongBank sponsor a "Seven Reservoirs Series" from September to March; and Asics Tiger sponsor cross-country races. There are also charity runs in the form of a Rickshaw Derby in August, and a Sedan Chair Race on the Peak in November.

Overseas entrants are welcome to all the above-mentioned events.

There are 18 running tracks in Hong Kong. Active organizations include:

Athletic Veterans of Hong Kong   GPO Box 10368, Hong Kong ☎891-6197

Hash House Harriers   c/o Community Advice Bureau, 8 Garden Rd., Central ☎524-5444, map **4C4**

Hong Kong Adventist Hospital Running Clinic   40 Stubbs Rd., Mid-Levels ☎740-6211, map **6F8**

Hong Kong Distance Runners Club   GPO Box 10368, Hong Kong ☎571-5512

Hong Kong Ladies Road Runners Club   GPO Box 20613, Hennessy Rd., Hong Kong ☎841-8223 (men can join as associates)

Bowen Rd. *(map 4 D4),* just above the business district, has a marked course and training obstacles and is the focal point for Hong Kong's joggers' each morning, evening and weekend. The **Hongkong Hilton** (see WHERE TO STAY) is such a short jog away that they provide maps for joggers in guests' rooms, and an early-morning minibus service up to Bowen Rd. for those who need a running start.

Other popular running courses include **Victoria Park** in Causeway Bay *(map 6 B8-9),* **Kowloon Park** in Tsimshatsui *(map 7E3)* and the **waterfront promenade** that hugs the harborfront from the Star Ferry's Kowloon concourse to the upper reaches of Tsimshatsui East *(map 7F2-8E4).*

There are, in all, 15 jogging tracks in the urban areas of Hong Kong and Kowloon run by the Urban Council.

SAILING AND WINDSURFING

The major yachting event in the region is the biennial **South China Sea Race**, run from Hong Kong to the Philippines. The event was originally based on a 1959 test cruise by the yacht *Morasum,* and the first race was held in 1962. Races are scheduled for 1992 and 1994, and it is possible to sign on as crew for experienced "yachties." Look for notices on marina boards. Alternate years, there is a race to Macau.

The **Royal Hong Kong Yacht Club** *(Kellet Island, Causeway Bay* ☎832-2817, *map 5 B7)* is the only club that has reciprocal arrangements with overseas clubs. If you can produce your own club membership card you are entitled to use their facilities. There are many other yacht clubs and marinas around Hong Kong, but their facilities can be used by members only.

For information on chartered junks and boats call the **Hong Kong**

Tourist Association *(☎ 801-7111)* for a list of boat-chartering companies.

Harbor tours are available on board the fleet of motorized Chinoiserie-crafts of **Watertours of Hong Kong Ltd** *(☎ 730-3031 for information, 525-4808 for reservations),* who operate the mock-junk with a huge Canon camera company sign atop it between Start Ferry Kowloon terminal and Blake's Pier in Central; on one of a dozen **Star Ferry Co. Ltd** ferries *(☎ 366-7024 for reservations);* or on the *Duk-ling,* billed as Hong Kong's only authentic sailing junk by her French owners, **Detours Ltd** *(☎ 311-6111).*

Windsurfing equipment can be rented at most beaches. Flying Fifteen World Championships windsurfing competitions are held in November at various beaches. For information on rentals and classes contact any of the following:

Cap Windsurfing   ☎367-1630
Cheung Chau Windsurfing Centre   ☎981-0719
Proshop   ☎801-0094
Windsurf Boutique   ☎366-9911

SNOOKER/POOL/BILLIARDS

Places where cue-and-ball games can be played are classified as clubs, and visitors will have to pay a small membership fee before they can play. They include the following:

Asia Billiard City Club   Flr 3, 14 Science Museum Rd., Culture Centre, Tsimshatsui East, Kowloon ☎369-3398, map **8E4**, open year-round 24 hours a day

Peninsula Billiard Club   Flr 3, Peninsula Centre, 57 Mody Rd., Tsimshatsui East, Kowloon ☎739-0638, map **7E3**

Prat Billiard Centre   Flr 2, 22-26 Austin Ave. and Grd Flr, Austin Tower, Kowloon ☎333-5591, map **7E3**

Woodland Lake Club   287-299 Queen's Rd., Central, Centremark Building ☎815-1166, map **3C3**

SOCCER

Several competitions are run during the year, including the Amateur Soccer Knock-out Competition and the Summer Youth Soccer League Competitions, at various grass pitches dotted around the city and at the Mongkok Stadium. For inquiries, contact the **Sports Promotion Centre** *(☎ 575-6793).*

There is a professional league that plays in season at the Hong Kong Stadium.

SWIMMING

There are 41 officially listed swimming beaches in Hong Kong, Kowloon and the New Territories, many of which can become seriously polluted. Beaches rated by the authorities as clean enough for swimming are listed in the daily newspapers during the season. There is no way to say in advance which will be clean. It depends on the tides, effluents *et al.* But they are tested regularly, rated scrupulously and

169

closed to public swimming if deemed a health hazard. Of the 41 bathing beaches, 12 are in Hong Kong and Kowloon and the rest in the New Territories.

In the urban districts, there are also 14 swimming pool complexes containing 92 pools (used by more than 4 million people a year), and a further four in the New Territories.

They include the following:

Kowloon Park Swimming Pool   ☎724-3577, map **7E3**
Kowloon Tsai Swimming Pool   ☎336-5817, map **8A4**
Morrison Hill Swimming Pool   ☎575-3028, map **5C7**
Victoria Park Swimming Pool   ☎570-4682, map **6B9**

For **disabled swimmers** there are particularly good facilities at the following:

Aberdeen Swimming Pool Complex   ☎553-3617, map **2E4**
Physically Handicapped and Able Bodied Association's Centre   Pokfulam ☎551-4161
Tai Wan Shah Swimming Pool   Kowloon ☎333-1335

Private pools are open to members and guests only. Some hotels have swimming pools (look for the 🏊 symbol in hotels listed in WHERE TO STAY).

There is an annual Cross-Harbour Swim in October, a course of about 1,500 meters (1,650 yards) from Kowloon Public Pier to Queen's Pier on Hong Kong Island. Both men's and women's records are just under 20 minutes, remarkable in view of the strong cross-currents in the harbor, plastic bags, ship's oil, garbage and sewage from urban outfalls with which the swimmers must contend.

TENNIS AND SQUASH

Major annual professional tennis and squash tournaments are held at **Victoria Park** and the **Hong Kong Squash Centre** in Hong Kong Park.

The Urban Council operates 7 tennis courts and 112 squash courts, but both sports are popular and the courts are very much in demand. For public courts inquire at **Victoria Park** (☎ 570-6186), which has both tennis and squash facilities. Other tennis centers are to be found at **Bowen Road Tennis Courts** (☎ 528-2983), the **Hong Kong Tennis Centre** (☎ 574-9122) and **Queen Elizabeth Stadium** (☎ 575-6793). The **Hong Kong Squash Centre** (☎ 869-0611/0088/0802) is in Hong Kong Park in Central district.

WALKING

A total of 21 country parks — protected areas of countryside covering 40 percent of the territory's landmass — exist in Hong Kong and her outlying territories. The cooler months of October to April are the best time to walk. For information call the **Agriculture and Fisheries Department, Country Parks Branch** (☎ 733-2235). The three best-known walks are the following:

- The **MacLehose Trail** in Saikung peninsula, a 60-mile route in full, which cuts through 8 country parks and can take 2 days to traverse.

- The **Lantau Trail**, which circles this large island for a distance of more than 40 miles from Silvermine Bay (a.k.a. Mui Wo).
- The **Taitam Reservoir** country park, around which one can walk an inner circle of Hong Kong Island that runs from Old Peak Rd. in Mid-Levels heading E to North Point, then S to the opposite coast of the island at Repulse Bay without ever seeing a single vehicle or hearing a single horn — while being often within 5 minutes' walk of a major urban thoroughfare.

There are two books of routes available: *Twelve Walks in Hong Kong* by Derek Kemp, the best known, and *Magic Walks* by Kaarlo Schepel. *Another Hong Kong: An Explorer's Guide* (Ed. Alan Moores) contains some interesting walks and guidance on other outdoor activities, including bicycling, diving, fishing and exploring the remote outer islands.

Excursions

Exploring the Hong Kong hinterland

The fascination of Hong Kong itself tends to forestall the desire to investigate other options outside the city area. Yet the tantalizing difficulty for the visitor is that Hong Kong is a superb base for exploring other parts of the region, starting with the colony's own hinterlands. In the following pages we look at some exciting possibilities for excursions. Some are close to Hong Kong, others farther afield.

THE ISLANDS — AN INTRODUCTION

Hong Kong has 235 offshore islands, most of them uninhabited, hard to get to and hardly worth the effort, since they offer little that cannot be found on the main islands of **Lantau**, **Cheung Chau**, **Peng Chau** and **Lamma**. These four are easy to reach by ferry from the **Outlying Islands Pier** in Central.

Lantau offers excellent walking and needs a full day, or half a day if you are not a walker. Cheung Chau merits half a day, Lamma and Peng Chau rather less.

All four islands have commuter populations, and ferries at commuting times are crowded. On summer weekends and holidays, ferries and islands alike can be incredibly crowded and frankly are best avoided, although the Hong Kong Yaumatei Ferry Co. (HYF), which runs all inter-island services under government franchise, adds extra sailings on crowded weekends and holidays. Normal schedules for most island services are either 40 minutes or hourly, and more frequent during busy commuting periods. HYF also operates hovercrafts, which cut travel times in half. Ferry services can be suspended on short notice at the approach of a typhoon.

LANTAU ISLAND
Map 1E1-D3.
Hong Kong's biggest island is a backwater — and that is its charm. Between three small towns and several big villages there are vast empty tracts of mountain slopes, gorges, hidden valleys and superb coasts. Here and there stands the occasional old village and its old people, very similar to parts of the SAIKUNG PENINSULA (see page 175), although Lantau's villages are far older.

Lantau's Buddhist monasteries are a special feature. The best known is **Po Lin** (see pages 23 and 75) at Ngong Ping, a high plateau below Sunset Peak (where you can also go horseback riding at the adjacent **Lantau Tea Gardens**). But others too are worth a visit.

The wooded slopes of **Keung Shan**, below Po Lin, leading down to the fishing town of Tai O, are studded with fine old monasteries and temples, where, according to the nuns, nothing has changed in 50 years. Take the Tai O bus from Silvermine Bay ferry pier and get off at the Po Lin stop; walk on down the road for a couple of hundred yards to a minor road on the right, leading to the monasteries.

The path rejoins the main road farther down, where you can catch another bus on to **Tai O**, an old fishing town built on a three-legged creek across a small peninsula. It's a picturesque place, with two long main streets of traditional shops and stores. Many of its buildings stand on stilts above the creek and were built by boat people moving ashore.

Another monastery walk continues from Po Lin via the Lantau Tea Gardens to the eastern gate, between Lantau and Nei Lak Shan Peaks, and on to the temples and monasteries of **Tei Tong Tsai**, from where a path leads down to Lantau's third town, **Tung Chung**, a rather sleepy place on the NW coast. The footpath from Tung Chung to Tai O offers some fine coastal walking (be quite sure to finish at Tai O rather than Tung Chung, where the last transportation leaves early). The coastal track leading NE from Tung Chung is equally good scenically, passing some fine villages and, after a few miles, turning S and inland to cross the mountains, emerging among the farms and villages of **Mui Wo**, not far from the Silvermine Bay ferry pier.

Ferries also leave Tai O and Tung Chung for Central, but less regularly.

Some of the best beaches and cleanest water in Hong Kong are found along the southern coast of the island at Pui O, Cheung Sha and Tong Fuk, all easily reached by bus or taxi. Silvermine Bay has a good beach, but the water may be polluted.

⇌ Food can be disappointing on Lantau, but the following restaurants have good reputations: **Charley's** (☎ *984-8329*) in Pui O, popular with Westerners and with a good selection of table wines; the **Good View** (☎ *984-8432*), a Chinese restaurant right on Pui O beach (a terrific setting, especially at sundown), which serves reasonable fare; and the serviceable Chinese restaurant of the **Silvermine Bay Hotel** (☎ *984-8295*). **Po Lin** monastery serves a well-known Buddhist vegetarian lunch in a soup-kitchen atmosphere, with quality to match.

CHEUNG CHAU
Map 1E3.

Much smaller than Lantau is the neighboring island of Cheung Chau, which has a fishing harbor that still stands out as one of the best in Hong Kong: a picturesque and vibrant floating community, staunchly conservative and still very traditional. For a tour of the harbor, you can hire a sampan water taxi at the quayside. This is one of the best vantage points from which to view the annual Dragon Boat race in mid-June (see page 51).

The town is still a charming place, its narrow streets crammed with all the colorful commercial life of a typical old Chinese town: traditional medicine halls, jade merchants, goldsmiths, old-fashioned rice shops with brass-bound grain barrels, porcelain shops, incense and funeral-paper shops, fishing-boat chandlers, general dealers, fruit and vegetable stalls, wet markets, Chinese cake shops, and kiosks selling cooling herbal teas. Only the occasional bank, boutique, supermarket or fancy new restaurant breaks the harmony.

There are two good temples: the 18thC **Pak Tai Temple** at the N end of the waterfront (a focus of the famous annual **Bun Festival** in late May (see page 51), and the **Kwun Yam Temple**, on the opposite side of the island.

A well-marked 4-kilometer ($2\frac{1}{2}$-mile) Family Trail for walkers is paved and quite safe for children. A useful purchase from HKTA, the *Cheung Chau Island Walking Tour Guide,* published in 1990, provides sound advice on exploring the island.

Cheung Chau's main beach has a magnificent nighttime view of Hong Kong Island. In the summer it is extremely popular and packed with people.

☙ There is one (almost) international-class hotel, the **Warwick** (☎ *981-0081* ▥), and many vacation flats that can be rented from picture albums at the ferry wharf. There are also many religious retreats and youth camps, which help swell the numbers of vacation travelers. Regrettably, the swell of tourism and the appeal of cheap rents to Hong Kong's growing community of working commuter couples has led to feverish development of tiny vacation "investment flats" in cheaply-made complexes on Cheung Chau.

LAMMA
Map 2E-F4.

This island, which lies between Cheung Chau and Hong Kong Island, has two main villages, each of which has a ferry service to Central. **Yung Shue Wan** is the larger village and has numerous charms, but is marred by the looming presence nearby of a large power station with two enormous chimney stacks.

The other village, **Sok Kwu Wan**, is in a deeply indented bay to the S. Not a very large place, it is famed for its row of seafood restaurants along the waterfront, which serve food harvested from the fish-farming platforms that almost fill the bay. This is a *de rigueur* dinner destination with local yachties and operators of pleasure junks.

A good beach on the other side of the island is reached after a short walk through the woods behind the village, via Lo So Sing, which stands at the opposite corner of the bay to Sok Kwu Wan.

═ Some 50 restaurants at the shoreline beside the public pier all offer much the same fare: fish, crab, shrimps, mussels, clams, octopus, lobster, squid. Their sole means of support is the expatriate clientele of pleasure boats, on summer evenings and all day on weekends and holidays. Wine lists are surprisingly sophisticated (although the WCs remain surprisingly primitive...). *Gaidos* ferry back and forth those visitors without the luxury of their own pleasure boats.

THE NEW TERRITORIES AND THE SAIKUNG PENINSULA

Top half of maps 1 and 2. The Saikung Peninsula is partly shown on map 2C5-6.

It is a shame that so few visitors to Hong Kong take away any clear impression of the city's rural hinterlands. These areas possess an abundance of wonderful scenery, much of it mountainous. They contain many ancient villages, some deserted, others still preserving a centuries-old way of life that has virtually disappeared from mainland China, as a result of modernization and the drift of young people to the cities. These settlements include remarkable walled villages, such as Kat Hing Wai and Wing Lung Wai in the Kam Tin area, enclosures fortified by a high wall and sometimes also by a moat. (Many of these are described on page 82 — see WALLED VILLAGES.)

A large proportion of the land is farmed, mostly as market gardens and fish ponds, and much of what remains has been made into a series of designated country parks (including four on Hong Kong Island itself). They contain rugged, inaccessible mountain and coastal terrain, with superb walks, terrific views, a rich subtropical flora, and abundant wildlife: barking deer, monkeys, foxes, porcupine, pangolin, civets, leopard cats, wild boar and hundreds of species of birds. There is a unique magic in the crystal air of the peaks on a clear October day as one rounds a steep shoulder to discover an old hill farm in the valley below, the silence broken only by the haunting cry of a male cuckoo calling for its mate, who never answers. These are moments of deep natural peace.

The Saikung Peninsula

Virtually the whole of this eastern peninsula is an area of rolling mountains and tor-topped hills, with some superb coastline and beaches. The total population numbers only a few thousand, mostly old people scattered among dozens of villages, more or less in decline. Few of them are served by the road that traverses the peninsula.

As is the case in much of Hong Kong's outlying areas, most of the local people are Hakkas. They arrived in the area later than the Cantonese settlers known as Punti, who had already taken up most of the best land. Saikung was one of the last areas to be settled, less than 300 years ago, and many of its village buildings and temples date from that time.

The s coast of the peninsula is accessible by road or by hired sampan from Saikung Town. The n coast can be reached by ferry from the pier at University Station (KCR) or from the eastern New Territories port of Tai Po *(map 2 B4)*.

It is advisable to take your own food and refreshments when setting out to explore most of the country parks. On Saikung, drinks can be bought in the villages and sometimes a bowl of noodles, but to be on the safe side, take your own sandwiches or a picnic lunch.

The Maclehose Trail

This 100km (63-mile) trail, a hiking and camping route of footpaths winding through eight country parks divided into ten stages from e to w, starts on the s coast of Saikung and winds counterclockwise around the peninsula before crossing it heading w to Ma On Shan Park.

The Trail is a good one, but can be swamped with hordes of city kids on summer outings. But they tend to stick to the route, and there is invariably an alternative path, which is just as good or better.

As in most of the parks, there is ample opportunity for both arduous and less strenuous hikes, ranging in duration from a few hours to a couple of days with camping overnight. It all depends on the route you choose and how it co-ordinates with ferries and buses.

Sampans are useful, since you can usually arrange for them to pick you up later. *Gaidos* (motorized junk ferries) run some useful routes from Saikung Town; routes and timetables are usually displayed at the quay-side. They are much cheaper than sampans and operate from any rural harbor, calling at some extremely out-of-the-way places.

Saikung Town

The original center of Saikung Town is still intact, surrounded by the developments of a modern market town serving prosperous farming valleys to the N and S. The narrow streets of the old town throng with traditional shops and stalls, still making a coherent unit with the market and the busy fishing harbor. Like other rural towns in the territory, Saikung Town still has its old teahouses, noodle shops and *daipai-dongs*, and you can get good seafood or sip wine and eat *al fresco* outside Cafferty's trendy and expensive little Sydneysider-style bistro.

Into the mountains

Farther W, between Saikung Peninsula and Shatin Valley, is Ma On Shan Country Park, reached by road from Saikung Town or by sampan or ferry from University Station pier. This is a mountainous area with superb views and good wildlife. The many old Hakka settlements are joined by ancient stone paths and surrounded by many abandoned paddies.

Pak Sha O is one such in Saikung country park, a 19thC hamlet, largely deserted, with houses rented to city folk as weekend retreats. The ancestral hall of the Ho family is like a walled village-within-a-village, with its own watchtower; inside, there is a profusion of decorative murals. A tiny Roman Catholic church nearby was built in 1930. There are several lime kilns, once a major source of bricks for the construction of urban Hong Kong. SHEUNG YIU (see page 82), a Hakka village whose name describes its purpose ("above the kiln"), was deserted 30 years ago. Together with a nearby lime kiln, it has been restored as a folk museum by the Regional Council (the rural equivalent of the Urban Council of Hong Kong).

In the high mountains there are also abandoned tea terraces and iron mines. Ma On Shan Park offers Hong Kong's best rock-climbing sites, some of them extremely difficult.

The Maclehose Trail continues W through Lion Rock and Kam Shan Parks to the highlands of Shing Mun, Tai Mo Shan (Hong Kong's highest peak) and Tai Lam Parks, each with something different to offer, each worth visiting.

Tai Po and the northern parkland

Access to the best northern parkland, in Pat Sin Leng and Plover Cove Parks, is via Tai Po in Tolo Harbour *(map 2 B4; train to Tai Po KCR)*. Here again there are rolling hills and hidden valleys embracing old villages, and some of the oldest *fung shui* (geomantically powerful) woods in Hong Kong. The E coast between the bay of Tolo Harbour and Starling Inlet (whose opposite shore is in China) offers some of Hong Kong's best swimming and beachcombing. The other northern park, Lam Tsuen, is arid, barren and deserted, a place only for serious walkers.

Tai Po is another old market town and fishing port. Its surviving traditional atmosphere is heavily beset by new developments, including a new town and an industrial park. The Old Tai Po Market Railway Museum was built in mock-temple style, the only architectural folly among the KCR's stations, albeit a rather modest affectation. It was replaced by a new station in 1983 and re-opened the next year by the Regional Council as a museum — as much for the lack of something better to do with it as for any inspired purpose. It is worth a visit only if you are in the area.

Tours of the New Territories

The Hong Kong Tourist Association arranges three New Territories tours. The shortest one, called simply the "New Territories Tour," is good value within its limitations, but it hardly scratches the surface. The "Land Between" tour takes 6 or 7 hours and explores many of the lesser roads.

Offering yet more scope is the "See For Yourself" tour. This is a self-organized tour using ferries, trains, local buses and your own two good feet. Alternatives are suggested at each point, and there is plenty of opportunity for detours short or long. It can be used as the basis for exhaustive and exhausting New Territories tours of your own.

Tsui Sing Lau

Ping Shan. Map 1C2.

Pagodas were brought to China along with Buddhism from India. Built in the 14thC, Tsui Sing Lau is the only ancient survivor in Hong Kong. Its hexagonal structure is 10m (nearly 33 feet) wide and was originally seven stories high. It is thought that typhoon damage wrecked the upper stories, taking it down to the existing 20m (66-foot) height of three stories, each of which has its own name.

Members of the Tang clan attribute to the structure geomantic influences that ward off evil influences from the N, and encourage scholarship.

**Tsui Sing Lau
pagoda**

Macau

Sometimes called these days the Las Vegas or Monaco of the East, Macau was founded as a trading center in 1557 for illicit dealings between Japan and China. It was operated by Portuguese middlemen, with the connivance of local *hoppos* (business leaders) and the Viceroy of Canton (today's city of Guangzhou, the provincial capital of Guangdong province). At that time, such trade was of dubious legality and more often than not illicit, largely because an Imperial decree of the Ming dynasty had closed China's borders to all unofficial trade or interaction with foreigners.

Portugal's fleet of caravels and carracks outgunned anything on the Eastern seas, and the Portuguese "discovered" China at an opportune time, in 1513. The Chinese had two strategic aims in mind in allowing a Portuguese territorial toehold at the mouth of the mighty Pearl river. They sought to protect the roadways upriver to Canton from rampaging Chinese and Japanese pirates who lived on the delta's many islands (especially on Lantau). They also wished to find a way acceptable to the emperor to continue Canton's lucrative trade with Japan. The deal had the added virtue of keeping Western "barbarians" preoccupied by their trading from attempting further penetration into continental China.

Canton's position at the top rim of the estuary of one of China's ten great rivers had made it an international trading city since at least the 2ndC AD. By the 10thC, the first Moslem mosque for Arab and Indian traders was built there. Authorities in the region were henceforth reluctant to embrace the notion of a closed kingdom.

The "black ships" of Portugal, in their time the only Europeans visiting Asian waters, sailed around Africa's Cape of Good Hope, traveling by way of fortified stations on the W coast, such as Ouidah (made famous by Bruce Chatwin's novel, *The Viceroy of Ouidah*) and Mombasa on the East African coast, and then crossed to Goa on the W coast of India. Working round from there to the Indian Ocean, they crossed to Malacca in the straits that connect the Indian Ocean and the South China Sea in what is now Malaysia, bartering and trading their way to Macau, from where they moved on fully laden E to Taiwan (which they called Formosa) and Nagasaki. The Goa-Nagasaki circle itself took several years to circumnavigate.

Although the Portuguese empire's glory days were over by the mid-17thC, after Japan evicted them in favor of the Dutch, Macau remained a center of trade for all Westerners throughout the 18thC. This was because, after being first admitted in 1714, Westerners were only allowed, under their agreement with China, to stay in their Canton "factories" on Shamian island for part of the year — and nowhere was closer or better to go, for the rest of the year, than Portuguese Macau. This waystation prominence finally evaporated when Hong Kong was ceded to the British after the first Opium War in the mid-19thC.

Some of the heroes who stormed "the heights of Canton" in May 1841, during the war, died later of disease or wounds and lie buried in Macau's Old Protestant Cemetery.

TEA AND OPIUM

The two Opium Wars had one thinly-veiled purpose. China was to be forced either to legalize the trading of India's opium by Her Majesty's merchants or to continue ignoring it. In the background loomed Britain's mammoth trade deficit, which resulted from the Victorians' passion for Chinese tea and the growing British middle-class who could afford to consume it.

And one drug habit begat another. Opium had been contraband in China since an edict was issued by Emperor Yung Cheng in 1729. But its enforcement was honored only in the breach — as was the fate of all such edicts that sought to strangle the accumulation of local wealth. The underlying thrust of Chinese law was (as it remains to this day) that its subjects should "tremble and obey," and the cruelty of punishments meted out to offenders was (and still is) repugnant to Westerners. But in reality, form was seldom troubled by substance when it came to local edicts carefully scripted and sealed by eunuchs empowered to speak for the Celestial Will in distant Beijing, which was all of 2,300km (1,440 miles) away.

Opium had entered the China trade in the late 17thC, but its huge economic significance only developed late in the 18thC. The 19thC Opium Wars were precipitated when a new imperial commissioner made the mistake of being more loyal to the Celestial Will than to his own personal enrichment, by actually enforcing the opium ban, seizing the traders' warehouses and burning over 20,000 chests of the expensive stuff. By 1841, when this calamity occurred, every country's traders were up to their necks in what the Chinese called "foreign mud" (opium) — and the impulse to break China's blockade assumed the character of a free-traders' holy war.

ROMAN CATHOLICISM

There was a time when Macau boasted the greatest density of churches per square mile in the world. It was the seat of Roman Catholic missionary activity in the whole of Asia, until the collapse of Jesuit influence in the 18thC, when a Pope caught up in court intrigues expelled the Jesuits from Macau and Asia in 1762 and eventually from the Americas (as depicted in the movie *The Mission*).

Matteo Ricci, the first and most illustrious of a generation of European Jesuit missionaries to be allowed access to the Ming dynasty imperial court, and every other major missionary sent to China's imperial court by the Pope, traveled by way of Macau.

St Francis Xavier, one of the founders of the Jesuit order who took Christianity to Japan, died on a nearby island upriver, and the bone of his right arm remains as a venerated relic in a chapel on Coloane Island.

GAMBLING

Nor does Macau excel in churches alone: there are seven casinos — more than any other city in Asia. Besides the usual run of baccarat, blackjack, craps and roulette, they all feature Chinese games: Fan Tan, Dai Siu, Pai Kao and Keno. Only the last of these is known in the West.

The *Macau AOA Gambling Handbook* is required reading.

The **Mandarin Oriental Hotel** casino is the most luxurious, followed by Macau's garish **Hotel Lisboa** casino. Most interesting is the casino in the **Jai-Alai Stadium**, where you can also take in (and bet on) a sport that is reputedly the world's fastest ball game. Pronounced "high-uh-lie" (called *pelota* in the Philippines), the game is a bit like racquetball or squash: it's not *where* the ball bounces but *how often* that makes the point. Players throw and catch with wicker baskets attached to leather gloves rather than strike with racquets. It is very popular in Cuba and Mexico, but only in the Philippines and Macau in Asia. (The Philippines lay within Mexico's jurisdiction in the days of the Spanish *conquistadors,* who picked up the game from local *indios. Pelota* is therefore the legacy of one subject people to another via their common conquerors.)

As elsewhere, casinos never close. Slummers are referred to the **Floating Casino** anchored at West Macau and **Kam Pec Casino** *(2 Travessa do Aterro Novo)*. Either of these makes the perfect setting for the start of a Triad murder mystery; they are good only for the anecdotes. The **Macau Canidrome** *(Avenida General Castelo Branco)* offers grayhound races four times a week with 14 races per night, starting at 8pm Tuesday, Thursday, Saturday and Sunday; it is located near the **Barrier Gate**, the arched gateway that leads by land to mainland China. In 1980, the **Macau Trotting Club** wagered its success on yet another bettable draw card: harness racing on Taipa Island.

A government-sanctioned cartel known as STDM (Sociedade de Turismo e Diversoes de Macau) runs legal gambling and pays a fixed percentage of its take to the Macau government. STDM holds shares in virtually all major hotels and several minor ones, plus associated restaurants, massage parlors and hostess nightclubs. It is a major employer of Macanese casino staff, Thai masseuses, Filipina hostesses, and French strippers in the nightly Crazy Paris Show. It also operates the jetfoil and helicopter services between Hong Kong and Macau; accounts for at least 25 percent of the territory's gross domestic product through its effective control of the tourism sector; and is run by a high-profile scion of Hong Kong's first *comprador* Eurasian family, the Hotungs.

Dr. Stanley Ho (the doctorate is honorary), chairman of STDM, is as close to being "Mr Macau" as anyone is ever likely to be. His role speaks volumes for how Macau works — which is as an entertainment and manufacturing extension of Hong Kong, "under Portuguese administration." It has no other economic life.

MACAU'S STATUS

The enclave, officially "a Chinese territory under Portuguese administration," is expected to return to full Chinese sovereignty in 1999, two years after its more glamorous and more than 10-times-larger neighbor, Hong Kong. It comprises three separate areas: Macau peninsula on the mainland, and the two islands of Taipa and Coloane offshore.

Some 450,000 people call Macau home, but the number of residents swells substantially each night when the jetfoil-loads of Hong Kong gamblers arrive in port. Today's language is officially Portuguese; tomorrow (after China resumes sovereignty) it will be Mandarin or *putonghua*. However, most people have always spoken the Cantonese and Chiu Chow dialects of Hong Kong, and some English is spoken as well.

Unlike the British in Hong Kong, the Portuguese have granted all native Macanese Portuguese citizenship after 1999 — which will make them citizens of the European Community entitled to live in Europe, if they elect to leave.

FURTHER INFORMATION

The best information sources on Macau in English are to be found in Hong Kong. There is a **Macau Information Desk** adjoining that of the HKTA at Kai Tak Airport's inner arrival hall, and the **Macau Tourist Office** *(Rm. 305, Shun Tak Centre* ☎ *540-8180)* is at the Macau Ferry Terminal in Hong Kong.

For all its long history, little has been written about Macau in English. There are a few novels: *An Insular Possession* by Timothy Mo, *City of Broken Promises* by Austin Coates and *Macau* by Daniel Carney; a few histories, the best of which are *Historic Macau* by C.A. Montalto de Jesus (published in 1919 but reprinted by OUP in 1984) and *A Macao Narrative* and *Macao and the British,* both by Austin Coates. An aged resident Jesuit, Fr. Manuel Texeira, has written many monographs on Macau history in English, which are available only in Macau. He himself became something of an historical curiosity in the mid-1980s, having been profiled in several in-flight magazines.

There are also two local guides, *Discovering Macau* by John Clemens (1983) and *Macau in 50 Ways* by Shann Davies, written for the Macau Government Tourist Office. Three good coffee-table picture books are *Macau* by Jean-Yves Defay, *Macau* by Leong Ka Tai and Shann Davies, and *Old Macau,* a sketchbook by Tom Briggs with text by Colin Crisswell. The **Hyatt Regency Macau** stocks a number of these in its lobby kiosk.

Virtually all Hong Kong travel guides carry sections on Macau of varying lengths, levels of accuracy, timeliness and thoroughness. At present, save for Formula Three followers, pretty well no one flies to Hong Kong or South China just to see Macau, although growing numbers add it to their existing itineraries. This may well change when Macau's airport opens in 1994-95, offering an alternative gateway to the region. A new airline, Air Macau, is proposed, and the existing East Asia Airlines, which operates the helicopter service to Hong Kong, may expand.

In the US   Macau Tourist Information Bureau, 3133 Lake Hollywood Dr., Los Angeles, CA 90068 ☎(213) 851-3402 or toll free (800) 331-7150 [Fx](213) 851-3684; Macau Tourist Information Bureau, 608 5th Ave., Suite 309, New York, NY 10020 ☎(212) 581-7465

In the UK   Macau Tourist Information Bureau, 6 Sherlock Mews, Paddington St., London W1M 3RH ☎071-224-3390 [Fx]071-224-0601

ENTRY REQUIREMENTS AND CUSTOMS

Visas are required by all nationals except citizens of the UK, US, Canada, Australia, France, West Germany, Spain, Sweden and some other European and South American countries. All visitors must have a passport. Macau customs officials allows almost anything to come in freely except hard drugs and assault rifles. Returning to Hong Kong, however, the Macau-tripper finds the normal international duty-free allowances cut by half: to wit, 100 cigarettes, 25 cigars or a quarter-pound of tobacco, and one bottle of wine.

HOW TO GET THERE

From Shun Tak Centre's **Macau Ferry Terminal** in Sheung Wan district *(map 3 A2)*, hydrofoils, jetfoils and ferries leave every $\frac{1}{2}$ hour from 7am-2.30am, with less frequent night sailings thereafter. There are more than 100 daily scheduled sailings each way. More than 13 million people traversed the 64km (40 miles) across the Pearl River estuary in 1991, making Macau the most heavily trafficked tourist destination in Asia and, save for the two US Walt Disney parks, probably the world.

Except on the large, high-speed ferries, luggage space is limited to carry-on bags. The 64km (40-mile) journey takes 50 minutes by jetfoil, 75 minutes by hydrofoil or 100 minutes by ferry. East Asia Airlines operates an expensive helicopter service six times daily from the roof of Hong Kong's Shun Tak Centre terminal, a short hop of 20 minutes.

WHEN YOU ARRIVE

The moment you exit the Macau terminal, the taxis, pedicabs and tour operators are waiting to escort you around town. Also available for rent are Avis Mini Mokes, a cross between a car and a golf cart run on electric power *(from Macau Mokes* ☎ *543-4190 in Hong Kong, 378851 in Macau)*. Their office is a short walk away in the adjacent parking lot on Av. Marciano Baptista.

Incidentally, the more "mini" the better as far as Macau's streets are concerned, for they are big on long Portuguese names (without English translations) and very short on space. Bicycles do very nicely if you happen to have the thighs to take on this tiny peninsula's seven hills.

SHADOWS FROM THE PAST

The whole of Macau peninsula can be toured in half a day, but it is far better savored slowly. Time moves on a Mediterranean sundial in Macau city and is banned altogether in its hermetically sealed casinos. It is a land modeled on Southern Europe, which still believes in 2- or 3-hour lunches and *vinho verde* for sundowners on the terrace, watching river silt rise in the harbor as the tide recedes at dusk.

It is as different from Hong Kong as Portugal is from England, but there is precious little left of its glorious history, and what remains is little known outside a small coterie of China Coast historians. Even this will be surgically removed once the Chinese mainlanders move in officially (there are already plans to remove all the commemorative sculptures of Portuguese officials from public places).

Macau's idiosyncratic allure derives from literary allusions and a very few actually ancient relics in the shadows of a past that has become mostly forgotten or ignored. They are as beguiling as a Druid stone or the grim gods of Easter Island.

Staring from the Estrada do Cemiterio at the color wheel of beautiful stained-glass windows of the chapel in **St Michael's Catholic Cemetery**, or out across the magnificent flocks of stone angels and madonnas who guard the graves of the peninsula's largest final resting place, the tragic madness of the whole enterprise we call the European Age of Discovery flashes across the mind like half-remembered messages from the past: death by fever... ; by falling from the ship's rigging... ; in childbirth... ; the much-loved only son of... ; while gallantly storming the enemy battery.... It seems as if the sole purpose of an entire age was to arrive at this tiny place, accrue honor and wealth, or die in the attempt.

That so much came from so few survivors in such unlikely circumstances beggars belief. Then, try conjuring a picture of Prince Henry the Navigator — he who began the Christian crusade to take control of the Eastern seas — standing on a promontory over the Atlantic in South Portugal, spurred by expectations encoded in captured Arab *cartolan* maps that depicted the currents of endless ocean in this distant Asian region, and declaring, "We shall find our own way to the gold and spices."

To Western eyes, it is either a miracle or an incredible accident of history that this improbable, tiny colony survives and even thrives, 450 years later, like a tattered battle flag that waved through local wars, two World Wars, innumerable pirate raids, and local and regional revolutions, to survive as the oldest Western settlement on the China Coast. To Chinese eyes, the forthcoming ending to this whole story is the final stitch that will close a wound which festered for almost half a millennium.

The whole place is a weird blend of sermons in stone, Iberian charms, and an urban China that still feels, in places, just like the officially "neutral" Portuguese enclave it was in World War II, when young Stanley Ho fled there for protection from the Japanese in Hong Kong. It still feels in many ways like the civilians' Chinese city it was during the wartime 1940s, filled with spies and counter-spies, refugees and intrigue, occasionally bombed by the Allies, where somewhere there must surely reside a man named "Rick" or "Bogie" running guns to the good guys while masquerading as a casino croupier, or running a "gin joint" in the warren of streets off Rua dos Lorchas, near the Macau-Guangzhou Ferry Wharf.

SIGHTS AND PLACES OF INTEREST

A STROLL AROUND MACAU

Spare at least a day for Macau. From the ferry pier, work your way s, along the Av. Amizade (the same seafront road of the Guia circuit down which Formula Three Grand Prix drivers and motorcyclists speed each November). On the left is the **Mandarin Oriental Macau** hotel, which has the newest casino, and at its end the entrance to the elegant bridge to Taipa Island, beside the city's grandest and most garish casino hotel, the **Lisboa**, with its bizarre roof modeled on a roulette-wheel spindle. On the right are the hills of Macau.

Follow the coast along the downtown business district below the daunting **Bank of China tower**, which here, as in Hong Kong, makes its statement by standing many stories taller than anywhere else in town.

Turning onto the Rua da Praia Grande, you pass the pastel-shaded buildings of **Government House**; the once creaky, colorful, much-loved, 110-year-old **Hotel Bela Vista**, now being renovated as a top-scale boutique hostel with only 8 suites for the Mandarin Oriental Group; and the exquisite all-suites **Pousada de Sao Tiago**, a hotel tastefully snuggled into the 17thC walls of the **Barra Fortress** (dating from c.1629) and furnished entirely with reproductions of Portuguese period furniture.

Finally, you reach the **A-Ma Temple** (actually Ma Kok Miu), set prettily into the rocky base of Penha Hill. It is named after Macau's protecting goddess, after whom Macau is also named by early settlers, in a tortuous twist of transliteration to *A Ma Gao* (in Hong Kong she's known as Tin Hau). The painting of a Chinese seagoing junk incised into a huge boulder at the entrance is, with the Sao Paulo facade, one of the two most popular landmarks in Macau. Across Calcada de Barra road is the **Maritime Museum**, containing actual boats, models and other artifacts of seaborne life on the China Coast.

THE CHINESE CITY

Having rounded the bottom tip of Macau and headed back up the w side, you pass the inner harbor and its floating casino. This is the "Chinese city" of Macau that so strongly evokes the 1940s, of a type so often seen in movie theaters and, since the 1960s, so seldom seen in real life. It is a world of shopfront factories, ships' provision stores, rundown hotels and hostels for the China traffic, pawnshops for casino losers and jewelry shops for jackpot winners. The opening sequence of

street scenes in *Indiana Jones and the Temple of Doom,* with sets by Hong Kong designer Basil Pao, was filmed here.

Turning up into the winding streets and ascending alleys (where you will definitely need a map if you are on your own) you will come to a congregation of churches: **St Lawrence** (Sao Lourenco), the **Church and Seminary of St Joseph**, **St Augustine** (Sao Agostinho) and the surviving facade of **St Paul's** (Sao Paulo), a magnificent remnant of a church built in the early 17thC with the help of Japanese Christians, which burned to the ground in 1835, leaving only this fragment (illustrated here). Those Christians had fled a massacre of Japanese Catholics ordered by the local nobles (the *daimyo*) of the Portuguese trading station of Nagasaki.

THE PROTESTANT CEMETERY

Next to St. Paul's is the **Monte Fort** (Citadel Sao Paulo do Monte), overlooking the harbor, from which vantage point it successfully defended Macau against Dutch invaders in 1622.

Also under the fort's gaze is the **Protestant Cemetery** (c.1921), containing graves gathered from older burial sites of many American, British, Scots and other seamen who lost their lives in nearby waters. It is the final resting place of two of the China Coast's most prominent European figures: George Chinnery, the portrait painter, and Robert Morrison, first translator of the Christian Bible into Chinese.

(In passing, one is struck by the ironical thought that a Chinese-language Bible is *still* viewed as a threat by Marxist ideologues in China and confiscated if found in your luggage. Christian fundamentalists, operating out of Hong Kong, still try to mount preaching campaigns in China, but are quietly and quickly evicted.)

Beside the cemetery is a superbly maintained colonial-style building that once housed the President of the Select Committee of the East India Company and, until 1990, a lovely art museum. It now houses a private cultural foundation.

Within its grounds is the **Camoes Garden and Grotto**, named after and sporting a bust of Luis Camoes (1524-80), Portugal's poet laureate. He is supposed to have spent a year in the colony and, according to an apocryphal account of the soldier-poet's tragic life, to have drafted stanzas here for the national epic *Os Lusiadas* (The Lusiads). There is no actual proof that he was ever in Macau.

LOU LIM IEOC GARDEN
Rua Ferreira de Almeida.

Also nearby is **Lou Lim Ieoc**, a Chinese walled garden modeled on the Suzhou literati style. Built by a wealthy Chinese gentleman of the Lou family in the 1920s, it has twisting walks, artificial ponds and mountains, decorative plants, pagodas, pavilions and bridges. The garden is only about half its original size, as much of it had been sold off and redeveloped before the government restored it as a tourist attraction in the 1970s. The original mansion is now the Pui Ching School.

This is the only such garden to be seen outside the Suzhou-Hangzhou environs (which are about 3 hours by train w of Shanghai), and one of only three outside mainland China. The other two are contemporary re-creations in the Metropolitan Museum of Art in New York City and in Vancouver's Chinatown district.

(Oddly, given their gift of gazebos, pagodas and moongate bridges to English landscapists and the endless books on Japanese Zen gardens, the only substantive English-language study of Classical literati gardens is *The Chinese Garden,* by Maggie Keswick, a China-coast child of the Jardine traders' clan. The best-illustrated survey is a Chinese-language book with a brief English summary inserted: *Soochow Gardens,* by

Professor Chuin Tung of Nanking. Both volumes are available in good bookstores in Hong Kong.)

SUN YAT-SEN'S HOME

Junction of Av. da Sidonio Pais and Rua de Silva Mendes 📷 *Open Mon, Wed-Fri 10am-1pm; Sat-Sun 10am-1pm, 3-5pm. Closed Tues.*

A short walk from the gardens is the home of Dr. Sun Yat-Sen, the father of modern China (who figures extensively in the introductory pages of this book). Dr. Sun studied Western medicine and revolution in Hong Kong and practiced both in Macau, before moving back to his home village, Cuiheng, just N of the peninsula. Tours to his home village are a staple of local travel agents.

The original house on the site blew up while used as an explosives store. This memorial house has photos, flags and other paraphernalia of the republican revolutionaries who eventually triumphed in 1911, when they engineered the abdication of the last Qing dynasty emperor, Pu Yi (the subject of Bertolucci's movie, *The Last Emperor*).

PANORAMIC VIEW ◀

The best panorama of Macau is to be seen from its highest point atop the **Guia Fortress** (1637), in the first **Lighthouse** (1865) to be built on the China Coast. Antique weather-forecasting equipment is on display. The 17thC chapel is dedicated to Our Lady of Guia (*guia* means guide in Portuguese). The uphill walk is severe, so best take a taxi.

KUN IAM TEMPLE

Av. do Coronel Mesquita.

This temple is, like the A-Ma temple, actually a complex of several shrines. Kuan Yin, to whom it is dedicated, is the Buddhist Goddess of Mercy. Its sooty, gilt sculptures of *lohan* (Chinese holy men) in the main altar room include one Westerner said to represent Marco Polo. Dynastic records suggest a temple has stood on this site for about 600 years, although this one is under 400 years old (it was built in 1627). It is popular for its fortune tellers.

Tucked in a corner garden is the stone table and benches at which sat the men who signed the first treaty of friendship and trade between Americans and Chinese, in July 1844 — two years after the signing of the Treaty of Nanking, which ceded Hong Kong to the British in perpetuity.

Although their first cargo on the *Empress of China* carried ginseng in 1784, the Americans had inherited their former British masters' tea habit; hence their ire over the Stamp Act, which led to The Boston Tea Party and revolution. With the habit came the same problem of trade imbalance: there was no means of buying enough tea from the Chinese to meet domestic demand without selling them cotton and opium, neither of which the Chinese, at least officially, wanted. Americans smuggled their "foreign mud" from Smyrna in Turkey, instead of Bengal in India, and their cotton was harvested by African slaves in the southern states. All in all, in 1844, the China Coast needed every bit of mercy their goddess Kuan Yin could muster.

✍   One of the pleasantest places to stay in Macau is the **Pousada de Sao Tiago** *(Av. de República* ☎ *378111* 📺), an award-winning inn of unique character built as a government-assisted demonstration project in architectural conservation. A large extension to be built behind it is planned, which may smother its present unique sense of intimacy, for it currently has only 23 rooms.

Hotels of more modern international style include the **Mandarin Oriental** *(Av. de Amizade* ☎ *567888* 📺*)* near the ferry terminal and the offshore **Hyatt Regency** *(Taipa Island* ☎ *83-1234* 📺*)*, which has good sports facilities. There are also some half-dozen international-class hotels on the island. Newest of them is the 18-story **New Century Hotel** *(Estrada Almirante, Taipa Island* ☎ *(853) 548-2213* 📺*)*, beside the Jockey Club; opened in February 1992, it boasts more food and beverage outlets to service its 600 rooms and 28 apartments than any other.

A pleasant, out-of-the-way inn, with only 22 rooms, a small, black sand beach and an excellent Sunday brunch of Portuguese cuisine is the **Pousada de Coloane** *(Praia de Cheoc Van* ☎ *32814/328144* 📺*)*.

Hotels are all fully reserved by gamblers on weekends, in November with Grand Prix auto racing enthusiasts, and by anyone who can get a room over long-weekend holidays in Hong Kong. Prices are also higher at these times. Weekday visits are highly recommended if you wish to get the rooms and restaurant reservations you want, while saving money on discounted room rates.

▬   Portuguese fare ranges from grilled sardines and African chicken to wonderful wines and hearty soups laced with rich olive oil. There are more than a dozen Portuguese restaurants. Several worth trying are: **Estrela do Mar** *(☎ 81270)*, beside the Governor's offices and those of the Macau tourism authority; **Henri's Galley** *(☎ 76207/83111)*, below the Bela Vista Hotel; **Pinocchio** *(☎ 327128/ 327328)*, on Taipa; **Grill Fortaleza** at the Pousada de Coloane *(☎ 328143)*; and **Solmar** *(☎ 574391)*, downtown on Rua da Praia Grande.

There are more than a dozen Chinese banquet restaurants besides those in hotels, and numberless noodle shops and *daipaidongs*. There are also serviceable Japanese, Korean, Thai, Vietnamese and Italian restaurants, and two international fast-food franchises: **MacDonald's** *(☎ 591499)* on Rua do Campo and **Pizza Hut** *(☎ 370840)* in the Hotel Lisboa.

FARTHER AFIELD

THE OFFSHORE DEPENDENCIES

If you have more time to spend here, rent a car or a moke or ride the buses to visit Macau's offshore island dependencies of **Taipa** and **Coloane**. Besides resorts astride heavily-silted, black sand beaches, they offer a ruddy, rural face of Macau's enigmatic ambience and history.

Taipa and Coloane towns are tiny warrens within which are tucked little Chinese temples and Catholic chapels. Here and there are cozy Macanese restaurants (try **Restaurante Panda** or **Taipa Comidas Portuguesa** on Taipa, or **Restaurante-Bar Pirao** near the Police Training Centre on Coloane). The **Taipa House Museum** re-creates household life as lived by China Coast Europeans circa the 1920s.

Coloane's main attraction is the **Chapel of St Francis Xavier** *(Av. de Cinco de Outubro),* built in 1928 to honor the sainted missionary to Japan who died nearby, on Shang Ch'an Island, in 1552. Beside his relic, a section of his right arm bone, there are boxes of other *memento mori:* bones of Japanese Catholics martyred in Nagasaki in 1597 (whose co-religionists built **St Paul's** on the peninsula), and of those killed later in a

17thC Japanese rebellion. The bones of Vietnamese Catholics killed in the early 17thC are also here.

Outside the chapel is a **cenotaph** surrounded by cannonballs. This commemorates the final battle fought and won against pirate fleets in Macau, on July 13, 1910. Again there swells the drum-roll of history: one reason the Portuguese were finally allowed to settle on the South China Coast was to help imperial customs ships rid the Pearl River delta of rapacious pirate fleets — a job which continued unabated for more than 350 years, from 1557 to 1910! Small wonder that the day of the pirates' final defeat is still a legal public holiday on the islands and still actively celebrated on Coloane.

MACAU'S HINTERLAND

Another option is to undertake a quick visit to China. Many tour operators offer packages that take in Macau and the Chinese counties of **Zhuhai** and **Zhongshan**. The latter city offers a championship golf course and a hot springs resort.

The opportunities for car travel between Macau, Guangzhou, Shenzhen and Hong Kong will improve dramatically when a massive superhighway, now under construction, is opened. The project, financed by Hong Kong's Hopewell Holdings, is scheduled to be completed in 1993. For the first time in their common history, Hong Kong and Macau will have a kind of hinterland most easily enjoyed by individual driving.

For Hong Kongers, with the world's highest density of Rolls Royces per mile of road and highest per capita level of Ferrari imports in the world, it should mean they will finally be able to get their beautiful luxury vehicles out of second gear.

BICYCLE TOURS

The very best way to see the w bank area of Taishan County, the birthplace of most Cantonese who have emigrated over the past century, is on a bicycle tour. **Bike China Tours** (*in Hong Kong* ☎ *984-7208, or c/o Flying Ball Bicycle Co., Grd Flr, 201 Tung Choi St., near Prince Edward Rd., Mongkok, Kowloon* ☎ *381-3661/381-5919, map 7B3)* operates a year-round schedule led by an affable Australian, Iain Dacre. The pace can be rigorous, but there is no better way, other than walking, to witness the amazing architectural follies built by wealthy returnees. Emulating Europe's medieval and Renaissance castles and cathedrals, the buildings emerge ghost-like from the rice paddies.

Sleeping is done in hotels, and a truck follows with spare parts, so there are no lengthy delays on the road — save when groups occasionally get lost, which can either be wonderful or simply awful if you're already tired. This happens because back roads are used as much as possible to avoid traffic and to see far more of the countryside, and Chinese maps are sometimes confused *and* confusing.

Tours of 3-5 days start with an overnight "slow boat to China" up one of many Pearl River tributaries along the w bank, traveling s back down toward the sea and eventually returning to Hong Kong via either Macau or Shenzhen.

South China

Hong Kong's neighboring Guangdong province is the 10th largest province in Communist China. It comprises 28 counties and has a total population of more than 62 million. The provincial capital is **Guangzhou** (a.k.a. Canton), which has a population of 5 million, and it also contains the Shenzhen, Shekou and Zhuhai Special Economic Zones, which have been in the forefront of Communist China's industrial development.

Many similarities exist with Hong Kong because the territory's people are overwhelmingly Cantonese. But there are even more differences. Despite the fact that Guangdong province is China's leading light in manufacturing and trading with the West, it retains an agrarian character and a low standard of living, which is all the more poignant when compared with the two tiny toeholds of Western capitalism and what China's ideologues refer to as "bourgeois decadence" in Hong Kong and Macau.

To the Cantonese, Hong Kong holds all to which they aspire: modernity, wealth and freedom. Their appetite is encouraged by the easy traffic in information and entertainment, such as Cantonese soap operas on Hong Kong television which are widely watched across the border, often on TVs purchased for them by their Hong Kong relatives.

To Hong Kongers, Guangzhou and its surrounding province are places from which they or their parents sought to escape — a repressive command economy wherein having the wrong parents is still potentially a crime against the state, and where the struggle to emerge from the cocoon of the globe's most ancient and continuous imperial past is still a reality. The province is also the center of ancestral villages to millions of Hong Kongers who, ironically, honor that fact more than do the mainlanders, since they are more free to cling to their Confucian ethos and its related practices of ancestor worship. Each Chinese New Year and on all traditional grave-tending holidays, all traffic arteries from Hong Kong to China are choked with gift-givers practicing filial piety.

To the Communist authorities in Beijing, Guangdong is more prosperous, more efficiently managed and more open to new ideas than most of the rest of China — attributes that make it at once most economically endearing and most morally suspect.

GUANGDONG AND THE PEARL RIVER

Guangdong province is China's longest, with a coastline measuring 4,314km (2,696 miles) and more than 1,000 islands (including the island of Hainan, which is 34,000sq.km/13,100 square miles in area). It comprises only 2.2 percent of China's entire land mass (212,000sq.km/82,000 square miles), and almost 60 percent of the terrain is mountainous. It has 600 rivers, 92 of which flow directly into the sea. The largest and most important is the Pearl River, China's fifth largest, with a total length of 2,129km (1,331 miles).

The Pearl River Delta is the province's most wealthy and populated area, and the city of Guangzhou sits on the upper reaches of the river

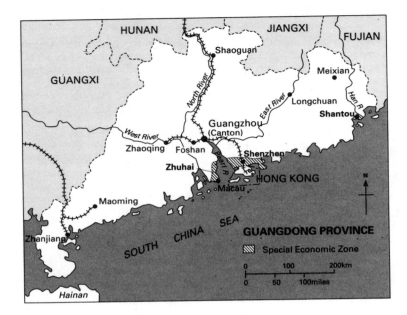

estuary. It has been the capital of North China's dominance over the wealthier south since a town was originally established on the site at about the time the Qin dynasty first imposed a single imperial rule over the whole of China in 221-207BC.

There had been trade with the Roman and Indian empires since at least the 2ndC of our era. Arabs, Armenians, Parsees and Indians acted as regular middlemen to markets in Southeast Asia and the Middle East during the Tang dynasty. For an entire millenium, the province has been the welcome mat for China's erratically swinging "open door" policy — and at times that mat has been rudely pulled from under the feet of foreigners.

GUANGDONG'S KEY ROLE IN DEVELOPMENT

These days about 60 percent of foreign-invested enterprises in China are based in Guangdong province, mostly in the Pearl River Delta region, where about 2 million workers are directly and indirectly employed by Hong Kong manufacturers operating some 20,000 enterprises. The province is also the most active area in China's foreign trade, ahead of Shanghai and accounting for 15-20 percent of the annual national total. It has been estimated to contain about half the country's almost 2,000 companies and enterprises formally authorized to trade with outsiders.

The biannual (April and October) Canton Trade Fair attracts about 30,000 visitors each session and remains the first port of call for most foreigners trading with China, and about a third of all China's exports are negotiated at the fair. To provide some perspective on how much of a star, in Chinese terms, Guangdong really is, bear in mind that this province achieves such superlatives while being but one of 30 provinces in China.

THE CRUCIBLE OF REVOLUTIONS
The downside is that it has always been the city of Guangzhou which, after Hong Kong, the Beijing bureaucrats loved to hate. It has a long history as a melting pot of economic change and of all revolutionary events in modern times, such as the Taiping Rebellion in the mid-19thC, the founding of the Republic in the early decades of the 20thC, and the Nationalist Party (Kuomintang) civil war, which the Chinese Communist Party called a revolution.

Besides temples, mosques, churches and parks, virtually the only official tourist sites in Guangzhou relate to the Republican or Communist revolutions (both the Nationalists now in Taiwan and the Communists on the mainland claim to have inherited the mantle of Dr. Sun Yat-Sen's Republic, which is why sites associated with Dr. Sun's activities are preserved and honored in both places). Some examples follow:

- The **Sun Yat-Sen Memorial Hall** *(Dongfeng Lu)*, built with Overseas Chinese contributions in 1921.
- The **Mausoleum of the 72 Martyrs & Memorial of Yellow Flowers** *(E of Garden hotel on Yellow Flower Hill)*, built in 1918, which honors fallen insurgents of an unsuccessful Republican uprising on April 27, 1911. In October that year, the Republic of China was declared in South China — while warlords still ruled North China.
- The **Memorial Garden to the Martyrs** *(main gate off Zhongshan 3-Lu, N gate off Dongfeng 4-Lu)*, opened in 1957 to celebrate the 30th anniversary of the abortive Canton Uprising against Chiang Kai Shek's Kuomintang Party (Nationalists) in December 1927.
- The **Peasant Movement Institute** *(Zhongshan 4-Lu)* was founded in 1924 to train Communist leaders. Here both Mao Zedong and Zhou Enlai lectured. It was restored in 1953.

OVERSEAS LINKS
China spent much of this century as a remittance economy, living, as does the Philippines today, largely on the backs of overseas workers sending their money home. Some argue that China's famous "Four Modernizations" since opening to the West in 1978 continue that tradition, with Hong Kong providing the linchpin. Until the Communist Revolution, all economic changes were financed from abroad — by foreign aid, foreign investors in the Treaty Ports, foreign missionaries in the hinterlands, and most of all by Overseas Chinese.

Almost all of the world's Chinatowns, from New York City to Panama City, are populated by the Cantonese scions of this province, children of the sojourners who ran off to "Golden Mountains" in America and Australia, "Sugar Mountains" in Hawaii, and the labor gangs of absolutely everywhere that used contract workers. Dr. Sun Yat-Sen's brother helped support him and his revolution from his own medical practice in Hawaii and, in fact, almost the entire Republican cause was financed from overseas, via Hong Kong.

Chinese Communism's core leaders, including the late Zhou Enlai, Deng Xiaopeng, Yang Shangkun and others, first developed a taste for Communism and croissants in Paris and later Moscow. This was courtesy of a work-study program founded to create interpreters to work with 175,000 Chinese laborers brought to dig Allied trenches near the end of the First World War. Most of those laborers would have been Cantonese.

It is estimated that half of today's 13 million Overseas Chinese, who now reside in 174 countries, are from Guangdong Province. Most live in Canada, Indonesia, Malaysia, the Philippines, Singapore, Thailand and the United States (this total excludes what the mainland calls "Chinese compatriots" resident in Hong Kong, Macau and Taiwan). Since 1978, they have contributed about 90 percent of foreign capital invested in the province (excluding their donations for construction or renovation of about 2,000 schools, 100 hospitals and other welfare projects).

WHERE TO OBTAIN VISAS

All visitors to China require entry visas. In Hong Kong, visas may be obtained from the following sources:

Ministry of Foreign Affairs   PRC Visa Office, China Resources Building, Flr 5 (low block), 26 Harbour Rd., Wanchai ☎585-1700, map **5C6**

China Travel Service (CTS)   China Travel Building, 77 Queen's Rd., Central ☎525-9121, map **3B3**; 78 Connaught Rd., Central, map **3B3**; Flr 1, 27 Nathan Rd., Tsimshatsui, Kowloon ☎366-7201, map **7E3**

China International Travel Service (CITS)   Unit 601-606, Flr 6, Tower II, South Sea Centre, Tsimshatsui East, Kowloon ☎721-5317, map **8E4**

— or from one of many travel agents offering China tours.

Visas normally take 1-2 days to process. Take your passport and one photo. Customs regulations for the short-term visitor are very simple. On entry, an itemized customs declaration is filled out (listing the amount of cash you are carrying, how many watches, what jewelry, and so on). One copy is given to the entry customs agent; the other copy is kept by you to be given as you exit China. "Cultural relics" may not be removed from China. Make certain that items purchased in China have a red-wax "approved for export" stamp on them and that you have a receipt. Duty-free allowances are 400 cigarettes or an equivalent assortment of tobacco, and two bottles of liquor or wine.

HOW TO GET THERE

You can get to South China from Hong Kong in many ways. Probably the easiest is via one of the numerous tours that operate out of Hong Kong into Macau and contiguous China. There are 1-day bus tours to Shenzhen and the border towns; 1-, 2- and 3-day hovercraft-and-bus excursions to Guangzhou, Shenzhen and Foshan; and there's a lovely traditional Chinese train (complete with lace doilies and tea service) that makes the 2- to 3-hour run from Tsimshatsui into Guangzhou.

Individual travel is a bit more difficult, but possible. There are about 10 regular Hong Kong-Guangzhou flights daily, which take just over half an hour, and many bus, hovercraft, jetcat, ferry and train services daily.

Shenzhen is scheduled to have an international airport built about 26kms (16 miles) from the city to open in 1992 at **Huangtian**, about 60kms (38 miles) N of Hong Kong — which means that by the middle of the 1990s there will be four international airports in the small circle of airspace above Guangzhou, Shenzhen, Hong Kong and Macau.

GUANGZHOU (Canton)

Guangzhou's population of 5 million makes it one of the largest cities in southern China, and the gateway to the region. Once a walled city, Guangzhou began to take its present shape in the 1920s.

A most surprising thing about the city of Guangzhou is how relatively little there is to see, given its very long history as an open city and equally long role as an international trading entrepôt. China's Great Cultural Revolution (c.1966-76) — an exercise in nihilism made manifest — is to blame for much of this. It became a major sport of "Red Guards" wielding Mao's "Little Red Book" to destroy every semblance of China's rich heritage upon which they could lay hands, along with the lives of anyone who dared question this ritualized cultural suicide.

SIGHTS AND PLACES OF INTEREST

The **Temple of Six Banyan Trees** (Liu Rong Si), with its 1,400-year-old **Flower Pagoda**, and the **Guang Xiao Si** (Bright Filial Piety Temple) are near each other, and are but two of several interesting temples that Guangzhou has to offer.

Others are the **Geniis Temple**, where the five rams that give the city its name are said to have appeared, and the **Smooth Pagoda**, first built by Arab traders in AD900. Guangzhou has plenty of parks, and the **Guangzhou Zoo** is one of the four largest in China. Naturally, it features pandas.

Despite the impulse to attract foreign tourists and hard currencies, the collective memory of "gunboat diplomacy" is still too fresh for any efforts to be made to create historical preserves of European outposts. Three such outposts in Guangzhou are all in decrepit condition: **Shamian Island** (only 900 meters/1,000 yards from E-W and 300 meters/330 yards from N-S on mostly reclaimed land), where the famous Canton factories were located; the **Sacred Heart Catholic Church**, a neo-Gothic structure built between 1863 and 1888; and the **Bogue Forts** on islets near the city once occupied by foreign troops or Jesuit missionary sites, such as the island where St Francis Xavier died. Perhaps after 1999....

Foshan, a short car ride from Guangzhou, is said to be almost as old as its neighbor, and was one of the most flourishing market towns in China by the 15thC. The porcelain industry thrives now as it has for centuries. For the temple-minded, there is the **Ancestral Temple**, with lovely landscaped grounds and elaborate bas-reliefs.

TOURS OF THE PROVINCE

A couple of days would provide enough time for a whirlwind tour of **Guangzhou** and one of the **Special Economic Zones (SEZs)**. These are actually of little interest except as curious examples of smaller communities trying to look and act like Hong Kong. In the case of Shenzhen's resorts, what they look and act like are laboratory efforts to cross the DNA of Disney amusement parks with Las Vegas entertainment centers sans gambling. Alternatively, you may prefer to spend both days in the provincial capital with a bit more time to explore. Added time will offer the chance to take in an SEZ, see Guangzhou *and* journey to Foshan (one of the four ancient cities of China, and a center for porcelain).

Shenzhen, center of one of the most impressive of the SEZs, is an instant city (population 600,000) of high-rises alongside traditional communes, not unlike Hong Kong's many New Towns in its New Territories. The high point of this stop, however, may well be the 30 minutes spent with the local kindergarten children, who sing and dance their welcome. The children have been thus exploited to charm the hearts of foreign tourists since the first tours to the town began in 1979.

Shekou, part of the Shenzhen SEZ, includes an exhibit of four of the **terra-cotta warriors** unearthed at Xian, and a stop at one of the many resorts catering to Hong Kong weekenders that have sprung up among the rolling hills and bays of Shekou. **Zhuhai** is most commonly visited as part of a Macau tour (see page 188) and is a center for oil rig suppliers and building materials. **Cuiheng Village**, in Zhongshan County, is the birthplace of Sun Yat-Sen; his former school and residence are now memorials.

✍ Offshore oil exploration and the open door have brought China traders to Guangzhou in herds, and several first-class hotels have sprung up to greet them, such as the **China Hotel**, the **Garden Hotel** and the **White Swan**. Most are joint ventures with Japanese or Hong Kong concerns. **Plum Flowers Hotel** has the virtue of providing the parking lot for an affiliated taxi company, and its restaurants are frequented by US Embassy personnel whose offices are nearby.

In the hot springs area of Zhuhai are the **Zhongshan International Hotel**, the **Zhongshan Hot Springs Resort** — which has a golf course designed by Arnold Palmer, and a Hong Kong manager, golf pro and office *(in Hong Kong* ☎ *521-0377/0378)* — the **Zhuhai Resort** and the **Zhuhai Holiday Resort**. The **Zhuhai International Golf Club** is run by the Japan Golf Promotion Co., as is a large amusement park nearby.

Since Hong Kong hotels are only about an hour away, Shenzhen SEZ has concentrated on building luxury resorts that offer golf, swimming, horseback riding, restaurants with floor shows, *et al.* **Honeylake Resort** w of the city has its own version of Disneyland as well. **Shenzhen Bay Hotel** is on the beach, with lovely views, although the best beach is at **Xiaomeisha Beach Resort** on Mirs Bay E of the city.

Shiyan Lake Hot Springs Resort, to the NW of the city, has good sports facilities. **Shenzhen Golf Course**, built in 1985 and designed by golf pro Isao Aoki, is a short taxi ride from Lo Wu rail station.

Hotels in China are usually fully reserved — so don't arrive without a reservation.

Taiwan

The Beautiful Island

The "real China" is how the Nationalists characterize the tobacco-leaf-shaped island of Taiwan (christened *Ilha Formosa,* "Beautiful Island," by the Portuguese sailors who sighted it in the 1600s). Traditional China thrives among Taiwan's 20 million people, 2.7 million of whom live in the capital city of Taipei. Yet the island is indisputably part of the modern world as well, and one of Asia's economic "dragons."

Taiwan's position on the world political stage is ambiguous. Officially calling it the Republic of China, its rulers claim sovereignty over the whole of China. Conversely, the government in Beijing, mainland China, itself claims in the name of the People's Republic of China to be the only legitimate government of the province of Taiwan.

The Taiwan government's main problem is that it is not officially recognized by most of the world community. It lost its UN seat and official contact with many countries in the early 1970s as the government in Beijing emerged from its period of hibernation. This makes it all but impossible for Taiwan to join an economic grouping, and in most matters the republic is isolated from the rest of the world.

However, these are not problems that need worry the traveler. For anyone interested in Chinese culture, and Chinese art in particular, there is a wealth to see — a wealth, indeed, that it may be impossible to see on the mainland. Among the main aims of Chiang Kai-shek, Taiwan's leader from 1945-75, was the promotion of traditional arts such as painting and calligraphy, and he brought with him to Taiwan the treasures that now reside in the National Palace Museum. The 600,000 *objets d'art* that pack its exhibition displays and underground vaults, which once occupied the Forbidden City in Beijing, are more than merely a collection of priceless artifacts: it is said that whoever controls *them* controls *China*. Little wonder so much effort was put in by the Nationalists to keep them from first the Japanese and then the communists.

LAND AND PEOPLE

Anyone lured to Taiwan because of its Portuguese name will be disappointed on arrival, for the flat, dull area where Taipei's international airport is sited can hardly be described as "beautiful." The western coastal plain, once the agricultural heartland of the island, is now becoming industrialized; to find the original beautiful island it is necessary to travel to the mountains and lakes of the interior and east coast and to the semitropical land of the extreme south.

Legend has it that the mountainous spine of Taiwan was thrown up by playful dragons as they cavorted down the length of the island. These mountains plunge down to the sea on the east, which makes for spectacular coastal scenery. The center of the island, with its misty vistas and reflective lakes, while not as splendid as Guilin in China, will still appear familiar to anyone interested in traditional Chinese landscape painting. The south paints an altogether different picture, with its palm trees, sandy beaches, virgin forest and grassy plateaux.

Unlike many other parts of Asia, including neighboring Hong Kong and Macau, Taiwan was not colonized long enough for Western influences to survive. The Dutch and the Spanish, and very briefly the French, occupied the island, but the last of the Europeans departed in the late 17th century. Just under 2 percent of the island's population has a history that goes way back beyond even the first Chinese settlers. The "aboriginal" tribes are thought to have originated from two sources. One, probably from Malayo-Polynesian stock, traveled north to Taiwan. The other is thought to have come from either South China or North Japan. For the past few centuries their descendants have been gradually pushed ever farther up into the hills, and many now live in special "cultural" villages.

Taipei, with its gleaming glass and concrete high-rises, is now far removed from the real China, but in the street markets and in particular the temples, the genuine article is easy enough to find. Temples continue to play an important role in Taiwanese society: they are local community centers, citizens' advice bureaus, social service offices and places to worship all rolled into one. No one will mind if you want to sit quietly in a cool corner. Local people will soon ignore visitors, who can watch the rhythm of life while taking a rest from the hot, traffic-choked streets.

Not so long ago, the "real China" was *so* Chinese as to be almost impenetrable to those who spoke no Mandarin. Today, as tourism and international trade become increasingly important, more and more Taiwanese travel and study abroad. English is becoming more common — or at least less uncommon. The main streets in Taipei now bear signs in Roman characters, and hotel staff in the international hotels speak acceptable English.

POLITICS AND THE ECONOMY

The Nationalists, or Kuomintang, trace their roots back to the Nationalist Party formed in 1912 by the Chinese revolutionary Dr Sun Yat-sen (1866-1925). Under the leadership of Chiang Kai-shek, they planted their flag on the island in 1945 after 50 years of Japanese rule. Taiwan became their last bastion after 1949, when they were ejected from the mainland.

Since then, relations between Taiwan and the People's Republic of China have been frigid, and at times fiery. Yet lately a thaw has been observed+, and unofficial contacts between the two now grow apace. Two-way trade between Taiwan and mainland China, channeled through Hong Kong, jumped to US$5.8 billion in 1991, representing a 43 percent increase over the previous year.

Despite its awkward political situation, Taiwan is opening up to foreigners, and as relations with China start to relax, the already booming economy seems set to continue its upward trend. This will generate much-needed cash to improve the infrastructure, which will enable Taiwan to consolidate its developing position as an important destination on the international tourism map.

Culture, history and background

A brief history of Taiwan

"Official" histories of Taiwan start noticeably late. There are passing references to the island as a protectorate of China in the **early 13thC**, but the story then jumps to the **17thC**, when the first of several waves of mass migration from the mainland took place. Until then, the island was virtually unknown in the West.

Archeological evidence, however, points to man's presence in the island as long as **10,000 years ago**. Similarities between finds here and in South China suggest some connections with the mainland. Little is known of the origins of the native peoples or "aborigines" of Taiwan, although it is thought that they are from two different sources. It is very likely that one group is of Malayo-Polynesian stock; its people have much in common with Malay and Filipino groups. The derivation of the other group is murkier: they have been linked to the southern Chinese Miao by some historians and anthropologists and to the northern Japanese Ainu ethnic group by others.

Taiwan's modern history is a tale of domination by foreign powers, China among them. Descendants of the Chinese, who crossed the straits in the **17th, 18th** and **19thC**, consider themselves to be the only true "Taiwanese." Even today, more recent immigrants are referred to as "mainlanders" or "late comers."

In February **1947** tensions between native Taiwanese and newcomers from the mainland boiled over into widespread demand for reforms on the part of the locals. During two bloody weeks in May a fragile truce was shattered when at least 10,000 Taiwanese are believed to have been massacred by KMT troops, an episode that still rankles today, a full generation later.

Although tensions between the two groups have diminished across the years, the differences between them remain an important facet of cultural, political and economic life on the island. The Taiwanese speak their own language, a dialect very similar to Fujian Chinese spoken on the mainland. This tends to leave many of the older residents, many of whom do not speak Mandarin, at a disadvantage in the labor market. Because of their contacts with the Kuomintang, the mainlanders who came across with the Nationalists were often given priority in securing the best jobs in the armed forces, politics and business. The Taiwanese were left behind in poorly paid, low-prestige agricultural jobs and were looked down on as simple country cousins.

ENTER THE EUROPEANS

Records indicate that Taiwan was known to the Chinese in the **3rdC BC**, but it was not until the **3rdC AD** that imperially authorized contact was made. Further expeditions were launched in the **7thC**, but as China lapsed into a long period of insularity, Taiwan was left to its native peoples, to the Japanese pirates that sheltered along its w coast and to the wandering Hakkas, the "gypsies" of China, who came to the island to farm.

And then on the horizon in the **16thC** appeared the ships of the Europeans — Portuguese, British, Spanish, Dutch and French — and the Japanese, all falling across one other to grab ports and trading rights in the Far East. The Portuguese were the first to visit Taiwan, but despite being obviously impressed (they named it *Ilha Formosa,* or the Beautiful Island), they did not stay and it was left to the Dutch to stake a claim. They arrived in **1624** and were granted permission by China to set up a trading post: China did not in fact control the island at that time.

Very few traces survive of the Dutch and the later Spanish settlements on Taiwan. In Anping, the Chih-kan Tower has been built on the remains of the Dutch Fort Providentia, destroyed by an earthquake in 1862. Outside the town there is a reconstruction of the main Dutch fort of Zeelandia. The Spanish also landed in the **mid-1620s** and established themselves in the N of the island. The so-called Red Fort at Tanshui — still standing today — was built by them, and was later occupied by the Dutch, who drove the Iberians out in **1642**.

The Dutch did not control the island for very long. In a foretaste of what was to happen nearly 300 years later, Cheng Cheng-kung, better known to the West as Koxinga, or Lord of the Imperial Surname, landed in **1661** with a force of 30,000 Ming troops from the mainland, fleeing the conquering Manchus. He set up a Chinese-style civil service and promoted traditional Chinese culture on the island, and for these efforts he is revered to this day.

The similarities with recent history are uncanny, although the glories of this earlier period were short-lived. Koxinga's descendants (he died aged only 38, just a year after he landed on the island) eventually lost power to the Manchus. With events on the mainland and on Taiwan finally running in tandem, the way was paved for thousands and thousands of immigrants to cross the Formosa Straits. Although there was a brief interregnum when the French occupied part of northern Taiwan following a dispute with China, the island was declared a fully-fledged province of China in **1887**.

As the Portuguese, Spanish and Dutch left the stage, the Russians and Americans took their place, and the Japanese, who had withdrawn into insularity, returned. Trading concessions on Taiwan were granted to foreign powers, similar to those granted at the mainland's treaty ports. A constant problem for the foreign powers, however, was China's self-admitted inability to exercise control over most of the island. Shipwrecked survivors were frequently beheaded, and protests to the imperial court had little effect.

One particularly nasty incident in the early 1870s led to the occupation of part of Taiwan by a Japanese military force, following unsuccessful negotiations with the Chinese emperor. This shock invasion brought the Chinese running back to the negotiating table, where they offered compensation for the murdered sailors, and the Japanese eventually withdrew.

THE JAPANESE OCCUPATION

Two decades later, however, the flag of the Land of the Rising Sun was to fly over the entire island, where it remained for another 50 years. Taiwan and the Pescadores islands were ceded in **1895** to the Japanese following China's debacle in a war between the two countries over Korea. Never particularly happy with life under the rule of distant Peking, the Taiwanese were even less enamored with their new colonial rulers, who governed the island harshly. Resistance lingered for years, and unrest among Taiwanese and the native tribes was regularly suppressed in a violent and heavy-handed manner. As late as **1930**, an uprising by tribespeople near Taichung was bloodily put down, and hundreds of tribesmen and 200 Japanese soldiers died, the former in mysterious circumstances.

The island's infrastructure — particularly its roads, rail and ports — was improved and food-processing plants were built to help the Japanese reap as much benefit as they could from their occupation. The island became Japan's rice bowl and sugar bowl. Japanese became the dominant language, and to this day many elderly residents still speak it. Education followed the Japanese model, Chinese institutions were dismantled, the culture was discouraged, and all residents were required to use Japanese names.

Following Japan's invasion of mainland China and the onset of **World War II**, Taiwan became gradually more self-sufficient as the Japanese developed heavy industry on the island to help fuel its own war effort. As shipping links between Japan and Taiwan grew increasingly tenuous during the war, Taiwan at last started to retain its own produce and ceased to be a colonial economy. Although the island was bombed extensively in **1944**, it was spared any major military action.

With Japan's defeat in **1945**, many Taiwanese looked forward to increased autonomy after centuries of foreign rule. But these hopes were dashed after it was returned to China under the terms of the Cairo Declaration on **October 28, 1945**. Led by Chiang Kai-shek, the Nationalists, who at that time formed the government on the mainland, took control.

THE KUOMINTANG ERA

Within four years of the end of World War II, Taiwan had become all that remained of the Nationalists' Republic of China. The Kuomintang (KMT) had been founded in **1912** by a handful of anti-Manchu revolutionaries. One of them was Dr Sun Yat-sen. Although the KMT was successful in the elections of **1913**, it was not until the **late 1920s** under the leadership of General Chiang Kai-shek that it became the legitimate government of China.

Following an uneasy truce during the war years and the Japanese occupation of part of China, fighting broke out between the KMT and the Chinese Communist Party. Despite possessing superior fire power, Chiang Kai-shek's armies came very close to defeat and eventually scrambled across the Taiwan Straits to the island refuge of Taiwan in **1949**, just as Koxinga had done 300 years before.

As the communists declared the People's Republic of China on the mainland, Taiwan became the last bastion of the Republic of China, a position that formally it still holds today. Chiang Kai-shek remained president and declared his republic to be the only legitimate government of the Chinese peoples. Reunification under the KMT was the ultimate aim. For its part, the communist government claimed sovereignty over Taiwan, a position that created an impasse between the two sides for more than 40 years.

Chiang Kai-shek died in **1975** and was succeeded by his son Chiang Ching-kuo. Following his death in **1988**, Taiwan was finally ruled by its first native-born president, Lee Teng-hui.

THE MODERN ERA

Taiwan's political status continues to be ambiguous. It is no longer recognized diplomatically as an independent state by most other countries. It lost its United Nations seat in **1971**, and the US cut diplomatic ties in **1979**. Yet Taiwan, belying its backwater position in world politics, has blossomed into a prosperous, vibrant land economically.

Today, along with Hong Kong, Singapore and Malaysia, it is described as one of the four dragons of Asia. In just four decades, Taiwan has been transformed from a backward agricultural land into one of the most dynamic economies in the world. A rapidly growing economy, burgeoning exports and expanding domestic market have been brought about by a combination of strong governmental management, enterprising individual companies and foreign investment.

As the manufacturing sector became increasingly diversified and import restrictions were liberalized, the economy matured. The result is the Taiwan we see today: a major producer of electronic appliances, petrochemicals, iron and steel, cars, airplanes, ships, textiles and sporting goods, footwear and toys. In 1990, Taiwan was the world's 15th largest importer and 12th largest exporter, and recorded the highest foreign exchange reserves in the world. Its per capita GDP at the end of 1991 was US$8,800, one of the highest in Asia.

Taiwan is by no means immune to the international trade cycle. Economic growth slowed to 5.2 per cent in 1990 from double-digit figures in previous years. 1990 also saw a major collapse in share prices on the country's highly speculative stock exchange.

But these are considered to be mere hiccups; the economy grew at a rate of 7.2 percent in 1991, a year in which Taiwan also embarked upon a new six-year economic plan at a cost of US$303 billion. The plan aims to improve the country's infrastructure by investing in new road and rail links and establishing a fourth nuclear plant. It is also designed to promote regional development in order to ease traffic congestion problems in the Taipei area, and to give tax and financial incentives to 10 key industries, including information technology and pollution control.

It is a strange paradox: for a country that is so successful economically — in **1991** it was the world's 15th-largest trading nation — Taiwan has remarkably little clout on the world stage. Although it is difficult to envisage any future Beijing government renouncing its avowed policy of unification with Taiwan, the political scene on the island itself is more fluid. The KMT may still remain in power, but several political reforms in recent years hint at a freer Taiwan.

In **1986**, martial law was lifted for the first time since 1949. One year later, in **1987**, residents were allowed to visit mainland relatives (via Hong Kong for now; but it is anticipated that direct flights will be allowed in the not too distant future). In recent years too, new political parties have been allowed to form and, in the legislative assembly, the opposition Democratic Progressive Party has become extremely vocal. In December **1991** all remaining sitting legislators representing mainland constituencies retired. In the following elections the KMT was returned to power with a huge majority, the DPP failing to turn rhetoric into votes.

In the same year, President Lee declared that Taiwan would "not use force as a means to seek reunification" with China. With trade, albeit "backdoor," between the island and China increasing steadily, it seems very likely that unofficial contacts between the two Chinas will increase.

Less certain is the political future of the island. Will it evolve into a Hong Kong-style one-country/two-systems model? Will there be full independence for Taiwan? Or will military — or, conversely, peaceful — unification be achieved with the mainland? All three possible outcomes are widely canvased.

Taipei architecture

Even the most loyal Taiwanese will hardly claim that Taipei is an architectural treasurehouse. Designated a city as recently as 1920, it has grown very quickly, and the level of new construction work currently in progress is widely thought to be the highest in Asia.

The Japanese, unlike the British, Dutch and Portuguese in other parts of the Far East, did not leave behind them in Taipei a distinctive legacy of bricks and mortar, their public buildings being mere copies of Western architecture. Moreover, as a backwater of various Chinese empires, the island has never garnered the palatial buildings to be seen on the mainland. However, there are two stylistically characteristic groups of buildings: **temples** and **public monuments**.

Most Taiwanese temples date from the 18th and 19thC, the oldest in Taipei being the **Lungshan Temple**. They vary in size from tiny, one-room affairs hardly big enough for more than one worshiper, to those consisting of several halls dedicated to what seem like hundreds of deities. The larger examples are usually built around a courtyard, with the main altar, which holds a representation of the temple's chief deity, located under a roof in the center. Smaller altars are positioned in halls around the outside. Characteristic of the temples is their roofs, which feature elaborate and frequently gaudy decorations, with exaggerated eaves and extravagantly curved ridges. Among the fishes, historical and mythical figures, phoenixes and flowers that adorn the roof, a favorite is the mighty dragon, who twists and pitches his way along the ridge: Lungshan, in fact, means "Dragon Mountain."

Temple roofline detail

Contemporary architects in Taiwan have turned to traditional Chinese imperial influences for inspiration for their important public monuments. Probably most impressive of these is the **Chiang Kai-shek Memorial Hall**, because of its size, its setting and the striking simplicity of its design. The white body of the 76m (250-foot) memorial with its strong, clean lines, topped by a brilliant blue-tiled and fluted roof, presents a graceful yet imposing structure (illustrated on page 226). When originally completed in 1980 this was the highest building in the city. It is flanked by a concert hall and an opera house, both of traditional design with red pillars and orange-tiled roofs. The entrance gate to the complex mirrors the memorial hall, with a white structure and blue-tiled roof. This portal, which is as wide as the memorial hall is high, features three arches and is likewise modeled on the Ming style, the grand Chinese architectural form named after the dynasty that ruled China between 1368 and 1644.

The long, low **Sun Yat-sen Memorial Hall** commemorates the Nationalists' other great hero. Although low-key in comparison with the majestic Chiang Kai-shek Memorial, it is hardly less impressive. Similarly based on traditional Chinese architecture, the design emphasizes the roof, with its yellow-glazed tiles and sweeping curves.

The **Martyrs' Shrine** is modeled upon the Ming and Ching palaces of Beijing, each building being styled after a particular hall or pavilion. Another in this traditional genre is the **Grand Hotel**, whose wholly Chinese character is emphasized by its red pillars and double-layered roof. The hotel, a landmark of Taipei, is described at length in WHERE TO STAY, on page 233.

Arguably the only imaginative modern building in the city is the **Fine Arts Museum**, illustrated below. The stacked-cube structure, designed by Kao Erh-pan, who was awarded the commission after several blueprints were considered, appears externally to be very Western. It does, however, owe as much to Chinese architecture as to Occidental, as the interior is modeled around a courtyard. Also worth visiting for its striking architecture is the **Taiwan Provincial Museum**, a replica of a Classical Greek building, built by the Japanese during their occupation.

Fine Arts Museum

The role of the arts

Taiwan, it is often said, is where the soul of true Chinese culture lies. As guardians of the treasures of China, in the form of the collection at the National Palace Museum, Taiwan believes it is protecting and preserving the arts so that, when the mainland returns to the fold — that is, to the Republic of China — traditional culture will flourish again throughout the land. Naive as this view may be, one has only to consider the destruction wrought in the name of the Cultural Revolution in the People's Republic on the mainland to understand this idealism. Culture has always been an emotive subject for the Chinese, for it has frequently been the single force that unifies a multitude of ethnic groups from a variety of geographical regions with very different dialects and no institutionalized religion.

This overriding cultural role might so easily have stifled the development of the arts in Taiwan. Instead, increasing social prosperity has made it easier for painters, sculptors, musicians and dancers to make a living and simultaneously to be more experimental. A good example is of this development is the **Cloud Gate Dance Group**, which has incorporated modern dance techniques into the traditional Chinese genre.

Another case in point is the success of the magnificent **Fine Arts Museum**. Housed in what is one of the few architecturally interesting modern buildings in Taipei (see ARCHITECTURE), the museum includes not only paintings and sculpture but a library, lecture rooms, a studio and an auditorium. Among its professed aims are the promotion of art education in Taiwan and collaboration with museums in other parts of the world. It stages exhibitions and retrospectives of major Western arts as well as transient and permanent collections of contemporary Chinese media. The mock-Tudor building next door is home to the **Artists' Club**, an information center and coffee shop that is open to the public.

The **National Palace Museum**, too, plays an important part in promoting the arts. Seminars are held in English on various aspects of Chinese painting and calligraphy. At the end of each lecture, museum guides conduct tours of exhibitions relevant to the talk *(for information* ☎ *881 2021, ext. 377).*

Away from the great museums, several small galleries where works of established and up-and-coming artists can be viewed and bought have congregated in **Chunghsiao E Rd. Sec 4.**

The soul of Chinese culture

Taiwan's spiritual life is similar to that of Hong Kong: a melting pot of **Buddhism, Taoism** and **Confucianism**, although temples are officially designated only as either Taoist or Confucian. The dominant deities of the island are **Kuan Yin** (or Goddess of Mercy), **Kuan Kung**, and **Matsu** or Goddess of the Sea (known in Hong Kong as Tin Hau). Taoist temple life is more vibrant than in Hong Kong, where firecrackers are banned; here, barrages of crackers regularly pierce the incensed-filled air. The buildings act as meeting houses for locals, where old people gather to doze in the shade and swap gossip, as well as to worship.

The question of **language** is vitally important to Taiwan. When mainland China slammed its door on the world, Taiwan became the only place where foreign students could study Mandarin in a native setting, and numerous language schools and institutions opened up to cater to the demand. Many have survived, despite the fact that mainland China is now more accessible.

In the post-World War II era, Taiwan's **film industry** took over from Shanghai the mantle of the "Hollywood of China." Movies were and continue to be produced not just for the home market but for Overseas Chinese communities from Manchester to Vancouver, from Singapore to Sydney and San Francisco. The 1960s saw the rise of the *kung-fu* genre, many produced in conjunction with Hong Kong companies. Lower production costs and a better choice of locations in Taiwan have allowed this co-operation to continue.

The sheer force of Chinese culture has obviously overshadowed that of the **indigenous Taiwan peoples**; it is impossible to sample the dance or music of these tribes outside of their own areas. The most accessible groups, for example the **Ami of Hwalien** on the E coast and the **Atayal of Wulai** N of Taipei, have been exploited mercilessly for tourist dollars, and the shows they produce are only pitiful imitations of what they must once have been. In general, the farther away they are from urban centers, the more authentic their dance, music, customs, rituals and living conditions, but even the loin-cloth-wearing **Yami of Lanyu** island 76km (47 miles) off Taiwan's SE coast are no strangers to camera-toting tourists.

Basic information

Before you go

DOCUMENTS REQUIRED

All foreigners must obtain a **visitor visa** from Taiwan diplomatic, consular and designated offices before they travel. These visas, which cover tourism, business and study, are valid for six months. Two extensions of 60 days can be obtained from various offices in Taiwan (see USEFUL ADDRESSES, page 216). **Health documents** are only needed if you have recently visited an infected country.

Those intending to drive in Taiwan must have a valid **international license** issued outside of Taiwan.

TRAVEL AND MEDICAL INSURANCE

Take out insurance coverage before you leave. **American Express** provides comprehensive travel and medical insurance including on-the-spot 24-hour emergency coverage. Contact **American Express Travel Service** offices for details. **Extrasure** also has a comprehensive package offering an emergency service. Check whether other insurance companies have a reciprocal agreement with companies in Taiwan for refund of medical expenses. (See also page 30 in HONG KONG).

The **IAMAT** (International Association for Medical Assistance to Travelers) is a nonprofit organization that has a directory of English-speaking doctors who will call, for a fixed fee. There are member hospitals and clinics throughout the world, including one in Taipei. Membership is free, and other benefits include information on health risks overseas.

For further information write to **IAMAT** headquarters in the US or in Europe *(417 Center St., Lewiston NY 14092 or 57 Voirets, 1212 Grand-Lancy, Genève, Switzerland).*

MONEY

The unit of currency is the New Taiwan dollar (NT$). Banks and newspapers provide daily exchange rates. Wait until you arrive in Taiwan before buying NT$; it is either unavailable abroad or exchange rates are unfavorable. Obtain and keep receipts when buying NT$; you will need them to exchange any leftover NT$ when you leave.

Travelers checks issued by American Express, Barclays, Thomas Cook and Citibank, and major **credit and charge cards** (American

Express, Diners Club, MasterCard, Visa) are widely accepted. Specialist travelers check companies such as American Express provide extensive local refund facilities through their own offices or agents.

Carry cash in small amounts only. Travelers checks issued by all major companies are widely recognized. Make sure you read the instructions included with your travelers checks. **It is important to note separately the serial numbers of your checks and the telephone number to call in case of loss.**

CUSTOMS
International allowances for alcohol and tobacco apply. You will need to declare gold, silver, foreign currencies and NT$ notes on arrival. **Airport tax** is NT$300 on departure.

GETTING THERE
By air   Most visitors arrive at Chiang Kai-shek airport, 40km (25 miles) from Taipei. A few international flights arrive at Kaohsiung in the s of the island.

By sea   The *Hiryu-3* sails once a week between Okinawa in Japan and Kaohsiung, a voyage of 37 hours. Accommodations includes first-class cabins and a variety of dormitories. Contact **Yeong-An Maritime** in Taipei (☎ *7715911)* or **Arimura Line** in Okinawa (☎ *(098) 869-1320)*. At the time of writing, a scheduled service between Macau and Kaohsiung was being withdrawn.

CLIMATE AND CLOTHES
Climate is very similar to Hong Kong. Winter temperatures in the N of the island can get down to 10˚C (50˚F), although the mean is 15˚C (59˚F), and it snows in the mountains. All-year-round swimming is possible in the s. The summer mean is 30˚C (86˚F). Taiwan's typhoon season matches that of Hong Kong, but being a much larger land mass the chances of a direct hit are much higher. The unprotected E coast is more prone to typhoons than the w.

Lightweight cotton clothes are best for summer months, but pack warm clothing for winter. Short-sleeved, open-neck shirts are suitable business attire for men, but jackets are required dress for formal occasions. Take either an umbrella or waterproof clothing at any time of year.

US INFORMATION SERVICES
Coordination Council for North America Affairs *(4201 Wisconsin Ave. NW, Washington, DC 20016-2137* ☎ *(202) 895-1800)*. This, the head office of the CCNAA, will provide contact addresses for other US cities. As the US has no official diplomatic ties with Taiwan, the CCNAA acts as the visa-issuing office.

UK INFORMATION SERVICES
Free Chinese Centre *(4/F Dorland House, 14-16 Regent St, London SW1Y 4PH* ☎ *(071) 930 5767)*. As the UK has no official diplomatic ties with Taiwan, the Free Chinese Centre acts as the visa-issuing office.

OBTAINING A VISA IN HONG KONG
Chung Wah Travel Service   #4, East Tower, Bond Centre, 89
Queensway, Hong Kong ☎525-8315, map 4C4

Getting around

There is only one way to cover the 40km (25 miles) from Chiang
Kai-shek (often abbreviated to CKS) airport to Taipei and that is by
road. Between 7.50am and 11.30pm, two public **buses** serve the airport at approximately 15-minute intervals. One line goes to the domestic airport on the NE of Taipei — useful for those who intend to fly
straight ahead to somewhere else in Taiwan — while the other deposits passengers at the main rail station in central Taipei. Some hotels
offer a shuttle-bus service to and from CKS, while others will arrange a
private limousine. Check when you make your reservation.

Taxis are available, but drivers will usually charge more than the
meter, making it about the same as or only marginally cheaper than a
private hotel limo. If you are thinking of using a limousine service get
someone at the hotel desk at the airport to write the name and address
of your destination in Chinese. Allow between 60-90 minutes for the trip.

PUBLIC TRANSPORTATION

Taipei's transportation system has not kept pace with its furious building and population boom. Streets are frequently choked with traffic,
especially during the evening rush hours, making traveling an unpleas-
ant experience. A **subway** system (to be called the MRT) is scheduled
to open its first line at the end of 1992 from Fuhsing N Rd. to Mucha in
the SE suburbs, with further lines coming on-stream in the following
couple of years. While residents eagerly look forward to this, they are
already fed up with the disruption caused by road repairs associated
with its construction. For the time being, however, that leaves only
taxis and buses.

Taxis are plentiful, easy to hail and inexpensive compared with those
in the West. Non-Chinese speakers should always carry a note of their
destination written in Chinese characters. **Buses** present more of a
problem: signs on vehicle fronts and at stops are only in Chinese,
although it is possible to purchase a book giving the routes in English.
How you pay depends on the line: either as you get on or off. You can
either pay the exact fare on the bus or buy a book of tickets from the
kiosk near stops.

Special **"Cultural Buses"** run on Sundays and public holidays only.
The **S Cultural bus** runs a circular route from the rail station opposite
the Hilton and takes in the Sun Yat-sen Memorial Hall, World Trade
Center, Flower Market, Postal Museum, National Museum of History,
Youth Park, Lungshan Temple and Armed Forces Museum. The **N Cul-
tural bus** also departs from the rail station and passes the Fine Arts
Museum, Chinese Culture and Movie Center, National Palace Museum,

Martyrs' Shrine, Hsingtien Temple and Chiang Kai-shek Memorial Hall in its loop.

Express buses run to all the major cities, towns and scenic spots on the island from Taipei.

GETTING AROUND BY CAR

This is not to be recommended in Taipei. The roads are crowded and the standard of driving not high, and apart from major thoroughfares all street signs are in Chinese. Cars drive on the right.

Self-drive is more attractive outside Taipei, especially in the extreme s, where jeeps or motorcycles can be rented to visit Kenting National Park. On major highways, be aware that lane discipline is virtually nil.

RENTING A CAR

Evidence that car rental is uncommon comes from the fact that none of the major international companies operate in Taiwan. The brave can contact **China Rental** (☎ *500 6088)*, **Tong Lu Car Rental** (☎ *521 7579)* and **Taipei Budget Rent-a-Car** (☎ *831 2906)*. Valid international licenses are required.

GETTING AROUND ON FOOT

The "pollution watch" in local newspapers and the face masks worn by scooter and motorcycle riders explain why Taiwanese are bemused by tourists who insist on walking around Taipei. However, several of the major sights are clustered together in the sw of the city and can comfortably be covered on foot. A word of warning for the unwary: scooters park — and therefore ride — on sidewalks, so keep an eye out for them.

GETTING AROUND BY TRAIN

This is a good, economical way to see Taiwan. Trains run to most tourist destinations except for the extreme s. Tickets can be reserved a couple of days in advance at the main rail station off Chunghsiao W Rd., Sec 1, opposite the Hilton hotel *(map 9 D3),* or through hotels and tour agents. Try to avoid traveling on weekends, especially to the resorts N of Taipei, when everyone else is on the go too. The **railroad information desk** can be contacted on ☎371 3558.

Trains are generally efficient and clean; free tea and hand towels are available, as are snacks. Express services are all air-conditioned. The fastest trains from Taipei to Kaohsiung take just under $4\frac{1}{2}$ hours, and from Taipei to Hwalien 3 hours.

DOMESTIC AIRWAYS

A number of companies operate routes all over Taiwan and to the outlying islands. For those with limited time, this is the best way to get around. The domestic airport is conveniently sited on the NE of the city.

- **China Airlines**   ☎715 1212
- **Far East Air Transport**   ☎712 1555
- **Formosa Airlines**   ☎514 9636

On-the-spot information

PUBLIC HOLIDAYS

Chinese holidays, based on the lunar calendar, vary from year to year, but the following provides a guide.

January 1, 2, founding of the Republic of China. **February** (usually), Chinese New Year (first 3 days of lunar new year). **March 29,** Youth Day. **April 4,** Children's Day. **April 5,** Tomb Sweeping Day and Commemoration of the Death of President Chiang Kai-shek (except in leap years, when it falls on **April 4**). **June,** Dragon Boat Festival. **September,** Mid-Fall Festival (Moon Festival). **September 28,** Birthday of Confucius (Teachers' Day). **October 10,** National Day (Double Tenth Day). **October 25,** Retrocession Day. **October 31,** birthday of President Chiang Kai-shek. **November 12,** Dr Sun Yat-sen's birthday. **December 25,** Constitution Day.

TIME ZONE

Taiwan is 13 hours ahead of Eastern Standard Time all year round with no daylight saving adjustment, so during Daylight Saving Taiwan is 12 hours ahead. It is 8 hours ahead of GMT all year round with no daylight saving adjustment, so during British Summer Time Taiwan is 7 hours ahead of the UK. (For further information on time zones, see pages 38-39 in HONG KONG.)

LANGUAGE

Mandarin is the official language, but Taiwanese (a Fujian dialect) is widely spoken, particularly in the s and in the countryside. Older residents, schooled during the Japanese occupation, speak Japanese. English is not widely spoken, except by those in the tourist industry, but as more young Taiwanese travel and study abroad it is becoming less uncommon. Few taxi drivers speak English — always have addresses written in Chinese.

Names of major streets in Taipei are written in English as well as Chinese. There is a great deal of confusion over spelling and style: thus Chungshan and Chung Shan, or Linsen, Linshen and Lin Shen. In this guide we adopt the most frequently used style for places and streets; hence Chungshan Rd., Nanking Rd., etc.

BANKS AND CURRENCY EXCHANGE

Banks are open Monday to Friday 9am-3.30pm and Saturday 9am-noon, and are closed on public holidays. Hotels change foreign currency and travelers checks, but sometimes only to room guests.

American Express has a **MoneyGram** ® money transfer service that makes it possible to wire money worldwide in just minutes from any American Express Travel Service Office. In Taipei you can receive money in this way, but cannot send it. This service is not limited to American Express Card members. Payment can be made in cash, or with an American Express Card with a Centurion Credit Line, or with other cards. For the location nearest you ☎**1-800-543-4080** (Canada and US).

SHOPPING AND BUSINESS HOURS

Department stores and large shops open seven days a week, from 10 or 11am to 10pm. Small, family-run businesses are open from early morning to late evening. Business and government offices' working hours are Monday to Friday 9am-5.30pm, with a lunch break from noon-1.30pm (this is taken very seriously: don't expect to get any help or answers at this time of day), and Saturday 9am-noon.

RUSH HOURS

Weekdays 8-10am and 5-7pm, and Saturday 8-10am and noon-2pm are times to avoid making long trips across the city. Buses and trains to popular resorts around Taipei, especially in the N, are crowded on weekends and on public holidays.

POSTAL AND TELEPHONE SERVICES

Post offices are open from 8am-5pm Monday to Saturday. When posting letters abroad at mail boxes, use the left slot of the red box (the other slot is for domestic express mail, the green box for domestic surface mail). Overseas phone calls can be made at **International Telecommunication Administration** (ITA) offices. Public pay phones are plentiful; pictorial instructions inside them are clear.

☎ The **area code** for Taipei is **02**.

LAWS AND REGULATIONS

Gambling is illegal, which explains why Macau with its casinos is a popular vacation destination for Taiwanese. It is illegal to bring communist literature or pornographic publications into Taiwan, or for that matter any article manufactured in a communist country, including, of course, mainland China. It is, however, unlikely that a foreign tourist would be stopped and searched at the airport.

SOCIAL CUSTOMS AND ETIQUETTE

Anyone who visits Taipei after Hong Kong will be pleasantly surprised by the relatively uncrowded streets, the welcoming smiles that greet them (even when nobody understands a word they say), and the lower noise level. Mandarin is much easier on the Western ear than Cantonese.

Name cards

It is a major *faux pas* for a business person to arrive in Taiwan without name cards. Even when on vacation it is a good idea to carry a handful around, as the Taiwanese love handing theirs out and appreciate them in return. To give your card to someone else hold it in both hands and bow slightly as you hand it over. Do the same when you receive theirs.

Meeting people

Taiwanese students don't get as much opportunity to practice their English as their Hong Kong equivalents, so they can be eager to engage foreigners in conversation. Some of their questions can be very direct: "Are you married?" "Why aren't you married?" "How much do you earn?" On the other hand, they may be reticent about discussing sensitive political issues — don't push them if they seem reluctant. If someone doesn't know the answer to your question, or doesn't have what you want, you'll probably get an embarrassed smile rather than a negative reply. Just learn to grin and bear it and avoid any temptation to shout at them. If a taxi driver claims his meter is not working, just get out and find another cab.

HEALTH AND HYGIENE
Although tap water is said to be safe, it is advisable to stick to the bottled variety.

DISABLED TRAVELERS
The government has been making an effort in recent years to improve facilities. Sidewalks in central Taipei have built-in ramps for the convenience of wheelchair users. Paradoxically, the only way to cross particularly busy intersections is by underground passage — and they are all steps. Museums, particularly the newer ones, are well equipped for disabled travelers, with special elevators, spare wheelchairs, etc.

LOCAL ENGLISH-LANGUAGE MEDIA
There are two local English-language newspapers, both very similar in content. The *China Post* and *China News* rely mainly on international news agency reports with a small amount of local reporting. They carry foreign exchange rates, television and movie theater listings, and advertisements for restaurants and clubs.

The *Directory of Taiwan*, published by *China News*, is an invaluable collection of addresses, phone and fax numbers, including trade and industry offices, chambers of commerce, trade associations, manufacturing companies and commercial offices, as well as government departments. It is available at bookstores, or contact ☎388 7931 or ⓕ381 5987. Hotel business centers may have a copy.

Trade Winds publishes a series of useful trade periodicals, including weekly and monthly general editions (usually to be found in major international hotels) and several annual titles organized by industry.

A local-run English-language radio station, **ICRT**, broadcasts 24 hours a day on AM 576MHz in Taipei, 1570KHz in Taichung and on FM 100.1MHz and 100.9MHz. See newspapers for details of English broadcasts on local television.

ENGLISH BOOKSTORES
Caves Books   103 Chungshan N Rd. Sec 2. Map **9**C3. By far the best, but unfortunately it is no longer able to sell cheap versions of reference books, which it was once famous for. Also sells tickets to concerts, etc.

Useful addresses

TOURIST INFORMATION
Tourism Bureau   #9, 280 Chunghsiao E Rd. Sec 4 ☎721 8541.
Map **10**D5.
Travel Information Service Center   Sungshan Domestic Airport
☎712 1212, ext. 471. Map **10**B5.
Tourist Information Hot Line   ☎717 3737. Map **10**B5. Travel information, emergency assistance, complaints, language problems, etc.
Pick up a card with the details at the passport control desk at the airport and keep it for handy reference. Open 8am-8pm.
American Express Travel Service   #1, 214 Tunhwa N Rd. ☎717
8600, or for lost cards ☎719 0606. Map **10**C5. A valuable source of information for any traveler in need of help, advice or emergency services.

VISA RENEWAL
Foreign Affairs Police   96 Yenping S Rd. ☎381 7475. Map
9D2.

POST OFFICE
Main post office   55 Chinshan S Rd. Sec 2 ☎392 1310. Map
9E3.

CABLE/TELEGRAPH
International Telecommunications Administration   28 Hangchou S Rd. Sec 1 ☎344 3780. Map **9**D3. Open 24 hours.
23 Chungshan N Rd. Sec 2   ☎541 7434. Map **9**C3. Open Monday
to Friday 8.30am-5.30pm, Saturday 8.30am-12.30pm.
118 Chunghsiao W Rd. Sec 1   ☎314 0250. Map **9**D2.
Sungshan Domestic Airport   ☎712 6112. Map **10**B5. Open Monday to Saturday 8am-6pm, Sunday and public holidays 8am-noon.
Taipei World Trade Center   ☎725 1111. Off map **10**E6. Open
Monday to Friday 8am-5pm, Saturday 8am-noon, Sunday and public
holidays same hours as exhibitions.

TOUR OPERATORS
China Express Transportation   70 Chungshan N Rd. Sec 2 ☎541
6466. Map **9**C3.
Edison Travel Services   #4, 190 Sungchiang Rd., Taipei ☎563
5313. Map **10**C4.
Huei-Fong Travel Service   #4, 50 Nanking E Rd. Sec 2, Taipei
☎551 5805. Map **10**C4.
Pinho Travel Service Co.   #3, 142-1 Chilin Rd. ☎551 4136. Map
10B4.
South East Travel Service   60 Chungshan N Rd. Sec 2 ☎571 3001.
Map **9**C3.
Taiwan Coach Tours   #8, 27 Chungshan N Rd. Sec 3 ☎595 5321.
Map **9**B3.

AIRLINES

Cathay Pacific   137 Nanking E Rd. Sec 2 ☎715 2333. Map **10**C4.
China Airlines 131 Nanking E Rd. Sec 3 ☎715 1212. Map **10**C4.
Delta Air Lines   #3, 50 Nanking E Rd. Sec 2 ☎551 0923. Map **10**C4.
Garuda Indonesia   #6, 82 Sungchiang Rd. ☎561 2311. Map **10**C4.
Japan Asia Airways   2 Tunhwa S Rd. Sec 1 ☎776 5151. Map **10**D5.
KLM Royal Dutch Airlines   1 Nanking E Rd. Sec 4, Taipei ☎717 3000. Map **10**C4.
Korean Air   53 Nanking E Rd. Sec 2 ☎521 4242. Map **10**C4.
Malaysia Airlines   #1/2, 102 Tunhwa N Rd. ☎716 8384. Map **10**C5.
Northwest Airlines   #1/2, 181 Fuhsing N Rd. ☎716 1555. Map **10**C5.
Philippine Airlines   #2, 90 Chienkuo N Rd. Sec 2 ☎505 3030. Map **10**C4.
Singapore Airlines   148 Sungchiang Rd. ☎551 6655. Map **10**C4.
South African Airways   #1, 205 Tunhwa N Rd. ☎713 6363. Map **10**C5.
Thai Airways International   152 Fuhsing N Rd. ☎715 2766. Map **10**C5.
United Airlines   #12, 2 Jenai Rd. Sec 4 ☎703 7600. Map **10**D5.

EMBASSIES, CONSULATES AND FOREIGN REPRESENTATIVES

Few countries have diplomatic relations with Taiwan, but the representatives listed below can issue visas, new passports and so on, although paperwork may take some time.
American Institute in Taiwan   7, Lane 134, Hsinyi Rd. Sec 3 ☎709 2000. Map **10**D4.
Anglo-Taiwan Trade Committee   #9, 99 Jenai Rd. Sec 2 ☎322 4242. Map **10**D4.
Australian Commerce and Industry Office   Rm 2605, 333 Keelung Rd. Sec 1 ☎757 6544. Map **10**E6.
Canadian Trade Office   #13, 365 Fuhshing N Rd. ☎713 7268. Map **10**C5.
New Zealand Commerce and Industry Office   Rm 0812, #8, 333 Keelung Rd. Sec 1 ☎757 7060. Map **10**E6.

USEFUL BUSINESS ADDRESSES

China External Trade Development Council   333, Keelung Rd. Sec 1. ☎725 5200 ⒻⓍ757 6653. Map **10**E6.
Taipei Chamber of Commerce   72 Nanking E Rd., Sec 2 ☎531 8217. Map **10**E6.
Taiwan Chamber of Commerce   158 Sungchiang Rd. ☎536 5455. Map **10**C4.

Emergency information

EMERGENCY SERVICES
Police ☎110
Fire ☎119
Tourist Information Hot Line ☎717 3737. Also deals with emergencies
Taipei Police HQ ☎381 7475, 381 8341. English-speaking service.

MEDICAL SERVICES
Adventist Hospital 424 Pateh Rd. Sec 2 ☎771 8151, map **10D5**
Cathay General Hospital 280 Jenai Rd. Sec 4 ☎708 2121, map **10D5**
Chang Gung Memorial Hospital 199 Tunhwa N Rd. ☎713 5211, map **10C5**
Mackay Memorial Hospital 92 Chungshan N Rd. Sec 2 ☎543 3535, map 9C3
Veterans General Hospital 201 Shihpai Rd. Sec 2 ☎871 2121

LOST PASSPORT
Contact the local police and your foreign representative office immediately.

LOST TRAVELERS CHECKS
Contact the local police and issuing bank immediately. Report stolen American Express travelers checks and cards at **214 Tunhwa N Rd.** ☎719 0606, map **10C5**.

LOST PROPERTY
Call the police and contact the **Tourist Information Hot Line** ☎717 3737.

Planning

Orientation

THE ISLAND

The island of Taiwan lies 100 miles off the SE coast of China. With an area of 36,000 square miles, making it slightly smaller than the Netherlands, it straddles the Tropic of Cancer, which puts the southern tip on the same latitude as Hawaii. Taiwan actually refers to the main island, the Pescadores group of islands (also known as Penghu) and at least 20 other islands, some mere dots in the ocean, others such as Quemoy, a few miles off the mainland coast, of strategic importance.

A chain of mountains runs through the main island from N to S, touching the coast on the E but leaving a fertile coastal plain on the W, now being exploited by industry as much as by agriculture. The highest peak is Yushan at 3,997 meters (13,113 feet) — the highest in this part of Asia, including Japan. There are tens of others above 3,000 meters.

Nomenclature can be tricky in Taiwan: to the Taiwanese (and mainland Chinese) Taiwan is simply a province of China — the Republic of China or the People's Republic of China, according to your point of view — but to most of the rest of the world it refers simply to the "land" (for it is not officially a sovereign state in its own right, and cannot be referred to as a nation). That is why most addresses in Taiwan have the letters ROC (Republic of China) printed at the end. The locals, however, have no objections to foreigners calling the place Taiwan. To complicate matters further, Taiwanese sporting teams competing around Asia are usually described as "Chinese Taipei" — for example at the Hong Kong International Rugby Sevens, where the Taiwanese appear frequently. Formosa, the name given to the island by the Portuguese, has now almost completely fallen out of use.

THE CAPITAL

Taipei, now a settlement of 2.7 million people, was not designated a city until 1920; it was declared the provisional capital of the Republic of China by the Nationalists in 1949 following their flight from mainland China. (Taiwan is a province of the republic, and Taipei is not actually the provincial capital; the small town of Chungshing in the center of the island has that honor.) Taipei lies in the N of Taiwan in the flat valley near the confluence of the Tanshui and Keelung rivers. The city has burgeoned in the past two decades, and is said to be the fastest growing in Asia in terms of building construction.

TAIWAN

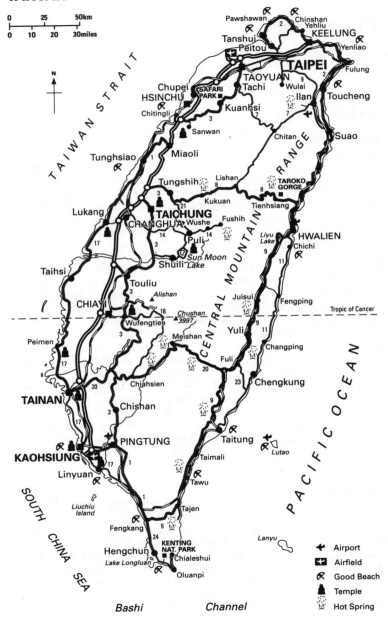

0   25   50km
0 10   20 30miles

N

TAIWAN STRAIT

Pawshawan
Chinshan
Yehliu
KEELUNG
Tanshui
Peitou
Yenliao
TAIPEI
Chupei
SAFARI PARK
TAOYUAN
Tachi
Wulai
Fulung
HSINCHU
Tachi
Ilan
Toucheng
Chitingli
Kuanhsi
Suao
Sanwan
Chitan
Tunghsiao
Miaoli
Lishan
Tungshih
TAROKO GORGE
Kukuan
Tienhsiang
Lukang
TAICHUNG
Wushe
Fushih
CHANGHUA
Liyu Lake
HWALIEN
Puli
Chichi
Taihsi
Sun Moon Lake
Shuili
Touliu
Alishan
Juisui
Fengping
CHIAYI
Chushan 3997
Tropic of Cancer
Peimen
Wufengtien
Yuli
Meishan
Fuli
Changping
Chiahsien
Chengkung
TAINAN
Chishan
PINGTUNG
Taitung
KAOHSIUNG
Lutao
Linyuan
Taimali
Tawu
Liuchiu Island
Tajen
Fengkang
Lanyu
KENTING NAT. PARK
Hengchun
Chialeshui
Lake Longluan
Oluanpi

CENTRAL MOUNTAIN RANGE

PACIFIC OCEAN

SOUTH CHINA SEA

Bashi   Channel

Airport
Airfield
Good Beach
Temple
Hot Spring

The city has developed along a gridiron pattern and is divided into four sectors by the N-S Chungshan Rd. and E-W Chunghsiao Rd., with all major roads being designated N, S, E or W according to their relationship with the two aforementioned. This isn't as complicated as it sounds, and actually makes searching for streets on a map or from the back of a taxi easy. Thus Nanking E Rd. runs E of Chungshan Rd., while Nanking W Rd. runs W of it. All long streets are divided into sections, building numbers starting anew with each section. Sidestreets, called lanes, are given numbers (not names) according to the nearest building on the main street they lead off from. Hence Lane 25, Shuangcheng St. means it is positioned near #25 Shuangcheng St.

Taipei does not really have a definable center, although the area around the **West Gate** (or Hsimending) and nearby **Snake Alley** and **Lungshan Temple** really come into their own at night and are probably the liveliest part of town. Fashionable **Chungshan N Rd.** was the Japanese center of town during the occupation, and many of the city's older hotels are to be found along or near this thoroughfare. Established businesses, in particular Japanese, maintain headquarters in this area, while newer concerns, including airline offices and international banks, occupy the gleaming new glass-and-concrete towers of **East Taipei**. An even newer quarter is that on the SE edge of the city, around the **World Trade Center**. Taipei's new city hall and other government offices have just moved to this sector.

To the N (and within easy reach) of Taipei lies **Yangmingshan National Park**, complete with lakes, mountain walks, volcanic craters, the hot-spring resort of Peitou and the smart suburb of Tienmou, popular with expatriates and well-to-do locals.

When and where to go

Taiwan's weather follows a similar pattern to Hong Kong's, making the summer months of July and August particularly hot and sticky. The wettest months are April, May and June; the best place to be in Taiwan during this period is the SW, where it rains less. Snow falls on the highest mountains during the months of December to February; typhoons hit in late summer and early fall.

SEEING THE CITY

Most of Taipei's main sights can be divided into two groups: those in the N of the city and those in the SW. It is perfectly possible to walk around this latter group, although if you mention this to a Taipei resident, the likely reaction will be a slightly hysterical laugh — they would never dream of voluntarily venturing out onto hot, traffic-choked streets for pleasure. Visitors to Taipei on Sundays and public holidays can make use of the **Culture Buses**, one of which covers the N route, the other the SW route. Both routes start and end at the main rail station opposite the Hilton.

- The NATIONAL PALACE MUSEUM, located out in the northern suburb of Waishuangshi, is an ideal starting point. True museum buffs and Chinese culture enthusiasts will want to linger a whole day here, but for most a morning spent taking in the exhibits is probably sufficient, followed by a stroll in the pretty gardens, and lunch either in the museum restaurant or at one of the establishments outside the main gates.

- Take a taxi to the MARTYRS' SHRINE (try to get there just before the hour to catch the changing of the guard), and then hop in another to the GRAND HOTEL. Built originally to house foreign heads of state, the Grand is a glorious monument to the Chinese palace-style of architecture, and offers a good view across the city. From the hotel it is a short ride to the tranquil CONFUCIUS TEMPLE and its neighbor, the much livelier BAO AN TEMPLE. There may be enough time to cross over to the other side of Chungshan N Rd. to visit the FINE ARTS MUSEUM — or save it for another day.

- LUNGSHAN TEMPLE in the SW of Taipei is the city's oldest temple; it is quite easy to while away an hour there, sitting in the shade, watching the comings and goings of worshipers.

- A walk to the NATIONAL MUSEUM OF HISTORY will take visitors along a street packed with animal shops and bird cages. The museum, which has a good collection of Chinese paintings, occupies a corner of the BOTANICAL GARDENS, a pleasant place for a stroll among the bamboo groves and palm trees.

- It is probably best to catch a taxi to the CHIANG KAI-SHEK MEMORIAL HALL, as the route crosses a couple of mammoth and daunting road intersections. The magnificent memorial with its dazzling white walls and blue-tiled roof is majestic in scale and occupies pride of place in a park also containing an opera house and concert hall built in traditional Chinese style.

- The nearby TAIWAN PROVINCIAL MUSEUM is probably most appealing for its Classical Greek building; few of the exhibits are explained in English. It, too, is in a park: NEW PARK, where visitors may catch a live concert and view two old steam engines.

- The SUN YAT-SEN MEMORIAL HALL is on the SE side of town, a 5-minute walk from the Taipei World Trade Center.

- For night-time strollers, there are two favorite areas: SNAKE ALLEY and adjacent streets in the S of the city, close to the Lungshan Temple, and the West Gate area a few blocks N; and the lanes off Shuangcheng St. and the night eating market of Chingkuang.

Calendar of events

Dates of Chinese festivals are decided by the lunar calendar and vary from year to year according to the Western calendar, so it is wise to check exact dates with the Taiwan Tourist Bureau. (See also PUBLIC HOLIDAYS, page 213.)

JANUARY TO FEBRUARY
‡ Late January to early February: **Chinese New Year**, the principal festival in the lunar calendar. Whereas in Hong Kong the only "bangs" to be heard are at the official fireworks display over the harbor, in Taiwan the New Year is ushered in in more traditional style with barrages of firecrackers all across the island. They are intended to ward off evil spirits. Lucky money, known as *laisee* in Hong Kong, is called *hung bao* in Taiwan.

Now that travel restrictions to the mainland have been eased, tens of thousands take the opportunity to visit relations, via Hong Kong. Take this into account if you intend flying between the two places at this time of year.

FEBRUARY TO MARCH
‡ Late February to early March: **The Lantern Festival**, held at the end of the first month of the year and traditionally an occasion when lamps were burned at night to keep bad spirits at bay, has been turned into a 6-day festival aimed at boosting tourism. The focus of the event is the square in front of the Chiang Kai-shek Memorial Hall and features Peking and Taiwanese opera, puppet shows, shadow plays, lion dances, martial arts performances and laser shows; 200,000 lanterns light up the memorial building itself. Fireworks events take place at Yenshui and Peikang in Central Taiwan and at Luerhman in the sw. This is a time for eating *yuan hsiao*, sweet rice dumplings filled with bean or date paste.

LATE MARCH
‡ **Kuan Yin Festival**, which celebrates one of Taiwan's most popular deities, the Goddess of Mercy. Ceremonies take place in temples such as the Lungshan Temple in Taipei.

EARLY APRIL
‡ **Tomb Sweeping Day** has a fixed date in Taiwan: April 5 (except leap years, when it falls on April 4), which is also the anniversary of the death of Chiang Kai-shek, the father of modern Taiwan, thus giving the day added significance.

LATE APRIL
‡ **Matsu Festival** is Taiwan's equivalent to the Tin Hau Festival in Hong Kong. A significant ceremony takes place in the Lungshan Temple, but the biggest ceremony is at the Matsu Temple in Peikang, near the Central Taiwan town of Chiayi.

MAY
‡ **International white-water rafting** competition on the Hsiukuluan River in eastern Taiwan.

JUNE
‡ Mid-June: **Dragon Boat Festival** is celebrated in Taiwan with international races, on the Tanshui River in Taipei as well as other venues in the island. *Dzung dze* — savory rice dumplings wrapped in banana leaves — are a popular delicacy during the festival. The town of Lukang on the w coast of Central Taiwan comes alive at this time of year with a Folk Arts Festival. As well as boat races, a whole host of folk arts can be seen, including top spinning, puppet shows, processions and a tug-of-war across the river. It is not unusual for local couples to marry in traditional ceremonies during the festivities. Most spectacular, though, is the "night patrol," when figures of gods are taken from their temples and paraded around town in a torch-lit procession for several hours late in the evening.

AUGUST TO SEPTEMBER
‡ Mid-August: Taipei's **Chinese Food Festival**.
‡ Mid-August: **Festival of the Hungry Ghosts**.
‡ Mid-September: **Mid-Fall Festival**.
‡ September 28: **Confucius' Birthday** (Teachers' Day). Temple ceremonies celebrate the anniversary of the great sage, philosopher and teacher, born in 551BC on the mainland, who still exerts a great influence over the lives of Chinese. Inquire at the Tourism Bureau about obtaining tickets to the event at Taipei's Confucius Temple.

OCTOBER
‡ October 10: Double Tenth celebrates the **anniversary of the October Revolution**, which put an end to the Chung Dynasty in China. It is celebrated with parades, mostly military in nature, which pass in front of the Presidential Building in Taipei.

DECEMBER
‡ December 25 is a public holiday, not because it is Christmas Day — although Westerners and Chinese Christians in Taiwan celebrate it as such — but because it is **Retrocession Day** and marks the anniversary of the end of the Japanese occupation of the island.

Sights and places of interest

How to use this section

In the following pages, Taipei's sights are arranged alphabetically. Look for the ★ symbol against the outstanding, not-to-be-missed sights. Buildings of architectural interest (🏛) and places of special interest for children (♣) are also indicated. For a full explanation of symbols, see page 7.

Some lesser sights do not have their own entries but are included within other entries: look these up in the INDEX.

Bold type is generally employed to indicate districts, buildings or other highlights. Places mentioned without addresses and opening times are often described more fully elsewhere in this chapter: check whether they are **cross-references**, which are in SMALL CAPITALS.

Taipei's sights A to Z

ARMED FORCES HISTORICAL MUSEUM
243 Kueiyang St. Sec 1 ☎ *331 5730. Map 9D2* 🚌 *Open 9am-5pm. S Cultural Bus.*
The history of the Kuomintang military, from its birth following the downfall of the Manchu/Ching dynasty to the present day.

BAO AN TEMPLE ★
61 Homi St. Map 9B3 🚌
As with all temples in Taipei, the gates are unlocked from dawn to late evening. This 240-year-old temple celebrates several deities including Bao Sheng Ta Ti, a doctor from Fukien province, the Goddess of Birth and the God of Luck. A great contrast from the serene and more famous neighboring CONFUCIUS TEMPLE, Bao An is a confusion of incense smoke and fragrance, burning candles, exploding firecrackers, yellow paper lanterns and the gossip of worshipers.

BOTANICAL GARDENS   See NATIONAL MUSEUM OF HISTORY.

CHIANG KAI-SHEK MEMORIAL HALL ★ 🏛
Chungshan S Rd. Map 9E3 🚌 *Hall open 9am-5pm. Park open 6am-midnight. N Cultural Bus.*

Without a doubt the most striking edifice in all Taipei, this monument is dedicated to Chiang Kai-shek, the former president of the Republic of China who died on April 5, 1975. It stands at one end of a large park, facing the 30m/98-foot-high Ming-style entrance gate. The memorial hall itself is made of dazzling white marble topped with brilliant blue tiles. It stands 76m (250 feet) high and contains a bronze statue of the former leader, weighing more than 25 tons. The lower floor of the structure contains memorabilia of the generalissimo. The park, with its landscaped gardens and parade ground, is also home to Taipei's **opera house** and main **concert hall**.

Chiang Kai-shek was born on October 31, 1887 in Chekiang Province on the mainland. As a military student in Japan in the early 1900s he met Sun Yat-sen and accompanied the revolutionary on missions to China. After the fall of the Manchus, Chiang settled in Shanghai and was sent as an adviser to Moscow by Sun. He won the power-struggle for leadership of the Kuomintang after the doctor's death, cementing the legitimacy of his succession by marrying a sister of Sun's widow. He remained at the head of the KMT until his death in 1975.

CHINESE CULTURE AND MOVIE CENTER

34 Chihshan Rd. Sec 4 ☎ *882 9010. Off map* **10A5** 🚌 *Open 9am-5.30pm. N Cultural Bus.*

Close to the NATIONAL PALACE MUSEUM, this is not quite a Hollywood movie studio, but there are plenty of traditional Chinese sets and costumes. Lucky visitors might see some filming.

CONFUCIUS TEMPLE

275 Talung St. Map **9B3** 📷

A great contrast to the usual bustle of a Chinese temple, the Confucian is devoid of worshipers and statues. For 364 days of the year it is a peaceful place where old men sit in the shade and students read books. But on September 28 it comes alive with music and processions, as a goat, pig and ox are sacrificed in honor of the great Chinese philosopher, teacher and statesman, Confucius. The style of the temple is similar to the original Confucius Temple in Chufu, the sage's native town in Shantung on the mainland.

Obtain tickets for the annual feast day from the Tourism Bureau.

FINE ARTS MUSEUM   See TAIPEI FINE ARTS MUSEUM.

GRAND HOTEL   Taipei's landmark hotel is described at length in WHERE TO STAY (see page 232). Map **9A3**.

HSINGTIEN TEMPLE
109 Minchuan E Rd. Sec 2. Map 10B4 🚻 *N Cultural Bus.*
This Taoist temple is dedicated to Kwan Kung, the warrior god. His figure can be picked out by his red face.

LIN-AN TAI HOMESTEAD 🏛
141 Szewai Rd ☎598 1572. *Map 10B4* 🚻 *Open Tues-Sun 9am-4pm. Closed Mon.*
The oldest residential building remaining in Taipei, this was moved from its original site to make way for a new road and reconstructed in Ping Chiang Park in 1978. It was built c.1822 in similar style, though smaller in scale, to houses in Fukien Province on the Chinese mainland, where many of the materials used in its construction came from. The homestead gives a good impression of living conditions in Taipei over a century ago.

LUNGSHAN TEMPLE ★ 🏛
211 Kuangchou St., Wanhua. Map 9D2 🚻 *S Cultural Bus.*
Also known as the Dragon Mountain Temple, this is Taiwan's oldest temple, built in the early 18thC, although parts had to be rebuilt following air-raid damage in World War II. It is dedicated to Kuan Yin and Matsu, two of Taiwan's principal deities. Kuan Yin, or the Goddess of Mercy, is the protector of just about everyone: women, the sick, the old, the poor, fishermen and sailors, farmers.... As with the BAO AN TEMPLE, Lungshan is a mix of Buddhist and Taoist influences and is a favorite sitting-out place for those who live in the neighborhood, particularly the elderly, who seek respite from the hot summer sun under its eaves. Note the exquisite dragon carvings on the roof.

MARTYRS' SHRINE   See NATIONAL REVOLUTIONARY MARTYRS' SHRINE.

NATIONAL MUSEUM OF HISTORY AND BOTANICAL GARDENS
49 Nanhai Rd. ☎361 0098. *Map 9E2* 🚻 *Open 9am-5pm* ⚹ ⚐ 🖭 *S Cultural Bus.*
A poor relation of the NATIONAL PALACE MUSEUM, this offers similar artifacts but without the latter's superb presentation. Very little is labeled in English, but those keen on Chinese painting, pottery, ceramics, jade and bronze should make an effort to pay the museum a visit. Children will find the exhibition on prehistoric Peking Man fun: a dark tunnel takes visitors past tableaux featuring lifesized models of man and beast.

The museum stands on the edge of the **Botanical Gardens**, full of specimens from tropical, subtropical and temperate climate zones. In summer the pond is covered with red-flowering lotuses. There is no café in the gardens, but canned drinks are available from the park's numerous vending machines.

NATIONAL PALACE MUSEUM ★
Waishuanghsi, Shihlin ☎881 2021/4. *Off map 10A5* ⚔ *(not compulsory)* 🚻
Open 9am-5pm 🎒 🍴 ⚐ 🚏 🖭 *N Cultural Bus.*
If visitors go nowhere else in Taipei they should make the trip out to

this museum, with its priceless collection of **Chinese art and artifacts** dating back 4,000 years. It is set among wooded hills, in the northern suburbs of the city.

The tale of how the rich treasure trove came to Taiwan is almost as fascinating as any of the 600,000 objects the building contains, only a fraction of which can be shown at one time. Most are stored in vaults beneath the museum and in underground caves in the mountainside. Exhibits are rotated regularly, so no matter how many times one visits Taipei, there will always be something new to see in the museum.

The original "palace museum" was founded during the Sung Dynasty in the 11thC, but was intended for aristocratic eyes only. With the fall of China's last dynasty in the early 20thC, eager art historians descended on Peking's Forbidden City to catalog its artifacts. A public museum was opened in 1925, but did not last long. In 1931 curators packed the exhibits into crates and shipped them to Nanking ahead of the invading Japanese. There followed a sojourn across the length and breadth of China, first to keep the precious cargo from falling into the hands of the invaders and then from the communists.

It is said by some that whoever guards the treasures of China is the guardian of China itself — hence the symbolic importance of the collection. It all survived miraculously intact, and 4,800 crates reached Taiwan in 1948. There are those who consider Chiang Kai-shek to have "stolen" the treasures, but the Taiwanese respond that in the light of the excesses of the Cultural Revolution this is not an altogether charitable view.

There is too much to take in one go: make more than one visit, or just pick collections that are of most interest. The exhibitions of painting and porcelain — a Chinese invention — are particularly fine. By following the chronological sequence of the exhibits in the porcelain rooms, the visitor can begin to appreciate the developments and refinements that have taken place throughout the centuries.

The apogee for **porcelain**, for many scholars and casual admirers, was probably during the Ming dynasty (1368-1644), and the museum carries many exquisite examples of the distinctive blue-and-white ware that was produced in the middle of the period. There is much more, though, including delicate celadon ware, red glazed vessels, fantastic pieces fashioned after dragons and phoenixes, and the garish colors of some of the later Ching dynasty ware.

Painting and **calligraphy** is again categorized by dynasty, and while a careful perusal of the latter may be of interest only to Chinese scholars, the paintings can be easily admired by anybody. There are two main traditions in Chinese painting: Huan Hua Pai, the fine-brush or meticulous style, and Wen Jen Hua Pai, which is characterized by bold, expressive brush strokes. These two divisions are sometimes referred to as the Northern and Southern schools respectively. Whatever the style, subject matter concentrates almost entirely on the beauty and serenity of nature, of mountainous landscapes, of birds and fish, of flowers, blossoms and bamboo. Ching dynasty artist Li Pei-yu's rare red and blue *Peonies* are a highlight, as are Chen Hsien-chang's *Thousand Plum Blossoms* (1437) and Ch'iu Ying's delicate *Narcissus and Plum* (1547).

While **figure painting** does not feature as highly as in the West, it is to be found here. Some of the best examples are the portraits of Tartar horsemen and archers depicted by Li Tsan-hua (c.10thC), himself a Tartar. The separate **modern art gallery** offers the visitor an interesting comparison.

Jade plays an important part in Chinese culture, as it is said to possess the virtues of benevolence, justice, wisdom, courage and modesty, and jewelry and *objets d'art* have been prized since Neolithic times. From the simple to the extravagant, the museum carries an extensive collection that includes pale blue, off-white, brown, gray, yellow and black jade as well as the more common green.

There is also an exhibition of "**Hindustan jade**," collected from India, via the silk road, during the Ching dynasty and featuring vessels of paper-thin jade. Other sections include **tapestry** and **embroidery**, **bronze carvings**, fascinating **curio cabinets**, **lacquerware**, **enamelware** and **books**.

Explanations in English appear throughout the museum, leaflets in English are available at the entrance to each collection, and in the tea shop visitors can browse through books on the museum. The museum shop is well stocked with books, postcards, slides and posters. The prints of Chinese paintings priced at only NT$50 must be the best bargain in Taiwan.

NATIONAL REVOLUTIONARY MARTYRS' SHRINE 血

Peian Rd. Map 10A4 ☷ *Open 9am-5pm* ⬤ *N Cultural Bus.*

On the northern outskirts of town, this shrine is dedicated to those who lost their lives fighting for the Republic of China. The design is based on a Ming dynasty palace and consists of an outer gate, pavilions set in a garden, inner gate, courtyard and memorial hall. In front of the main gate is a pair of marble lions; the one with its paw resting on a ball is male, the other, embracing the lionet, is female. Murals on the gate depict heroic scenes from the Canton Uprising of 1911 and the 1937 Battle of Shanghai.

The outer gate and memorial hall are guarded by soldiers who keep so still they almost look like store-window dummies. Their self-discipline in maintaining a straight face as tourists jostle to have their picture taken beside them is remarkable. "Minders" mop the sweat from their brows, straighten clothing and ensure that the soldiers' feet is the regulation number of centimeters apart. They only have to put up with this for an hour at a time; the photogenic guard-changing ceremony, which occurs on the hour, features much twirling and throwing of rifles.

NEW PARK   See TAIWAN PROVINCIAL MUSEUM AND NEW PARK.

POSTAL MUSEUM

45 Chungking S Rd. Sec 2 ☎ *394 8064. Map 9E3* ☷ *Open Tues-Sun 9am-4.30pm. S Cultural Bus.*

The history of the Chinese postal service going back to the days of the Mongols — the original Pony Express. A must for philately buffs.

SNAKE ALLEY ★
Huaxi St., Wanhua. Map 9D1. S Cultural Bus.
Much of the charm of Snake Alley has disappeared over the years as it has become more touristy, but it remains a "must see" in Taipei.

Wait until nightfall to see the alley and its neighboring streets at their best. The bright neon lights of the restaurants, trinket stalls and hawkers' carts attract locals and tourists like moths, but the big attraction is the snakes. Those of a queasy disposition may find the spectacle puts them off their dinner, as the snake handler goes through a routine that is as polished as any circus performer's. Running commentaries are in Chinese only, but no translation is needed as the poor creature has bulldog clips applied to it to straighten it out while its skin is slit and the blood extracted. Snake restaurants sell the blood and dishes containing the meat (it will improve your virility, it is said); those protesting a more delicate constitution can head off for a more palatable seafood meal.

SUN YAT-SEN MEMORIAL HALL 血
Jenai Rd. Sec. 4 ☎702 2411. Map 10D6 🖼 Open 9am-5pm ✈ S Cultural Bus.
If the monument to Chiang Kai-shek is imposing and regal, then the memorial to the Republic of China's other hero, founder Sun Yat-sen, is understated and serene. With its classical Chinese lines, it makes a fitting backdrop for the early-morning *tai-chi* practitioners who gather in the surrounding gardens. A bronze statue of Dr Sun, who died in 1925 and is as revered on the mainland as he is in Taiwan, stands inside the hall's entrance, which also houses a library and lecture and exhibition rooms. Later in the day children flying gaily colored kites replace the *tai-chi* crowd.

Dr Sun came from Guangdong Province in South China but had been educated in Honolulu, an experience which put some distinctly rebellious ideas into his head. Exiled for his actions, he traveled the world rallying support for the overthrow of the "foreign" Manchu dynasty. Back in China, numerous attempts at rebellion failed, until 1911, when a Sun-inspired (he was actually in the US at the time) military revolt at Wuchang in Central China succeeded. The date was October 10, which came to be known as "Double Tenth," its anniversary still celebrated with military parades in Taiwan today. On January 1, 1912, Dr Sun was declared president of the republic — a post he soon relinquished although he was to remain immensely influential and presided over the formation of the Chinese Nationalist Party, or Kuomintang, in 1919.

His "Three Principles of the People" — nationalism, democracy and economic security — remain the guiding ideas of Taiwan, and of the governmental system he pioneered, consisting of five "yuan" — executive, legislative, judicial, examination, inspectorate.

TAIPEI FINE ARTS MUSEUM 血
181 Chungshan N Rd. Sec 3 ☎595 7656. Map 9B3 ⚟ 🖼 Open Tues-Sun 10am-6pm ✈ ⚹ ▣ N Cultural Bus.
A must for all art lovers, this distinctive cubist-style building is home to not just contemporary Chinese art and sculpture, but to European

works as well. The permanent collections are supplemented by retrospectives of major Western and Chinese artists and other theme exhibitions. The museum's shop is well stocked with catalogs, books, postcards and posters.

TAIWAN PROVINCIAL MUSEUM AND NEW PARK 🏛

2 Hsiangyang Rd. ☎381 4700. Map ***9****D3* *(not compulsory)* *(free on Mon). Open 9am-5pm*

The oldest museum on the island, a Classical Greek structure built in 1908, it houses zoological and anthropological exhibits. It is not as well organized as most of the city's other museums, and there is very little information in English. What is signposted as the ground floor is actually the basement! Of most interest to travelers is the collection of Taiwanese aboriginal artifacts.

The museum is on the edge of **New Park**, a lively and well-patronized garden that frequently features live music. A statue stands in honor of an American Air Force Chief, Claire Chennault, who assisted the Taiwanese in the defense of their island in World War II. Space has also been found for two steam locomotives, one built in Dusseldorf in 1887 and the other manufactured at the Avonside Ironworks in the UK in 1895.

Where to stay

Making your choice

The proud old ladies of Taipei — the **Grand** and **Ambassador** hotels
— have not had it their own way for some time now. The choice of
accommodations has been increasing steadily across the years. It does
seem as if the Grand's cavernous lobby has set a trend among Taipei
hotels that continues to this day: take the large entrance hall of the **Lai
Lai Sheraton**, for instance, or the palatial lobby of the **Grand Hyatt**.
Ten to 15 years ago, major hotel chains moved into Taipei to offer
franchises, but only recently did service begin truly to match the best
international standards.

A third tier of hotels has recently appeared, with the opening of **The
Regent**, the **Grand Hyatt** and the **Sherwood** in 1990. They are now the
standard by which others are judged.

There is not much to choose from in service and facilities; elevators
and air conditioning are universal, as are IDD telephones and televisions
in every room. Location and price are probably the most important factors
when deciding where to stay, especially when taking into account
Taipei's dreadful traffic jams. Note that hotels with outdoor swimming
pools close them from October to May.

The Taiwan Tourism Bureau divides tourist hotels into two categories:
international and tourist. Instead of stars it awards "plum blossoms";
international class is either four or five, tourist class either two or three.

TAIPEI'S LANDMARK HOTEL — THE GRAND
☎596 5565 ⊠11646 ⊠594 8243. *Map* **9A3** ⅢⅢ *to* ⅢⅢ 530 *rms* ⇌ ꔢ ⊙ ꔅ ꔆ ꔇ
ꔈ ꔉ ꔊ ꔋ
Location: On the slopes of Yuanshan hill, N of Taipei. So well known in Taiwan is
this hotel that it doesn't have a proper address and is regarded as one of Taipei's
tourist sights in its own right. Modeled on the Forbidden City in Beijing, it was
intended to be the place where heads of state would stay, but as so few countries
recognize Taiwan it sees far more tour groups than it does kings and presidents.

The Grand is an imitator of the "Chinese palace" school of architecture. A hotel
it may be, but its size, position and guest list do almost put it into the palace class.
The establishment of a prestigious hotel capable of housing heads of state was the
pet project of Madame Chiang Kai-shek, who took great personal interest in the
Grand. Yuanshan hill was deliberately chosen as the site because of the splendid
views it affords across the Keelung River to the northern sector of Taipei. However,
the imposing main wing of the hotel, with its distinctive Chinese roof and red pillars,
was not part of the original, which was built in the 1950s.

The 14-story main wing (or new wing, as it is still referred to) was finished in the early 1970s, and is topped by a two-tier roof with curved eaves covered in gold-colored tiles, which glisten in the sunlight. The *pièce de résistance,* though, is the enormous lobby, which covers nearly 17,000 square feet. The thick red pillars support a ceiling of painted panels depicting traditional Chinese motifs and landscapes. The main front doors are bronze, many of the interior doors are fashioned from teak, and the main staircase is marble.

Built to house visiting dignitaries, the guest list has become somewhat less distinguished since the early 1970s as a result of Taiwan's awkward political status, but the King and Queen of Thailand, President Lyndon B. Johnson and King Hussein of Jordan are among those who have occupied the state rooms.

The location is inconvenient and the service reputedly somewhat rusty, yet the views are magnificent, the building palatial and sporting facilities truly excellent. Some rooms in the center of the building have no windows, but they are half the price of outer rooms, which come with attractive, airy balconies. Rooms are available in connected buildings: the Chi-Lin Pavilion and the Golden Dragon.

Taipei's hotels A to Z

AMBASSADOR
63 Chungshan N Rd. Sec. 2 ☎*551 111*
🕿*11255, 11184* 🖷*561 7883. Map* **9C3**
▥ *471 rms* ═ AE ⊡ ⊙ ▥ ⇔ 🍴 ⛄
🖵

Location: N Central Taipei, on one of city's main thoroughfares. One of the first hotels to be built in the city as a

result of the government's tourism development policy, the Ambassador may no longer be number one, but it retains a charm and warmth that is lacking in newer, more palatial establishments. Rooms are currently being renovated. As well as the usual Cantonese Chinese restaurants that almost every hotel boasts, the Ambassador has a Szechuan restaurant. Past guests include the then Governor of California, Ronald Reagan. The hotel has executive floors, plus a karaoke bar.

ASIAWORLD PLAZA

100 Tunhwa N Rd. ☎715 0077 ⊠26299 ⊠713 4148. Map **10C5** ▥ 1,057 rms

≡ 🎫 ◉ ⓘ 📺 ☷ ≈ ☂ ↔ ⚓

Location: In the new business district of East Taipei, close to the domestic airport. A huge hotel with attached conference center. As well as all the usual facilities, it houses a large shopping arcade.

BROTHER

255 Nanking E Rd. Sec 3 ☎712 3456 ⊠25977 ⊠717 3334. Map **10C5** ▥

268 rms ≡ 🎫 ◉ ⓘ 📺 ☷

Location: In the new business district of East Taipei, close to the domestic airport.. One of a number of hotels that has now found itself in a booming district. The Brother's ORCHID ROOM Taiwanese restaurant (see page 240) has a good reputation with locals. Not as packed with facilities as neighboring hotels, but correspondingly cheaper.

COSMOS

43 Chunghsiao W Rd. Sec 1 ☎361 7856 ⊠21887 ⊠311 8921. Map **9D3** ▥

269 rms ≡ 🎫 ◉ ⓘ 📺 ☘ ☷

Location: Near to the rail station and several tourist sights. A well-appointed hotel in downtown Taipei. Its main restaurants serve Shanghainese and French cuisine.

FIRST ♣

63 Nanking E Rd. Sec 2 ☎541 8234 ⊠21533 ⊠551 2277. Map **10C4** ▥

173 rms ≡ 🎫 ◉ ⓘ 📺 ☷ ⚓

Location: The new business district of East Taipei. A good-value hotel with a choice of restaurants, including Hunan, Shanghainese and Japanese *Teppanyaki,* and a business center.

FORTUNA ♣

122 Chungshan N Rd. Sec 2 ☎563 1111 ⊠21578 ⊠561 9777. Map **9C3** ▥

300 rms ≡ 🎫 ◉ ⓘ 📺 ☷ ☂ ↔

Location: N central Taipei, on one of the city's main thoroughfares. Close to shops and Taipei's pub area and within easy reach of tourist sights, the Fortuna has a lot going for it, with (for the price) a surprising number of facilities, including a beauty salon. It boasts Taipei's only revolving restaurant, the **Fortuna Grill**, serving continental cuisine.

GALA

186 Sungchiang Rd. ☎541 5511 ⊠28453 ⊠531 3831. Map **10C4** ▥

200 rms ≡ ☷ ◉ ⓘ 📺 🎫

Location: Between downtown Taipei and the new business district. A small hotel with a Taiwanese restaurant and a coffee shop that serves Western dishes.

GRAND   Illustrated and described on page 232.

GRAND HYATT

2 Sungshou Rd. ☎720 1234 ⊠12738 ⊠720 1111. Off map **10D6** ▥ 872 rms

≡ 🎫 ◉ ⓘ 📺 ₺ ☷ ≈ ☂ ↔ ⚓

Location: SE Taipei, next to the World Trade Center and 5 minutes from the Sun Yat-sen Memorial. Vying with THE REGENT for the best-in-Taipei spot, the Grand Hyatt opened in late 1990. It has managed to "out-Grand" other Grand Hyatts with an enormous marble-and-brass lobby that is quite easy to get lost in, and which features what must be the world's biggest flower arrangement. The **Regency Club** floors are popular with business people; the special lounge serves a buffet breakfast and evening cocktails and has its own business center. Certain floors are designated nonsmoking. As well as Cantonese and Japanese cuisine, the hotel has the **Shanghai Court** Shanghainese restaurant and the interesting **Bel Air** outlet (see RESTAURANTS, page 239) serving a mix of Californian and Asian dishes. The hotel's bars and restaurants have become "in" places for the glitterati of Taipei, who love strolling around the palatial lobby showing off their fashionable garb.

HILTON

38 Chunghsiao W Rd. Sec 1 ☎*311 5151*
☒*11699* ☒*331 9944. Map 9D3* ▥
394 rms ☲ ☒ ☉ ☒ ☒ & ☀ ☝ ☞ ☞
Location: Opposite the rail station and close to several tourist sights. Once a prime site, this part of Taipei has been looking scruffy in recent years, but the redevelopment of the area around the station, which is to include a park, will improve it. Not as grand as many of the other international-class hotels in the city, the hotel nevertheless has a cozy atmosphere and a good Hunanese restaurant (see HUNAN, page 240). Certain floors are designated nonsmoking. Three executive floors cater to business travelers, and facilities include rooftop whirlpools and sundeck.

HOWARD PLAZA ♣

160 Jenai Rd., Sec 3 ☎*700 2323*
☒*10702* ☒*700 0729. Map 10D5* ▥
606 rms ☲ ☒ ☉ ☒ ☒ ☀ ☚ ☝ ☞ ☒
Location: E of the city center, in a mainly residential area. One of Taipei's newer hotels, it is built around a huge atrium, rooms either looking onto this or facing the street. The pièce de resistance of the atrium is a 4-story waterfall. All the facilities one expects for the price are here. Among the shops in the basement is an interesting tea house selling different types of tea and tea accouterments. The hotel has six Oriental and Western restaurants.

IMPERIAL

600 Linshen N Rd. ☎*596 5111* ☒*11382*
☒*592 7506. Map 9B3* ▥ *328 rms* ☲
☒ ☉ ☒ ☒ ☀ ☝ ☞ ☒
Location: A block along from Chung-shan N Rd., one of Taipei's main thoroughfares. In operation since 1969, the Imperial's **Palace** caters to the tourist rather than the business traveler. The Piano Bar features live music, while on the 12th floor is the **Galaxy Disco.**

LAI LAI SHERATON

12 Chunghsiao E Rd. Sec 1 ☎*321 5511*
☒*23939* ☒*394 4240. Map 9D3* ▥
705 rms ☲ ☒ ☉ ☒ ☒ ☀ ☚ ☞
☒ ☒

Location: A few blocks E of the rail station, close to downtown Taipei. "Lai Lai" means "come, come," or welcome. Looking rather old-fashioned compared with Taipei's glamorous new hotels, the Sheraton remains a popular meeting place for locals and tourists. It has 12 restaurants (including two Japanese), plus four cafés and bars and the **Elysée Nightclub.** Facilities for guests include two nonsmoking floors and two that are set aside for women. All the usual business facilities are here, and fitness facilities include a rooftop jogging track, golf practice areas and squash courts. The hotel will arrange golf outings for guests.

LEOFOO ♣

168 Changchun Rd. ☎*507 3211*
☒*11182* ☒*508 2070. Map 10C4* ▥ *to*
▥ *237 rms* ☲ ☒ ☉ ☒ ☒ ☚ ☀
Location: Between downtown Taipei and the new business district. Restaurants include Japanese, Western and Chinese (serving afternoon *dim sum*). A good no-frills hotel.

MAGNOLIA ♣

166 Tunhwa N Rd. ☎*712 1202* ☒*11386*
☒*712 2122. Map 10C5* ☚ ▥ *343 rms*
☲ ☒ ☉ ☒ ☒ ☀ ☚ ☚ ☞ ☞ ○
Location: The new business district of East Taipei, close to the domestic airport. Another hotel decorated in the imperial-palace style, although from the outside it looks rather drab. There is even a small Chinese garden at the back complete with pavilion and pond. This is just about the only hotel in town where guests can play tennis (indoor and outdoor courts). It also boasts a Mongolian barbecue restaurant and a beauty salon. Rooms at the back have balconies. The **Kiss disco** is open until 3am (see NIGHTLIFE AND ENTERTAINMENT, page 243).

NEW ASIA ♣

139 Changshan N Rd. Sec 2 ☎*511 7181*
☒*23394* ☒*522 4204. Map 9C3* ▥
120 rms ☲ ☒ ☉ ☒ ☒
Location: On Taipei's main N-S thoroughfare, close to the pub area. No

business or fitness facilities here, but this is good value for those who want a central location without the frills.

ORIENT
85 Hankow St. Sec 1 ☎*331 7211* 📠*26504* 🖷*381 3068. Map* **9D2** ▯
120 rms ═ ▦ ▣ ▦ ▦
Location: Downtown Taipei. Well-placed for shopping and sight-seeing, this is a no-frills hotel.

PRESIDENT
9 Tenhwei St. ☎*595 1251* 📠*11269* 📠*591 3677. Map* **9B3** ▨ *423 rms* ═
═ ▦ ▣ ▦ ▦ ○
Location: One block from Chungshan N Rd., one of Taipei's main thoroughfares. One of the city's oldest hotels, with a friendly atmosphere. Appropriately for a hotel in a nightlife district, it has a disco, the **Champagne Room Nightclub.**

REGENT
41 Chungshan N Rd. Sec 2 ☎*523 8000* 📠*20385* 🖷*523 2828. Map* **9C3** ▨
550 rms ═ ▦ ▣ ▦ ▦ ▦ ⚓ ♥ ♥
▥
Location: N Central Taipei, on the city's main thoroughfares. One of Taipei's newest establishments, this is part of the prestigious Regent Hotels International organization. If the young fashionable set go for the GRAND HYATT, business people flock to the lobby area and restaurants of The Regent (see, for example, TSAI FUNG SHUEN on page 240).

The Court on the atrium's ground floor has tables grouped around a podium where musicians offer jazz-type music from lunch through till late evening. Among its guest facilities are ladies' and nonsmoking floors. The basement-level shopping areas include a duty-free emporium and some of the swankiest names in fashion.

RITZ
41 Minchuan E Rd., Sec 2. ☎*597 1234* 📠*27345* 🖷*596 9222. Map* **10B4** ▨
283 rms ═ ▣ ▦ ⚓ ♥ ♥ ▥
Location: The new business district of East Taipei, close to the domestic airport. The Ritz's position as the city's premier hotel has been usurped by the grander newcomers, but it is still a place where the service and facilities are first-class.

SHERWOOD
111 Minsheng E Rd. Sec 3 ☎*718 1188* 📠*13630* 🖷*713 0707. Map* **10C5** ▨
350 rms ═ ▦ ▣ ▦ ▦ ⚓ ♥ ▥
Location: The new business district of East Taipei, close to the domestic airport. Another of Taipei's newest hotels, the Sherwood makes a pleasant change from the enormous marble palaces. It has a European feel to it, an ambience enhanced by the attractive **Toscana** Italian restaurant and by **Henry's Bar**, which comes complete with a (working) fireplace. The Sherwood's pool is indoor, so it is open all year round.

Eating and drinking

Where to eat in Taipei

The Taiwanese frequently claim that the quality and variety of Chinese food available in Taipei makes it the best in the world. They acknowledge that Hong Kong comes close, but chauvinistically explain that in Taiwan the different cuisines have remained "pure." A decent case can be made for this extravagant assertion — and yet, curiously, it is common for Taiwanese restaurants to boast that their kitchen is staffed by "Hong Kong chefs."

Migrants from all across China have brought their styles of cooking and lists of ingredients with them, and restaurants serving all types of food are represented in the capital, including **Pekingese**, **Mongolian barbecue**, **Shanghainese**, **Cantonese**, **Chaozhow**, **Hakka**, **Fuchou**, **Szechuan** and **Hunanese**.

The island has also developed its own style — **Taiwanese** — based loosely on Fuchou cooking from Fukien Province, just across the Taiwan Straits in mainland China. It is characterized by stewed soups and fresh seafood, with mild seasoning.

Readers wishing to find out more about regional Chinese cuisines should turn to EATING AND DRINKING in HONG KONG, page 107.

HOTEL RESTAURANTS
Hotel restaurants in Taipei, as in most of Asia, command a much higher reputation than they do in the West. When it comes to Western food, in particular, few private restaurants can afford to bring in foreign chefs and to buy unfamiliar foodstuffs from overseas, as can their rivals in the hotels.

STREET STALLS
But starting at the bottom of the scale, the simplest and cheapest food in Taipei is to be enjoyed at street stalls, particularly in the evenings. Noodles, fried rice, dumplings and sausage are popular dishes. Night markets can be found in the quadrant between **Linshen N Rd.** and **Nanking E Rd.** close to the pub area *(map 9 C3)*, at **"Food Circle"** by Chungking N Rd. and Nanking W Rd. *(map 9 C3)*, around **Snake Alley** *(map 9 D1)*, and at **Jaoher** near Sungshan rail station. Hygiene is usually good at these places, but anyone concerned about cleanliness can take their own chopsticks along.

See also NIGHTLIFE AND ENTERTAINMENT, page 243.

WESTERN-STYLE

Western-style fast food from the likes of **McDonald's**, **Pizza Hut**, **Burger King** and **Kentucky Fried Chicken** has taken off much faster than other foreign food. There are branches of these outlets all across the city: just look out for the familiar bright neon signs. Steak houses offer another "safe" alternative for Westerners seeking sustenance. Again, almost every street has a steak house — which is advertised as such outside.

In the basement of one of the Hilton hotel's neighbors is **FM Station**, a collection of eateries ranging from noodle stalls to pizza parlors at very reasonable prices: not great on atmosphere, but good for a midday snack.

COFFEE HOUSES

Coffee houses are popular with Taipei's younger set. They often have a peculiarly Continental air about them, and with their air conditioning can offer a welcome haven to hot and foot-weary sightseers. Cheap the coffee isn't, but there's a good choice of coffee from all across the world — Blue Mountain, Colombian, etc. — with snacks, particularly desserts, and other beverages, including alcohol, also available.

PUBS

British-style pubs are a good source of affordable, filling food. Burgers, pies, sandwiches, chili, pizza, steaks, fried fish and French fries and so on are usually available.

SELECTING A RESTAURANT

Ask a Taipei resident which is his or her favorite restaurant and you will receive a variety of answers. Taipei people nearly always recommend a neighborhood restaurant; they eat out frequently and don't want to go to the bother of driving all the way across town (and with Taipei traffic being as it is, that's not surprising) when there is something very reasonable around the corner.

Cuisine from other Asian countries, apart from Japan, has not yet made as much of an impact as in Hong Kong or Singapore, although as more and more Taiwanese travel and study abroad the culinary base is becoming wider. A sprinkling of Thai and Indian restaurants can be found. Some of Taipei's best Western restaurants are actually in **Peitou/Tienmou**, a suburb N of the city that is popular with expatriates, but it's a bit of a trek for someone staying in a central Taipei hotel.

Japanese restaurants have been a familiar sight in Taiwan since the days of the Japanese occupation. From small neighborhood *sushi* bars to elegant hotel restaurants, the whole gamut is available in Taipei.

AT THE TABLE

Equipment, etiquette and menus for Chinese meals are the same as in Hong Kong (see page 115 for further essential information about how to conduct yourself at a Chinese table). When a large party sits down at a traditional circular table for a meal, the host sits with his back to the door. Unlike the West, where the guest of honor sits next to the host, in

Taiwan he or she sits opposite. The second most important guest sits on the main guest's right, and so on.

At a traditional banquet, tea, beer and Chinese rice wine (usually *Shao Hsing*) are served. The Taiwanese are not great drinkers, but banquets will frequently be punctuated by double-fisted toasts, in which the glass is clasped with one hand and rests on the fingers of the other. One is expected to drain the glass in one go, and shout *kanpei* ("Bottoms up!") beforehand. Any excuse is used for a toast — catching the eye of someone else on the table, discovering two guests were born in the same year.... Local beer (labeled simply Taiwan Beer) is a light lager-type drink and extremely palatable — and cheaper than imported brands.

As elsewhere in Asia, wine drinkers will be disappointed by both price and choice. Hotel restaurants are just about the only places with a wide range of European, Pacific and American wines — but be prepared to pay through the nose for that good bouquet.

Taipei restaurants A to Z

888 RESTAURANT *Seafood*
Snake Alley (Huahsi St.) ☎ *308 1689. Map 9D1* ▥ *No cards.*
Although less well known than the exotically named Flour Meal of Tainan, or Tainan Tan Tsu Man, across the alley, this is cheaper. It specializes in barbecued seafood; diners point out what they want at the display counter at the front. The decor is basic (apart from one elaborate chandelier), but the people are friendly, and it makes a good spot to sit and watch the comings and goings in the alley.

ANCIENT AND MODERN *Chinese*
8 Lane 223, Nanking E Rd. Sec 3 ☎ *717 2680. Map 10C4* ▥ ▨
An intriguing name for a restaurant serving Shanghainese cuisine. Specialties include sliced croaker with almonds, mountain duck with mushrooms.

BEL AIR *Californian*
Grand Hyatt, 2 Sungshou Rd. ☎ *720 1234. Off map 10D6* ▥ ▰ ▨ ▣ ▣ ▨
Although this exquisitely decorated restaurant describes itself as "Californian," it is really all about East meets West. Similar menus in Hong Kong have not always taken off, but in Taipei, where many locals are still unfamiliar with

Western cuisines, Bel Air's menu is highly popular. Lunchtime is dominated by business people and wealthy women taking a break from shopping; the atmosphere is somewhat more intimate in the evening.

CHALET SWISS *Western*
47 Nanking E Rd. Sec 4 ☎ *715 2051. Map 10C5* ▥ ▰ ▣ ▣ ▨
A long-established Swiss restaurant complete with fondue dishes. The Chalet's *crêpes suzette* are also a favorite with diners.

GENGHIS KHAN *Mongolian*
176 Nanking E Rd. Sec 3 ☎ *711 4412. Map 10C5* ▥ *No cards.*
Mongolian barbecues have long been popular in Taipei, and Genghis Khan is just one representative of several restaurants offering this filling fare. Diners pick what they want from the meat, vegetables and seasonings on offer and hand it to the chef, who fries it on an enormous hotplate; be warned that those who don't go back for seconds look like wimps. The decor is not exactly smart, but that's not what diners are here for; as a magazine article the English-speaking manager will proudly produce for interested eaters puts it,

239

"the buffet way is favority [sic] by greedy people." No wonder this place is called the Genghis Khan.

HUNAN Chinese
3/F Hilton Hotel, 38 Chunghsiao W Rd. Sec 1 ☎311 5151. Map 9D3 ▥ ▨ ▣ ▣ ▨
Hunanese cooking is spicy and rich; steamed dishes are a specialty, which the Hilton's Hunan restaurant does well. Set menus as well as à la carte are available.

LA LUNE VAGUE French
7 Alley 7, Lane 290 Chungshan N Rd. Sec 6 ☎837 2214 ▥ No cards.
A cozy restaurant with a romantic ambience in the Tienmou suburb, to the N of the city. The decor is eclectic but elegant.

ORCHID ROOM Chinese
2/F Brother Hotel, 255 Nanking E Rd. Sec 3 ☎712 3456. Map 10C5 ▥ ▨ ▣ ▣ ▨
The Orchid Room has a reputation as one of the city's best Taiwanese restaurants. Soups and seafood figure prominently on the menu in this restaurant decked out in traditional Chinese style.

PLOWMAN'S COTTAGE Western
305 Nanking E Rd. Sec 3 ☎713 4942. Map 10C4 ▥ ▨ ▣
Take the rickety old elevator up to the 2nd floor. Hunting prints and portraits of Queen Elizabeth II line the walls in this old-fashioned dining room; and the food is unpretentious but well prepared. The downstairs pub is popular with Taiwanese and expatriates; live music features there most nights.

ROYAL THAI Thai
49 Jenai Rd. Sec 2 ☎351 0960. Map 10D4 ▥ ▨ ▨
All the usual Thai favorites are on offer here, but with the fire toned down to suit local taste.

RUFFINO ONE Italian
15 Lane 25, Shuangcheng St. ☎592 3355. Map 9B3 ▥ ▨ ▨

Decor: Italian *trattoria*, with a bit of Chinese thrown in. The fare: fairly authentic Italian, including antipasto, garlic snails, pastas and meat. Salads are prepared to your liking at the table. There is a limited wine list. In the same area you will find Ruffino Two and Three.

SEASON'S GARDEN Chinese
342 Tunhwa S Rd. Sec 1 ☎708 3110. Map 10D5 ▥ ▨ ▣ ▣ ▨
There's plenty of choice on the big menus of this Szechuan restaurant. But it is very popular, and reservations are recommended.

TAU TAU Chinese
57-1 Chungshan N Rd. Sec 2 ☎564 1277. Map 9C3 ▥ ▨ ▣ ▣ ▨
An elegant but friendly restaurant done out in wood, brass and mirrors evokes Shanghai's heyday. The staff is helpful, and there's always someone on hand who speaks English. It is almost worth taking the children along just to use the beautifully crafted wooden highchairs. Recommendations include crabmeat with preserved mushrooms, steamed scallops with white gourd, and the smashed date paste bun dessert.

TSAI FUNG SHUEN Chinese
Regent Hotel, 41 Chungshan N Rd. Sec 2 ☎523 8000. Map 9C3 ▥ ▬ ▨ ▣ ▣ ▨
Cantonese food is regarded as the most refined of the Chinese cuisines and is therefore the first choice for smart dining and banquets. In the elegant setting of the REGENT hotel, the emphasis at Tsai Fung Shuen is on seafood, and as one would expect from a hotel of this standing, the wine list is excellent — something missing in independent restaurants in Taipei.

WALTZING MATILDA Pub fare
3 Lane 25 Shuangcheng St. ☎594 3510. Map 9B3 ▥ ▨ ▣ ▣ ▨
Situated in Taipei's pub district, between Chungshan N Rd. and Linshen N Rd., Waltzing Matilda provides typical pub atmosphere, with a long bar and tables (and even a couple of outside

tables) and a dart board. Live music features most nights. Sister to the Hong Kong Kowloon pub of the same name, it is popular with expatriates. The food on offer includes fish, chicken, steaks, chilis, pizzas and sandwiches. Friendly staff.

ZUM FASS *German-Swiss*
55 Lane 119, Linshen N Rd. ☎*531 3815.*
Map 9C3 ▨ ▧ ▣ ▣ ▨ *Closed Sun.*
One of the first European restaurants to open in Taipei, the Zum Fass concentrates on German-Swiss fare. The menu changes daily.

The autumn winds have risen
The snakes are in good form
It's time to nourish yourself
*(Old Chinese saying referring to
the practice of eating snakes in winter)*

Nightlife and entertainment

Taipei by night

Taipei does not have the racy nighttime reputation of Manila or Bangkok, nor the variety of Hong Kong. However, it is only a decade or so since, it is rumored, it was impossible for an unaccompanied foreign male to get from the door to the check-in desk of one of the city's top hotels without being propositioned at least once. The seamier side of after-dark life in Taipei has faded with increasing affluence, the disappearance of American military on R&R from the Vietnam war, and US diplomatic recognition of mainland China. What sex industry does remain is essentially for visiting Japanese businessmen.

Increasing prosperity also brought about an expansion in the city's cultural life. But since most of the population is Chinese-speaking, there are not so many options among the performance arts for foreigners. All the same, there is still a lively night scene that should cater to most tastes.

PUBS AND BARS

The area behind the Imperial hotel centered on Shuangcheng St. between Chungshan N Rd. and Linshen Rd. is a pub crawler's dream. So many establishments are crammed into such a small area that it's a wonder they all manage to stay in business, given the high level of competition. Most serve food, and several feature live music. Among those worth checking out are **Waltzing Matilda** (*3 Lane 25* ☎ *594 3510, map 9 B3*), the small but popular **Mariners** (*6 Lane 25* ☎ *594 3510, map 9 B3*), **Plowman's** (*9 Lane 25* ☎ *594 9648, map 9 B3*), the **Farmhouse** (*5 Lane 32* ☎ *595 1764, map 9 B3*), **Sam's Place** (*9 Lane 32* ☎ *594 2402, map 9 B3*), which serves Mexican food, and the late-closing **Hsaling** (*2/F #20* ☎ *591 8995, map 9 B3*). Unaccompanied women should encounter no problems in any of these pubs, which are all located off Shuangcheng St.

In other parts of town are the **Plowman Inn** (*8 Lane 232, Tunhwa S Rd. Sec 1* ☎ *773 3268, map 10 D5*), which includes a Mongolian barbecue among its restaurants and features a live rock band several nights a week, and the **Plowman's Cottage** (*305 Nanking E Rd.* ☎ *712 4965, map 10 C4*).

More refined — but pricier — surroundings are to be found at hotel bars, including the cozy **Galleon Pub** at the HILTON, **Henry's Bar** at the SHERWOOD, and the **Lobby Bar** of the LAI LAI SHERATON, a popular meeting place. (See WHERE TO STAY for all these hotels.)

DISCOS, LOUNGES AND KARAOKE

Hostess bars are an ubiquitous feature of the night scene in Southeast Asian cities, and Taipei is no exception. Catering, as usual, mainly to visiting businessmen, many feature live music — either professional musicians or amateur karaoke. For those who can't resist displaying their singing skills, one with a karaoke lounge (or MTV, as it is often known in Taiwan) is the **Barcelona** *(B1, 432 Keelung N Rd. Sec 1* ☎ *758 1288)*, not far from the Grand Hyatt and World Trade Center. The **Blue Star** *(615 Linshen N Rd.* ☎ *591 4837, map 9 B3)* is a piano lounge and hostess club situated in the pub district, as are the **Mayflower** *(23-1 Shuangcheng St.* ☎ *591 7377, map 9 B3)*, **Romeo Club** *(23-3 Shuangcheng St.* ☎ *591 7779, map 9 B3)* and the interestingly named **High Heel Club** *(23 Lane 13, Shuangcheng St.* ☎ *597 2629, map 9 B3)*.

Among the venues in town designed to help revelers dance the night away with disco music and laser shows is the **Kiss** at the Magnolia hotel, which describes itself as a "superdisco/livehouse/videotheque." Other hotel nightspots include the **Galaxy** at the IMPERIAL, the **Elysée** at the LAI LAI SHERATON and the **Champagne Room** at the PRESIDENT.

Karaoke enthusiasts have an almost endless choice; lounges open and close down again more frequently than traffic jams occur in Taipei's streets. Neon signs advertising "karaoke" or "MTV" are everywhere. Most of the songs are in Mandarin or Japanese, but there's usually a small section of Western pop hits. Strangely popular — to Western eyes and ears — among the Japanese list are marching songs featuring movie clips of World War II Japanese soldiers.

NIGHT MARKETS

Great for eating, browsing, bargaining or just strolling, Taipei's brightly lit night markets offer the traveler an intoxicating glimpse of Chinese life, even in the more "touristy" locations such as **Snake Alley** (see page 230). Snake Alley once had a dubious reputation as a prostitute haunt, but has since been cleaned up. Foreigners, including unaccompanied women, should experience no difficulties at this or other markets, although the usual precautions against pickpockets should be observed.

Apart from Snake Alley, night markets can be found at **Shilin**, in an area N of the Grand Hotel, the city's largest and oldest such venue; **Jaoher market**, on the E side of the city near Sungshan rail station; and **Kunghuan market**, in the vicinity of the National Taiwan University, and therefore popular with students.

CHINESE OPERA

The colorfully elaborate and highly stylized makeup of a character from Chinese (or Peking) Opera frequently does duty as a national symbol of Taiwan. Stories are based on legend and folklore, accompanied by high-pitched music and song that can be difficult for ears attuned to Western tones to appreciate. Locals know the plots by heart and recognize instantly the symbolism used by the actors. Visitors wishing to see a performance should try to find out the story in advance if they wish to get the most out of Peking Opera.

Performances of Peking Opera can be seen at the **Chinese Armed Forces Cultural Activities Center** *(69 Chunghwa Rd. Sec 1 ☎371 6832, map 9 D2)* and the **National Theater** at the **Chiang Kai-shek Memorial** *(☎ 758 8014, map 9 E3)*.

Especially at festival times, it is possible to stumble across backstreet opera performed outdoors; this is known as **Taiwan Opera**.

MOVIE THEATERS

There about eight theaters showing English-language movies in Taipei. Check the *China Post* and *China News* English-language newspapers for titles and times. Other sources of movies are foreign organizations such as the **AmVet Post 3** *(☎833 3916)*.

BARBERSHOPS

Sometimes known to provoke a nudge and a wink, "barbershops" offer more than a simple haircut, and some offer a great deal more. Respectable ones will provide shampoo, cut and blow-dry, manicures, head-and-shoulder massages and ear cleaning; others are fronts for brothels. Those who don't want to end up in a house of ill-repute should check with their hotel desk for recommendations.

CONCERT HALLS

Western and Chinese performances of music, dance and opera can be seen at the National Theater and Concert Halls at the **Chiang Kai-shek Memorial** *(map 9 E3)*. For other venues, see the English-language papers or inquire at **Caves** bookstore *(103 Chungshan N Rd. Sec 2 ☎ 537 1666, map 9 C3)*.

Shopping

Where to go

Taipei, while not being the emporium that Hong Kong is, nevertheless offers a good selection of Chinese arts and crafts, and bargains in casual clothes. The days when foreigners flocked to **Caves** bookstore *(103 Chungshan N Rd. Sec 2* ☎*537 1666, map 9 C3)* for cut-price "pirated" reference books, however, are long since gone. But the shop still carries an excellent stock of books on every aspect of China, from paintings to politics.

Taipei's main shopping areas are along **Chungshan N Rd.** *(map 9 D3-B3),* in the vicinity of the hotels; **Chunghsiao E Rd.** *(map 9 D2-10 D6),* in East Taipei; and **Chunghwa Rd.** *(map 9 E2-D2),* near the West Gate. Places range from cheap market stalls and small family-owned shops to multistory, air-conditioned department stores and hotel arcades. Needless to say, the latter group is more expensive, but they accept credit and charge cards, will usually exchange faulty goods, may be willing to arrange shipment of goods, and are generally more reliable.

CRAFTS

The **Chinese Handicraft Mart** *(1 Hsuchow Rd.* ☎*321 7233, map 9 D3),* near the Chiang Kai-shek Memorial, is a government-sponsored organization selling Chinese porcelain, jade, bronze, lacquer, wood carvings, jewelry, painting and furniture. Major credit and charge cards are accepted.

The **Taiwan Crafts Center** *(#7, 110 Yenping S Rd.* ☎*331 5701, map 9 D2; closed Mon)* is another government-operated store selling locally produced goods. Like the Handicraft Mart, the center will ship goods to anywhere in the world.

DEPARTMENT STORES

Top department stores in Taipei include the following:-
Evergreen   6 Nanking E Rd. Sec 2 ☎561 7181, map **10**C4, and 246 Tunhwa S Rd. ☎777 4428, map **10**D5
FIT   14 Nanking W Rd. ☎564 1111, map **9**C3
HOT   337 Nanking E Rd. Sec 3 ☎715 3777, map **10**C5
Ming Yao   200 Chunghsiao E Rd. Sec 4 ☎777 1266, map **10**D5
Shin Shin   247 Linshen N Rd. ☎521 2201, map **9**C3
Worth noting is that a number of these stores have supermarkets in their basements.

FASHION

Men's custom-made suits can be ordered from tailors shops in most of the upscale hotels; cheaper are the shops along Chungshan N Rd. *(map 9 B3-D3).*

Women will be attracted by the rich array of silks and brocades, which tailors can make up into garments in a short time. Some famous overseas fashion houses have clothing manufactured in Taiwan, some examples of which find their way into local shops and markets.

There is a great abundance of cheap and cheerful casual clothing for both sexes, particularly T-shirts. But watch out for sizes: small means Asian small!

GOLF

Taiwan is golf mad, and this means not only plenty of places to play but also a good array of golfing equipment for sale, including clubs, bags and clothing. In Taipei, department stores and specialist sports shops are the places to find them.

JADE

The outdoor **jade market** under the overpass (flyover) at Pateh Rd./Hsinsheng Rd. *(map 10 D4)* is open on Sundays only, but is worth visiting just for a browse, if not to buy. As well as jade, the stalls sell jewelry, pottery and knickknacks. In the arcade directly under the overpass are numerous shops selling cheap computer software and components, although how long many of them will stay in business is questionable now that the authorities have been persuaded to clamp down on pirated software.

MARBLE AND WOODEN CARVINGS

Most of the Chinese arts and crafts items on sale here are identical to those found in other Chinese centers such as Hong Kong and Singapore, but there is a huge array of marble goods and wooden carvings that can be truly described as "Made in Taiwan." Marble is mined near the Taroko Gorge in eastern Taiwan, and the wood carvings come from Sanyi in western Taiwan.

Sadly, it seems to be virtually impossible to find Taiwanese aboriginal artifacts and art for sale in Taipei.

PRINTS

An excellent source of prints of traditional Chinese paintings is the **National Palace Museum** (see page 229). The **Fine Arts Museum** also has a good selection of art books, prints and cards (see page 231).

SHOPPING FOR BARGAINS

The key is to look for anything made locally, as import duties make overseas items pricey. (The Taiwanese themselves love shopping in Hong Kong.)

Cheap clothing can be found in the **Dinghao** area on either side of Tunhwa S Rd., N of its intersection with Chunghsiao E Rd. *(map 10 D5).*

Reproductions of antiques are often a good buy, as are jewelry and ornaments made from local jade and coral, as well as marble. Taiwanese-made gold pieces can also be a bargain, but much of it is made from 24-carat "pure" gold, much prized by the Chinese but actually too soft for jewelry.

Computers are comparatively cheap, but investigate whether you will be able to obtain spare parts easily and inexpensively in your home country. Many of these computers find their way onto the Hong Kong market.

Sports and recreation

No fewer than 12 golf courses are within easy reach of Taipei, catering to one of the city's great passions. Some have special days for non-members. Opportunities for playing tennis and bowling are also reasonable.

Outside of Taipei the most popular sports likely to appeal to visitors are scuba diving, mountaineering and hiking.

The major hotels have fitness centers for guests: look for the ♈ symbol in the hotel listings on pages 233-36.

BOWLING
Bowling facilities can be found at **Chia Chia Bowling Center** (*223 Sungkiang Rd.* ☎ *503 7216, map* **10** *C4*) and **Yuan Shan Bowling Center** (*6 Chungshan N Rd. Sec 5* ☎ *881 2277*).

GOLF
If Hong Kong is Japan's shopping mall and Manila its bordello, then Taiwan is its golf course. It is a game that is also extremely popular among the Taiwanese: more than 300,000 play regularly. Several courses near Taipei set aside days, usually during midweek, when nonmembers can play a round or two. The clubs include the **Taoyuan Golf Club** (*Taoyuan* ☎ *03-322 1786*), **Taipei Golf Club** (*Luchu, Taoyuan Hsien* ☎ *03-324 1311*) and the **Marshal Golf & Country Club** (*Taoyuan Hsien* ☎ *03-322 1786*). Check with the individual course for the days when they accept visitors; another source of information is the **Golf Association of Taiwan** (*75 Lane, 187 Tunhwa S Rd. Sec 1* ☎ *711 7482, map* **10** *D5*).

RUNNING
The **Hash House Harriers** is a worldwide running and social club with branches in Taipei. The *This Month In Taiwan* publication, available free in most hotels, carries the phone numbers you need.

SKIING
January and February see the short snow-skiing season in Taiwan. **Hohuanshan**, in the center of the island, offers the only facilities, although they are unlikely to tempt anyone used to the flash resorts of the Alps or the Rockies: St Moritz this isn't. Information can be gained from the **Chinese Taipei Ski Association** (*50A Lungchian Rd.* ☎ *771 2374*).

TENNIS

There are public tennis courts at the **Taipei Tennis Club** *(285 Chunghsiao E Rd. Sec 4* ☎ *711 7482, map 10D6)* and the **Youth Park Tennis Club** *(199 Shuiyuan Rd.* ☎ *303 2451, map 9F2).* The latter also has a public swimming pool.

WALKING AND CLIMBING

Central Taiwan with its mountainous scenery offers plenty of scope for those keen on mountain climbing or plain hard walking. One drawback is that permits often need to be obtained in advance. They are available from the **Alpine Association** *(#3, 30 Lachou St., map 9 B3).*

Taiwan's highest mountain is **Yushan** (also known as the Jade Mountain or Mt. Morrison), at 3,997m (13,113 feet). It is within a national park and is easily accessible from Alishan, a popular resort. **Tungpu** and **Hsinglungshan** are two other peaks for experienced hikers, while those preferring a less daunting summit can try those in the **Yangmingshan national park**, N of Taipei, for which no passes are needed. All these areas offer excellent opportunities for walkers.

WATER SPORTS

The southern tip of Taiwan has a coral coastline that is excellent for scuba and snorkeling. The **China Diving Association** in Taipei *(114 Mingshen E Rd. Sec 2* ☎ *596 2341, map 10C4)* has information on where to go and how to rent equipment. Beaches in the area have windsurfers and motor scooters for rent.

WHITE-WATER RAFTING

A 22km (14-mile) section of the Hsuikuluan River that tumbles down from Taiwan's central mountain range has been developed as a whitewater rafting course. The trip across the rapids takes about 4 hours. There are about 10 companies operating the trips, which include transportation to and from Hwalien, a major town on the E coast. Rafters are provided with life jackets and helmets but need to bring a set of dry clothing. More information is obtainable from the **Jueisui Visitors' Service Center** *(*☎ *038-873651)* and the local branch of the **Tourism Bureau** *(*☎ *089-281217/089-281237).*

Excursions

INTRODUCTION

With Taiwan's excellent internal airways system it is easy to travel long distances quickly and really get away from the big city. **Taroko Gorge** is probably the island's most spectacular natural sight, and by flying to and from Hwalien, visitors can see it in one day. The southern tip of Taiwan with the coral seas and tropical scenery of **Kenting National Park** are a world away from the rest of the island; its attractions (which include luxury resort hotels) make a relaxing contrast to the cultural sights of Taipei, and it is well worth the effort to see it.

One recommended itinerary is to fly to **Hwalien** early morning, visit Taroko, stay overnight and catch an early flight direct to Kaohsiung for a 2-day stay in Kenting Park, returning to Taipei at the end. Kenting can be easily visited over a weekend, but make hotel reservations in advance, especially during holiday periods, and ask the hotel to arrange car-rental for a trip around the park.

The **central mountainous region** is more difficult to visit if your schedule is tight, but those with the time should consider a trip along the East-West Cross-Island Highway. A trip to **Sun Moon Lake** and the surrounding mountains requires at least 4 days to do the area justice. **Northern Taiwan** is very accessible by train or bus or by rental car from Taipei: among the attractions are mountains, lakes, hot springs and seaside resorts, all of which make ideal one-day trips.

Refer to the map of the island on page 220 for locations of place names mentioned in this chapter.

TAROKO GORGE

Taiwan's most spectacular natural sight is the Taroko Gorge, which lies at the E end of the East-West Cross-Island Highway near the coastal town of **Hwalien**. It is perfectly feasible to make a day trip of the gorge by taking an early-morning flight to Hwalien, going on an organized tour of Taroko and returning to Taipei late afternoon. Several tour operators in Taipei offer just this as a package. An alternative is to take a more leisurely train ride back to the city. Don't try this the other way round: you should strive to see Taroko as early as possible, for the clouds close in after noon.

The last 19km (12 miles) of the highway runs through a steep ravine formed by the **Liwu River**. The Taiwanese had long been aware that there was marble in the mountains around Taroko, but not until the road was blasted through the area in the 1950s did they discover how extensive it was. Moves were then made to turn the entire area into one big marble mine, but the conservationists won the day and the area is now protected under the national park scheme.

The road itself, opened in 1960, cost US$15m to build — and the lives of 400 men. The western section ends at **Tungshih**, but it is the eastern end that is of most interest to the traveler, although for those with time the complete drive is well worth doing.

The first stop on any tour of the gorge is at the ceremonial **archway** that marks the beginning of the highway. The bridge carrying the coastal road that branches off to the right here was destroyed by Typhoon Dot in September 1990 — one of the worst tropical storms to hit Taiwan in several years — and was out of action for more than a year.

The E coast is home to the Ami and Taiya indigenous peoples, and it can be guaranteed that there will be a handful on hand to be photographed by tourists — for a fee. The going rate seems to be around NT$20. The traditional costumes are somewhat spoiled by the baseball caps sported by the two old ladies from the Taiyu (along with their face tattoos, which signify they are married) and the high-heels worn by the red-clad Ami girls.

A more appealing spot is the **Shrine of the Eternal Spring**, built in memory of those who died building the highway. On the opposite side of the ravine to the road, the small temple perches on a rock ledge above a waterfall. The river bed is wide here, with the water a narrow ribbon among the gravel. Farther up the road the valley bottom is narrow and filled with boulders across which the turquoise water bubbles and gushes. The road regularly disappears into tunnels hollowed out of the marble and limestone cliffs. The **Swallow Cave** is named after the hundreds of swallows that nest in it; tour buses disgorge passengers here for them to walk through and peer out of the "windows" looking down onto the river many, many meters below. From one of these natural portholes can be seen Indian Face Rock, so-called because the profile is reminiscent of a Native American.

The gorge finishes at **Tienhsiang**, where a pretty monastery and photogenic pagoda nestle among the wooded slopes, accessible via a swaying pedestrian suspension bridge, and the national park headquarters and a lodge. Those with time to spare and a penchant for the quiet life can stay the night here; the facilities are sparse, but it's a beautifully peaceful spot and it is hardly surprising that the place is so popular with Taiwanese honeymooners. Anyone interested in hiking could easily base themselves at Tienhsiang and spend a couple of days walking around the area.

Those continuing on a bus tour will be driven back down through the canyon and on to the **Retired Servicemen's Engineering marble factory** close to the airport. There's a dining room, museum and large store here as well as the actual factory, and Ami dance performances are also put on for the benefit of tour groups, although the performance can best be described as lackluster. Better shows can be seen at the **Ami Cultural Village**, although connoisseurs of aboriginal culture believe the best Ami performances take place at the **Ami Cultural Center** in the town of Feng-Pin, 30km (19 miles) s of Hwalien.

Hwalien itself is a pleasant coastal town, although the beach is rather scruffy and the sea on the E coast is generally too rough for swimming in. It has a colorful street market, an impressive **Martyrs' Monument** and a couple of interesting temples. Outside of town is **Liyu Lake**, or Carp Lake, where boats can be rented.

The best hotels in Hwalien are the **Marshal** (☎ 038-326 123 ☒ 038-326 140 ▥), **Chinatrust Hwalien** (☎ 038-221 171 ☒ 038-221 185 ▥) and **Astar** (☎ 038-326 111 ☒ 038-324 604 ▥). At Tienhsiang the standard of accommodations is much simpler; there's **Tienhsiang Lodge** (☎ 038-691111-3 ▥) and the **Catholic Hostel** (☎ 038-691122 ▢).

KENTING NATIONAL PARK

The southern tip of Taiwan is a world away from the traffic-choked streets of Taipei or the cool mountain resorts of Central Taiwan. If the rest of the island is the "real China," then the s must belong to some other land. Bound by the Pacific Ocean on the E and the South China Sea on the w, the **Hengchun Peninsula** has long been settled by farmers; Kenting actually means "plowmen."

The National Park itself occupies 336 square kilometers (130 square miles), of which just over a half is land, the rest consisting of coral-rich coastal waters. The balmy, tropical climate of the peninsula helps make it home to 220 species of bird (and temporary home to several migratory species in the winter), 216 kinds of butterfly and 43 types of reptiles and amphibians. The Kenting National Park offers an amazing array of environments and sights: coral outcrops, sandy beaches, surf seas, lakes, woodland, grassland, virgin forest, meadows, caves, lighthouses.... Hiking, bicycling, scuba diving, windsurfing or simply soaking up the sun, it's all there.

The easiest access is by 40-minute flight from Taipei to **Kaohsiung**, while those who want to see some of the country on the way can take the $4\frac{1}{2}$-hour train ride. Travelers from Hong Kong and Singapore can bypass Taipei and fly direct to Kaohsiung. Kaohsiung is essentially an industrial city and seaport, and anyone just arrived from Taipei will find little cause to linger before heading off for the beaches and wide open spaces farther s. The Caesar Park Hotel in Kenting runs a shuttle bus service to and from the airport; otherwise travelers need to take a bus to **Hengchun**, 9km ($5\frac{1}{2}$ miles) from Kenting and from there catch another bus or taxi.

Most travelers choose to base themselves in Kenting village itself, either at one of the deluxe resort hotels with their myriad facilities, or at one of the simpler hotels or guest houses. (See below for examples at both levels.) Close to sandy beaches, Kenting has a real seaside air about it, with its main street lined with shops selling all the brightly colored paraphernalia of a beach vacation. While the rest of Taiwan is content to sit inside in air-conditioned splendor, visitors to Kenting can sit out in the open air to eat seafood, sip cold drinks and watch the world go by at several of the town's cafés. At nighttime the parking lot above **Little Bay** beach is turned into an informal eating area when small vans convert themselves into mini barbecue joints selling grilled seafood.

The landscape around Kenting is dominated by the huge sugarloaf shape of **Big Stone Slab**; from other angles it looks sharper, hence its alternative name of Big Pointed Mountain. The surefooted can climb to the top of the 318m/1,043ft-high peak and look down on the surrounding meadowland, complete with Texan cattle belonging to the livestock research station. The nearby forest recreation center provides trails through woodland and jungle, along limestone ravines and through caves. There are said to be more than 1,200 species of plant life in the 435ha (1,075 acres) of this special conservation area. Birdwatchers, too, get more than their fair share of species to keep them occupied.

More weird rock formations — with names to match — are found along the coast: **Frog Rock** near Kenting, **Sail Rock** at the entrance of Banana Bay, and **Maopitou**, or Cat's Nose, in the w of the park. The fortified lighthouse at **Oluanpi**, built in 1882, still sends its guiding beam out to shipping on the high seas; it is now surrounded by a park offering panoramas of the ocean and enjoyable walks through limestone and coral rock formations.

The road turns N after Oluanpi, which is the southernmost settlement in Taiwan, and runs on top of the cliffs along the wilder, wave-pounded E shore. Farther N the cliffs yield to a gentler coastline. The road ends at **Chialeshui**, a specially protected stretch of shore. Strata of sandstone have formed layer upon layer of huge, flat, angled slabs, and sea water breaks across the coral at the front of the shore to fill rock pools in the sandstone.

At the opposite side of the park lie the tranquil surroundings of **Lake Longluan**, a staging post for thousands of migratory birds in the fall and winter as they make their way from Siberia to South Asia. This is the best time for birdwatchers to visit, but at any time of year it is a haven for native Taiwanese birds and wildfowl.

Caesar Park Hotel (☎ 08-886 1888 08-886 1818) is a short walk out of Kenting, opposite the beautiful Little Bay beach. It has a landscaped pool, tennis courts, an archery area, rents out watersports equipment and will arrange scuba lessons. It offers Chinese, Japanese and Western restaurants as well as Kenting's only disco. **Kenting House** (☎ 08-886 1370 to) has two branches: one up the hill away from town and a set of cottages along the beach. **Kenting Youth Activity Center** is modeled on a Fukien village, and offers youth hostel type accommodations ( ). *Smaller hotels are to be found along the main street of Kenting, and in the back lanes toward the beach.*

Those who want to stay overnight in Kaohsiung have a good choice of hotels. **The Ambassador** (☎ 07-211 5211), sister to the Taipei establishment of the same name, the lakeside **Grand** (☎ 07-383 5911) and the **Holiday Garden** (☎ 07-241 0121) are all top-class hotels with a swimming pool. A step below are the **Kingdom** (☎ 07-551 8211), **Kingwang** (☎ 07-281 4141), **Major** (☎ 07-521 2266) and **Summit** (☎ 07-384 5526).

Kenting has plenty of restaurants selling everything from prawns to pizza; **Oluanpi** also has several restaurants and cafés. **Kaohsiung** has a good array of restaurants, from fast food and pub-style Western to every shade of Chinese.

253

CENTRAL TAIWAN

One of the most picturesque parts of Taiwan — certainly one of the most photographed — is **Sun Moon Lake**, 726m (2,382 feet) up in the Central Highlands. It is reputed to be Taiwan's top honeymoon destination, but it isn't just romantically inclined couples who visit the place — there are times when it seems as if the whole of Taiwan has made a trip there.

You are best advised therefore to avoid the lake on weekends and public holidays.

A further recommendation is that if you wish to see the lake and its surrounding hills at their best even during the week, it is a good idea to arrive in the evening, stay overnight at the Sun Moon Hotel and get up early the next morning — when the light is at its best — and tour around the lake before the tourist buses arrive. The rest of the day can then be spent venturing up into the hills or out to the **Formosan Aboriginal Cultural Village**.

The highlight of a visit to Sun Moon Lake is the **Wen-Wu temple**, dedicated to Confucius and Kuan Kung, the Warrior God. This palatial building, guarded by two enormous stone lions, is a maze of halls, and offers stunning panoramic views of the lake.

Good views are also to be had from the 46m/151ft-high **Tzu En**, or Temple of Filial Virtue. This is one of Taiwan's most enduring symbols, and was built in 1971 as a memorial to Chiang Kai-shek's mother; hence its title.

The **Hsuan Chuang Temple** contains the bones of a 7thC priest who made a Buddhist pilgrimage to India. During the Japanese occupation, some of Hsuan Chuang's bones were taken to Japan, but they were returned in the 1950s and lodged in a special golden pagoda. Boats can be taken out on the lake.

In the southern part of the Central Mountain range lies **Alishan**, best known as the base for an early-morning trip to see the sunrise from **Chushan**. At 2,200m (7,218 feet), the weather at Alishan can be cool, even at the height of summer — so bring warm clothing (and rainwear: there is usually an afternoon downpour), especially if you plan to make the assault on Chushan at dawn to see peaks piercing the Sea of Clouds. You can walk to Chushan (it takes about an hour), or take a mini-bus or the train.

In fact, sunrises aside, trains are a good reason in their own right for coming to Alishan, for the **narrow-gauge railway** built by the Japanese from **Chiayi** up to Alishan is still in use. It spirals its way up for 72km (45 miles), crossing 77 bridges and ducking into 50 tunnels.

Other excursions from Alishan include **Monkey Rock**, with its panoramic views, the hike to **Two Sisters Ponds**, and, farther afield, to the peaks of **Fengshan** and **Shanlinhsi**. ("Shan," incidentally, means mountain.) Chiayi can be reached by direct train from Taipei, and there are express buses from Taipei direct to Alishan.

✍   The **ChinaTrust Sun Moon Lake** (☎ 049-855 911 ▯) overlooks the lake; facilities include a pool (swimming in the lake is not allowed) and a 9-hole golf course. At Alishan, the top hotel is **Alishan House** (☎ 05-267 9811 ▯).

NORTH TAIWAN

For a quick getaway from Taipei, the best destination is **Yangming-shan National Park**, a 40-minute drive N of the city, with its volcanic peaks and sulfurous craters, lakes and rivers. The park is famous for its hot springs, several of which can be bathed in. **Hell Valley** is not one of these: locals boil eggs in it. To try a hot-spring bath, check into one of the old-style inns outside the park in neighboring **Peitou**; the once dubious reputation of this place has long since been cleaned up.

NE of Taipei, near the mouth of the Tanshui River, is **Tanshui**, (sometimes spelt Tamsui or Tansui), an important port before it silted up in the early 20thC, which contains one of the few European colonial relics on the island, in the form of the 17thC Spanish fort, **Fort San Domingo**. Standing next to it is the old **British consulate**, abandoned in 1972 when the British cut off diplomatic ties with Taiwan. While Europeans built forts, the later colonial power of Japan built golf courses: Tanshui's course is the oldest on the island. There are several antique stores in town to browse through.

A pleasant way to reach Tanshui is via river boat from Minsheng W Rd., Taipei *(map 9 C2)*. Boats run on the hour between 9am and 5pm. A few miles away is Shalun beach, but being so close to Taipei it gets very crowded on summer weekends. Farther N along the coast are other beach resorts at **Chowtzuwan, Chienshuiwan** and **Pawshawan**, and, on the E coast, at **Chinshan**. Some of the weirdest rock formations on the island, easily rivaling those in the S, are to be seen at **Yiehliu**, also on the E coast. Some of the strangely shaped coral rocks, sculpted by the ocean, are so distinctive that they have been given appropriate names, such as **Queen's Head**.

Keelung is one of the largest ports on the island, as well as being a city with a long history. Unfortunately very little evidence of its past survives, partly because of a devastating earthquake in 1887. Apart from the imposing statue of **Kuan Yin**, the goddess of mercy, 22m (72 feet) high and overlooking the harbor, there is not much to keep a visitor occupied at Keelung.

☙   The only hotel of international standard in Peitou is the modern **Communications Palace** (☎ *891 3031* ▢), which has hot-spring baths. Linked to this hotel is a smaller inn called the **Insular**, also with hot-spring baths *(same* ☎ *number* ▢ *)*.

▬   Thanks to the presence of expatriate communities in **Peitou** and neighboring **Tienmou**, there is an abundance of restaurants, including French, Italian and Indian.

Index

Page numbers in **bold** indicate the main entry; page numbers in *italic* refer to illustrations and maps.

Hong Kong

Taiwan

List of street names

All streets mentioned in this book that fall within the area covered by our maps are listed below. Map numbers are printed in **bold** type. Some smaller streets are not named on the maps, but the map reference given below will help you locate the correct neighborhood.

Hong Kong

Albany Rd., **3**C3
Arbuthnot Rd., **3**C3
Argyle St., **7**B2-**8**A5
Ashley Rd., **7**E3
Austin Ave., **7**E3
Austin Rd., **7**D2-**8**E4

Barnton Court, **7**E2
Battery St., **7**D2
Blue Pool Rd., **6**E8-9
Bonham Strand East, **3**B2
Bonham Strand West, **3**A1-B2
Boundary St., **7**A1-**8**A4

Caine Rd., **3**B1-C3
Cameron Rd., **7**E3
Canton Rd., **7**B2-F2
Carnarvon Rd., **7**E3
Cat St., **3**B2
Chatham Rd., **7**E3-**8**C5
Cheong Wan Rd., **8**E4
Chico Tce., **3**B2
Cleveland St., **6**B8
Cleverly St., **3**B2
Cochrane St., **3**B3
Connaught Pl., **4**B4
Connaught Rd., **3**A1-**4**B4
Coombe Rd., **4**E5
Cotton Tree Dr., **3**C3-**4**C4

D'Aguilar St., **3**C3-B3
Des Voeux Rd., **3**A1-C3
Duddell St., **3**C3

Edinburgh Pl., **4**B4
Electric Rd., **6**A9

Elgin St., **3**B2
Exchange Sq., **3**B3

Fenwick St., **4**C5
Food St., **6**B8

Garden Rd., **3**D3-**4**C4
Glenealy St., **3**C3
Gloucester Rd., **5**C5-**6**C9
Graham St., **3**B2
Granville Rd., **7**E3
Great George St., **6**C8

Haiphong Rd., **7**E2-3
Hankow Rd., **7**E3
Hanoi Rd., **7**E3
Harbour Rd., **5**C5-7
Harcourt Rd., **4**C4-5
Harlech Rd., **3**D1-2
Hart Ave., **7**E3
Heard St., **5**C7
Hennessy Rd., **5**C5-7
Hillier St., **3**B2
Hillwood Rd., **7**D3
Hollywood Rd., **3**B2-3
Hospital Rd., **3**B1
Hysan Ave., **6**C8

Ice House St., **3**C3-B2

Jaffe Rd., **4**C5-**6**C8
Jardine's Crescent, **6**C8
Jervois St., **3**B2
Johnston Rd., **4**C5-**5**C7
Jordan Rd., **7**D2-3

Kadoorie Ave., **7**A3-B3

Kai Chiu Rd., **6**C8
Kansu St., **7**D3
Kennedy Rd., **3**C3-**5**D6
Kimberley St., **7**E3-D3
King Kwong St., **6**E8
Kingston St., **6**B8
Ko Shing St., **3**A1
Kowloon Park Dr., **7**E2-F3

Ladder St., **3**B2
Lai Chi Kok Rd., **7**A2-B2
Lam Kam Rd., **2**C4-B4
Lan Fong Rd., **6**C8
Lan Kwai Fong, **3**C3
Leighton Rd., **6**C8
Li Yuen St., **3**B3
Lock Rd., **7**E3
Lockhart Rd., **4**C5-**6**C8
Lok Ku Rd., **3**B2
Lower Albert Rd., **3**C3
Lower Lascar Row, **3**B2
Luard Rd., **5**C6
Lyndhurst Tce., **3**B3

MacDonnell Rd., **3**C3-4D4
Man Lok St., **8**D5-C5
Man Wah Lane, **3**B2
Man Yue St., **8**D5
Market St., **7**D3
Marsh Rd., **5**B7-C7
Matheson St., **5**C7-**6**C8
Middle Rd., **7**E3
Mody Rd., **7**E3-**8**E4
Morrison Hill Rd., **5**C7
Mosque St., **3**C2

Taipei

Clothing sizes chart

LADIES
Suits and dresses

Australia	8	10	12	14	16	18
France	34	36	38	40	42	44
Germany	32	34	36	38	40	42
Italy	38	40	42	44	46	
Japan	7	9	11	13		
UK	6	8	10	12	14	16	18
USA	4	6	8	10	12	14	16

Shoes

USA	6	$6\frac{1}{2}$	7	$7\frac{1}{2}$	8	$8\frac{1}{2}$
UK	$4\frac{1}{2}$	5	$5\frac{1}{2}$	6	$6\frac{1}{2}$	7
Europe	38	38	39	39	40	41

MEN
Shirts

USA, UK Europe, Japan	14	$14\frac{1}{2}$	15	$15\frac{1}{2}$	16	$16\frac{1}{2}$	17
Australia	36	37	38	39.5	41	42	43

Sweaters/T-shirts

Australia, USA, Germany	S	M	L	XL
UK	34	36-38	40	42-44
Italy	44	46-48	50	52
France	1	2-3	4	5
Japan		S-M	L	XL

Suits/Coats

UK, USA	36	38	40	42	44
Australia, Italy, France, Germany	46	48	50	52	54
Japan	S	M	L	XL	

Shoes

UK	7	$7\frac{1}{2}$	$8\frac{1}{2}$	$9\frac{1}{2}$	$10\frac{1}{2}$	11
USA	8	$8\frac{1}{2}$	$9\frac{1}{2}$	$10\frac{1}{2}$	$11\frac{1}{2}$	12
Europe	41	42	43	44	45	46

CHILDREN
Clothing

UK

Height (ins)	43	48	55	60	62	
Age	4-5	6-7	9-10	11	12	13

USA

Age	4	6	8	10	12	14

Europe

Height (cms)	125	135	150	155	160	165
Age	7	9	12	13	14	15

CONVERSION FORMULAE

To convert	Multiply by
Inches to Centimeters	2.540
Centimeters to Inches	0.39370
Feet to Meters	0.3048
Meters to feet	3.2808
Yards to Meters	0.9144
Meters to Yards	1.09361
Miles to Kilometers	1.60934
Kilometers to Miles	0.621371
Sq Meters to Sq Feet	10.7638
Sq Feet to Sq Meters	0.092903
Sq Yards to Sq Meters	0.83612
Sq Meters to Sq Yards	1.19599
Sq Miles to Sq Kilometers	2.5899
Sq Kilometers to Sq Miles	0.386103
Acres to Hectares	0.40468
Hectares to Acres	2.47105
Gallons to Liters	4.545
Liters to Gallons	0.22
Ounces to Grams	28.3495
Grams to Ounces	0.03528
Pounds to Grams	453.592
Grams to Pounds	0.00220
Pounds to Kilograms	0.4536
Kilograms to Pounds	2.2046
Tons (UK) to Kilograms	1016.05
Kilograms to Tons (UK)	0.0009842
Tons (US) to Kilograms	746.483
Kilograms to Tons (US)	0.0013396

Quick conversions

Kilometers to Miles	Divide by 8, multiply by 5
Miles to Kilometers	Divide by 5, multiply by 8
1 meter =	Approximately 3 feet 3 inches
2 centimeters =	Approximately 1 inch
1 pound (weight) =	475 grams (nearly $\frac{1}{2}$ kilogram)
Celsius to Fahrenheit	Divide by 5, multiply by 9, add 32
Fahrenheit to Celsius	Subtract 32, divide by 9, multiply by 5

KEY TO MAP PAGES

KEY TO MAP SYMBOLS

City Maps

▨ Place of Interest or Important Building

▬ Built-up Area

▨ Park

[↑ ↑] Cemetery

▲ Temple

☾ Mosque

† Church

✿ Synagogue

▦ Hospital

i Information Office

✉ Post Office

☙ Police Station

☞ Parking Lot / Garage

◉ MTR Station

→ One-way Street

▶5 Adjoining Page No.

Area Maps

■ Place of Interest

▬ Built-up Area

▨ Park

▨ Natural Vegetation

═○═ Expressway (with access point)

══ Expressway (under construction)

━━ Main Road / 4-Lane Highway

━━ Secondary Road

- - - Ferry

═══ Railway

---- MTR Line

✈ Airport

▲ Temple

𝒳 Good Beach

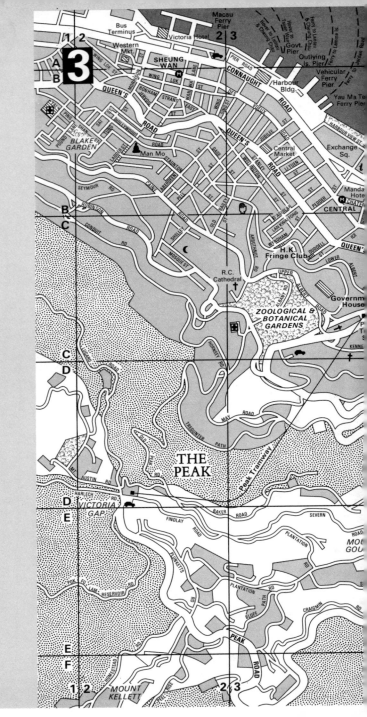

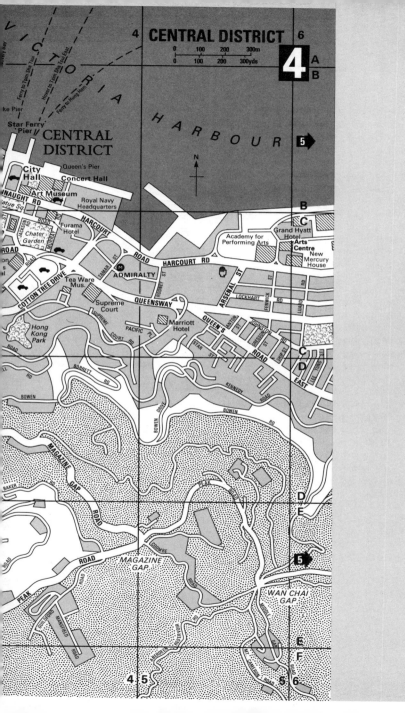

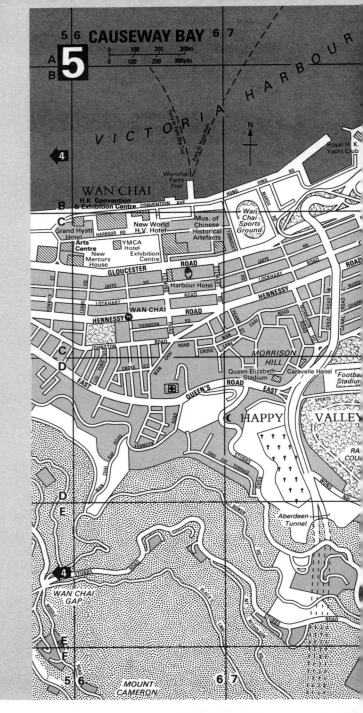

A

B

5

0 100 200 300m
0 100 200 300yds

VICTORIA HARBOUR

N

Royal H. K.
Yacht Club

Ferry to Tsim Sha Tsui

Ferry to Hung Hom

Wanchai
Ferry Pier

HUNG HING RD

HUNG HING RD

MARSH

WAN CHAI
H.K. Convention
& Exhibition Centre   CONVENTION   AVE

Wan
Chai
Sports
Ground

Grand Hyatt
Hotel   HARBOUR RD

New World
H.V. Hotel

Mus. of
Chinese
Historical
Artefacts

**Arts
Centre**
New
Mercury
House

YMCA
Hotel
Exhibition
Centre

JAFFE   ROAD

ROAD

GLOUCESTER   ROAD

STEWART   RD

LOCKHART

ROAD

JAFFE   RD

Harbour Hotel

FENWICK ST

LUARD RD

JAFFE

LOCKHART

WAN CHAI

HENNESSY ⓜ   **WAN CHAI**   ROAD

THOMSON

ROAD

JOHNSTON   ROAD

CROSS ST

CROSS ST

HENNESSY

ROAD

HENNESSY   ROAD

MORRISON HILL RD

CHAN STREET

CANAL ROAD W

CANAL ROAD E

BURROWS

SHARP

MORRISON
HILL

WAN
LANE

CROSS LANE

C

D

EAST   LUEN TUNG

Queen Elizabeth
Stadium

Caravelle Hotel

Footba
Stadiur

QUEEN'S   ROAD

EAST

SPORTS

HAPPY

VALLE

WAN CHAI GAP ROAD

KENNEDY RD

SHIU FAI TERRACE

STUBBS ROAD

WONG NAI

RA
COU

D

E

Aberdeen
Tunnel

4 STUBBS

**WAN CHAI
GAP**

BOWEN

BLUE

STUBBS

MT. NICHOLSON

MORRISON

ROAD

E

F

◀ **4**

5 6   6 7

**MOUNT
CAMERON**

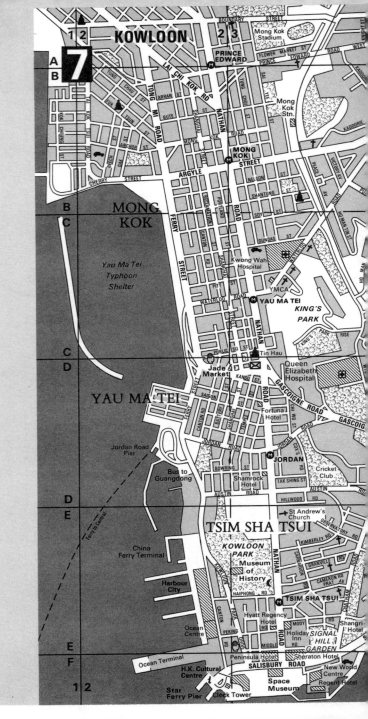

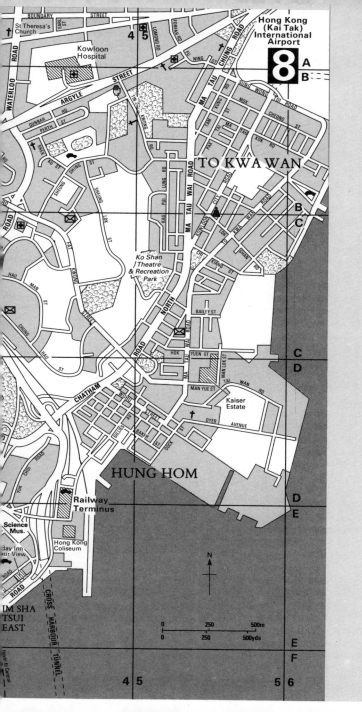

HONG KONG
KCR & MTR systems

©TCS Designed by R.Woods

Map authorised user number D/CAS/WW/AM/1013

NEW TERRITORIES

KOWLOON

HONG KONG ISLAND

CHINA

Sheung Wan
Central
Admiralty
Victoria Harbour
Wan Chai
Causeway Bay
Tin Hau
Fortress Hill
North Point
Quarry Bay
Lei Yue Mun
Tai Koo
Sai Wan Ho
Shau Kei Wan
Heng Fa Chuen
Chai Wan

Tsuen Wan
Tai Wo Hau
Kwai Hing
Kwai Fong
Lai King
Mei Foo
Lai Chi Kok
Cheung Sha Wan
Sham Shui Po
Shek Kip Mei
Prince Edward
Mong Kok
Yau Ma Tei
Jordan
Tsim Sha Tsui

Kowloon
Kowloon Bay

Kowloon Tong
Lok Fu
Wong Tai Sin
Diamond Hill
Choi Hung
Kowloon Bay
Ngau Tau Kok
Kwun Tong
Lam Tin

Tai Wai
Sha Tin
Racecourse
University
Fo Tan
Tai Po Market
Tai Wo
Fanling
Sheung Shui
Lo Wu (Restricted to passengers with suitable visas)

LEGEND
■ Island Line
⋯ Kowloon-Canton Line (KCR)
Kwun Tong Line
Tsuen Wan Line
○ Interchange with other lines

What the papers said:

• "The expertly edited American Express series has the knack of pin-pointing precisely the details you need to know, and doing it concisely and intelligently." (*The Washington Post*)

• "*(Venice)* ... the best guide book I have ever used." (*The Standard* — London)

• "Amid the welter of guides to individual countries, American Express stands out...." (*Time*)

• "Possibly the best ... guides on the market, they come close to the oft-claimed 'all you need to know' comprehensiveness, with much original experience, research and opinions." (*Sunday Telegraph* — London)

• "The most useful general guide was *American Express New York* by Herbert Bailey Livesey. It also has the best street and subway maps." (*Daily Telegraph* — London)

• "...in the flood of travel guides, the *American Express* guides come closest to the needs of traveling managers with little time." (*Die Zeit* — Germany)

What the experts said:

• "We only used one guide book, Sheila Hale's *Amex Venice,* for which she and the editors deserve a Nobel Prize." (Eric Newby, London)

• "Congratulations to you and your staff for putting out the best guide book of *any* size *(Barcelona & Madrid).* I'm recommending it to everyone." (Barnaby Conrad, Santa Barbara, California)

• "If you're only buying one guide book, we recommend American Express...." (*Which?* — Britain's leading consumer magazine)

What readers from all over the world have said:

- "The book *(Hong Kong, Singapore & Bangkok)* was written in such a personal way that I feel as if you were actually writing this book for me." (L.Z., Orange, Conn., USA)

- "Your book *(Florence and Tuscany)* proved a wonderful companion for us in the past fortnight. It went with us everywhere...." (E.H., Kingston-on-Thames, Surrey, England)

- "I feel as if you have been a silent friend shadowing my time in Tuscany." (T.G., Washington, DC, USA)

- "We followed your book *(Los Angeles & San Francisco)* to the letter. It proved to be wonderful, indispensable, a joy...." (C.C., London, England)

- "We could never have had the wonderful time that we did without your guide to *Paris*. The compactness was very convenient, your maps were all we needed, but it was your restaurant guide that truly made our stay special.... We have learned first-hand: *American Express — don't leave home without it.*" (A. R., Virginia Beach, Va., USA)

- "Much of our enjoyment came from the way your book *(Venice)* sent us off scurrying around the interesting streets and off to the right places at the right times". (Lord H., London, England)

- "It *(Paris)* was my constant companion and totally dependable...." (V. N., Johannesburg, South Africa)

- "I could go on and on about how useful the book *(Amsterdam)* was — the trouble was that it was almost getting to be a case of not venturing out without it...." (J.C.W., Manchester, England)

- "We have heartily recommended these books to all our friends who have plans to travel abroad." (A.S. and J.C., New York, USA)

- "Despite many previous visits to Italy, I wish I had had your guide *(Florence and Tuscany)* ages ago. I love the author's crisp, literate writing and her devotion to her subject." (M. B-K., Denver, Colorado, USA)

- "We never made a restaurant reservation without checking your book *(Venice)*. The recommendations were excellent, and the historical and artistic text got us through the sights beautifully." (L.S., Boston, Ma., USA)

- "We became almost a club as we found people sitting at tables all around, consulting their little blue books!" (F.C., Glasgow, Scotland)

- "This guide *(Paris)* we warmly recommend to all the many international visitors we work with." (M.L., Paris, France)

- "It's not often I would write such a letter, but it's one of the best guide books we have ever used *(Rome)* — we can't fault it!" (S.H., Berkhamsted, Herts, England)

American Express Travel Guides

spanning the globe....

EUROPE
Amsterdam, Rotterdam
  & The Hague
Athens and the
  Classical Sites ‡
Barcelona & Madrid ‡
Berlin ‡
Brussels #
Dublin and Cork #
Florence and Tuscany
London #
Moscow & St Petersburg *
Paris #
Prague *
Provence and the
  Côte d'Azur *
Rome
Venice ‡
Vienna & Budapest

NORTH AMERICA
Boston and New
  England *
Los Angeles & San
  Diego #
Mexico ‡
New York #
San Francisco and
  the Wine Regions
Toronto, Montréal and
  Québec City ‡
Washington, DC

THE PACIFIC
Cities of Australia
Hong Kong & Taiwan
Singapore &
  Bangkok ‡
Tokyo #

* Paperbacks in preparation   # Paperbacks appearing January 1993
‡ Hardback pocket guides (in paperback 1993)

Clarity and quality of information, combined with outstanding maps — the ultimate in travelers' guides

Buying an AmEx guide has never been easier....

The *American Express Travel Guides* are now available by mail order direct from the publisher, for customers resident in the UK and Eire. Payment can be made by credit card or cheque/P.O. Simply complete the form below, and send it, together with your remittance.

New paperback series (£6.99)   # Available from January 1993

☐ Amsterdam, Rotterdam
  & The Hague
  1 85732 918 X

☐ Brussels #
  1 85732 966 X

☐ Cities of Australia
  1 85732 921 X

☐ Dublin & Cork #
  1 85732 967 8

☐ Florence and Tuscany
  1 85732 922 8

☐ Hong Kong & Taiwan
  0 85533 955 1

☐ London #
  1 85732 968 6

☐ Los Angeles & San Diego #
  1 85732 919 8

☐ New York #
  1 85732 971 6

☐ Paris #
  1 85732 969 4

☐ Rome
  1 85732 923 6

☐ San Francisco and
  the Wine Regions
  1 85732 920 1

☐ Tokyo #
  1 85732 970 8

☐ Vienna & Budapest
  1 85732 962 7

☐ Washington, DC
  1 85732 924 4

Hardback pocket guides (£7.99)

☐ Athens and the Classical Sites
  0 85533 954 3

☐ Barcelona & Madrid
  0 85533 951 9

☐ Berlin
  0 85533 952 7

☐ Mexico
  0 85533 872 5

☐ Singapore & Bangkok
  0 85533 956 X

☐ Toronto, Montréal
  & Québec City
  0 85533 866 0

☐ Venice
  0 85533 871 7

While every effort is made to keep prices low, it is sometimes necessary to increase them at short notice. American Express Travel Guides reserves the right to amend prices from those previously advertised.

Please send the titles ticked above.   **HKT**

Number of titles @ £6.99 ☐   Value: £

Number of titles @ £7.99 ☐   Value: £
Add £1.50 for postage and packing   £_____1.50

Total value of order: £_____
I enclose a cheque or postal order ☐ payable to Reed Book Services Ltd, or
please charge my credit card account:

☐ Barclaycard/Visa   ☐ Access/MasterCard   ☐ American Express

Card number ☐☐☐☐☐☐☐☐☐☐☐☐☐☐☐☐☐☐☐☐

Signature _____   Expiry date _____

Name _____

Address _____

_____   Postcode _____
Send this order to American Express Travel Guides, Cash Sales Dept,
Reed Book Services Ltd, PO Box 5, Rushden, Northants NN10 9YX.